readings
on the
sociology
of small
groups

prentice-hall international, inc., London

prentice-hall of australia pty. ltd., Sydney

prentice-hall of canada ltd., Toronto

prentice-hall of india private ltd., New Delhi

prentice-hall of japan, inc., Tokyo

# readings
# on the
# sociology
# of small
# groups

Theodore M. Mills

State University of New York at Buffalo

WITH

Stan Rosenberg

Dartmouth College

prentice-hall, inc./englewood cliffs, new jersey

**prentice-hall readings in modern sociology series**
Alex Inkeles, Editor

© 1970 by
PRENTICE-HALL, INC., Englewood Cliffs, N.J

13–761932–4

Library of Congress Catalog Card Number: 74–97155

Printed in the United States of America

Current printing (last digit)
10  9  8  7  6  5  4  3  2

# preface

We present in this volume readings which together, should prove valuable to those interested in the newly developing field of the sociology of small groups. They represent a variety of approaches, cast new light on current thought in the field, and contain imaginative leads for future development.

Within the past fifty years or so, the social scientist has turned his attention to small groups for several reasons. One is that the social scientist as humanist has been struck by the intimate and pervasive interrelation between the individual—his growth, his beliefs, his values, and his habitual ways of acting and feeling—and the groups which surround him. These groups are so fundamental a part of his "life space" (at home, the playground, school, the neighborhood, or the shop) that their existence is taken for granted and their dynamics and properties are rarely considered consciously. Second, on a broader scale, the community's history is heavily influenced by certain groups which exert great power and control such as the President's Cabinet, the Joint Chiefs of Staff, the Supreme Court, and city councils. And third, experience in limited contexts has supported the belief that man can better order his social world and his relation to it by a fuller, more self-conscious understanding of how groups operate. The possibility of altering existing structures to achieve our ultimate goals is increased through reflexive awareness. Man's active control over his environment—physical or social—cannot be achieved until the nature of that environment has been understood.

The social scientist as empirical researcher and builder of theoretical constructs finds the small group a convenient context in which to explore the principles governing how the individual copes with immediate social realities. Those interested in broad generalizations about the operations of social systems have been attracted to the study of small groups for several different reasons. First, the myriads of these groups which exist in every collectivity and institution known to man are clearly fundamental substructures the operations and influences of which must be understood if the larger systems are to be understood. And second, small groups have been seen as "microsystems" exhibiting, in miniature, many of the features and processes of larger collectivities or entire societies. We believe that the selections in our anthology not only exemplify reasons for studying groups, but because of their substance and insight demonstrate the quality of work through which the field is likely to advance. This is our primary reason for presenting them.

The secondary purpose is to provide a companion volume to *The Sociology of Small Groups*, by the senior editor (Prentice-Hall, Inc., 1967). Taken together, the two books emphasize current needs and future directions of development. In the other volume, for instance, it is suggested that modern investigators must: (1) expand their scope of inquiry so as eventually to encompass all human groups on the globe; (2) broaden the range of processes considered for any one group to include the domain of the less obvious—emotional undercurrents, unconscious motives and fantasies, implicit assumptions and latent culture; (3) recognize and somehow incorporate into their technology the fact that the growing knowledge that members have of the dynamics of their own group is becoming a more substantial causal factor in their group's life; and (4) devise a new theory which anticipates the far-reaching implications of the capability of system self-awareness and by so doing seriously entertain the notion that, due to new capabilities, the small group may become subject to transformation from one type of system to a more advanced type, from a relatively stable type to one capable of rapid growth into new and more sophisticated levels of operation.

In seeking readings which are resonant with these needs for wider scope, greater depth, and a more dynamic theory of system transformation, we quite naturally arrive at a collection with features of its own. For one thing, its emphasis is theoretical—it presents a variety of theoretical views, from the elemental distinctions between personality, social system, and culture in Parsons *et al.* to the cybernetic model of Deutsch to the controversial conception of the structure of unconscious collective processes presented by Brown. Second, throughout the readings the view is taken that the small group is the interface between the individual and the larger society. And related to this, the selections invite a more relaxed consideration of just what relevance psychoanalytical thought has to the universal sociological issues of authority relations, intimacy among members, role differentiation, and the significance of the "social-whole" for group members' feelings, thoughts, and actions. In general, the collection presents a set of variables—personal, social, cultural, and contextual—that comprise the "field of forces" which, in combination, cause observable processes. Particular selections suggest how these variables are dynamically related to one another. Finally, and in more personal terms, the papers reflect our values, at least in the sense that after having first been read they have not only remained in our thinking but have made it impossible for us to return to our habitual ways of thinking about groups. We hope they will be equally exciting to the reader.

THEODORE M. MILLS
STAN ROSENBERG

# table of contents

the relevance
of
small groups

# the group as interface between the individual and his society

## chapter one

While highlighting some of the empirical generalizations that have emerged from the study of groups, Verba's presentation, exerpted from *Small Groups and Political Behavior*, establishes the subject area of small groups in a broader social science perspective.

Primary groups—whether families, work groups, or informal social, economic, or political cliques—are seen as a central element in even advanced societies, providing an essential link between the social system on the one hand and the individual participant on the other. Both early and adult socializations take place in the face-to-face units that can be discovered in any community or organization. Some are centers of power, whereas others are sources of affection and support for their members. Such groups not only influence the attitudes and behavior of their members but also affect the history of the communities and organizations of which they are a part. Because of these effects and because many functions served by small groups are necessary for the maintenance and effective operation of the larger systems, Verba argues that any analysis of large-scale organizations or social systems must include an examination of the structure and function of the smaller primary units that have developed within the system. The social context in which the small group develops, on the other hand, exerts a strong influence on the nature of the group by representing a social environment to which the groups must adapt.

# The Small Group and Political Behavior

SIDNEY VERBA

## The Small Group and Political Behavior

The fact that individual group members will, under certain circumstances, suppress their own views in order to conform to the dominant group position brings us to the first level of analysis of the impact of the face-to-face group on the political process—its impact on the attitudes, opinions, and behavior of group members. The face-to-face groups to which an individual belongs exert a major influence on him. This influence may be looked upon as taking place in two time periods. In the first place, the primary group plays a major role in the political socialization of the individual before he enters the political process. It forms the predispositions that an individual brings with him into his participation in political affairs. Secondly, the primary groups to which an individual belongs continue to shape his political behavior after he has begun to participate in the political process.

An individual does not enter the political arena totally unprepared. The nature of his first political act—whether it be a vote or the equally significant political act of not voting when the opportunity arises; obeying a law or disobeying a law; showing interest in political affairs or avoiding political affairs—will to a large extent have been

Reprinted from Sidney Verba, *Small Groups and Political Behavior: A Study of Leadership* (Princeton, N.J.: Princeton Univ. Press, 1961), pp. 29-60, by permission of the author and Princeton University Press. Copyright © 1961 by Princeton University Press.

determined by the set of predispositions he brings with him from his experience in primary groups. "Whatever changes the New Age may bring, person-to-person relationships and primary groups will remain the basic character-forming agencies of society."[1] Primary group experiences influence an individual's political behavior in several ways. In such groups individuals develop non-political personality traits and general expectations from interpersonal relations. These traits and interpersonal expectations first receive specifically political content when the individual faces a particular political situation. Or the influence of the primary group can be more directly and manifestly political. Within the primary group, individuals may learn generalized attitudes toward government and the state. These general attitudes include trust and confidence in government, respect for the state and its symbols, respect for law, and the like. On the other hand, the political attitudes learned in the primary group may be quite specific. These may be support for a particular party or issue.

### The Political Personality

The influence of personality traits on political behavior has been stressed in political science for a number of years. The early works of Harold Lasswell, as well as recent works on the authoritarian personality, suggest that much political behavior is a projection of private needs and emotions onto the

[1] Karl Mannheim, *Freedom, Power and Democratic Planning* (London: Routledge, 1951), p. 181.

political sphere.[2] What is of particular interest here is the way in which the authority system in the primary group (what one might call the political system of the family) influences the expectations of the individual in regard to authority in the larger political system. Within the primary group, the individual receives training for roles that he will later play within society. This training consists in both the teaching of certain standards of behavior that can be applied to later situations and, perhaps more significantly, the playing of roles in the family and in other primary gorups that are similar to roles later to be played in the political or economic system.

The type of political structure the child experiences in the family will affect the type of participation that the child will have in other social structures. In a study of ethnocentrism among children, Else Frenkel-Brunswik found that the degree of prejudice among children was related to the family atmosphere. Ethnocentric children tended to come from families in which the authority figure (the father) was strict and rigid, and in which the parent-child relationship was one of dominance and submission. Unprejudiced children came more often from families characterized by a more affectionate and less rigid relationship. It is especially significant that the prejudiced and non-prejudiced children had expectations in non-family role relationships similar to those developed in the family. When asked to describe the "ideal teacher," the two types of children gave quite different answers. Frenkel-Brunswik cites the typical responses of two non-prejudiced boys:

Would carefully listen to your viewpoints and explain what's wrong and what's right about it, and let you argue it out instead of flatly telling you you are wrong. . . . If she can relate her own experiences in relation to some topic you are studying, it is interesting. Has the personality to keep order in the classroom and not afraid the pupils will dislike her if she does. Should accept a joke, but not let it go too far.

Fair in her attitude toward all pupils, doesn't favor one, explains the lessons and helps you within reason.

On the other hand, a highly ethnocentric girl replied: "Someone that is strict. If she asks for homework, you have to have it done. Most teachers are not strict enough. If the assigned work is not in you should be given a zero. She shouldn't let the class get out of hand."[3] Similarly, Baldwin, in a long-term and continuing study of power structure in the home, found that where the political system of the home was an open one—free communication in both directions between parents and children, some participation by children in family decisions, "fair" (not arbitrary) behavior on the part of parents—the children were better prepared to show initiative and participate fully in other role systems.[4]

Numerous writers have attempted to trace styles of political participation and types of political expectations back to early experiences in the family. Both Mannheim and Fromm emphasize that

[2] Harold Lasswell, "Psychopathology and Politics," in *The Political Writings of Harold Lasswell* (New York: The Free Press, 1951); and T. W. Adorno *et al.*, *The Authoritarian Personality* (New York: Harper & Row, Publishers, 1950).

[3] Else Frenkel-Brunswik, "Further Explorations by a Contributor to 'The Authoritarian Personality,'" in Richard Christie and Marie Jahoda, eds., *Studies in the Scope and Method of "The Authoritarian Personality"* (New York: The Free Press, 1954), p. 239.

[4] A. Baldwin, "Socialization and the Parent-Child Relationship," in D. McClelland, ed., *Studies in Motivation* (New York: Appleton-Century-Crofts, 1955).

a stable and independent "democratic" personality, upon which at least to some extent democratic government depends, develops basically in the primary group.[5] Perhaps the major body of literature dealing with the impact of family training on political behavior is that of the "national character" school.[6] A large group of anthropologists and psychologists have attempted to find certain dominant psychological patterns within national societies. The patterns that characterize the "modal" person in that society are developed during earliest childhood experiences. Early childhood experiences may result in a personality that desires a submissive relationship to authority,[7] a personality that alternates between acceptance and rejection of authority,[8] or a personality that thrives on signs of love and acceptance.[9] And these different personalities result in different political behavior in later life. Germans raised in authoritarian families, for instance, will want and expect political leaders to stand in such an authoritarian relationship to them.[10]

Many of the studies of the effects of early family experiences on political behavior have generalized too easily from childhood experiences to adult attitudes. The step from early socialization to political attitudes is a long one and, as we shall suggest below, can be fully understood only in terms of the intervening effects of other intermediate face-to-face contacts and of the political system itself.

## Training for Political Participation

Small group experiences in childhood not only provide certain generalized expectations from political relationships; they also provide training for participation in these relationships. Much of this training of course takes place within the family, but it takes place in other face-to-face situations as well—in the classroom and, especially during adolescence, in the peer group. Furthermore, the training for political participation that takes place in face-to-face groups continues beyond childhood and adolescence.[11]

Participation in decisions in small face-to-face groups where the individual can have some grasp of the alternatives available for choice is a preparation for participation in decisions that are more complex, less immediate,

[5] Mannheim, *Freedom, Power* . . . , p. 181; and Erich Fromm, *Escape from Freedom* (New York: Holt, Rinehart & Winston, 1941), pp. 287 ff.

[6] For a general discussion of this school, see Nathan Leites, "Psychocultural Hypotheses About Political Acts," *World Politics*, I (1948), 102-19; and Margaret Mead, "The Study of National Character," in D. Lerner and H. Lasswell, eds., *The Policy Sciences* (Stanford, Calif.: Stanford Univ. Press, 1951).

[7] David Rodnick, *Postwar Germans* (New Haven: Yale Univ. Press, 1948); and Bertram Schaffner, *Fatherland: A Study of Authoritarianism in the German Family* (New York: Columbia Univ. Press, 1948).

[8] Geoffrey Gorer, *The People of Great Russia* (London: Cresset Press, 1949); and Dinko Tomasic, *The Impact of Russian Culture on Soviet Communism* (New York: The Free Press, 1953).

[9] Geoffrey Gorer, *The American People* (New York: Norton, 1948).

[10] Rodnick, *op. cit.* The same point is made by Fromm, *op. cit.*; Schaffner, *op. cit.*; and Kurt Lewin, *Resolving Social Conflicts* (New York: Harper & Row, Publishers, 1948).

[11] Cf. A. S. Maslow, "Power Relationships and Patterns of Personal Development," in Arthur Kornhauser, ed., *Problems of Power in American Democracy* (Detroit: Wayne State Univ. Press, 1957). The influence of the peer group is discussed in M. Sherif and H. Cantril, *Psychology of Ego-Involvements: Social Attitudes and Identifications* (New York: Wiley, 1947), pp. 156-347. John Dewey argues that democratic techniques must permeate the family, the school, and the community to be effective (*The Public and Its Problems* [Chicago: Gateway Books, 1946], Chaps. 5 and 6).

and engage only a small part of an individual's attention. According to Bryce, "An essential ingredient of a satisfactory democracy is that a considerable proportion of the people should have experience of active participation in the work of small self-governing groups, whether in connection with local government, trade unions, cooperatives, or other forms of activity."[12] Some writers have, in fact, maintained that democracy is possible only in situations in which relations are predominantly face-to-face in nature.[13]

Much of the literature on the authoritarian family suggests that a democratic political system is difficult, if not impossible, to achieve unless there is experience in democratic participation within the family. Levy, for instance, on the basis of his studies of Nazis and anti-Nazis, concluded that democracy could not be introduced into Germany simply by removing authoritarian controls, since there was not sufficient training for democratic participation among the German people.[14] Similarly, it can be argued that an absence of participation in decisions in other face-to-face situations outside the family will affect the level of participation in the broader political system. Crozier, on the basis of a study of administration in French government agencies and industrial organizations, notes a complete absence of participatory leadership. Social distance between different levels in the various organizations is great, and there is little communication. Organizational relations are characterized by a "fear of face-to-face contacts" and a "constant recourse to impersonality."[15] Charles Micaud, who cites the Crozier work, suggests that this lack of face-to-face participation is one reason for the combination of a highly centralized state and highly atomized society in France. Lack of participation leads to an *espoir millénariste* and a desire to escape from political activity. If there were greater participation in primary groups, there might be greater political participation.[16]

---

[12] James Bryce, *Modern Democracies* (New York: Macmillan, 1921), Vol. I, p. 132.

[13] G. D. H. Cole, for instance, maintains that men "can control great affairs only by acting together in the control of small affairs, and finding, through the experience of neighborhood, men whom they can entrust with larger decisions than they can make rationally for themselves. Democracy can work in the great States (and *a fortiori* between great States or over Europe or the world) only if each State is made up of a host of little democracies, and rests finally, not on isolated individuals, but on groups small enough to express the spirit of neighborhood and personal acquaintance. . . . Democracies have either to be small, or to be broken up into small, human groups in which men and women can know and love one another." G. D. H. Cole, *Essays in Social Theory* (London: Macmillan, 1950), pp. 94-95. Cf. J. J. Rousseau, *The Social Contract* (London: Everyman's, 1931), p. 55.

[14] David M. Levy, "Anti-Nazis: Criteria of Differentiation," in Alfred H. Stanton and Stewart E. Perry, eds., *Personality and Political Crisis* (New York: The Free Press, 1951). The importance of primary group participation as a basis for a democratic political system is stressed in Lewin, "The Special Case of Germany," in *Resolving Social Conflicts.*

[15] Michel Crozier, "La France, Terre de Commandement," *Esprit*, XXV (1957), 779-98; and Crozier, "Pour une Sociologie de l'Administration Publique," *Revue Française de Science Politique*, VI (1956), 750-69.

[16] Charles Micaud, unpublished manuscript on the French Left, Chap. 2. Micaud cites Charles Bettelheim and Suzanne Frère, who point out the low level of participation in face-to-face relations in *Une Ville Française Moyenne: Auxerre en 1950* (Paris: Armand Colin, 1950). Only 18 per cent of the men and 38 per cent of the women of Auxerre visit each other. They do belong to a large number of interest groups, but these are centrally organized with headquarters in Paris. This is supported by Roy V. Peel, *The Political Clubs of New York* (New York: Putnam, 1945), who found that France had none of the diffuse, social-political local clubs found in American cities. A similar finding is

Participation in decisions on levels below that of the political system is a requisite or, at least, a desirable adjunct to a democratic political system. In the first place, insofar as significant political decisions are made in such sub-groups, effective participation in the political system will not exist unless members can participate on these lower levels. Furthermore, participation in decisions is much easier within smaller units. In larger units, the organizational necessities associated with a larger structure make participation difficult, if not impossible. Bureaucratic structures, introduced to bring rationality into the organization, limit participation. The decision process and the effects of decisions are less visible. Communication on an organization-wide basis requires the use of formal media, more easily controlled by the hierarchy. And the complexity of decisions is likely to limit the ability of the individual members to comprehend the

issues involved.[17] Evidence of the rarity of participation by members in organization decisions is found in numerous studies.[18] The proposition is also supported by the finding in numerous small group studies that as the size of the group increases, there is a tendency toward less free participation on the part of group members and toward the concentration of group activities in the hands of a single leader.[19]

The most complete study of the relationship between the existence of small

---

reported by Lawrence Wylie, *Village in the Vaucluse* (Cambridge, Mass.: Harvard Univ. Press, 1957). See also Edward C. Banfield, *The Moral Basis of a Backward Society* (New York: The Free Press, 1958), for a similar, but more extreme, situation in a southern Italian village.

The view that the type of participation in the face-to-face group will be similar to the type of participation on other levels is supported by some findings in a different context from the one discussed above. It has been found in military and industrial situations that leaders of lower-level, face-to-face groups tend to stress participation of the group members in decisions if the leaders in the hierarchy above them also stress participation. The style of leadership in the higher levels of the organization is directly related to the style on lower levels. See Stanley Seashore, "Administrative Leadership and Organizational Effectiveness," in Rensis Likert and Samuel P. Hayes, eds., *Some Applications of Behavioral Research* (Paris: UNESCO, 1957), p. 57; and Edwin A. Fleischman, "Leadership Climate, Human Relations Training and Supervisory Behavior," *Personnel Psychology*, VI (1953), 205-22.

[17] These reasons why participation is difficult, if not impossible, in large organizations are essentially the ones suggested by R. Michels, *Political Parties* (New York: The Free Press, 1949), pp. 2-44, 130-35, 185-204, and *passim*. Cf. Seymour M. Lipset, Martin A. Trow, and James S. Coleman, *Union Democracy: The Internal Politics of the International Typographical Union* (New York: The Free Press, 1956), pp. 9-10.

[18] Michels (*op. cit.*) is still the classic study on the German Socialist Party and trade unions. See also M. Duverger, *Political Parties* (London: Methuen, 1954), pp. 151-68; Oliver Garceau, *The Political Life of the AMA* (Cambridge, Mass.: Harvard Univ. Press, 1941); and David Truman, *The Governmental Process* (New York: Knopf, 1951), pp. 139-55.

[19] Carter and his associates found that as group size is increased from four to eight members, a more restricted atmosphere develops. "In the group of four, each individual has sufficient latitude of space in which to behave and thus the basic abilities of each individual can be expressed; but in the larger group only the more forceful individuals are able to express their abilities and ideas, since the amount of freedom in the situation is not sufficient to accommodate all the group members." Launor Carter *et al.*, "The Relation of Categorization and Rating in the Observation of Group Behavior," *Human Relations*, IV (1951), 250.

Similar results are reported by R. F. Bales *et al.*, "Channels of Communications in Small Groups," *American Sociological Review*, XVI (1951) 461-68; and by F. F. Stephan and E. G. Mischler, "The Distribution of Participation in Small Groups: An Exponential Approximation," *American Sociological Review*, XVII (1952), 598-608.

sub-units in which individuals can participate and organizational democracy is that of the International Typographical Union carried on by Lipset, Trow, and Coleman. Unlike most other unions, the ITU has maintained a democratic system. This is attributed by the authors to the existence of numerous formal and informal sub-groups to which the members belong. Most of these sub-groups are formally apolitical and deal with social affairs, but they perform a number of important political functions. They are centers of communication about what is going on in the union. Through them, members develop interest in union affairs and are drawn into participation in union politics. Participation in the sub-units also trains potential leaders for union office—training that otherwise would have to take place within the organizational hierarchy. Thus a pool of potential leaders not necessarily committed to the existing leadership is developed. Furthermore, the sub-units serve as possible alternate power centers to challenge the leadership hierarchy. The maintenance of democracy in the large organization—the ITU—is, therefore, highly dependent upon the existence of sub-groups in which members can participate, even though these groups are not formally political.[20]

## Small Group Roles and Political Roles

Though experiences within primary groups profoundly influence political behavior, one cannot accept any simple primary group monism and look for the explanation of all political behavior within the family, the peer group, and other primary groups. Political behavior is not determined solely by the predispositions that an individual brings

into the political process from his experiences and training in primary groups. It is also affected by the way in which the political system interacts with these predispositions. The political system can channel political behavior in a number of directions. Insofar as political predispositions are molded in childhood, they are developed in essentially non-political situations. The point is obvious but significant. It means that predictions that can be made about adult political behavior on the basis of childhood experiences will be limited to a rather general set of predispositions that an individual brings into the political process—in a sense, to an individual's psychological orientation to politics. We may be able to predict some of the psychological satisfactions that he will seek from political participation, but we will know little about the political content of that participation. This content will depend, among other things, upon the position of the individual within the political structure and the alternatives that the political structure offers him. As Shils has pointed out in his commentary on the Berkeley studies of authoritarianism, similar authoritarian personality traits may be directed toward the Left (Communism) or the Right (Fascism), depending upon the political environment in which the individual finds himself.[21]

The limitation in the range of choices that any political system offers an individual means that particular predispositions and expectations developed in early primary group situations may be directed into diverse political activities, depending upon the political environment. But the range of choices within the political system may also direct the individual seeking to satisfy

---

[20] Lipset, Trow, and Coleman, *op. cit.*, Chaps. 4-9.

[21] E. A. Shils, in Christie and Jahoda, eds., *Studies in the Scope . . .* , p. 24.

expectations developed in the primary group in another direction—out of politics. This situation will arise if the political system cannot satisfy the needs developed in primary groups. Much of the literature that attempts to link childhood experiences and political behavior assumes that the political system will be congruent with the patterns in the primary group and will satisfy the needs developed there. Authoritarians will find an authoritarian political system, and non-authoritarians will participate in democratic relationships. But this assumption is not necessarily valid. This can be seen if we compare the relationship between family training and political participation in France and Germany. According to Schaffner, the political orientation of the German people is a reflection of the respect for authority learned within the family. Thus the Germans readily accepted Hitler, "whose manner was that of the traditional German father: it inspired confidence."[22] The French family system, according to Rodnick, has a similar pattern and develops expectations similar to those of the German family. "Individuals [are] conditioned to expect guidance and a dependency relationship from their authority figures."[23] But, unlike the German political system, the French system has produced (at least, until recently) no authority figures who inspire such confidence. The individual cannot find satisfaction in the political sphere for needs developed in the family. "The reaction against authority has been because it has been weak rather than because it has been strong."[24]

Similar role experience in primary groups may, therefore, lead to quite different political behaviors. The question as to whether there is pressure toward homogeneity among the various political systems to which a person belongs is still open. Do those who experience one type of authority in the family, school, and peer group desire the same type of authority in their economic and political relations? Some of the evidence we have cited suggests that such will be the case, but it may well be that in certain situations there is a high degree of autonomy among the various authority systems in which a person participates. Further research is needed on the relationship between primary group training and political predispositions.[25]

## Political Attitudes and the Small Group

The impact of the primary group on politics has been discussed so far in terms of the political structure of the primary group. Participation in families, peer groups, work groups, and

---

[22] Schaffner, *Fatherland*, p. 75.
[23] David Rodnick, *An Interim Report on French Culture* (Maxwell Air Force Base, Ala.: Human Resources Institute, 1953).
[24] *Ibid.* This section does not necessarily agree with the accuracy of the descriptions by Schaffner and Rodnick. Their works are used merely as examples of the type of interaction that may take place between primary group training and political structures to influence the political behavior of the individual.
[25] The problem of connecting roles in small face-to-face groups with roles in larger systems is a thorny one about which little is known. Roles in face-to-face groups—say, the role of participant in decisions or the role of leader—may be quite different from participant or leadership roles in larger systems. Authority patterns in a small group where all members communicate directly are clearly not the same as authority patterns in systems in which communication is indirect and authority figures are distant. On the question of moving from analysis of roles on the small group level to analysis of roles in larger systems, see Talcott Parsons, "The Small Group and the Larger Social System," in Roy R. Grinker, ed., *Toward a Unified Theory of Human Behavior* (New York: Basic Books, 1956), and S. Verba, *Small Groups and Political Behavior*.

other formally apolitical groups influences the individual's style of political behavior by developing certain expectations of political roles and certain skills for political role-playing. But the impact of the face-to-face group on political affairs can be more direct and have a more specific political content. The explicit political attitudes with which an individual comes into contact in the face-to-face group have a significant impact on his political views and behavior. This is especially so in the light of the strong influence that the primary group has on the attitudes of its members. This primary group influence does not involve the development of a political "personality" or of generalized role expectations that receive political content only when brought into contact with the political system, but the impact of the primary group may be on quite general political attitudes as well as on specific political opinions. Thus children may learn by direct teaching, or by observing the political attitudes and behaviors of their parents, certain general attitudes toward the state, toward law, and toward other political groups. They may learn to have trust and confidence in political figures, or to look with distrust and disdain on politics. They may learn respect or disrespect for law. This aspect of political socialization has been little explored, but there is reason to believe that it is very significant. French *incivisme* was explained by Rodnick in terms of the disappointment of the individual Frenchman at not finding in the political system the strong authority figure that he had been led to expect by his experience in the family; and by Crozier and Micaud in terms of the lack of primary group training for participation. But *incivisme* is probably also influenced by the explicit attitudes toward the political system that young people hear from the adults around

them. Wylie reports that the children in the French village he studied ". . . constantly hear adults referring to Government as the source of evil and to the men who run it as instruments of evil. There is nothing personal in this belief. It does not concern one particular Government composed of one particular group of men. It concerns Government everywhere and at all times—French Governments, American Governments, Russian Governments, all Governments. Some are less bad than others, but all are essentially bad."[26]

The development of political attitudes begins in the family. The relations between the attitudes of parents and those of their children have been most widely explored in the fields of intergroup relations and voting behavior. Studies of grade-school children as well as of college students have found that the racial attitudes of parents are a major influence on the attitudes of children.[27] Voting behavior is also influenced by early family experiences: "Indeed it would not be inappropriate to consider the family as the primary unit of voting analysis. . . ."[28] The

---

26 Wylie, *Village in the Vaucluse*, p. 208. It is interesting to note that this political education is effective despite the fact that it is in direct conflict with the teachings of the school civics textbooks. *Ibid.*, pp. 106-7. This is another example of the greater effectiveness of informal as against formal communications.

27 The study of grade-school children is by E. L. and R. L. Horowitz, "Development of Social Attitudes in Children," *Sociometry*, I (1938), 301-8. The college student study is by G. W. Allport and B. M. Kramer, "Some Roots of Prejudice," *Journal of Psychology*, XXII (1946), 9-39. These and other corroborative studies are discussed in John Harding *et al.*, "Prejudice and Ethnic Relations," in G. Lindzey, ed., *The Handbook of Social Psychology* (Reading, Mass.: Addison-Wesley, 1959), Vol. II, Chap. 27.

28 B. R. Berelson *et al.*, *Voting* (Chicago: Univ. of Chicago Press, 1954), p. 93.

panel studies of voting behavior indicate that between two-thirds and three-quarters of the American voters vote for the party for which their fathers voted.[29] The family may also influence the general tendency of an individual's political affiliation, rather than the specific party for which he votes. Thus members of the Communist Party show a tendency to come from radical and left-wing, but not necessarily Communist, families.[30] The emphasis in much of the literature on the connection between family experience and such implicit personality-oriented attitudes as authoritarianism may have led to an underestimation of the more manifest and direct political training that an individual receives in primary groups. On the basis of an analysis of numerous studies of political socialization, Herbert Hyman concludes that socialization into party affiliation seems to take place earlier than that into ideological orientation. Similarly, while there is little evidence for an implicit personality-oriented authoritarianism among children, studies have found that manifestly political authoritarian attitudes (say, opposition to civil rights) are more highly developed at a young age.[31]

The influence of the primary group on voting extends beyond that of the family during childhood. The face-to-face contact that a voter has during a campaign has a significant effect on his voting choice. This was the "discovery" made in the Erie County voting study: that not only does one's class, religion, occupation, and residence affect one's voting choice, but the small face-to-face groups in which one participates play an important role.[32] A major finding in relation to the role of the small face-to-face group in voting and other decisions is that the mass media of communication, rather than acting directly upon the individual audience member, act upon individuals through a "two-step communication process." Certain community members, it was found, are more receptive to the communications of the mass media. These "opinion leaders," in turn, pass on the content of these media to those with whom they have face-to-face contact.[33] The discovery of the intermediary role of face-to-face communication between the individual and the mass media serves as a strong qualification of the conception of modern society as a "mass society"—a place where lone individuals stand naked and defenseless before the mass media. The two-step process of communication has been found in voting and community studies in this country. It has also been found as a major determinant of the lack of impact of hostile propaganda on the *Wehrmacht* and as an important tech-

29 *Ibid.*; and P. F. Lazarsfeld *et al.*, *The People's Choice* (New York: Columbia Univ. Press, 1948). Of course, since children usually share certain politically relevant characteristics with their parents—residence, class, religion, ethnic group—the relationship between vote of father and vote of child may not be due to family influence. The Elmira voting study attempted to test the relative weight of family influence and social characteristics. Among those having family influences and social characteristics that led in different political directions (members of the working class whose fathers had voted Republican; members of the middle class whose fathers had voted Democratic), family influence was found to play as large a role as social position. Berelson *et al.*, *Voting*, pp. 88-93.
30 Gabriel A. Almond, *The Appeals of Communism* (Princeton, N.J.: Princeton Univ. Press, 1954), pp. 221-24.

31 Herbert Hyman, *Political Socialization* (New York: The Free Press, 1958), p. 47.
32 Lazarsfeld *et al.*, *op. cit.* Chap. 15, and Berelson *et al.*, *op. cit.*, pp. 137-38.
35 See Elihu Katz, "The Two-Step Flow of Communications," *Public Opinion Quarterly*, XXI (1957), 61-78.

nique of propaganda and agitation in the Soviet Union.[34]

The face-to-face communication groups found by Lazarsfeld and his associates in the voting studies and the Decatur study, as well as the primary group in the *Wehrmacht*, are informal parts of the communication process. These groups did not come together with the explicit purpose of linking the individual and the mass media. They are not planned parts of the communication process. But, as was mentioned earlier, face-to-face groups are not necessarily informal. Their communication functions may be explicitly planned. One of the major sources of the strength of the Communist Party, it has been suggested, is the fact that it is organized on the basis of cells, for which the optimum size is about 15-20 members.[35] The strength of the cell system lies not only in its greater adaptability to clandestine action, but in the greater influence that such small meetings can have on the attitudes of the members. For many members, Micaud points out, the cell is a substitute for primary ties in family or church. Furthermore, it performs the intermediary function in the two-step process of communication. The Party literature is available in the cell, and its transmission in the small group context gives it an especially strong impact.[36]

The process of transmitting communications from the mass media through the face-to-face group is not merely one of amplification. Communications from the group's external environment do not reach the group unchanged by the process of face-to-face transmission. The views of the opinion leader will, of course, affect the content of the transmitted message. So will the nature of the group. Communications that challenge the solidarity of the group, for instance, tend to be rejected by group members.[37]

The participation of an individual in politically relevant face-to-face groups affects not only the content of his political attitudes, but the intensity of these attitudes as well. There are two variables to be considered here: (1) the range of primary groups in which there is political participation; and (2) the homogeneity of that participation. The wider the range of primary contacts that are politicized, the greater the intensity of political participation. In a survey in France, voters were asked: "Before voting, do you discuss the election with others in your circle?" The percentage answering "yes" is shown in Table 1, broken down into party affiliation.[38] The interesting point of these figures is that not only do the Communist supporters report discussion within the family more frequently than do the supporters of the other parties, but unlike the other parties there is no falling off in the frequency of discussion among Communists as one moves from family to friends to colleagues on the job. The political intensity of the Communist supporter is manifested in the high degree of politicization of the range of primary groups to which he belongs.

Secondly, the greater the homogeneity of primary group contacts, the greater the intensity of political participation. In *Voting* it was found that

[34] E. A. Shils and M. Janowitz, *Public Opinion Quarterly*, XII (1948); and Alex Inkeles, *Public Opinion in the Soviet Union* (Cambridge, Mass.: Harvard Univ. Press, 1950), Chaps. 5-8.

[35] Duverger, *Political Parties*, pp. 28-30.

[36] Charles Micaud, "Organization and Leadership of the French Communist Party," *World Politics*, IV (1952), 318-55; and Inkeles, *op. cit.*, p. 84.

[37] See Shils and Janowitz, *op. cit.*

[38] From Jean Stoetzel, "Voting Behavior in France," *British Journal of Sociology*, VI (1955), 119.

TABLE 1     **Per Cent Saying They Discuss Politics**

| Party preference | With family | With friends | With colleagues |
|---|---|---|---|
| Communist | 68% | 65% | 69% |
| Socialist | 53 | 49 | 42 |
| Radical | 58 | 49 | 31 |
| MRP | 51 | 43 | 40 |
| Moderates | 53 | 53 | 36 |
| RPF | 58 | 51 | 32 |

voters with friends of various political persuasions were less strong in their voting intentions than those whose friends were all of the same persuasion. McCloskey and Dahlgren report similar findings, both for relations within the primary group and for those among primary groups. The greater the political homogeneity of a particular primary group—for instance, the more solid a family is in one political direction—the more likely the individual is to be a stable voter in that direction. And the greater the political homogeneity among the family of origin, the present family, and the peer group, the more likely the individual is to be a stable voter in that direction.[39]

**The Small Group and the Political System**

That the face-to-face group plays a significant role in the political process is now clear. The process of decision-making in small groups has been described, as has the influence of the small group on the political attitudes and behaviors of its members. What remains is to consider the small group

———

[39] Berelson et al., Voting, p. 98; and Herbert McCloskey and Harold E. Dahlgren, "Primary Group Influence on Party Loyalty," American Political Science Review, LIII (1960), 757-76.

from the point of view of the operation of the political system as a whole. That face-to-face relationships have an impact on the political system because these groups influence the attitudes of their members is not to say what that impact is likely to be. To relate the face-to-face group to a theory of the political system, we shall look at (1) the effect of the discovery of "pre-modern" primary structures in the modern political system on the theoretical distinction between modern and traditional political systems and (2) the relationship between face-to-face contacts and political stability.

*Face-to-Face Groups in Traditional and Modern Systems*

The discussion so far indicates clearly that there is no absolute distinction between modern and traditional systems in terms of the absence or presence of significant primary structures. In both systems, primary, face-to-face contacts play an important role. But if the contrast between the traditional and the modern was once too sharply drawn, the discovery of these pre-modern primary structures in modern society does not justify the opposite conclusion that an analysis of primary group phenomena cannot be used to distinguish these two types of system. Though both types of system contain primary structures, distinctions can be drawn in two ways: (1) in terms of the *types* of politically significant primary structures and (2) in terms of the relative *importance* of primary and secondary structures.

(1) *Types of Primary Structure.* Though primary structures persist in modern systems, they tend to be penetrated and modernized by the larger organizations of which they are a part. It was a significant finding of the "rediscovery" of the primary group that these groups regulate behavior within the larger systems to which they belong. But the primary group is in turn regulated by these larger systems. Though the primary groups discovered in the modern factory and army are often informal and unplanned in relation to the larger organization, the structure of these groups is greatly influenced by the framework set for them by the organization. The composition and location of these informal primary groups are largely determined by the formal structure of the organization. Informal groups in factories or in the army usually develop only where the formal organizational structure facilitates frequent contact—at certain locations in the plant or in the squads of the army. Thus to a large extent the formal rules determine who interacts with whom. More important is the fact that the formal organization impinges on the informal, internal interaction of the group. If, for instance, some of the members of the informal face-to-face group have higher statuses within the formal organization, this will affect the structure of interaction as well as the degree of solidarity within the group. Similarly, the degree to which the group members are oriented to the norms of the formal organization in contrast to those of the group—for instance, are interested in promotional opportunities—affects interaction within the group.[40]

Relations within primary groups tend to be affective, diffuse, and particularistic. But they differ greatly in the extent to which they approach this pattern. The informal, face-to-face group in a modern organizational context is pre-modern in orientation when contrasted with the secondary system of which it is a part, but it tends to be quite modern when contrasted with primary groups in a traditional society. The work group discovered in the Western Electric Hawthorne plant is in this respect quite different from the traditional family. And within the industrial society there is wide variation in the degree to which primary structures approach the traditional pattern. Thus the street corner gang studied by Whyte is much more inclusive and intimate than the industrial work group in the Bank Wiring Room of the Hawthorne plant. The commitment of the individual member is much greater in the former group. In contrasting the modern and traditional systems it is thus important to note what types of primary groups are politically relevant.

(2) *The Relative Importance of Primary Structures.* The relative importance of primary structures differs from society to society, with a tendency for them to be more important in traditional societies. This can be measured in two ways: (1) the relative weight given to primary and secondary group norms and (2) the relative degree to which political functions are performed in primary and secondary structures. Though in both the traditional and the modern societies, pri-

---

[40] See Leonard R. Sayles, *Behavior of Industrial Work Groups: Prediction and Control* (New York: Wiley, 1958), Chap. 3.

mary groups are significant reference points for norms and attitudes, the weight of loyalty to primary norms differs. Ike writes of the situation that would arise in Japanese politics if an individual were caught between ". . . conflicting loyalties: loyalty to his political principles and convictions and his obligation or *on* to an individual" —*on* being the sense of obligation developed in an intimate face-to-face relationship. In a conflict situation of this sort, the dominant norms in Japanese society would require that the individual fulfill his personal, particularistic obligation rather than follow the universalistic criteria associated with his loyalty to the rules of the impersonal political system. If he did not follow the norms associated with his loyalty to an individual, he would be ". . . subjected to social disapproval and criticism."[41] One can imagine a similar conflict in the American political system between obligation and loyalty to one's primary group—family and friends—and loyalty to the abstract rules of political principle. And no one can deny that often the particularistic criteria will prevail, and that bureaucrat, voter, or legislator will behave according to standards other than those prescribed by the rules of the formal political system. But though such behavior is likely to exist, it would receive blame in the United States, rather than the praise it receives in Japanese politics. Thus, though primary loyalties exist in both systems, the weight placed on these loyalties differs.[42]

In the modern system, furthermore, the number of significant political functions performed within primary groups will not be as great as in the traditional system. Face-to-face groups will tend to share the performance of political functions with secondary structures. Thus, while in the modern system the face-to-face group plays a significant role in political communication as a mediator between the mass media and the individual, it shares the communication function with these media. And insofar as primary groups in modern systems tend to be more functionally specific, greater demands are placed upon secondary structures to regulate the relations among these groups.

Thus an analysis of primary group phenomena as they appear in traditional and modern systems is still useful in drawing distinctions between these two systems if the types of primary structure and their relations with the larger system are elaborated.

The next question we shall deal with in placing the analysis of the primary group within the context of the political system is the relationship between face-to-face contacts and political stability. Do face-to-face groups act to support the political system, or are they destructive and subversive forces from the point of view of the central political structure? Clearly a question of this sort when asked in such general terms can only be answered in such terms. The specific content of the impact of any face-to-face group—the particular attitude influenced, the particular decision made—depends of course upon the specific group and the specific situation. It is, however, possible

---

[41] Nobutaka Ike, *Japanese Politics* (New York: Knopf, 1957), pp. 31-33. Cf. Chitoshi Yanaga, *Japanese People and Politics* (New York: Wiley, 1956), p. 69.

[42] Apter points out the extent to which primary groups are more important in a traditional system such as that of the Gold Coast than in a Western system. David Apter, *The Gold Coast in Transition* (Princeton, N.J.: Princeton Univ. Press, 1955), p. 288. But

even among primitive societies, the weight given face-to-face loyalties varies with, among other things, the size of the tribe. See I Schapera, *Government and Politics in Tribal Societies* (London: Watts, 1956).

---

to describe some general effects that the face-to-face group has as both subverter and supporter of the political system, as well as to suggest some variables that affect the direction in which primary group pressures will go.

## The Small Group in Conflict with the Political System

The face-to-face group may conflict with the larger political system of which it is a part in several ways. In the first place, the very existence of primary groups which have an effect on the political system may be regarded as a source of conflict with the development of a rational, efficient system. Secondly, the face-to-face group may support particular behaviors or attitudes that are deviant in terms of the norms of the larger system. We shall look at these in turn.

(1) The "Irrationality" of Small Group Behavior. It was once a common view among sociologists, as Shils has pointed out, to consider the primary group and modern society ". . . logically antithetical and empirically incompatible. . . . The persistence of traditionally regulated informal and intimate relations was regarded as an archaism inherited from an older rural society or from a small-town handicraft society."[43] This view that informal relations are *per se* in conflict with larger structures is found among those administrative theorists who view organizations as essentially rational and formal. Though the organization planner will have to consider the informal relations that exist within an organization, he will look at them as deviations from the formal pattern and will try to minimize them. Urwick describes

the process of designing an organization:

He [the planner] should never for a moment pretend that these difficulties don't exist. They do exist; they are realities. Nor, when he has drawn up an ideal plan of organization, is it likely he will be able to fit in all the human material perfectly. There will be small adjustments . . . in all kinds of directions. But those adjustments are deliberate and temporary deviations from the pattern in order to deal with idiosyncrasy. . . .

What is suggested is that problems of organization should be handled in *the right order*. Personal adjustments must be made insofar as they are necessary. But fewer of them will be necessary and they will present fewer deviations from what is logical and simple, if the organizer first makes a plan, a design. . . .[44]

Insofar as the face-to-face groups in larger structures are informal—that is, perform unplanned functions—they are here looked on as in conflict with what is felt to be the essential planned rationality of the larger structure.

Similarly, it was pointed out earlier that the face-to-face voting groups are informal in the sense that their function in influencing voting decisions is a form of influence which has not been considered by traditional theories of the way in which a democracy operates.[45] In this sense, face-to-face contacts in voting can be considered to be in conflict with the operation of a "rational" democratic system in which voting choices are made on the basis of principle or a rational calculation of interests, or both. V. O. Key contrasts the voting decision made on the basis of party or issue with that made on a

[43] Shils, in Lerner and Lasswell, eds., *Policy Sciences*, p. 44.

[44] L. Urwick, *The Elements of Administration* (New York: Harper & Row, Publishers, 1953), pp. 36-39.

[45] Bernard Berelson, "Democratic Theory and Opinion," *Public Opinion Quarterly*, XVI (1952), 313-30; and Berelson *et al.*, Voting, Chap. 14.

"friends and neighbors" basis. The support of a candidate by his "friends and neighbors who know him" is an indication of ". . . the absence of stable, well-organized, state-wide factions of like-minded citizens formed to advocate measures of a common concern. In its extreme form, localism justifies a diagnosis of low voter interest in public issues and a susceptibility to control by the irrelevant appeal to support the hometown boy. . . . If the factions within the Democratic Party of Alabama amounted to political parties, a candidate's strength in the vote from county to county would not be appreciably influenced by his place of residence. A well-knit group of voters and leaders scattered over the entire state would deliver about the same proportion of vote to its candidate wherever he happened to live. A concern for issues (or at least group success) would override local attachments. In well-developed two-party situations, localism is minimized, if not erased, by a larger concern for party victory. The classic case is that of Duchess County, New York, the home of Franklin D. Roosevelt, a Democrat of some note. The county, traditionally Republican, stubbornly held to its party attachments and repeatedly failed to return a majority for even its most distinguished son. Radically different voting behavior characterizes battles within the Alabama Democratic primaries. A candidate for governor normally carries his own county by a huge political majority, and the harshest criticism that can be made of a politician is that he cannot win his own beat or precinct. If his friends and neighbors who know him do not support him, why should those without this advantage trust a candidate?"[46]

In this view, personal influence in the voting decision is looked at as the antithesis of a voting decision made on the basis of party or issue; the passage cited above would seem to reflect a belief that such face-to-face influence is inconsistent with political choices made on a rational democratic basis. This view of a conflict between the primary group and the rational political system or the rational organization may, however, be more a reflection of an artificial, rational model than a reflection of actual conflict between primary and secondary structures.[47]

(2) *Deviant Small Groups.* Face-to-face participation will also be in conflict with the larger political system if the particular norms of that system differ from those of the face-to-face group. Thus conformity to the face-to-face group, when that group is a deviant one, will mean non-conformity to the norms of the larger system.

I . . . have been, am still, a criminal. But there is a sense in which I have been an almost abjectly law-abiding person. From my very first years I adapted myself wholeheartedly to the community I lived in, accepting its values, obeying its imperatives, observing its customs. Submissiveness could go no further. If, then, law-abidingness is acting according to the dictates of the community you were born into, there never was a more law-abiding person than myself.

But, unfortunately or otherwise, the community I was born into was a small one at variance with the larger community containing it. In obeying the laws of the criminal quarter I incurred the disapproval of the law courts.[48]

[46] V. O. Key, *Southern Politics* (New York: Knopf, 1949), pp. 37-38.

[47] As the studies of Berelson and Lazarsfeld have shown, face-to-face contact is not necessarily in conflict with political choice on the basis of party or issue. Even decisions based on party or issue are made in a face-to-face context.

[48] From an autobiographical novel by Mark Benney, *Low Company* (New York

Similarly, the people with radical family backgrounds who join in radical political movements will be conforming to their primary group background, though they are deviants from the point of view of the larger political system.

Conversely, the absence of strong face-to-face commitments on the part of the individual strengthens the norms of the general political system. As illustrated in the Elmira voting study, in a dominantly Republican community, this dominant norm has its least effect where the face-to-face group is "solid"; that is, where one participates in face-to-face groups of homogeneous political composition. Where the face-to-face group is "solid,"

. . . the strong community majority for the Republicans has little effect because it has little access to persons within homogeneous Democratic groups.

But when the primary environment is internally *divided*, the effect of the distant community can be seen. Then the Republicans get a higher proportion of the vote. . . . The impact of the larger community is thus most evident among voters with discordant or disagreeing primary groups. When the voter's close associates do not provide him with a single, clear political direction—when instead they offer an alternative—then wider associations in the surrounding community reinforce one position over the other.[49]

Attachments to face-to-face groups may thus lessen the impact of the overall political culture on the individual. This fact is especially relevant in totalitarian societies. Insofar as such societies demand total loyalty to the state, loyalties to primary groups are in conflict with the dominant political norm. Attachment to a family or other primary group places an area of behavior outside government control. Thus, in Soviet theory, loyalty to primary groups is "deemed intolerable."[50] "Family circles" (informal cliques of local officials) have often come under severe criticism in the Soviet Union because of the many illicit activities that go on in them. Fainsod reports the exposure of such a "family circle" in Smolensk which had been formed for the self-protection of the local leaders against the demands placed on them by Moscow. The important point about these "families" is that while they were for the central government "the mortal enemy of control," they performed significant functions for the members in providing them with a

---

[50] Raymond Bauer, Alex Inkeles, and Clyde Kluckhohn, *How the Soviet System Works* (Cambridge, Mass.: Harvard Univ. Press, 1956), p. 81. See also Margaret Mead, *Soviet Attitudes Toward Authority* (New York: McGraw-Hill, 1951), pp. 55-57. On the attempts of totalitarian societies to atomize interpersonal relations below the level of the state, see Robert A. Nisbet, *The Quest for Community* (New York: Oxford Univ. Press, 1953), Chap. 8; and Hannah Arendt, *The Origins of Totalitarianism* (New York: Harper & Row, Publishers, 1951).

That attachment to a primary group is a possible challenge to the state has long been realized. Thus Plato argues in *The Republic* that communal property and families will prevent the guardians of the state from having divided loyalties. They can then serve the state better. "Both the community of property and the community of families, as I am saying, tend to make them more truly guardians; they will not tear the city in pieces by differing about 'mine' and 'not mine'; each man dragging any acquisitions which he has made into a separate house of his own, where he has a separate wife and children and private pleasures and pains; but all will be affected as far as may be by the same pleasures and pains because they are all of one opinion about what is near and dear to them, and, therefore, they will all tend towards a common goal." *The Republic*, Book V, Jowett translation.

---

Avon, 1952), quoted in Morton Grodzins, *The Loyal and Disloyal* (Chicago: Univ. of Chicago Press, 1956), p. 42.

[49] Berelson *et al., Voting*, pp. 100-101.

sanctuary. The main reason why the "family" system grew in the local area studied by Fainsod was an "almost desperate desire for relaxation and security" in the face of the overwhelming production demands of the central government.[51]

## The Small Group and Political Stability

Face-to-face groups are not necessarily in conflict with the political system. They also perform significant supportive functions. The norms they support, for instance, may be norms that are congruent with those of the larger system. They may supply the individual member with affective outputs, the absence of which might place burdens on the political system. And they are a source of flexibility in running the system. Let us look at these functions in turn.

(1) *Socialization for Citizenship.* The major supportive role played by the primary group is the socialization of children to take adult roles in the political process. We have emphasized above some ways in which socialization into deviant political roles may take place. But it is highly probable that unless a large proportion of the population is socialized into behaviors that support the political system, that system will be highly unstable. In any case, even totalitarian states, afraid of competition from the family for the loyalty of their citizens, have had to

revise doctrine so as to accept the basic role the family plays in socialization.[52]

Political socialization, furthermore, continues beyond childhood. Face-to-face contacts have a continuing effect on the individual's political attitudes and behavior. These face-to-face groups may, it was pointed out, support norms that are deviant from the point of view of the political system. They may, on the other hand, foster norms that are supportive of that system. What determines whether the pressures placed upon the individual in his face-to-face contacts—both as a child and later—will act to further the goals of the larger system? The question is a difficult one, but some tentative hypotheses may be offered.[53]

(a) Insofar as the leaders of the political system can directly penetrate and control the interaction process within the face-to-face group, the norms set by that process will tend to support the larger system. The ability of the totalitarian system to influence norm setting within the family is the clearest example. In the first place, the political system may directly penetrate the family communication process. Interviews with Soviet *émigrés* reveal that it is a norm of Soviet family conduct that one does not express non-conforming attitudes in front of the children because of the possibility of inadvertent betrayal. Thus even if the political system cannot completely control the norms held by adult family members it can limit their transmission to the children. Secondly, insofar as the political system firmly controls the other norm-setting institutions to which the child is exposed—the school, the media and so on—the parents are limited i

---

[51] Merle Fainsod, *Smolensk Under Soviet Rule* (Cambridge, Mass.: Harvard Univ. Press, 1958), pp. 48-50, 92, 111. . . . See also Barrington Moore, *Terror and Progress: USSR* (Cambridge, Mass.: Harvard Univ. Press, 1954), p. 161. Moore writes: "From the point of view of the rulers, a 'good' friendship clique is one that aids in the execution of policy, while from the point of view of the population a 'good' clique is one that aids in the evasion of policy."

[52] See Moore, *op. cit.*, pp. 158-60.
[53] For a similar discussion in the context of organization theory, see James March and Herbert Simon, *Organizations* (New York: Wiley, 1958), pp. 78-81.

the choice of norms that they may pass on to the children.[54]

(b) The greater the degree of cultural fusion between the primary and secondary structures, the more the norms of the small group will support the larger system. The fusion of the standards of the small group and the larger system may come from the "modernization" of the primary group by the larger system, or it may come from the diffusion upward of the primary group's particularistic and diffuse values into the political system. Whichever the direction of influence, this interpenetration of the two systems will increase the probability that the face-to-face group will further norms that support the political system. Almond suggests that it is the degree of fusion between the informal, traditional group component and the modern, secondary component of the political system that differentiates French from British politics. In the former the two components are isolated and antagonistic; in the latter they are fused and supportive.[55]

(c) The more the face-to-face group perceives itself as participating in the decisions of the political system, the more the sub-group will tend to support the norms of the political system. The "participation hypothesis" is one of the basic hypotheses of small group research. It appears to have a wide range of political applicability, though its generality may be limited to cultures with value systems that support such participation. . . . [W]e will merely cite it here.

(d) The more the face-to-face group perceives itself as receiving valued outputs from the political system, the greater will be its support of that system. This hypothesis merely states that those who perceive themselves as being highly rewarded by the activities of the political system are more likely to support that system.

(2) *The Small Group as a Source of Affect.* Just as the face-to-face group may support the political system by its furtherance of supportive norms, so may it support that system by providing affective outputs to its members. Relations in large organizations that engage only a part of the individual and that are specifically goal-oriented afford the individual insufficient emotional and affective ties.[56] The political system can offer some satisfaction for the individual's affective needs through emotional attachments to the symbols of the state, to a charismatic leader, or to some "cause" for which the state stands. But the specific demands that the larger system places upon the individual and the distance of the center of authority from the individual make it difficult for the system to satisfy his affective needs adequately. Argyris suggests that there is an inevitable conflict between the formal organization and what he calls the "healthy" personality, and that the more intimate face-to-face group in organizations is an adaptive mechanism whereby the affective gap is filled.[57] In political systems, such "gap-filling" face-to-face groups may also be found. Local politi-

---

54 See Kent Geiger, "Changing Political Attitudes in Totalitarian Society: A Case Study of the Role of the Family," *World Politics*, VIII (1956), 187-205.

55 Gabriel A. Almond and James C. Coleman, eds., *The Politics of the Developing Areas* (Princeton, N.J. Princeton Univ. Press, 1960), pp. 24-25.

56 Cf. Nisbet, *Quest for Community*; and E. Kahler, *The Tower and the Abyss* (New York: George Braziller, 1957).

57 Chris Argyris, *Personality and Organization* (New York: Harper & Row, Publishers, 1957), p. 139 and *passim*. The fact that in large organizations affective satisfactions can be found within informal small groups is one of the major findings of the rediscovery of the small group.

cal organizations, for instance, give the individual a feeling of attachment to the political system that is not gained from participation in the larger, more formal processes. Writing of the political clubs of New York, Peel states: "Since in the modern democratic state the participation of the individual in the actual working of government is reduced to a minimum, the [local political] clubs might give him what the primaries, general elections, initiative, referendum, recall, assembly, and petition have failed to give him—the feeling that he is an important part of the self-governing community."[58]

The important point is that affective ties to the primary group have significant latent effects on the political system. Loyalty to the face-to-face group may lead an individual to behave in such a way as to support the larger system. Thus, studies of wartime behavior in the American and German armies indicate that soldiers were motivated to fight by loyalty to the primary group. The results as far as the larger systems were concerned were the same whether the soldiers fought for the democratic or the Nazi ideology. The affective security and emotional rewards given by the primary group were directly related to the soldier's ability to act effectively in regard to the larger system. As Shils and Janowitz point out: "It appears that a soldier's ability to resist [enemy propaganda] is a function of the capacity of his immediate primary group (his squad or section) to avoid social disintegration. When the individual's immediate group and its supporting formations met his basic organic needs, offered him both affection and esteem from both officers and comrades, supplied him with a sense of power, and adequately regulated his relations with authority, the element of self-concern in battle, which would lead to disruption of the effective functioning of his primary group, was minimized."[59] And it is important to note that though the attachment to the primary group was essentially a non-political attachment, it functioned directly to support the political goal of the organization. "The solidarity of the German army was discovered by these studies . . . to be based only very indirectly and very partially on political convictions or broader ethical beliefs. Where conditions were such as to allow primary group life to function smoothly, and where the primary group developed a high degree of cohesion, morale was high and resistance effective or at least very determined, *regardless in the main of the political attitudes of the soldiers*."[60] Thus, in this case, the unplanned functions of the small group served the purposes of the formal organization by performing functions of which the formal organization was incapable.

The proposition that satisfactory affective ties within the primary group will lead to behavior on the part of the individual that supports the larger political system finds confirmation in a number of studies that link radical be-

---

[58] Peel, *The Political Clubs of New York*, p. 136. Rousseau maintained that a large state could not be proportionately as strong as a small one. One of the reasons he advanced for this is that in a large state an individual will not have the face-to-face contacts that make his political participation affectively satisfying. In large states, he wrote, ". . . the people has less affection for its rulers whom it never sees, for its country, which, to its eyes, seems like the world, and for its fellow citizens, most of whom are unknown to it." *The Social Contract*, p. 38.

[59] Shils and Janowitz, *Public Opinion Quarterly*, XII (1948), 281; and Shils, in R. K. Merton and P. F. Lazarsfeld, eds., *Studies in the Scope and Method of the American Soldier* (New York: The Free Press, 1950).

[60] *Ibid.*, p. 314. Italics mine.

havior with the absence of such ties. Several authors have argued that one of the major appeals of participation in the Communist Party is that its deep political ties satisfy affective needs left unsatisfied by the secondary relationships in an industrial society. The Communist cell often replaces weakened face-to-face ties in family or church.[61] A lack of face-to-face ties has been shown to be related to political instability in a number of other situations. Ringer and Sills found that political extremists in Iran tended to have fewer family, religious, and friendship ties. They engaged in individualistic recreation and reported that they received communications through the mass media rather than through visiting and talking.[62] Davies and Wada, in a study of the background characteristics of rioters and non-rioters, present tentative evidence that rioters tend to have fewer family and other primary group ties.[63]

Even the face-to-face group whose norms conflict with the formal organization may perform supportive affective functions. Thus Argyris has shown that even those informal work groups whose norms (limiting production) operate to hinder the goal attainment of the larger organization perform positive functions for that organization by satisfying needs of the workers that the organization itself cannot satisfy.[64] Similarly, Fainsod suggests that the "family group" in Russia, even though it fosters behavior overtly opposed to the central regime, performs a supportive function by serving as an "escape valve." He suggests that the Bolshevik attempts to transform the country rapidly under harsh conditions despite the opposition of many Russians would have led to stronger negative reactions than the formation of "family groups" if these informal, self-seeking groups had not developed.[65]

(3) *Source of Flexibility.* Lastly, face-to-face communications may aid the achievement of the goals of the larger system by introducing an element of flexibility into the operation of the formal system. Over-conformity to the rules and directives of the formal system is a form of deviant behavior that can harm the larger system. And as Blau points out, the over-conforming bureaucrat—the stickler for rules—may behave in that manner because of ". . . lack of security in important social relationships within the organization."[66] The face-to-face group, often developing outside the structure of the formal organization, allows a flexibility in interpreting rules not possible within formal bureaucratic channels. Formal systems will, therefore, develop a tolerance for these informal structures. Thus, though the Soviet system is officially opposed to informal arrangements among administrators, it has become tolerant to some extent of these arrangements as a means of introducing flexibility into an otherwise highly formal and bureaucratized struc-

---

[61] See Philip Selznick, *The Organizational Weapon* (New York: McGraw-Hill, 1952), pp. 283-87; Almond, *The Appeals of Communism*, pp. 272-79; and C. Micaud, *World Politics*.

A similar argument is made by Fromm in *Escape from Freedom*, and by Mannheim in *Man and Society in the Age of Reconstruction* (New York: Harcourt, Brace, 1950).

[62] Benjamin B. Ringer and David L. Sills, "Political Extremists in Iran: A Secondary Analysis of Communications Data," *Public Opinion Quarterly*, XVI (1952-53), 689-701.

[63] James C. Davies and George Wada, "Riots and Rioters," *Western Political Quarterly*, X (1957), 864-74.

[64] Argyris, *Personality and Organization*, Chap. 4.

[65] Fainsod, *Smolensk* . . . , p. 450.

[66] P. Blau, *The Dynamics of Bureaucracy* (Chicago: Univ. of Chicago Press, 1955), p. 188.

ture.[67] And the discovery of the importance of the informal organization in American administrative studies has led to attempts to put the informal structure to the use of the formal organization.

## Conclusion

The case for the primary group as a subject of political study has now been made. Face-to-face relationships—their absence or presence, the kinds of relationships—play a significant role in the political process. But the specification of the small groups that affect politics and the type of effect they have is only a first step in increasing our knowledge of political affairs through small group analysis. Small groups have a characteristic that differentiates them from most other subjects of political analysis —they can be studied by techniques and methods not available for use with larger social systems. Small groups can be created by researchers in experimental laboratories, and can be manipulated in ways not possible in other systems.

On-going small groups are important in the political process. Can studies of experimental small groups increase our understanding of that process? [Our argument] may be looked at as one part of a two-part justification of the study of small group experiments by a political scientist. It has attempted to show the relevance of the small group to political affairs. We have still to justify our interest in the experimental method as an approach to small groups.

---

[67] Bauer, Inkeles, and Kluckhohn, *How the Soviet System Works*, p. 79; and Fainsod, *op. cit.*, p. 151.

Part 2

theoretical
perspectives

# personality, social system, culture, and their interplay

## chapter two

From Verba's discussion, one can draw a first inference that if groups are significant to political processes they must be equally important in other areas, such as economics, religion, education, recreation, and so on, and a second inference that if this is true in one society then it must be true for most societies. When one considers all societies on the globe, one discovers that there are billions of small face-to-face groups that nurture and influence individuals and affect the operation and the social situation around them. The task of the sociology of groups is to clarify both the internal dynamics of such groups and their function for other social orders.

Simply in numbers the task is immense. Yet the theoretical scope is potentially greater still, for in the view of Parsons *et al.*, presented in the first selection in this section, the small group is but one form of a much larger class of social phenomena called action systems. Other forms include the community, the school, the corporation, and the total society. Even the single individual (when his internal processes are conceived as actions) is considered an action system. Assuming that one task of social science is to explain the dynamics of these systems, Parsons *et al.* begin with a most elemental set of theoretical constructs: personality, social system, and culture. Though analytically distinct, they are interdependent, and their interplay is a major feature of system dynamics.

It is important to note that Parsons *et al.* do not intend to present a theory of system dynamics. Instead they attempt (1) to establish the fundamental distinctions between personality, social system, and culture (which often become blurred) and (2) to consider the interdependence among the three types of systems (which is often ignored for the sake of concentrating upon one type of system at a time). In this respect their closing comments can serve the reader as a guide:

[What] we have presented . . . is a highly general and abstract scheme. We are fully aware that *by itself* it cannot do justice to the immense richness and particularity of the human scene. But it can help us to analyze that scene and organize our knowledge of it. . . . The empirical complexity is immense, and the unexplored areas are, in the light of present knowledge, Stygian in their darkness.

From their perspective, it can be seen that the study of the small group can contribute to an understanding of action systems in general. First, because an action system is the dynamic interplay among personality, social system, culture, and an environment, a large proportion of small groups fulfill these conditions. Second, it is relatively easy to observe the interaction that occurs in many groups. Third, because this interaction is the result of the interdependence among the three types of systems, findings about the small group can suggest hypotheses about the dynamics in other larger action systems, providing, of course, good judgment is used in transposing from one context to the other. It is in this sense that the small group represents an ideal microcosm of action systems.

## Fundamental Concepts

TALCOTT PARSONS et al.

The present statement and the volume which it introduces are intended to contribute to the establishment of a general theory in the social sciences. Theory in the social sciences should have three major functions. First, it should aid in the codification of our existing concrete knowledge. It can do so by providing generalized hypotheses for the systematic reformulation of existing facts and insights, by extending the range of implication of particular hypotheses, and by unifying discrete observations under general concepts. Through codification, general theory

Reprinted from Talcott Parsons, Edward A. Shils, Gordon W. Allport, Clyde Kluckhohn, Henry A. Murray, Jr., Robert R. Sears, Richard C. Sheldon, Samuel A. Stouffer, and Edward C. Tolman, "Some Fundamental Categories of the Theory of Action: A General Statement," in Talcott Parsons and Edward A. Shils, eds., *Toward a General Theory of Action* (Cambridge, Mass.: Harvard University Press. Copyright 1951 by the 27, by permission of the authors and Harvard University Press. Copyright 1951 by the President and Fellows of Harvard College.

in the social sciences will help to promote the process of cumulative growth of our knowledge. In making us more aware of the interconnections among items of existing knowledge which are now available in a scattered, fragmentary form, it will help us fix our attention on the points where further work must be done.

Second, general theory in the social sciences should be a guide to research. By codification it enables us to locate and define more precisely the boundaries of our knowledge and of our ignorance. Codification facilitates the selection of problems, although it is not, of course, the only useful technique for the selection of problems for fruitful research. Further than this, general theory should provide hypotheses to be applied and tested by the investigation of these problems. If research problems are formulated in terms of systematically derived theoretical hypotheses, the resulting propositions will in turn contribute toward both the validation and revision of the theory.

Third, general theory as a point of departure for specialized work in the social sciences will facilitate the control of the biases of observation and interpretation which are at present fostered by the departmentalization of education and research in the social sciences.

This statement does not itself purport to be the general theory which will adequately fulfill these three functions. It is rather a formulation of certain fundamental categories which will have to enter into the formulation of this general theory, which for many years has been developing through the convergence of anthropological studies of culture, the theory of learning, the psychoanalytic theory of personality, economic theory, and the study of modern social structure.

## The Frame of Reference of the Theory of Action

The present discussion will begin with an exposition of the fundamental concepts from which it is intended to develop a unified conceptual scheme for theory and research in the social sciences. In accordance with already widespread usage, we shall call these concepts the *frame of reference of the theory of action*. In order to make the rest of the exposition comprehensible, we shall define a considerable number of the concepts[1] and state their more general bearing on our problem.

---

[1] The authors are fully aware of the difficulty of standardizing terminology in the present state of social science. The difficulty is great particularly in view of the heterogeneity of the sources from which the terms here used have been drawn and the new emphasis we have often given them. We are not all equally satisfied with every term, and we do not regard ourselves as bound to use exactly this terminology each in his own work. We have merely endeavored to be as clear as possible, to avoid violent neologisms, and to use terms which would be as nearly acceptable to all members of the group as possible.

## *Orientation and Situation*

In the theory of action the point of reference of all terms is the action of an individual actor or of a collectivity of actors. Of course, all individual actors are, in one aspect, physiological organisms; collectivities of actors are made up of individual actors, who are similarly physiological organisms. The interest of the theory of action, however, is directed not to the physiological processes internal to the organism but rather to the organization of the actor's orientations to a situation. When the terms refer to a collectivity as the acting unit, it is understood that it does not refer to all of the actions of the individuals who are its members, but only to the actions which they perform in their capacity as members. Whether the acting unit is an individual or a collectivity, we shall speak of the actor's *orientation of action* when we describe the action. The concept *motivation* in a strict sense applies only to individual actors. The motivational components of the action of collectivities are organized systems of the motivation of the relevant individual actors. Action has an orientation when it is guided by the meaning which the actor attaches to it in its relationship to his goals and interests.

Each orientation of action in turn involves a set[2] of *objects of orientation*. These are objects which are relevant in the situation because they afford alternative possibilities and impose limitations on the modes of gratifying the needs and achieving the goals of the actor or actors.[3] A situation provides

---

[2] The word *set* is used to designate a plurality of entities determinately limited in number and range of variation but not necessarily conceived as interdependent so as to constitute a system.

[3] The establishment of a definite relationship with objects (e.g., their possession or modification) or the creation of objects may

two major classes of objects to which the actor who is the point of reference may be oriented. These are either (1) nonsocial, that is, physical objects or accumulated cultural resources, or (2) social objects, that is, individual actors and collectivities. Social objects include the subject's own personality as well as the personalities of other individuals. Where collectivities are objects, sectors of the action systems of a plurality of individual actors form a system which is an object for the actor or actors who are our point of reference. A specific combination of selections relative to such objects, made from among the possibilities of selection which were available in a specific situation, constitutes an orientation of action for a particular actor. The organized plurality of such orientations of action constitutes a system of action.[4]

The orientation of action to objects entails selection, and possibly choice. Selection is made possible by *cognitive* discriminations, the location and characterization of the objects, which are simultaneously or successively experienced as having positive or negative value to the actor, in terms of their relevance to satisfaction of drives[5] and their organization in motivation. This tendency to react positively or negatively to objects we shall call the *cathectic mode of orientation*. Cathexis, the attachment to objects which are

gratifying and rejection of those which are noxious, lies at the root of the selective nature of action.[6] Furthermore, since selection must be made among alternative objects and gratifications at a single point of time or through time, there must be some evaluative criteria. The tendency of the organism toward integration requires the assessment and comparison of immediate cognized objects and cathectic interests in terms of their remoter consequences for the larger unit of evaluation. *Evaluation* rests on standards which may be either cognitive standards of truthfulness, appreciative standards of appropriateness, or moral standards of rightness. Both the motivational orientations and the value-orientations are modes of distinguishing, testing, sorting, and selecting. They are, in short, the categories for the description, on the most elementary level, of the orientation of action, which is a constellation of selections from alternatives.

It is essential to point out that a description of a system of action must refer not only to the particular constellation of orientations and sets of objects actually selected but also to the alternative sets from which the selections might have been made but were not. In other words, we are concerned not only with how an actor actually views a situation but also with how he might view it. This inclusiveness is required for the purposes of a dynamic

---

be among the goals sought by actors. Objects once created may in turn become objects of orientation in ensuing actions.

[4] The word *system* is used in the sense that determinate relations of interdependence exist within the complex of empirical phenomena. The antithesis of the concept of system is random variability. However, no implication of rigidity is intended.

[5] By *drive* we mean the *organic energy* component of motivation with whatever elements of organization and directionality may be given with the *genetic constitution* of the organism.

[6] Human beings do much which is inhibiting or destructive of their interests in its consequences; hence the naïve hedonism which maintains that the gratification of a wish explains every overt act is clearly untenable. However, to deny that even self-destructive acts are motivated equally fails to make sense The postulate that the course of behavior, at least at certain points where alternatives were open, has had motivational significance to the actor, that in some sense he "wanted" to do it, is essential to any logical theory of behavior.

theory of action which would attempt to explain why one alternative rather than another was selected.

The range of the alternatives of action orientation is determinate; it is inherent in the relation of the actor to the situation and derives ultimately from certain general properties of the organism and the nature of objects in their relation to such organisms. This determinate range of the alternatives which are available for selection marks the limits within which variability is possible.

.  .  .

## Personality, Social System, and Culture

The frame of reference of the theory of action applies in principle to any segment of the total round of action or to any process of action of any complex organism. The elaboration of behavior to which this conceptual scheme is especially appropriate, however, occurs above all in human action. In the formation of systems made up of human actions or the components of human action, this elaboration occurs in three configurations. First, the orientation of action of *any one* given actor and its attendant motivational processes becomes a differentiated and integrated system. This system will be called the *personality*, and we will define it as the organized system of the orientation and motivation of action of one individual *actor*.[7] Second, the action of a plurality of actors in a common situation is a process of interaction, the properties of which are to a definite but limited extent independent of any prior common culture. This interaction also becomes differentiated and integrated and as such forms a social system. The social system is, to be sure, made up of the relationships of individuals, but it is a system which is organized around the problems inherent in or arising from social interaction of a plurality of individual actors rather than around the problems which arise in connection with the integration of the actions of an individual actor, who is also a physiological organism. Personality and social system are very intimately interrelated, but they are neither identical with one another nor explicable by one another; the social system is not a plurality of personalities. Finally, systems of culture have their own forms and problems of integration which are not reducible to those of either personality or social systems or both together. The cultural tradition in its significance both as an *object* of orientation and as an *element* in the orientation of action must be articulated both conceptually and empirically with personalities and social systems. Apart from embodiment in the orientation systems of concrete actors, culture, though existing as a body of artifacts and as systems of symbols, is not in itself organized as a system of action. Therefore, culture as a system is on a different plane from personalities and social systems.[8]

Concrete systems of action—that is, personalities and social systems—have psychological, social, and cultural aspects. For one thing, the state of the system must be characterized in terms of certain of the motivational properties of the individual actors. The description of a system of action must

---

[7] The physiological aspect of the human organism is relevent to action theory only as it impinges on the orientation system. However, phantasies and imaginative productions, though they may not refer directly to any realistic situational objects, are unequivocally part of the orientation of personality as a system of action.

[8] Mr. Sheldon dissents from this view. His grounds are stated in Chapter II [of the original volume].

employ the categories of motivational orientation: cognition, cathexis, and evaluation. Likewise, the description of an action system must deal with the properties of the system of interaction of two or more individuals or collective actors—this is the social aspect—and it must note the conditions which interaction imposes on the participating actors. It must also take into account the cultural tradition as an object of orientation as well as culture patterns as internalized patterns of cognitive expectations and of cathectic-evaluative selection among possible orientations that are of crucial significance in the personality system and in the social system.

Cultural elements as constituents of systems of action may be classified in two ways. First, they may be differentiated according to the predominance of types of interests corresponding to the predominance of each of the modes of motivational orientation. Second, culture patterns as objects of the situation may be distinguished from culture patterns as internalized components of the orientation system of the actor. These two classifications cut across each other.

In the first method of classification it is convenient to distinguish the following three major classes of culture patterns. (1) Systems of ideas or beliefs. Although cathexis and evaluation are always present as orientational components, these cultural systems are characterized by a primacy of cognitive interests. (2) Systems of expressive symbols; for instance, art forms and styles. These systems are characterized by a primacy of cathectic interests. (3) Systems of value-orientations. Here the primary interest is in the evaluation of alternatives from the viewpoint of their consequences or implications for a system of action or one of its subsystems.

With respect to the second classification, it is quite clear that culture patterns are frequently objects of orientation in the same sense as other types of objects.[9] The actor knows their properties (for example, he understands an idea); he responds to them (that is, he is attracted or repelled by them); and he evaluates them. Under certain circumstances, however, the manner of his involvement with a cultural pattern as an object is altered, and what was once an object becomes a constitutive part of the actor. When, for example, he cannot violate a moral rule without intense feelings of guilt, the rule is functioning as a constitutive part of his system of orientation; it is part of his personality. Where this occurs a culture pattern has been internalized.

Before we continue with an elaboration of each of the above three major types of system into which the components of action become organized and differentiated—personality, cultural systems, and social systems—it is essential to review briefly certain other categories of action in general, particularly those that have been developed in behavior psychology.

## Some Fundamentals of Behavior Psychology

### Needs and the Organization of Behavior

Certain trends in psychological theory have placed the primary sources of

---

9 A special position is occupied by physical artifacts which are the products of action. Like the objects of the natural environment they do not *interact* with the actor. They are situational objects which cannot be internalized into the orientation system of the actor. They might serve as instrumental objects of action systems or they might have meaning conferred on them by value-orientation systems, in the same way that meaning is conferred on objects of the natural environment.

the organization of behavior into the constitution of the organism. They have done this through some version of the "instinct" theory. This tendency has continually been challenged by demonstrations of the range of plasticity of the organism and the corresponding importance of "learning"—a challenge which has been greatly accentuated by the cultural relativity disclosed through the work of social anthropology and sociology.

The present analysis will observe a rule of parsimony with regard to assumptions about the constitutional organization of the tendencies of behavior. There is certainly a system of viscerogenic needs which are grounded in the interchange of the organism as a physiological system with its environment. Some of them are highly specific: the need for food is relatively specific; the needs for sleep and for breathing are much more so. The object which is constitutionally most appropriate for the cathexis of a viscerogenic need is, however, seldom absolutely specific. But, on the other hand, the range of variability open to action and cultural definition always has some limits. Among these needs which come to be of primary importance for action, however, the degree of specificity usually tends to be slight, particularly in the mode as distinct from the fact of gratification. In general, there is a wide range of variability of the objects and modes of gratification of any constitutionally given need. In addition to the viscerogenic needs there seem to be certain needs for "social relationships." These might be constitutionally given or they might, by being indirectly necessary for the gratification of viscerogenic needs, be derivative in their origin and come subsequently to acquire autonomy.

We assume then a set of needs which, although initially organized through physiological processes, do not possess the properties that permit these physiological processes to be exclusively determinative in the organization of action. In other words, the direction and modes in which these needs can determine action is modifiable by influence emanating from the situation of action. Moreover, the needs themselves can be modified, or at least their effect on action is modifiable, by the process of becoming embedded into need-dispositions.

However, even though the set of viscerogenic needs has initially a physiological organization, it possesses one persistent property which plays a central role as the set of needs evolves into the system of need-dispositions. It is incipiently organized with respect to a positive-negative discrimination; that is, it discriminates between need-gratifying and need-blocking or need-depriving aspects[10] of the situational object system. This discrimination is the point of departure of a complex process of further differentiation into need-dispositions[11] which might possess vary-

---

[10] *Deprivation* is to be understood here as subsuming: (1) the withdrawal of gratifying objects already possessed by the actor; (2) the obstruction of access to gratifying objects which the actor does not possess and for which he is striving; (3) the enforced relationship with objects which are not gratifying, e.g., physical or psychological suffering of positive pain or injury (this category includes both actively encountering and passively receiving pain, etc.); (4) the threat of any of the foregoing. Responses by the actors to each of these types of deprivation might vary considerably.

[11] The term *need-disposition* has been chosen to emphasize that in action the unit of motivation faces two ways. On the one hand, it is involved in the equilibrium of the actor as a personality (and organism), and on the other, it is a disposition to act in relation to one or more objects. Both references are essential. It is to be distinguished from *need* by its higher degree of organization and by its inclusion of motivational and evaluative elements which are not given by viscerogenic needs.

ing degrees of specificity. In addition to the specific viscerogenic needs and the wider discrimination between gratification and deprivation, the human organism has a constitutional capacity to react to objects, especially other human beings, without the specific content or form of the reaction being in any way physiologically given. This reactive capacity or potentiality may be likened to the capacity to learn language, which is certainly not constitutionally specific to any particular language, and if the individual is not exposed to speech of other human beings, may not be activated at all. The human organism has a sensitivity to other objects, a potentiality of cathecting them as objects in various ways, depending on the context of orientation and situation.

This sensitivity extends to nonsocial objects but it is especially significant where *inter*action is involved. Moreover, this sensitivity is, like the discriminatory tendency to which we have already referred, inherently responsive to experience in interactive relationships. On the one hand, gratifying experience with an object engenders a positive attachment-seeking and -forming tendency; on the other, deprivation from an object predisposes the actor to a reaction of flight, escape, or aggression, a tendency to avoid or injure the object in order to control or forestall the deprivational effect of its action.

### Cognitive and Cathectic Orientation in the Organization of Action

Impelled by its drives and needs, the acting organism is oriented to social and nonsocial objects in two essential, simultaneous, and inseparable modes. First, it "cathects" particular objects or classes of objects through attributing to them significance for direct gratification or deprivation of impulse-

needs.[12] It may become attached to an object as a source of gratification[13] or repelled by it as a source of deprivation. Second, it cognizes the object field, discriminating any particular object from others and otherwise assessing its properties. Only when the actor knows the relations of objects to one another and to his own needs can his behavior become organized with reference to cathectic-cognitive discriminations.

The essential phenomena in motivational orientation are thus cognitive and cathectic discriminations among objects. When these discriminations become organized in a stable way, they form a system of orientation. The actor *selects* or is *committed* to culturally imposed selections among accessible objects with respect to their potentialities for gratification; he also selects from among the modes of their possible significance to him. The most primitive forms of this selectivity are

---

12 A distinction between *affect* and *cathexis* is desirable for present purposes. *Affect* refers to a state of the organism—a state of euphoria or dysphoria or qualitative variants thereof. *Cathexis* refers to a state of the organism—a state of euphoria or dysphoria—*in relationship to some object*. Thus the term *cathexis* is broader in its reference than the term *affect*; it is *affect* plus *object*. It is *object-oriented affect*. It involves attaching affective significance to an object; although it involves attachment to one or more properties of the object, as used here it does not itself refer to a property of the object, but to a *relation* between actor and object. Furthermore, there is no connotation either of activity or passivity in the actor's relation to the object implied in the concept.

13 The content of the gratifications need not be specified here. Gratifications may of course include those experiences or states which are normally viewed as pleasures, such as love, physical comfort; they may also under certain conditions include certain experiences ordinarily conceived as deprivational such as pain, horror, disgust, but which because of the organization of a given personality system may have gratifying consequences.

perhaps acceptance—for instance, incorporation of food, remaining in a comfortable place, etc.—and rejection —spitting out, withdrawal from, or avoidance.

Cathectic-cognitive orientation toward the object world, in any system of behavior extending through time, always entails *expectations* concerning gratifications or deprivations receivable or attainable from certain objects and classes of objects. Action involves not merely discrimination and selection between immediately present objects, and the directly ensuing striving, acceptance, or rejection, but it involves also an orientation to *future* events with respect to their significance for gratification or deprivation. A discrimination between immediately available and future gratifications and the assessment of their relative value is an essential aspect of action.

## Expectations and Evaluations

Where there are alternative opportunities for gratification in a present situation and alternatives distributed among present and expected situations, the actor must have some means of deciding which of the alternatives or combinations of alternatives he should follow. The process of deciding among alternatives, of assessing them in the light of their ramified consequences, is called *evaluation*. Evaluation is the more complex process of selection built upon the discriminations which make up the cognitive-cathectic orientation.

There is a variety of possible ways in which action can be organized with respect to expected events. One of the most important categories of reaction to expectations is that of activity-passivity. On the one hand, the actor may *actively* seek out objects and ma-

nipulate them in the interest of his goals,[14] or he may explore the situation seeking previously unrecognized opportunities. Alternatively, he may passively *await* the impact of expected situations and renounce interest in positive but still unattained goals. (There are various possible combinations of active and passive elements, such as the positive effort to escape from a situation expected to be threatening or enlisting the aid of others to cope with a threat.)

## Learning

Learning[15] becomes relevant at this point in the development of the frame of reference of the theory of action. Learning is not merely the acquisition of "information" (that is, specific items of cognitive orientation) about the properties of the object world; it is also the acquisition of new "patterns of orientation." That is, it involves acquiring new ways of seeing, wanting, and evaluating; these are predispositions to approach or avoid, to seek actively in certain types of situation or to "lie low" and wait, to keep away from noxious objects or to control them.

Of fundamental importance in learning is the degree and incidence of generalization[16] which is introduced into

---

[14] The cognitive-cathectic and evaluative orientations are connected by the "effort" of the actor. In accordance with a value standard and/or an expectation, the actor through effort manipulates his own resources, including his own body, voice, etc., in order to facilitate the direct or indirect approximation to a certain cathected goal—object or state.

[15] Learning is the acquisition of changed modes of orientation to the object world, including in the latter the actor's personality, ideas, culture, social objects, etc.

[16] It is recognized that the term generalization has two principal current meanings: (1) the discrimination of the objects in what had previously been a single undifferentiated category to constitute two or more classes still

the actor's orientations to his object world. Generalizations are modes of defining the actor's orientations to particular objects of which he has not yet had experience. This entails the categorization of the particular, concrete objects of his situation into general classes. In the acquisition of systems of cultural symbols, generalization is perhaps the most important of the learning mechanisms. As frames of reference, as the content of communication, and as the foci of common orientations, cultural patterns must possess content with a degree of generality which transcends the particularity of all concrete situations and experiences. Generalization through a cognitive process has consequences for the cathectic aspect of orientation. For example, through generalization it is possible to cathect categories of objects as well as particular objects.

Generalization as a cognitive mechanism orders the object world and thereby defines the structure of alternatives open to the orientation of action. The world in the actor's expectations comes to be composed of classes of objects, as well as particular objects, defined and differentiated by properties significant to the actor. Furthermore, the experiences of gratification or deprivation from particular objects may be generalized to other objects which are, in the actor's definition of the situation, classified with the original objects.

*   *   *

possessing certain common features, and (2) the discernment of common properties in a group of events previously discriminated as different. The common element of the two meanings is the organization of the object world into categories. If it is important to distinguish the two meanings, the applicable meaning will be made clear.

## Interaction and the Development of Personality

The *inter*active element in the system of action, when joined with the fundamental variables of the organization of behavior . . . accounts for the enormously complicated differentiation and organization of the social and personality systems. In interaction we find the basic process which, in its various elaborations and adaptations, provides the seed of what on the human level we call personality and the social system. Interaction makes possible the development of culture on the human level and gives culture its significance in the determination of action.

*   *   *

### Personality as a System

The child's development of a "personality" (or an "ego structure") is to be viewed as the establishment of a relatively specific, definite, and consistent system of need-dispositions operating as selective reactions to the alternatives which are presented to him by his object situation or which he organizes for himself by seeking out new object situations and formulating new goals. What will be needed, therefore, for the coherent description and analysis of human personality *as a system* will be the categories and hypotheses bearing on four main sets of variables

1. Fundamentals of behavior psychology of the sort discussed above: motivation, the gratification-deprivation balance, primary viscerogenic and possibly social-relational needs, cognition and learning, as well as the basic mechanisms of cognitive and cathectic-evaluative learning and adjustment. The latter involves the examination of such learning mechanisms as differentiation and generalization, where cognitive interests have primacy, and reinforcement, extinction, inhibition, substitution, identification, and imitation

where cathectic or evaluative interests have primacy.

2. The allocative processes,[17] by which the strivings toward gratification are distributed among the different available objects and occasions and gratification opportunities are distributed among the different need-dispositions. These processes keep conflict and anxiety within the limits necessary for the working of the personality system; the failure of their smooth operation calls the special mechanisms of defense and adjustment into play.

3. The mechanisms, classifiable as those of defense and adjustment,[18] by which the different components of need-dispositions are integrated internally as a system and directed toward objects.

4. The integration of the various need-dispositions into an on-going personality capable of some degree of self-control and purposeful action. The character of the on-going personality cannot be understood without reference to the relatively independent sub-integrations within the personality structure and the adjustive mechanisms which relate them to each other.

The constitutional foundations of the need-disposition structure of personality continue to function throughout life. But because of the plasticity of the human organism they directly determine the behavior of the human adult far less than in many other spe-

cies. Through learning and interactive experience they become integrated with the symbolic structures of the cultural tradition to form an interdependent system of acquired need-dispositions, many of the latter being closely fused into specific object attachments and systems of role-expectations. In comparison with its physiological base, the structure of human personality is highly autonomous and socialized. In addition, the personality usually has a high degree of autonomy vis-à-vis the social situation at any particular moment, in the sense that the variations in the social situation do not bring about completely corresponding variations in the personality systems.

*Personality and Social Role*

One particular crucial aspect of the articulation of personality with the social system should be mentioned briefly. Once an organized system of interaction between ego and alter becomes stabilized, they build up reciprocal expectations of each other's action and attitudes which are the nucleus of what may be called *role-expectations*. Alter expects ego to behave in given situational conditions in certain relatively specific ways, or at least within relatively specific limits. Alter's reaction will then, contingent on the fulfillment or nonfulfillment of his expectations, be different, with fulfillment leading to rewards and/or favorable attitudes and nonfulfillment leading to the reverse. Alter's reaction is in turn meaningfully interpreted (not necessarily correctly—distortion is of course possible and frequent) by ego and this interpretation plays a part in shaping the next stage in the process of his action toward alter (all this, of course, takes place in reverse too). The pattern of expectations of many alters, often generalized to include all of those in the status of ego, constitutes in a

---

[17] By *allocation* we mean the distribution of significant components *within* a system in such a way as to be compatible with the functioning of the system in a given state. The term is borrowed from economics.

[18] By *mechanisms of defense* we mean the motivational processes by which conflicts internal to the need-disposition system of a personality are resolved or the severity of their consequences mitigated. *Mechanisms of adjustment*, on the other hand, are the processes by which *strains* on the actor's relations to objects are coped with. Complete resolution may occur through normal learning, but short of this special mechanisms operate.

social system the institutionalized[19] definition of ego's roles in specified interactive situations.

Ego's system of need-dispositions may or may not predispose him to conform with these expectations. There are, of course, many complex possibilities of variation between dispositions to complete conformity and to drastic alienation—that is, predispositions to avoid conformity, to withdraw, or to rebel. There are also many complex possibilities of accommodation between dispositions not to conform, in varying modes and degrees, and interests in avoiding the sanctions which nonconformity might incur.

Moreover, alienative and conformist responses to institutional role-expectations do not exhaust the possibilities. Some actors possess, to a high degree, the potentialities of elaborating their own goals and standards, accepting the content of institutional role-expectations but simultaneously modifying and adding something new to them. These are the creative personalities whose conformity or alienation is not motivated mainly by a need-disposition to accept or reject the given institutional role-expectations, but rather by the need to discover, elaborate, and conform with their own ego-ideal.

The group of problems centering around conformity, alienation, and creativity are among the most crucial in the whole theory of action because of their relevance to problems of social stability and change. It is essential, in order to make progress in this area, to have conceptualized both the personality and social system adequately so that the points of empirical articulation where integration and unintegratedness are in balance can be analyzed.[20]

## Cultural Aspects of Action Systems

### Internalized Orientations and Cultural Objects

We have already stated that the organization of the basic alternatives of selective orientation is fundamental to any system of action. Without this organization, the stable system of expectations which are essential to any system of action could not exist. Not only does the child receive the major organization of his own selective orientations from adults through the socialization process, but consensus with respect to the same fundamental selections among alternatives is vital to a stable social system. In all societies the stabler and more effective patterns of culture are those which are shared in common—though in varying interpretations with varying degrees of conformity, idiosyncrasy, creativity, and persistence—by the members of societies and by groups of societies. The pattern of "commitment" to a particular set of such selections among the potentially open alternatives represents

---

19 By *institutionalization* we mean the integration of the expectations of the actors in a relevant interactive system of roles with a shared normative pattern of values. The integration is such that each is predisposed to reward the conformity of the others with the value pattern and conversely to disapprove and punish deviance. Institutionalization is a matter of degree, not of absolute presence or absence.

20 Although many schemes will allow the *ad hoc* analyses of some of the points of articulation, the scheme presented here seems to have the advantage of proceeding systematically from the elements of orientation. This permits the formulation of concepts which reveal the points of conceptual correspondence among the different types of systems— and this in turn offers a basis for a more comprehensive and more rigorous analysis of the points of empirical articulation.

the point of empirical articulation of systems of actions.

Once the analysis of the organization of systems of action is pursued to the levels of elaboration which are necessary for the analysis of the structure of personalities, it also becomes necessary to examine the direct articulation with the patterns of cultural orientation, which have come to be one of the principal objects of anthropological study. The same basic set of categories of the selective alternatives which is relevant for the analysis of personality structures will also be involved in the macroscopic differentiation and classification of the cultural orientations or traditions of social systems.

## The Organization of Culture Patterns in Systems

A cultural system is a highly complex constellation of elements. We may refer here to the two parallel classifications of the actor's modes of motivational orientation as cognitive, cathectic, and evaluative, and of the basic cultural orientations as systems of ideas or beliefs, systems of expressive symbols, and systems of value-orientation (as set forth above). Each type of culture pattern might then be regarded as a solution of a type of orientation problem—systems of ideas are solutions of cognitive problems, systems of expressive symbols are solutions of problems of how "appropriately" to express feelings, and systems of value-orientations are solutions of problems of evaluation, particularly but not exclusively in social interaction.

Value-orientation patterns are of particularly decisive significance in the organization of systems of action, since one class of them defines the patterns of reciprocal rights and obligations which become constitutive of role-expectations and sanctions. (Other classes of value-orientation define the *standards* of cognitive and appreciative judgments.)

Cultural patterns tend to become organized into systems. The peculiar feature of this systematization is a type of integration which we may call *consistency of pattern*. Whether it be the logical consistency of belief system, the stylistic harmony of an art form, or the rational compatibility of a body of moral rules, the internal coherence of a body of cultural patterns is always a crucial problem for the student of culture.

The determination of the extent of the consistency of pattern and deviations from it in a given culture presents serious difficulties to the analyst. The overt or explicit culture almost always appears fragmentary at first, and its parts seem disconnected. Only under special conditions—for example, in highly sophisticated systems of ideas or legal systems—is explicit systematization carried out by the creators and bearers of the culture themselves. In order, therefore, to determine the existence of systematic coherence where there has not been explicit systematization, it is necessary for the student of culture to uncover the implicit culture and to detect whatever common premises may underlie apparently diverse and unconnected items of orientation. Very close approximations to complete consistency in the patterns of culture are practically never to be found in large complex social systems. The nature and sources of the mal-integration of cultural patterns are as important to the theory of action as the integration itself.

## The Internalization of Culture Patterns

It has already been made clear that, whatever its systematic form, a cultural pattern may be involved in action either as an object of the actor's situation or it may be internalized to become part of the structure of his personality. All types of cultural patterns may be internalized, but particular importance is to be attributed to the internalization of value-orientations, some of which become part of the superego structure of the personality and, with corresponding frequency, of institutionalized role-expectations.[21]

Cultural patterns when internalized become constitutive elements of personalities and of social systems. *All concrete systems of action, at the same time, have a system of culture and are a set of personalities* (or sectors of them) *and a social system or subsystem.* Yet all three are conceptually independent organizations of the elements of action.

Because of this empirical interrelatedness, there is a dynamic theory of culture which corresponds to that of the dynamic theory of personality and social systems. It is concerned with the conditions under which certain types of systems of culture can exist in certain types of personalities or societies. It analyzes the processes of cultural innovation and change in terms of their motivational determinants, as these operate in the mechanisms of the social system and in the mechanisms of personality. It is concerned with the imperfections in the integration of cultural patterns and accounts for them in terms of the empirical interdependence of culture orientations with the

___

[21] This fact of the internalization of values was independently and from different points of view discovered by Freud in his theory of the superego and by Durkheim in his theory of the institutionalization of moral norms. The fact that the two men, working from different premises, arrived at the same conclusion is one of the landmarks of development of modern social science.

strains and processes of the social and personality systems.

## The Social System

When, in the above discussion of action, we reached the point at which interaction of an actor with other persons or social objects became crucial, we disclosed the nucleus of the development of social systems. Personality as a system has a fundamental and stable point of reference, the acting organism. It is organized around the one organism and its life processes. But ego and alter in interaction with each other also constitute a system. This is a system of a new order which, however intimately dependent on them, does not simply consist of the personalities of the two members.

## Role as the Unit of Social Systems: Social System and Personalities

In the present terms a social system is a system of the interaction of a plurality of persons analyzed within the frame of reference of the theory of action. It is, of course, composed of relationships of individual actors and only of such relationships. The relationships themselves are constellations of the actions of the parties to the relationship oriented toward one another. For most analytical purposes, the most significant unit of social structures is not the person but the role. The role is that organized sector of an actor's orientation which constitutes and defines his participation in an interactive process. It involves a set of complementary expectations concerning his own actions and those of others with whom he interacts. Both the actor and those with whom he interacts possess these expectations. Roles are institutionalized when they are fully congruous with the prevailing culture patterns and are organized around expectations of conformity with morally sanctioned patterns of value-orientation shared by the members of the collectivity in which the role functions.

The abstraction of an actor's role from the total system of his personality makes it possible to analyze the articulation of personality with the organization of social systems. The structure of a social system and the functional imperatives for its operation and survival or orderly change as a system are moreover different from those of personality.[22] The problems of personality and social structure can be properly treated only if these differences are recognized. Only then can the points of articulation and mutual interdependence be studied.

When we recognize that roles rather than personalities are the units of social structure, we can perceive the necessity of an element of "looseness" in the relation between personality structure and the performance of a role. Role situations are situations with potentially all the possible significances to an actor that situations can have. Their significance and the resultant effect on the motivation of behavior will be different with different personalities. But, in the organization of the latter's reactions where the stability of the sector of the social system in question is maintained, there are certain "control mechanisms" which serve to keep the potential dispersion of the actor's reactions within limits narrower than would be produced by the combi-

nation of the total situation and the actor's personality without this specificity of role expectations.

An important feature of a large proportion of social roles is that the actions which make them up are not minutely prescribed and that a certain range of variability is regarded as legitimate. Sanctions are not invoked against deviance within certain limits. This range of freedom makes it possible for actors with different personalities to fulfill within considerable limits the expectations associated with roughly the same roles without undue strain. It should also be noted that role-expectations and sanctions do exert "pressures" on individual actors which may well generate types of strain which have important repercussions in various parts of the personality. These will be manifested in types of action which in turn have a variety of social consequences and often result in either the development of further mechanisms of social control or the generation of pressures toward change, or in both. In this manner, personality and role structure constitute closely interdependent systems.

### Role Types and the Differentiation and Integration of Social Systems

The structural roles of the social system, like the structure of need-dispositions of the personality system, must be oriented to value alternatives. Selections are of course always actions of individuals, but these selections cannot be interindividually random in a social system. Indeed, one of the most important functional imperatives of the maintenance of social systems is that the value-orientations of the different actors in the same social system must be integrated in some measure in a *common* system. All on-going social systems do actually show a tendency toward a general system of common

---

[22] A further distinction between social and personality systems lies in the fact that a social system is not tied to any one *particular* aggregate of organisms. Furthermore, there is no reason to believe that when, having undergone a change of personnel, the social system remains the same, the new actors who have replaced those which were lost are necessarily identical in all the details of their personality with their predecessors.

cultural orientations. The sharing of value-orientations is especially crucial, although consensus with respect to systems of ideas and expressive symbols are also very important determinants of stability in the social system.

The range of variation and the shape of the distribution of the types of roles in a social system is neither parallel to nor fully congruous with the range of variation and the distribution of the personality types of the actors filling those roles. The actual operation of this structure of roles as an on-going system is, of course, possible in the last analysis only because the component personalities are motivated to act in the requisite ways and sufficient gratification is provided to enough individuals within the immediate system of roles itself or in the more embracing system of roles. There are functional imperatives limiting the degree of incompatibility of the possible kinds of roles in the same action system; these imperatives are ultimately related to the conditions of maintenance of a total on-going social system of the type in which the more constitutive of these roles are found. A social system, like a personality, must be coherently organized and not merely a random assortment of its components.

As in the case of personality, the functional problem of social systems may be summarized as the problems of allocation and integration. There is always a differentiation of functions within any action system. There must accordingly be an allocation of such functions to different classes of roles; the roles must be articulated for the performance of collaborative and complementary tasks. The life span of the individual being limited, there must be a continual process of replacement of personnel within the system of roles if the system is to endure. Furthermore, both the facilities necessary to perform functions and the rewards which are important to the motivation of individual actors are inherently scarce. Hence their allocation cannot be left to an unregulated competitive process without great frustration and conflict ensuing. The regulation of all these allocative processes and the performance of the functions which keep the system or the subsystem going in a sufficiently integrated manner is impossible without a system of definitions of roles and sanctions for conformity or deviation. With the development of a considerable complexity of differentiation there emerge roles and subsystems of roles with specifically integrative functions in the social system.

· · ·

The general requirement for integration demands that the control of allocative and integrative processes be associated with the same, or with closely interacting, roles; and that the mechanisms regulating the distribution of power and prestige apportion sufficient power and prestige to these allocative and integrative roles. And finally, it is essential that the occupants of these roles perform their allocative and integrative functions with a view to conforming with the value consensus of the society. These allocative and integrative roles (whether they be roles filled by individuals or by subcollectivities) may be considered to be important integrative mechanisms of the society. Their absence or defectiveness causes conflicts and frustrations.

It must be recognized that no social system is ever completely integrated just as none is ever completely disintegrated. From the sectors of unintegratedness—where expectations cannot be fulfilled in institutional roles or where need-dispositions are frustrated by institutionalized expectations or where the strain is not absorbed in safety-valve mechanisms—from these sectors some of the most important sources of change and growth are to be found.

Any system of interactive relationships of a plurality of individual actors is a *social system*. A *society*[23] is the type of social system which contains within itself all the essential prerequisites for its maintenance as a self-subsistent system. Among the more essential of these prerequisites are (1) organization around the foci of territorial location and kinship, (2) a system for determining functions and allocating facilities and rewards, and (3) integrative structures controlling these allocations and regulating conflicts and competitive processes.

With the institutionalization of culture patterns, especially value-orientation patterns, in the social structure, the threefold reciprocal integration of personality, social system, and culture comes full circle.[24] Such value patterns, institutionalized in the social structure, through the operation of role mecha-

nisms and in combination with other elements organize the behavior of adult members of society. Through the socialization process, they are in turn constitutive in establishment of the personality structure of the new adult from the plasticity of early childhood. The process of socialization, it is clear from the above, is dependent upon social interaction. Adults in their orientation to the child are certainly acting in roles, very largely institutionalized, and almost from the beginning the child himself develops expectations which rapidly become role-expectations. Then within the framework of the personality structures thus formed, adults act both to maintain and to modify the social system and the value patterns in which and by which they live, and to modify or keep within the pattern the personality structures of their living descendants.

The reader should bear in mind that what we have presented in the foregoing pages is a highly general and abstract scheme. We are fully aware that *by itself* it cannot do justice to the immense richness and particularity of the human scene. But it can help us to analyze that scene and organize our knowledge of it.

The general outlines of the nature of action systems sketched here, the interrelations of the various components and the interdependence of the system levels of organization of those components, seems to be quite clearly implied in much contemporary theory and research. But the empirical complexity is immense, and the unexplored areas are, in the light of present knowledge, Stygian in their darkness. To us, progress toward unraveling that complexity and illuminating some of the obscurity depends, along with empirical investigation, on more precise and explicit conceptualization of the components of action and of the ways in which they are interrelated.

---

[23] Partial social systems, so long as their relation to the society of which they are parts is made clear, are certainly legitimate objects of empirical investigation.

[24] Although—as must almost inevitably be the case with each individual signer—there are some things I should prefer to see said somewhat differently, there is only one point on which I remain slightly uncomfortable. This is the relation of social structure, social system, role, and culture. Many anthropologists (and certainly the undersigned) will agree today that there is an element in the social (i.e., interactive) process which is not culturally patterned, which is in some sense autonomous from culture. Nevertheless, one whose training, experiences, and prejudices are anthropological tends to feel that the present statement does not give full weight to the extent to which roles are culturally defined, social structure is part of the cultural map, the social system is built upon girders supplied by explicit and implicit culture. On the other hand, whatever my reservations, I welcome the publication of the statement in its present form because I am convinced that in the present stage of social science it is highly useful to behave experimentally with reference to conceptual schemes—Clyde Kluckhohn.

# the interaction system

## chapter three

Starting from the same basic perspective presented in the preceding article, Bales presents a view of the group as an interaction system. In his terms,

the idea of an interaction system is a key theoretical starting point. From it one can derive the ideas of personality, social system, and culture as particular sub-types of systems, distinguishable by abstracting in different directions from the same concrete observable phenomena: interaction. On the other hand, the characteristics of interaction as we observe it cannot be deduced from even our most general ideas about any one of the sub-systems—personality, social system, or culture.

What is largely *visible* in the concrete sequence of overt acts members perform when meeting together is the interplay among personality, social system, culture, and situation. In order that the interplay may continue and the interaction system may function effectively, a set of problems, common to all action systems, must be solved to a minimum degree, at least. These problems may be broadly categorized as *instrumental*—that is, relevant to the group task or its relation to the external environment—or *social-emotional*—that is, relevant to internal needs of group members or the relations between members. By specifying these problems and by devising a simple set of categories to be used in observing interaction, he is able to record the relevance of each observable act to the system problems. Such scores are an empirical representation of how the interaction system is operating. Although research experience shows less order, less simplicity, and less regularity in interaction systems than was at first hoped, techniques like those of Bales are necessary if we are to bridge the gap between our theoretical notions and actual group processes. His statement of system problems provides a simple yet highly useful guide in organizing observations and interpretations of group process.

# Interaction Process Analysis

ROBERT F. BALES

## Actor and Situation as a Frame of Reference

In the present conceptual frame, every action is treated as an interaction. The action is regarded as an interaction because it is conceived to fall between, to connect, or to relate a subject to some aspect of situation or object. Usually, but not necessarily, the observed interaction will involve at least two separate biological individuals in addition to the observer. We assume that because of the ability to manipulate symbols which is characteristic of socialized human beings, any given person may be an object to himself. That is, in his capacity as a thinker, evaluator, or actor, he can think about himself, have emotional reactions or evaluate judgments about himself, and act in one way toward another part of himself which is tending to act in a contrary way. As examples, we often speak of a person as talking to himself, feeling ashamed of himself, expressing himself, trying to talk himself into something, as agreeing with himself, disagreeing with himself, etc. In cases of this kind, under the present scheme, the self is regarded as a situational focus or object, and that part or aspect of the same concrete individual which is taking the momentary reflexive role is regarded as the subject or actor. A single biological individual in a room

Reprinted from Robert F. Bales, *Interaction Process Analysis* (Reading, Mass.: Addison-Wesley Publishing Co., 1950), pp. 42-62, by permission of the author. Copyright 1950 by Robert F. Bales.

working at a problem, talking to himself or thinking out loud, is thus technically regarded as engaged in interaction, and insofar as the interaction is with the self—a social object—the actor is regarded as engaged in social interaction.

The personality, then, in the present conceptual frame, is not treated as an irreducible unit, but is conceived by the observer as a complex of sub-parts or sub-aspects not all of which are in overt action at once. The conception of the actor as only a part (the presently managing aspect of the personality) implies that the actor is not coextensive with the biological individual we observe. It is thus impossible to locate in any exact physical sense the author of the acts we observe. The author or actor involved in any present act is, for conceptual purposes, only a point of reference adopted for the analysis of that particular act. If the observer demands a more concrete way of looking at the problem, he may think of the author of a given act as that part of the person, or that coalition of parts, which for the moment is in command and is managing the motor apparatus. For technical purposes it is probably more satisfactory to say that the actor is simply the subjective or internal aspect of the present act itself, but this way of conceptualizing brings the referent of the term actor almost to the vanishing point and seems to be unnecessarily refined or rarified for the observer in his practical job of recording. The postulation of an actor in a somewhat more substantive sense is a conceptual convention adopted by the observer in order to allow him to think of each act as having an author, which is somehow not quite identical with the overt act he sees. This author or actor stands behind the overt act, persists through it, and ties the present act to acts which have gone before and to acts which are to come, but it is nevertheless not identical with the more extended self seen as object by the actor.

When the standpoint of the actor is taken as the point of reference for a given act, everything else relevant to that act becomes, for conceptual purposes, a part of the situation. Actor and situation thus constitute the two poles of a major conceptual dichotomy. The actor, as the subject pole of the dichotomy, is treated as an irreducible point of reference (although the categories on the interaction list constitute a classification of things which the actor does). The situation, however, as the other or object pole of the dichotomy, is differentiated into a set of major foci. These foci (or target objects as they will be called later) are considered to group into two major target areas, which may be called the inner situation and the outer situation. The target objects in the inner situation include the self, and the other(s) or in-group. The target objects in the outer situation include the other(s) not present or belonging to the out-group, and all of the residual physical objects, spatial and temporal relationships, etc., which may be relevant to action but which are not subjectively identified by the actor as a part or aspect of self or in-group.

Before presenting a diagram which may help to make these relations clearer, we have to consider the fact that the process of action itself, regarded as a chain or progression of activities, past, present, and anticipated future, may be viewed as object from the point of view of actor—this as another result of the ability of the socialized human being to manipulate symbols. Some assumptions about the nature of this process will be presented in a later section. Just now we are concerned merely with making a place for it in our conceptual framework. Since the process of action in itself is intrinsically time-involved and transitive, it cuts across the subject-object dichotomy which is the primitive basis for all of the above distinctions. In other words, from the point of view of the actor, the process of action may be felt subjectively to be peculiarly a part or aspect of self; or a part or aspect of the other or in-group; or a somewhat external affair which, so far as subjective involvement is concerned, is a part of the outer situation.

The diagram presented in Fig. 1 is a crude representation of the relationship of the various aspects of the actor-situation frame of reference.

It does not seem possible to represent all of the relationships properly on a two-dimensional diagram. The diagram is meant to be only roughly illustrative of certain assumptions and may very well imply things that are not meant. The essential things it is meant to represent, however, are these:

The observer does not appear on the diagram, since we cannot state in general whether the actor will be aware of his presence at all or, if so, whether the actor will see him as a part of the outer situation, as a part of the in-group, or as a part of the self (as he would in the case where the observer is participating as a member of the in-group and is scoring his own present activity). The reader of the diagram is taking the point of view the observer takes as he analyzes a given momentary act.

The actor, designated by the number 1 in this particular case, is given a special place on the diagram in an attempt to represent the fact that he is conceived as separated from the situation proper. However, we also wish to represent him as having no determi-

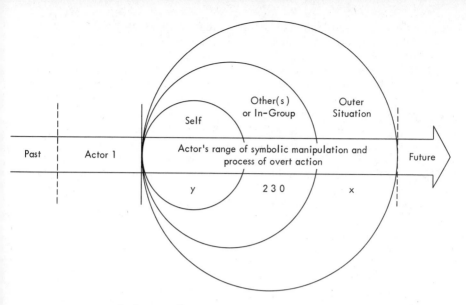

FIG. 1. Actor and situation as a frame of reference.

nate position in the time dimension, or rather, as having a range through it by symbolic manipulation and overt action. Aside from the position designated actor, all the rest of the diagram represents the other side of the dichotomy, i.e., the situation. The time dimension as perceived by the actor reads from left to right, from past, through present, to future. Only the present is drawn in as actual. It is desired to represent the assumption that the past and the future can be reached (i.e., constructed or reconstructed) by the actor only through the channel of symbolic manipulation, which in itself is present activity. Similarly, the actor can only reach (i.e., perceive, evaluate, or change through overt action) the various foci in the situation through the channel provided by the process of action itself, which includes both symbolic activity and overt action. The process of action itself is represented as cutting through past, present, and future situations and is transitive in nature, passing from subject pole to object pole as indicated by the arrow-like

form. The process of action is the generalized means through which the various factors influencing action are related to each other by the actor. The situation is represented by three progressively inclusive circles, with the innermost circle representing the self, the next innermost the other or in-group, and the outermost representing the bounds of the outer situation.

Thus, from the point of view provided by the concept "actor," the situation includes not only the outer situation—past, present, and future, external to the group as a whole, which we ordinarily think of when we say the word "situation"—but also all other persons of the in-group—and their past, present, and potential future activity, which is the inner, peculiarly social part of the actor's situation—and finally, the self, which includes the effects left in the personality by past actions, the memories, the desires, all the more permanent structure of the personality formed through genetic endowment and past experience, and the future possible actions which the actor regards in the present moment as object. The total situation, then, embraces the outer situation, all other persons of the in-group, and the self.

The rough similarity of these concepts to certain basic psychoanalytic concepts is evident: The similarity of actor to ego; of outer situation to reality; of inner or social situation to super-ego and ego-ideal; and of the self, regarded as object, to the id. However, the present writer is not prepared to say how far this similarity goes. It is his impression that the cognate psychoanalytic concepts are similar in logical origin but are designed for a somewhat different purpose, are ordinarily used in a more substantive sense, and carry with them assumptions about the genetic sources, the particular kind of content, and the semipermanent character of parts of the personality which imply a stability of reference to the terms which are not characteristic of the present concepts. The terms actor and situation in the present conceptual scheme do not have stable referents through a time span of any length. At best, the observer can point to their concrete referents only for a given momentary act which he chooses to isolate for analysis. In the next act of the same person, another part or aspect or balance of forces may be uppermost in the personality, in the sense of steering action, and what the observer a moment ago regarded as actor now becomes object or a part of the self. Furthermore, a second source of instability of referent consists in the fact that when another person speaks or acts in relation to the first, the referents of actor and situation reverse as the observer changes to a point of view in which the second person now in action is actor, and the first person and his now past activities become a part of the situation. In other words, actor and situation, as the observer uses the terms, are two poles of a conceptual framework which the observer uses to characterize certain aspects of each act as it comes along. The referents of these concepts change both as action proceeds with the same person acting and also as the observer changes his point of view to a new person. For the observer, the act itself is the center of attention; the actor and the situation are descriptive aspects of the act.

There is a further source of instability of referent of the concepts. This consists in the fact that the actor in a given momentary act, even in the abstract sense described, may be acting with regard to the outer situation in one or both of two different capacities. The actor, regarded as the executive agent of the self, may at the same time be acting as the momentary executive agent of the other or in-group. The first instability of referent mentioned above arises out of the fact that the present act (which is identified with the actor) in the next moment may become a part of the self seen as object. The present instability of referent arises out of the fact that the actor is capable of regarding the object—group or other person—as a part of the self or as extensions of the self. For example, when the actor "asks for help" (Category 11) [see below, p. 53], he may be acting primarily as the agent of the self *vis-à-vis* the other. However, when he "suggests a course of action" (Category 4), he may be acting as an agent both of the self and of the other or in-group *vis-à-vis* the outer situation, since he envisages cooperative action. The observer regards the actor as capable of identifying himself with the other group members in such a way that a larger psychological unit is formed, and this larger unit *vis-à-vis* the outer situation may constitute the psychologically relevant subject-object polarity. This last fact does not present any additional difficulty in scoring "who to whom" since the number assigned to the person is used to designate the actor, whether the actor is acting on behalf of the self only, or on behalf of both the self and the other.

The problem of scoring "who to whom" as a part of the present method is a matter essentially of identifying the actor and the target object for a given act. The target object may be defined as that area or focus in the situation (i.e., self, other or in-group, or outer situation) which the actor aims to affect or change, or which is affecting and changing him, and to which he is therefore giving primary attention in the present momentary act. To return to the diagram in Fig. 1, the reader can represent a single act or interaction by drawing an arrow, beginning at the point designated actor, signified by the number 1, passing by way of the process of action, and ending in any one of the three target objects. For example, if the act under analysis were the question "I wonder where I put my glasses?" asked by the actor of himself, an arrow passing from "1" to "y" would locate the act. The act would be recorded on the Interaction Recorder or on a paper form by putting the symbols 1-y (read one to y) following Category 7 on the list of categories. In later reconstruction we would be able to say what preceded and followed this act, whose act it was, and that it was a question asked by this person of himself, asking for some kind of information or report; in short, that he was trying to remember something. The topical content—the fact that it was his glasses he was trying to remember—we could get only by checking through the sound recording or written transcription.

The method employs conventional symbols to stand for the actor and the various foci in the situation. Each individual in the group is assigned an identification number by the observer. These, and the symbols O, x, and y (to

be explained below) are chosen to fit in with the positions on the columns of IBM punch cards, so that they can be punched in directly without an intermediate coding. Thus, the IBM punch card code and, at the same time, the key to the symbols on Fig. 1, is as follows:

The *actor* is designated by his assigned number, 1, 2, 3, etc.
The *self* is designated by the letter "y."
The *other* is designated by his assigned number, 1, 2, 3, etc.
The *in-group* as a whole is designated by a zero.
The *other(s) not present and in the out-group,*
    the *outer situation,* and
    the *observer* are all designated by the letter "x."
The *process of action itself* is designated according to its psychological location, as a part of self, other, or in-group, using the same symbols as above, generally as "y."

Thus, an interaction recorded 1-y, 2-y, etc. is identified as some interaction addressed by the actor to himself. An interaction recorded as 1-2, 2-3, etc. is identified as some interaction addressed by a given actor to some other specific person in the group, that is, the in-group. An interaction recorded as 1-0, 2-0, etc. is identified as some interaction addressed generally to several members or the in-group as a whole. An interaction recorded as 1-x, 2-x, etc. is identified as some interaction by the given actor addressed to or directed toward some other person not physically present in the in-group, but only recalled or symbolically represented.

## The Problem-Solving Sequence as a Frame of Reference

The preceding section presented a set of concepts dealing with certain aspects of the context within which any given act takes place and in terms of which the act may be located and scored. The concepts in that section are all derived from the subject-object polarity which we assume to be a descriptive characteristic of any human interaction. One of the target objects within this frame of reference was called the process of action itself. The purpose of the present section is to carry the analysis of the content of action a step further by introducing further assumptions about the process of action and by presenting further concepts in terms of which the observer can think about the process of action not simply as a target object, but as a *differentiated* target area. As a differentiated area, the total process of action in itself becomes a context within which a given act may be placed or located in a way similar to that in which the act is located in the subject-object polarity, as described in the preceding section.

The observer assumes that the total process of action is complex in a variety of ways. In this section we are concerned with three aspects of this complexity. First, we think of the process as complex in that it involves a distribution of phases, or parts, or aspects in the time dimension. This assumption made, we find that we have to think of the process as having an internal complexity at any given point in time. Finally, we find that the process is complex in that it involves a distribution of parts or phases between persons. All three of these assumptions are interlocking, and in certain respects identical.

With regard to time involvement, the total process of action as a system of acts is conceived as proceeding from a beginning toward an end, from a felt need or problem toward a solution, from a state of tension toward tension reduction, from a state of heightened motivation toward motivation reduction, or in an instrumentally oriented or meaningful way which may be described in terms similar to these. Action is conceived to have a sense or direction such that any given act is relevant, either logically or causally or both, to what has gone before or what the actor expects to come or both. A given act is thus regarded as a part of a larger context which is distributed in the time or process dimension, and the act is given its character in certain measure by its particular location in this context.

This forward and backward reference of action in the time dimension is assumed to rest largely on the ability of the normally socialized human animal to deal with his situation by the manipulation of symbols. This ability, we postulate, makes it possible to remember the consequences of his past action and to foresee the consequences of his present activity, or rather, to build up expectations as to what the consequences will be. In human action, we assume, both the remembered consequences and the expected consequences can become a part of the effective causation of action. The manipulation of symbols is conceived to be not simply an epiphenomenon, but an aspect of action as "real" as any other in its causal role. The manipulation of symbols, we assume, can operate to steer the ongoing act; it is through the manipulation of symbols that the present act can bear a *meaningful* as well as a causal relation to what has gone before, and that the anticipated future can play a *causal* as well as a meaningful role in the present. In short, the manipulation of symbols or the imputation of meaning on the part of the actor is, insofar as it is present, a part or an aspect of the causal process.

We thus assume that every act has important ties at least to what has gone before and usually to what the actor expects will come. As a remark about our conceptual scheme, we recognize that in postulating an actor who is the author of an act and momentarily differentiated from the self, we implicitly make the assumption that *all* behavior we observe has important ties in the forward and backward directions through the concurrent manipulation of symbols, since in a technical sense the referent of the concept "actor" is the present process of symbol manipulation. This is a heuristic assumption. We do not fully accept it, even within our conceptual scheme, recognizing that some of the behavior items we score (as examples, some of those in Category 11) may be almost entirely without symbolic content for the actor. We choose nevertheless to retain the terminology in which we attribute every behavior item to an actor as if the act had symbolic content, and we make the exception explicitly in those few instances where it is necessary.

When we wish to make a distinction regarding a predominant weight of emphasis on the backward or forward reference of action, we shall use the terms "expressive" and "instrumental," respectively, to designate the proper weight of emphasis. If the act is judged by the observer to be steered by cognitive orientation primarily to the past, or if it is felt to be caused in a non-meaningful manner by some existing state of emotion or motivational tension in the self, and if the results which follow it are judged not have been specifically anticipated by symbolic manipulation, we shall speak of the act as primarily expressive. On the other hand, if the act is judged to be steered by a cognitive orientation to the future as well as the past and to be caused in part by the anticipation of future consequences, we shall speak of the act as instrumental. This distinction is recognized in our everyday habits of speech:

in what we have called primarily expressive activity, the individual is said to act "because" of some immediate pressure, tension, or emotion. In the instrumental act, the individual is said to act "in order to" realize certain ends. Thus, we might drum our fingers on the table *because* we are nervous or tense, or we might raise our eyebrows *in order to* summon the waiter. The difference lies in the degree to which anticipated consequences enter in as a steering factor. All instrumental activity is also expressive, as we view it, but not all expressive activity is necessarily instrumental. All behavior is considered to be at least expressive, as viewed by the other and as apprehended and scored by the observer.

The point was made that in addition to its reference forward and backward in time, the total process of action is conceived as involving an internal complexity in a given period or at a given point of time. According to our conception of the matter, the reference forward and backward would be impossible without the internal complexity of symbolic manipulation and, conversely, the internal complexity of symbolic manipulation is intrinsically (i.e., both genetically and logically) bound up with the forward and backward reference.

The internal complexity of any given act at a given time can be conceived by the observer in terms of elements or aspects of the action process which are traditionally designated as the cognitive, affective, and conative modes of orientation. As we shall use the term "cognitive" aspects, it will subsume a range of "adaptive" variations of behavior which emphasize the manipulation of symbols. These variations include perception, apperception, memory and recall, observation of and inference about the object, and communication with social objects. By the term "affective" aspects, we will understand a range of "expressive" variations, including emotional and optative reactions of all kinds to the object and evaluation—liking, disliking, approval, disapproval, etc.—of social objects. Finally, by the term "conative" aspects, we shall designate a range including decision about the object and active, overt, goal-oriented or instrumental attempts to withdraw from, adapt to, change, or control the object, including the potential activities of social objects. The socially oriented referents of the above terms are not generally given in their traditional definitions. The reasons for adding them will be apparent shortly.

It seems clear that individual acts differ in the degree of emphasis they place on one or another of these aspects; it is also clear that there is a variation in time. But no act is clearly made up of just one aspect and there seems to be no sure uniformity with which the variations in emphasis may appear in time. The most satisfactory assumption seems to be that *every act* involves some characteristics which we can abstract and call cognitive or symbolic, some characteristics we can abstract and call affective, and some we can abstract and call conative. (For certain other purposes these analytical characteristics can be designated by a cognate trio of terms: adaptive, expressive, and instrumental.) The ongoing process of action is assumed to require description in terms of all three aspects and is conceived to be responsive to deficiencies in the articulation or "support" of any of the three aspects or to surpluses, especially of an affective sort. Thus, as we shall think of the matter, when the articulation of any of these aspects fails for any reason to be adequate to maintain or support the ongoing process as a total stream or where affect is sufficiently strong, there is a sudden modification of the cognitive-affective-conative stream or process directed toward a mending or further development of the deficient aspects or an expression of the surplus affect. This deficiency or surplus removed, the stream modifies to mend another deficiency or to overcome another barrier to its free flow. The acts which we conceptually isolate and observe are these sudden modifications of the total stream, and our classification of them is in terms of the deficiency or surplus we judge to be present, or the kind of support to the ongoing process which they offer, or the kind of barrier they remove (not in terms of what they "are").

Although it seems impossible to make a direct deduction from the categories cognitive, affective, and conative, in the traditional sense, to a series of categories which formulate phases in the problem-solving process, the assumptions which we have made just above about the nature of the process, along with certain other assumptions about the social and cultural nature of the process, do give us a base from which deductions can be made. If we assume that the process of action which we are trying to describe takes place in a social context, and if we assume that implicitly or explicitly it is divided among persons and is shared by them, we can derive a fundamental sequence which will serve our purpose. As we conceive it, the process of action, from its genesis in the personality of any given individual and in its very nature, logically and ontologically, is a *social* process. Under these assumptions, we conclude that in the interaction of any small group the problem of maintaining adequate cognitive support or articulation of the total process of action is a problem of joint or shared cognitive orientation to or articulation of the problem elements (or target areas) Similarly, the problem of maintaining an adequate affective support of articulation of the total process is a problem of a *joint* or *shared* evaluation of the problem elements or target areas. And finally, the problem of maintaining an adequate conative support or articulation of the total process is a problem of *joint* or *shared* decision or consensus about the direction of instrumental activity.

From these assumptions about the social—i.e., the joint, shared nature of interaction—we can derive a set of categories which will describe the verbalized and overt problem-solving activities of a single individual, but we are unable to reverse the procedure. That is, we are unable to derive a set of categories that will describe adequately the problem-solving activities of either a single individual or a small group if we start simply from the categories of cognition, affection, and conation in their most general sense as a deductive base. It appears that the concepts of cognition, affection, and conation are relatively high order abstractions from the concrete matrix of interaction and are to be derived from more generic process-related concepts of interaction, rather than vice versa. They are abstracted in such a way as to ignore the fact that the processes to which they refer are essentially social, and distributed between persons in the interaction process.

From the assumption that the process of action is a process which goes on *between* social objects (actor and other where more than one individual is involved, or actor and self in the case of the single individual) we conclude that *communication* between the two foci is an indispensable feature of the process if it is to proceed in other than an expressive way. Communication between the two or more foci, however, as we view it, is in itself an achievement, i.e., it is a result of interaction and requires interaction if it is to be maintained or sustained. This seems to imply that at least in some sense interaction is prior to communication. This

indeed is what we do imply, along the lines suggested by George H. Mead, but this is an area of problems which we can by-pass by assumptions for the present.

If we by-pass for the moment the problem of how communication is achieved, and assume that at some given time it has been achieved and that action is proceeding in a small group as a joint or shared process, we also assume that insofar as communication does exist, the essential elements of the process are reproduced, repeated, or represented symbolically, separately in the minds of each of the participants. We also assume that each person proceeds with an awareness, or at least an assumption, that the process is being shared with the other. The "sense" (i.e., the intuition of appropriate cognitive, expressive, or instrumental consonance) of the activity of each of the participants, both from his own point of view and the point of view of each of the others, depends upon the way the present act fits into the total shared process. Insofar as the process is shared or is felt to require a sharing by each of the participants, any failure of sufficiently exact reproduction in the mind of any *one* of the participants (as to the thinking, feeling, or intention of the others) may be felt by him and by the others to constitute an impairment of the integrity of the total process and may constitute the occasion for one of the sudden modifications of the total process, as mentioned above, in an effort to restore its shared integrity.

Such repairs as we observe them empirically seem to involve at least three separable acts or interactions. The observer can distinguish an "initial act" which signals at least to him (the observer) and often to the other participants that the impairment is present. Such an act is sometimes primarily expressive (such as a startled or bewildered expression on the face of one of the participants) but often is an act which is apparently *meant* by the actor to signal a difficulty or need, such as a question, a disagreement, a request for repetition, or the like. If the signal is noted by another participant, the next act is often a kind of attempted answer to the problem indicated by the signal. This attempted answer we shall call a "medial act." Again, the "medial act" may be primarily expressive, but often is an instrumental act which has a problem-solving relevance to the problem signaled by the initial act; examples of such instrumental acts would be an answer to a question or the giving of a requested repetition. Following the medial act, the first participant usually gives a signal as to whether the attempted answer of the other has or has not solved the problem signaled by the initial act and this permits the other to determine whether the process is again integrally shared. This third act we shall call the "terminal act." It is conceived to be terminal simply in a logical · or communicative sense, not necessarily (in fact, we believe, usually not) terminal in an empirical sense; i.e., there are few impairments of process which are repaired to the satisfaction of all in a simple three-act sequence. A nod of understanding or an agreement might be terminal in both a logical and an empirical sense. A disagreement following an initial act and medial act would be logically terminal with regard to the two prior acts but it might at the same time empirically constitute the initial act of a new three-

phase sequence. The terminal act, as we define it, may be either positive or negative. In any sequence we shall call a terminal act positive if it signals that the actor apprehends the attempted answer of the other as a successful solution to the problem raised by the initial act; we shall call it negative if it signals that the actor apprehends the attempted answer of the other as an unsuccessful solution to his own problem. Figure 2 shows the categories arranged in a problem solving sequence according to this conception.

In applying the method, the observer should keep in mind this idealized three-phase sequence as a logical context which will help him to locate and classify the act. The sequence will often be observed to follow through empirically as described but this does not always occur. Sometimes initial acts are ignored. Often medial acts continue autonomously and are interrupted by an initial act of another logical sequence from another participant before terminated by the first actor. Sometimes no discernible terminal act is given. When the terminal act is negative, the sequence necessarily becomes more extensive and complicated, overlapping with the next.

The problem-solving sequence—initial act, medial act, and terminal act— is presented here not as a characterization of the way interaction always goes but as a specification of the *minimal* number of interactions logically necessary to restore the integrity of the total process of action when a single impair-

FIG. 2. The problem-solving sequence as a frame of reference. The numbers are the numbers of the twelve categories. For category titles, see Fig. 3, p. 53.

| Initial acts | Medial acts | Terminal acts | | |
|---|---|---|---|---|
| 7 | 6 | 10 | 3 | |
| 8 | 5 | 11 | 2 | Future |
| 9 | 4 | 12 | 1 | |
| Questions | Attempted Answers | Negative Reactions | Positive Reactions | |
| Forward reference | Forward and Backward reference | Backward reference | Backward reference | |

ment has appeared in interaction between the minimal two participants. These three phases may be thought of as a conceptualization by the observer of a problem-solving sequence at a minimal degree of articulation. As such, the three concepts taken as a sequence constitute a "context" in terms of which we can classify or locate any given empirical act. Stated another way, the three concepts taken as a sequence constitute one of the conceptual dimensions which we shall use to generate or deduce, or rationalize the set of categories in terms of which observations are made in the present method. This dimension, it may be repeated, is deduced not simply from the general assumptions that the process of action has cognitive, affective, and conative aspects (which we retain as an additional specification) but rather it is deduced from probably more essential or basic assumptions about the social, joint, or shared nature of the action process as we observe it and about its distribution in time. The logically minimal distribution in time and the logically minimal distribution between actors is merged into the one conceptual sequence: initial act, medial act, and terminal act. The frame of reference is thus applicable even though we are observing the verbalized problem-solving activities of a single individual.

The recognition that we are dealing with interaction and not simply with solipsistic acts of conceptually isolated individuals involves the recognition that there are certain fundamental characteristics of action which we cannot deduce from the conception of action in terms of cognitive, affective, and conative aspects. The idea that an act is a part of an *interaction system* which is distributed both in time and between numbers is a fundamental idea and must be accepted as axiomatic. It is not a conclusion that can be deduced logically from more elementary principles or properties of action. These *are* the most elementary properties, as we view the matter, and can be observed or at least apprehended or grasped from first-hand observation.

To make this idea more concrete and to extend it a bit beyond the three-act sequence, let us suggest an experiment. First we would have to accept provisionally the system of categories and observation method as the set of concepts in terms of which our observations were to be made. Suppose then we set up a standard problem. . . . We obtain a number of groups of a given size, say five people each, and observe each of them according to standard procedures until they complete the problem. Suppose we then found that for each group taken as a whole the profiles were very similar.

Then suppose that for one group we were to break down the total period they required to solve the problem into six or eight sub-periods, and made a profile for each sub-period. Suppose we found these sub-periods were very different from each other. If the profiles for these sub-periods differed from each other more than the total profiles of the series of groups differed from each other, we would have some justification for saying that there is a system-influence which is distributed in time, so that one discovers the pattern of the system only by observing through a complete "cycle of operations" and not by smaller samples.

Now suppose we were to take a total profile for one of our groups again and, instead of a time breakdown, we make a breakdown to show the profile of each individual member. Suppose these profiles turned out to be very different from each other and yet fitted together to make a total group profile just like the other total group profiles. If the profiles for these individual members differed from each other more than the total profiles for the series of groups differed from each other, we would have some justification for saying that there is a system-influence which is distributed between members, so that one discovers the pattern of the system only by looking at the total activity of all members put together over the total time or, in other terminology, by looking at the social system and not simply at the individual roles.

This is a concrete illustration of one meaning of the proposition that each act is a part of an *interaction system*, distributed in time and between members. . . .

Figure 3, which should be compared with Fig. 2, illustrates the positions of the twelve categories in the problem-solving sequence conceived in this way. The problem-solving sequence is visualized as a system of interaction distributed in time and between members, with a general tendency to move from an initial state in which some problem is recognized to a terminal state in which the problem is solved. By abstracting in one way we can visualize certain problems as growing out of the relation of the members of the system to a situation that impinges on their adjustment. We can designate these problems in the traditional way as problems of cognitive orientation—"what is it?"; problems of affective orientation—"how does it affect us?"; and problems of conative orientation—"what shall we do about it?"

These three types of problems may be said to arise quite directly out of the nature of the relationship between the interaction system and the outer situation. These are problems of "foreign policy" or external relations. But the interaction system has an "internal extensity" also—its distribution in time and between members—and this internal extensity gives a different twist to the problems just mentioned.

With regard to the problem of cognitive orientation, one recognizes that there is a temporal dimension ranging from the appearance of a cognitive lack of some kind to the appearance of a solution in terms of understanding, and a "social" dimension (member to member) which makes the problem one of *communication* leading to decision, and not simply one of perception.

So far as the problem of affective orientation is concerned, again there is a temporal dimension leading from tension reduction in some sense, as well as a social dimension which makes the problem one of *evaluation* leading to decision in a more social, rounded sense and not simply one of diffuse emotional reaction of isolated individuals.

Similarly, for the problem of conation there is both a temporal and a social dimension ranging from vaguely stirring impulse through communication, evaluation, *decision*, and the *control* of overt action calculated in turn to control the situation and result in tension reduction.

Each of the problems mentioned above—roughly in order, the problems of communication, evaluation, control, decision, and tension reduction—is "nested" into the next, as shown in Fig. 3, by the nesting brackets on the right. That is, the solution of problems of evaluation assumes an ongoing successful solution to the problem of communication; the solution of the problem of control assumes an ongoing successful solution of both the problems of communication and evaluation; and so on. The solution of each problem in turn can be regarded as a functional prerequisite to the solution of the next. In this sense, each in turn becomes a more complicated or higher order problem than the last, since each involves all of those preceding and something more. Finally, all of the preceding problems are nested into the problem of social integration or reintegration.

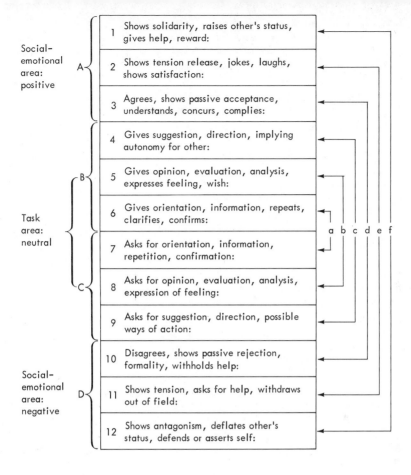

FIG. 3. The system of categories used in observation and
their major relations.

This last point requires more comment than we have prepared the ground for to this point. However, a few things can be said. . . . We start with the recognition that the interaction system is distributed in time and between persons, and is in contact with a situation which is a constant source of problems.

We recognize tension reduction and re-integration as the state of affairs toward which the system tends but also as a state of affairs which demands the intermediary solution of a nesting series of sub-problems which may fail of solution at any point and for any number of reasons external to the system as such. If there is a failure of solution of any of the sub-problems we assume there is by so much a failure of tension reduction, and the integration of the system is threatened. Even in cases of successful solution of the sub-problems we assume that there is a "wear and tear" involved in the solution of sub-problems which demands periodic activity oriented more or less directly to the problem of distributing the rewards accruing from productive activity back to individual members of the system and re-establishing their feeling of solidarity or integration with it. In particular we believe that the necessities of control or modification of activity in order to control the outer situation productively is likely to put the existing integration of the system under strain, no matter how successful the attack on the situational problem may eventually be. In order to show more fully why the effort to adapt to the outer situation creates tendencies toward malintegration, it would be necessary to give a more complete treatment of interaction as constituting a social system. . . .

To sum up certain aspects of the point of view presented here, one can say that the process of problem-solving in a group involves a series of social processes. Conversely, those phenomena in social systems referred to as social processes are or should be regarded as problem-solving processes. One can go further and say that what we usually regard as individual problem-solving, or the process of individual thought, is essentially in form and in genesis a social process; thinking is a re-enactment by the individual of the problem-solving process as he originally went through it with other individuals. It can probably be maintained with considerable success that the best model we have for understanding what goes on *inside* the individual personality is the model of what goes on *between* individuals in the problem-solving process. The component parts—acts in a system of interaction—are identical.

In short, the idea of an interaction system is a key theoretical starting point. From it one can derive the ideas of personality, social system, and culture as particular sub-types of systems, distinguishable by abstracting in different directions from the same concrete observable phenomena: interaction. On the other hand, the characteristics of interaction as we observe it cannot be deduced from even our most general ideas about any one of the sub-systems —personality, social system, or culture. Nor can the characteristics of interaction systems be entirely deduced from our most general ideas as to the characteristics of the single act in any isolated sense. This starting point, however, is more general than the others. Although it may not be entirely clear from the short exposition here, the writer is convinced from his attempts to solve the theoretical problems posed by the present method of observation that the idea of an interaction system is a generic concept toward which we shall be forced as we attempt to integrate our theory concerning personality, social systems, and culture. Apparently there is no single logical criterion or axiomatic base from which we can deduce its properties, although the properties we assign to it must be consonant with what we observe at first hand and with what we believe theoretically about personality, social systems, and culture. . . .

# consciousness in groups

# chapter four

In basic agreement with Parsons *et al.* that societies, groups, and personalities are usefully conceived as action systems, Deutsch distinguishes two sectors in such systems: (1) the high energy-low control and (2) the low energy-high control. The first is analogous to the power plant in an ocean liner and the second to its steering apparatus. In human systems the first involves needs, drives, fears, moral compulsions, and so on, whereas the second involves communication networks, the information transmitted through them, the use made of the information, decision-making procedures, and so on. In his model, Deutsch applies the concepts and learning from cybernetics to this second sector in human action systems. To him, the group is an information processing-steering system. His discussion implies that regardless of how existing groups are found to operate, the potential for increasing their capabilities to process information is enormous. He conceives of groups capable not only of self-steering (as Parsons *et al.* and Bales do) but also of self-monitoring, self-reorganizing, and becoming conscious of themselves. Building on concepts of *information, goal-seeking feedback* (which enables the system progressively to diminish errors until its goal is reached), and *goal-changing feedback* (which enables the system to reorganize itself so that it can seek alternative goals), he develops the far-reaching notion of a system capable of consciousness. By *consciousness* is meant the process whereby messages about the normal and regular processes are collected and organized, so as to indicate how the system as a whole is operating, and then fed back into the system where they become a new component in the regular processes, as well as a possible basis for altering the entire system. In other words, while operating, the system scans itself, selects indicators of how it operates, reads those indications, and takes them into account in its operation.

That human systems might be capable of "consciousness" in this sense is a revolutionary idea. Indeed, according to Boulding, it is precisely in the development of man's consciousness of himself that a new revolution is occurring: "this movement of the social system into self-consciousness is perhaps one of the most significant phenomena of our time, and it represents a very fundamental break with the past. . . ."[1]

---

[1] Kenneth E. Boulding, *The Impact of the Social Sciences* (New Brunswick, N.J.: Rutgers Univ. Press, 1966), p. 4.

Within the small group context it can be argued that one function of sociology is to contribute to group consciousness. If the sociologist as an outside observer can scan and assess groups in operation and over time is able to develop a sociology about their dynamics, then there is no inherent reason those capabilities cannot be transmitted to and incorporated by the group members themselves. They can scan, assess, interpret, and reorganize their own group according to the learning they import from the sociologist. In this respect Deutsch's model anticipates a close collaborative relation between sociologist and group member.

## A Simple Cybernetic Model

KARL W. DEUTSCH

Mechanic, organismic, and historical models were based, substantially, on experiences and operations known before 1850, even though many of their implications were worked out more fully only later. A major change in this situation began in the 1940's. Its basis was in the new development in communications engineering, with its extensive use of self-monitoring, self-controlling, and self-steering automatic processes. By making equipment that fulfills the functions of communication, organization, and control, significant opportunities were gained for a clearer understanding of the functions themselves.

These new developments in science and engineering were the beneficiaries of long-standing developments in social organization. Communication was social before it became elaborately technological. There were established routes for messages before the first telegraph lines. In the nineteenth cen-

Reprinted from Karl W. Deutsch, *The Nerves of Government: Models of Political Communication and Control* (New York: The Free Press, 1963), pp. 75-85, 88-102, 103-5, by permission of the author and The Free Press, a Division of The Macmillan Company. Copyright © 1963 by The Free Press, a Division of The Macmillan Company.

tury, factories and railroads required accurate coordination of complex sequences of human actions—a requirement that became central in the assembly-line methods and flow charts of modern mass production. The same age saw the rise of general staffs, and of intelligence organizations for diplomatic as well as for military purposes. These staffs and organizations, just as the modern large-scale industrial research laboratory itself, represent in a very real sense assembly lines of information, assembly lines of thoughts. Just as the division of manual labor between human hands preceded the division of labor between human hands and power-driven mechanisms, so the increasing division of intellectual labor between different human minds preceded today's divisions of labor between human minds and an ever-growing array of electronic or other communications, calculating, and control equipment.

What have the new machines of communication and control to offer for a further understanding of historical and social processes? For thousands of years, the operations of communication and control were largely carried on inside the nerve systems of human bodies. They were inaccessible to direct observation or analysis. They could be neither taken apart nor reassembled. In the new electronic machines of communication and control, messages or control operations can be taken apart, studied step by step, and recombined into more efficient patterns.

## The Viewpoint of Cybernetics

The science of communication and control, which has been derived from his technology and which Norbert Wiener has called "cybernetics," is therefore a new science about an old subject. In investigating the old subject of communication and control, it uses the facilities of modern technology to map out step by step the sequence of actual events involved.[1]

Cybernetics, the systematic study of communication and control in organizations of all kinds, is a conceptual scheme on the "grand scale," in J. B. Conant's sense of the term.[2] Essentially, it represents a shift in the center of interest from drives to steering, and from instincts to systems of decisions, regulation, and control, including the noncyclical aspects of such systems. In its scope, it is comparable to Lavoisier's stress on quantitative chemistry, or to Darwin's concept of evolution. As to its performance and success, the future will have to tell, but it is perhaps safe to say that social science is already being influenced by the interests implicit cybernetics at this time.

The fundamental viewpoint of cybernetics and its relevance to social science have been well expressed by Norbert Wiener:

The existence of Social Science is based on the ability to treat a social group as an organization and not as an agglomeration. Communication is the cement that makes *organisations*. Communication alone enables a group to think together, to see together, and to act together. All sociology requires the understanding of communication.

What is true for the unity of a group of people, is equally true for the individual integrity of each person. The various elements which make up each personality are in continual communication with each other and affect each other through control mechanisms which themselves have the nature of communication.

Certain aspects of the theory of communication have been considered by the engineer. While human and social communication are extremely complicated in comparison to the existing patterns of machine communication, they are subject to the same grammar; and this grammar has received its highest technical development when applied to the simpler content of the machine.[3]

In other words, the viewpoint of cybernetics suggests that all organizations are alike in certain fundamental characteristics and that every organization is held together by communication. Communication is a process different from transportation on the one hand and from power engineering on the other. Transportation transmits physical objects such as liquids in pipelines, or boxes, or passengers in trains or on escalators. Power engineering transmits quantities of electric energy. Communication engineering, by contrast, transmits neither tons of freight

---

[1] N. Wiener, *Cybernetics*, 2nd ed. (New York: Wiley, 1961); and *The Human Use of Human Beings* (Boston: Houghton Mifflin, 50). Cf. also W. Ross Ashby, *An Introduction to Cybernetics* (New York: Wiley, 56); and, for a brief account, G. T. Guilaud, *What Is Cybernetics?* trans. Valerie McKay (New York: Grove, 1960).

[2] *Science and Common Sense* (New Haven: Yale Univ. Press, 1961), pp. 47-49. Cf. Conant, *On Understanding Science* (New Haven: Yale Univ. Press, 1947), pp. 20, 23-28.

[3] Wiener, personal communication, M.I.T., 1955.

nor kilowatts of power. It transmits messages that contain quantities of information, and I shall say more about this concept of information later in this chapter. It is communication, that is, the ability to transmit messages and to react to them, that makes organizations; and it seems that this is true of organizations of living cells in the human body as well as of organizations of pieces of machinery in an electronic calculator, as well as of organizations of thinking human beings in social groups.[4] Finally, cybernetics suggests that steering or governing is one of the most interesting and significant processes in the world, and that a study of steering in self-steering machines, in biological organisms, in human minds, and in societies will increase our understanding of problems in all these fields.

## Analogies and Convergent Developments

Why should anyone think that this viewpoint represents a conceptual scheme and not a mere analogy? Actually, the meaning of the term *analogy* is often poorly understood. Analogy means limited structural correspondence. All mathematics is based on analogies, and so is a large part of every science. Darwin himself tells us that it was his perception of the analogy between Malthus' theory of human population and certain processes in the animal kingdom that led him to his theory of evolution. When scientists speak disparagingly of "mere analogies," they mean, more accurately, "false analogies" or "poor analogies." The test by which we discriminate between a false analogy and a good analogy consists in the extent of actual structural correspondence between the two systems from which the analogy is drawn.[5] How many and how significant are the instances in which the analogy holds good, and how numerous and how important are the instances in which it fails to work? These are the questions by which we test analogies and which serve to unmask the many false analogies which look plausible at first glance but fail completely after the early stages of the application. The test of a good analogy, conversely, is that it continues to be confirmed after we have penetrated more deeply into the subjects it purports to connect and that it becomes more fruitful of new ideas and of new investigations as we continue to apply it. Darwin's analogy with the work of Malthus was a good analogy in this sense, and so was Torricelli's analogy between the atmosphere and a "sea of air." It is suggested that cybernetics is currently proving itself a good analogy or conceptual scheme in a similar manner.

The rise of the viewpoint of communications in the present period has not been fortuitous. Rather, it has been the result of convergent development in a whole series of different sciences. Among these trends is the development of mathematical and statistical methods for the study of randomness and order, and thus of probability, leading to the mathematical theory of communication as developed by Norbert Wiener, Claude Shannon, and

---

[4] Cf. Wiener, *Cybernetics* and *The Human Use of Human Beings*, both *passim*; Colin Cherry, *On Human Communication* (Cambridge, Mass.-New York: M.I.T. Press-Wiley, 1957); and J. Ruesch and G. Bateson, *Communication: The Social Matrix of Psychiatry* (New York: Norton, 1951).

[5] Cf. G. Polya, "Analogy," in *How to Solve It* (Princeton, N.J.: Princeton University Press, 1945), pp. 37-46.

others. During the same decades the concept of homeostasis was developed by Claude Bernard, and later by Walter B. Cannon and Arturo Rosenblueth in physiology. This medical work found its parallel in the mathematical and empirical studies of control mechanisms, from Clark Maxwell's early paper on the governor in steam engines to the highly developed automatic control engineering of today. Problems of flow in various organizations were studied in production engineering, traffic engineering, city planning, and the design of telephone systems. Advances in the design of automatic switchboards eventually merged with the long-standing efforts to design effective calculating machines, from the early days of Leibniz and later of Charles Babbage to the analogue computer constructed by Vannevar Bush and the big digital computors of today. These advances in mathematics and the study of physical systems were paralleled by Ivan Pavlov's emphasis on the material nature of psychological processes, and on the discrete structure of the conditioned reflexes on which many of them were based. This emphasis was balanced by the rise of the school of *Gestalt* psychology led by Kurt Koffka and Wolfgang Köhler, emphasizing the importance of pattern and order, and the rise of the depth psychology of Sigmund Freud and his followers.

It is the experience of this new group of sciences that finds its reflection in some of the major ideas of cybernetics, such as the notion of the physical reality of patterns and of information and of the statistical nature of the latter, as well as the related notions of the physical nature of control processes, memory, and learning. Taken together, the new experiences and notions promise to replace the classic analogues or models of mechanism, organism, and process, which so

long have dominated so much of scientific thinking. All three of these models have long been felt to be inadequate. Mechanism and the equilibrium concept cannot represent growth and evolution. Organisms are incapable of both accurate analysis and internal rearrangement; and models of historical processes lacked inner structure and quantitative predictability.

In the place of these obsolescent models, we now have an array of self-controlling machines that react to their environment, as well as to the results of their own behavior; that store, process, and apply information; and that have, in some cases, a limited capacity to learn.

None of this is *thought* in the human sense of the word, as we find it in the behavior of individuals or groups, but it has significant parallels to it. Above all, the storage and treatment of information in machines, and its application to the control of the machines themselves, are taking place under conditions where every step can be traced distinctly and where every system can be taken apart for study and reassembled again. This is a research advantage that it would be neither easy nor entirely desirable to parallel in the case of human beings.

The test of the usefulness of this new science, as that of any science, must be its results. In the field of scientific theory it must offer new concepts rather than mere explanations. The analogies cybernetics may suggest between communication channels or control processes in machines, nerve systems, and human societies must in turn suggest new observations, experiments, or predictions that can be confirmed or refuted by the facts. They must be meaningful, that is, capable of being tested by practicable operations, and they should be fruitful, that is, lead to new operations and new concepts.

## The General Concept of a Self-Controlling System

To the extent that we can demonstrate that such analogies exist, and that they are fruitful in research, we may derive from them a generalized concept of a *self-modifying communications network* or *"learning net."* Such a "learning net" would be any system characterized by a relevant degree of organization, communication, and control, regardless of the particular processes by which its messages are transmitted and its functions carried out—whether by words between individuals in a social organization, or by nerve cells and hormones in a living body, or by electric signals in an electronic device.[6]

How does a modern communications mechanism look and what concepts can be derived from it?

Let me refer here to a brief sketch I gave elsewhere:

A modern radar tracking and computing device can "sense" an object in the air, interacting with its beam; it can "interpret" it as an airplane (and may be subject to error in this "perception"); it can apply records of past experience, which are stored within its network, and with the aid of these data from "memory" it can predict the probable location of the plane several seconds ahead in the future (being again potentially subject to error in its "recollections" as well as in its "guess," and to "disappointment," if its calculation of probability was correct, but if the airplane should take a less probable course); it can turn a battery of antiaircraft guns on the calculated spot and shoot down the airplane; and it can then "perceive," predict, and shoot down the next. If it should spot more than one airplane at the same time, it must become "infirm of purpose," or else decide ("make up its mind") which one to shoot down first. . . .

Man-made machines actually operating or designable today have devices which function as "sense organs," furnish "interpretations" of stimuli, perform acts of recognition, have "memory," "learn" from experience, carry out motor actions, are subject to conflicts and jamming, make decisions between conflicting alternatives, and follow operating rules of preference or "value" in distributing their "attention," giving preferred treatment to some messages over others, and making other decisions, or even conceivably overriding previous operating rules in the light of newly "learned" and "remembered" information.

None of these devices approach the overall complexity of the human mind. While some of them excel it in special fields (such as the mechanical or electronic calculators), they are not likely to approach its general range for a long time to come. But, as simplified models, they can aid our understanding of more complex mental and social processes, much as sixteenth century pumps were still simpler than the human heart, but had become elaborate enough to aid Harvey in his understanding of the circulation of the blood.[7]

6 On this whole subject, see also A. Rosenblueth, N. Wiener, and J. Bigelow, "Behavior, Purpose and Teleology," *Philosophy of Science*, X (January, 1943), 18-24; W. S. McCulloch and W. Pitts, "A Logical Calculus of the Ideas Immanent in Nervous Activity," *Bulletin of Mathematical Biophysics*, V (1943), 115-33; F. S. C. Northrop, "The Neurological and Behavioristic Psychological Basis of the Ordering of Society by Means of Ideas," *Science*, CVII, No. 2782 (April 23, 1948), 411-16; J. Ruesch and G. Bateson, "Structure and Process in Social Relations," *Psychiatry*, XII, 2 (May, 1949), 105-24. On the learning aspects, cf. also N. Wiener, *Cybernetics*, 2nd ed. (New York: Wiley, 1961), pp. 169-80; W. Ross Ashby, *Design for a Brain*, 2nd ed. (New York: Wiley, 1960), pp. 11, 113, 234. Cf. also the essays in Peter Laslett, ed., *The Physical Basis of Mind* (Oxford: Blackwell, 1957); and W. Russell Brain, *Mind, Perception and Science* (Oxford: Blackwell, 1951).

7 K. W. Deutsch, "Higher Education and the Unity of Knowledge," in L. Bryson *et* eds., *Goals for American Education* (New York: Harper & Row, Publishers, 1950), 110-11.

What are some of the notions and concepts that can be derived from this technology? Perhaps the most important is the notion of information.

## The Concepts of Information, Message, and Complementarity

Power engineering transfers amounts of electric energy; *communications engineering transfers information.* It does not transfer events; it transfers *a patterned relationship between events.* When a spoken message is transferred through a sequence of mechanical vibrations of the air and of a membrane; thence through electric impulses in a wire; thence through electric processes in a broadcasting station and through radio waves; thence through electric and mechanical processes in a receiver and recorder to a set of grooves on the surface of a disk; and finally played and made audible to a listener—what has been transferred through this chain of processes, or channel of communication, is not matter, nor any one of the particular processes, nor any significant amount of energy, since relays and electronic tubes make the qualities of the signal independent from a considerable range of energy inputs. Rather it is *something* that has remained unchanged, invariant, over this whole sequence of processes.

The same principle applies to the sequence of processes from the distribution of light reflected from a rock to the distribution of black or white dots on a printing surface, or the distribution of electric "yes" or "no" impulses in picture telegraphy or television. What is transmitted here are neither light rays nor shadows, but information, the pattern of relationships between them.

In the second group of examples, we could describe the state of the rock in terms of the distribution of light and dark points on its surface. This would be a *state description* of the rock at a particular time. If we then take a picture of the rock, we could describe the state of the film after exposure in terms of the distribution of the dark grains of silver deposited on it and of the remaining clear spaces, that is, we should get another state description. Each of the two state descriptions would have been taken from a quite different object—a rock and a film—but a large part of these two state descriptions would be identical whether we compared them point by point or in mathematical terms. There would again be a great deal of identity between these two descriptions and several others; such as the description of the distribution of black and white dots on the printing surface, or of the electric "yes" or "no" impulses in the television circuits, or the light and dark points on the television screen. The extent of the physical possibility to transfer and reproduce these patterns corresponds to the extent that there is "*something*" unchanging in all the relevant state descriptions of the physical processes by which this transmission is carried on. That "*something*" is *information—those aspects of the state descriptions of each physical process that all these processes had in common.*[8]

_____

[8] Somewhat differently phrased, a communications *network* is "a system of physical objects interacting with each other in such a manner that a change in the state of some elements is followed by a determinate pattern of changes in other related elements, in such a manner that the changes remain more or less localized, and independent of changes in the system from other sources" (W. Pitts); a communication *channel* is a "physical system within which a pattern (or *message*) is more or less isolated from other changes in the system" (Norbert Wiener); "A *state description* of a network or part of it" (Pitts); or again, somewhat differently stated, "a message is a reproducible pattern regularly followed by determinate processes

To the extent that the last state description in such a sequence differs from the first, information has been lost or distorted during its passage through the channel. From the amount of information transmitted as against the information lost, we may derive a measure of the *efficiency* of a channel, as well as of the relative efficiency or *complementarity* of any parts or states of the channel in relation to the others.

These patterns of information can be measured in quantitative terms, described in mathematical language, analyzed by science, and transmitted or processed on a practical industrial scale.

This development is significant for wide fields of natural and social sciences. Information is indeed "such stuff as dreams are made on." Yet it can be transmitted, recorded, analyzed, and measured. Whatever we may call it, information, pattern, form, *Gestalt*, state description, distribution function, or negative entropy, it has become accessible to the treatment of science. It differs from the "matter" and "energy" of nineteenth-century mechanical materialism in that it cannot be described adequately by their conservation laws.

But it also differs, if not more so, from the "idea" of "idealistic" or metaphysical philosophies, in that it is based on physical processes during every single moment of its existence, and in that it can and must be dealt with by physical methods. It has material reality. It exists and interacts with other processes in the world, regardless of the whims of any particular human observer; so much so that its reception, transmission, reproduction, and, in certain cases, its recognition can be and sometimes has been mechanized.

These, then, were the main developments that came to a head after 1940. Cybernetics as the science of communication and control arose in response to a technological and social opportunity. It was made possible by advanced and parallel developments in neurophysiology and psychology, in mathematics, and in electrical engineering, and by the growing need for cooperation among these and other sciences.[9] The result of these developments was a new body of experience, going beyond classic organism in its rationality, that is, in its ability to be retraced step by step in its workings.

The concept of information grew out of this new body of experience, and particularly out of the separation of communications engineering from power engineering. Information is what is transferred in telephony or television: it is not events as such, but a patterned relationship between events. Information has physical, "material" reality; without exception, it is carried by matter-energy processes. Yet it is not subject to their conservation laws. Information can be created and wiped out—although it cannot be created from nothing or destroyed completely into nothingness.[10] Finally, it differs from the classic notion of "form" in that it can be analyzed into discrete units that can be measured and counted.

Information consists of a transmitted pattern that is received and evalu-

---

depending on that pattern" (Wiener)—personal communication, M.I.T. (Spring, 1949). Cf. also Claude E. Shannon and Warren Weaver, *The Mathematical Theory of Communication* (Urbana, Ill.: Univ. of Illinois Press, 1949), pp. 99-106.

[9] For a discussion of this entire subject, see N. Wiener, *Cybernetics*; and Shannon and Weaver, *op. cit.*; for a much simplified account, cf. E. C. Berkeley, *Giant Brains* (New York: Wiley, 1949).

[10] On "Information" and "Matter," see also John E. Burchard, ed., *Mid-Century The Social Implications of Scientific Progress* (Cambridge, Mass.-New York: M.I.T. Press, Wiley, 1950), p. 228, n. 52.

ated against the background of a statistical ensemble of related patterns. The classic example for this is the standardized birthday telegram transmitted by telegraphing a single two-digit number indicating the message to be selected from the limited set of prefabricated messages held ready by the company. All information at bottom involves the indication of some pattern out of a larger statistical ensemble, that is, an ensemble that is already stored at the point of reception.

From this it follows that recognition can be treated as a physical process and can, in fact, be mechanized in many instances. Current mechanical devices embodying operations of matching and recognition range all the way from the lowly fruit-grading and candling machines to the Moving Target Indicator and the Friend and Foe Identification device of the Armed Forces.[11] Similar standardized recognition processes are embodied in processes that have been only partly mechanized thus far and that still embody standardized human operations at some stages. Examples of such semimechanized recognition processes include qualitative analysis in chemistry and the Crocker-Henderson odor classification scheme and its successor, the flavor profile, according to which each of five hundred well-known smells can be identified by a four-digit number.[12] These recognition devices

have grown up empirically, but the application of the theory of information forms part of the current development work on more complex devices of recognition—devices that are to be used to permit the deaf to understand spoken messages and the blind to read printed books, as well as for work on machines that will transcribe dictation or translate printed matter from one language into another.[13] Work on all these problems has been under way since the 1950's at several institutions of research.

.　　.　　.

### Feedback and Equilibrium

Another significant concept elaborated since the 1940's is that of the "feedback." The feedback pattern is common to self-modifying communications networks, whether they are electronic control devices, nerve systems, or social organizations.

In a broad sense [feedback] may denote that some of the output energy of an apparatus or machine is returned as input. . . . [If] the behavior of an object is controlled by the margin of error at which the object stands at a given time with reference to a relatively specific goal . . . [the] feedback is . . . negative, that is, the signals from the goal are used to restrict outputs which would otherwise go beyond the goal. It is this . . . meaning of the term feedback that is used here.[14]

---

[11] Peter B. Neiman, "The Operational Significance of Recognition," B.S. thesis, M.I.T., 1949 (unpublished). Cf. also Cherry, On Human Communication, pp. 256-73.

[12] Cf. S. E. Cairncross and L. B. Sjöström, "Flavor Profiles—A New Approach to Flavor Problems," Food Technology, IV, No. 8 (1950), 308-11; Sjöström, Cairncross, and Jean F. Caul, "Methodology of the Flavor Profile," ibid., XI, No. 9 (1957), 20-25; Caul, Cairncross, and Sjöström, "The Flavor Profile in Review," Perfumery and Essential Oil Record, XLIX (March, 1958), 130-33,

and "Physicochemical Research on Flavor," Analytical Chemistry, XXX (February, 1958), 17A-21A; Caul, "Geruchs- und Geschmacksanalysen mit der Profilmethode, II. Welche Rolle spielt der Geschmack bei Verbrauchsgütern," Die Ernährungswirtschaft, VII, No. 9 (1960), 398-402.

[13] For this last topic, cf. W. N. Locke and A. D. Booth, eds., Machine Translation of Languages (Cambridge, Mass.-New York: M.I.T. Press-Wiley, 1955).

[14] Rosenblueth, Wiener, and Bigelow, op. cit., p. 19. A more refined definition would

By output is meant any change produced in the surroundings by the object. By input, conversely, is meant any event external to the object that modifies this object in any manner.[15]

In other words, by feedback—or, as it is often called, a servomechanism—is meant a communications network that produces action in response to an input of information, and *includes the results of its own action in the new information by which it modifies its subsequent behavior.* A simple feedback network contains arrangements to react to an outside event (for example, a target) in a specified manner (such as by directing guns at it) until a specified state of affairs has been brought about (the guns cover the target perfectly, or the automatic push-button tuning adjustment on a radio has been accurately set on the wavelength approached). If the action of the network has fallen short of reaching fully the sought adjustment, it is continued; if it has overshot the mark, it is reversed. Both continuation and reversal may take place in proportion to the extent to which the goal has not yet been reached. If the feedback is well-designed, the result will be a series of diminishing mistakes—a dwindling series of under- and over-corrections converging on the goal. If the functioning of the feedback or servomechanism is not adequate to its task (if it is inadequately "dampened"), the mistakes may become greater. The network may be "hunting" over a cyclical or widening range of tentative and "incorrect" responses, ending in a breakdown of the mechanism. These failures of feedback networks have specific parallels in the pathology of the human nervous system ("purpose tremor") and perhaps even, in a looser sense, in the behavior of animals, men, and whole communities.[16]

This notion of feedback—and its application in practice—is at the heart of much of modern control engineering. It is a more sophisticated concept than the simple mechanical notion of equilibrium, and it promises to become a more powerful tool in the social sciences than the traditional equilibrium analysis.

If we say that a system is in *equilibrium*, we make a number of rather specific suggestions. We suggest that it will return to a particular state when "disturbed"; that we imagine the disturbance is coming from outside the system; that the system will return with greater force to its original state the greater has been the disturbance; that the high or low speed with which the system reacts or with which its parts act on each other is somehow irrelevant (and we term this quality "friction" to denote that it is a sort of imperfection or blemish that has no proper place in the "ideal" equilibrium); and finally we suggest that no catastrophes can happen within the limits of the system, but that, once an equilibrium breaks down, next to nothing can be said about the future of the system from then on.

Such equilibrium theories are based on a very restricted field of science,

put "output information" in place of "output energy," in accordance with the distinction between "communications engineering" and "power engineering." Cf. Wiener, *Cybernetics*, 2nd ed., pp. 39, 42.

[15] Rosenblueth, Wiener, and Bigelow, *op. cit.*, p. 18. There is also another kind of feedback, different from the negative feedback discussed in the text: "The feedback is . . . positive [if] the fraction of the output which reenters the object has the same sign as the original input signal. Positive feedback adds to the input signals, it does not correct them . . ."—*ibid.*, p. 19; see also Wiener, *Cybernetics*, 2nd ed., pp. 95-115. Only self-correcting, i.e., negative, feedback is discussed here.

[16] Wiener, *loc. cit.*

called *steady-state dynamics*. They are not well-suited to deal with so-called *transients*; that is, they cannot predict the consequences of *sudden* changes within the system or in its environment, such as the sudden starting or stopping of a process. Altogether, in the world of equilibrium theory there is no growth, no evolution; there are no sudden changes; and there is no efficient prediction of the consequences of "friction" over time.

On all these points the feedback concept promises improvements. Instead of pushing the effect of "friction" into the background, feedback theory is based on the measurement of *lag* and *gain*. *Lag* is the time that elapses between the moment a negative feedback system reaches a certain distance from its goal and the moment it completes corrective action corresponding to that distance. *Gain* means the extent of the corrective action taken. An inexperienced automobile driver tends to have slow reflexes: he responds tardily to the information of his eyes that his car is heading for the right-hand ditch. His lag, in feedback terms, is high. Yet when he acts, he may turn his steering wheel sharply—with a high gain—and head for the left-hand ditch until he notices the overcorrection and corrects his course again. If we know three quantities—the speed of his car and extent of his lags and of his gains—we can try to predict the wobbliness of his resulting course.

*Lag* and *gain*, in the feedback approach, are the most important variables to work on. Of the two, *lag* is the more important. It can be reduced by improving the system, as when our novice driver learns to react faster; or lag can be compensated for by a lead—a prediction of a future distance from the goal—as when an experienced driver compensates for an anticipated skid at the first sign of its onset. What *lag* still remains will permit control

engineers to calculate just how much gain—how drastic a self-correction at each step—the system can afford under known conditions without endangering its stability.

To sum up, equilibrium analysis is based on a restricted part of dynamics; it is restricted to the description of steady states. Cybernetics is based on full dynamics including changes of state; and it combines these full dynamics with statistics. Cybernetics is the study of the full dynamics of a system under a statistically varying input. The potential usefulness of this approach to such economic problems as, for example, the so-called "cobweb theorem" has been stressed by some economists.[17]

From a historical point of view, the rise of equilibrium analysis meant the neglect of problems of purpose. Cybernetics offers not only a gain in technical competence but also a possibility of restoring to problems of purpose their full share of our attention.

## Learning and Purpose

Even the simple feedback network shows the basic characteristics of the "learning process" described by John Dollard in animals and men. According to Dollard, "there must be (1) drive, (2) cue, (3) response, and (4) reward." In a man-made feedback network, "drive" might be represented by "internal tension," or better, by mechanical, chemical, or electric "dis-

---

[17] Harry G. Johnson, Review of Norbert Wiener's *Cybernetics*, in the *Economic Journal*, LIX, No. 236 (December, 1949), 573-75. For an early attempt to apply feedback analysis to economics, see A. Tustin, *The Mechanism of Economic Systems* (Cambridge, Mass.: Harvard Univ. Press, 1953). Cf. also the special issue on "automatic control" of *Scientific American*, CLXXXVII, No. 3 (September, 1952).

equilibrium"; input and output would function as "cue" and "response"; and the "reward" could be defined analogously for both organisms and man-made nets as a "reduction in intensity" (or extent) of the initial "drive" or internal disequilibrium.[18]

A simple feedback mechanism implies a measure of "purpose" or "goal." In this view a goal not only exists within the mind of a human observer; it also has relative objective reality within the context of a particular feedback net, once that net has physically come into existence. Thus a *goal* may be defined as "a final condition in which the behaving object reaches a definite correlation in time or in space with respect to another object or event."[19]

This definition of a goal, or purpose, may need further development. There is usually at least one such external goal (that is, one relation of the net as a whole to some external object) that is associated with one state encompassing the relatively lowest amount of internal disequilibrium within the net. Very often, however, an almost equivalent reduction of internal disequilibrium can be reached through an internal rearrangement of the relations between some of the constituent parts of the net, which would then provide a more or less effective substitute for the actual attainment of the goal relation in the world external to the net. There are many cases of such surrogate goals or *ersatz* satisfactions, as a short circuit in an electronic calculator, intoxication in certain insects, drug addiction or suicide in a man, or outbursts against scapegoat members of a "tense" community. They suggest the need for a distinction between merely internal readjustments and those that are sought through pathways that include as an essential part the reaching of a goal relationship with some part of the outside world.

This brings us to a more complex kind of learning. Simple learning is goal-seeking feedback, as in a homing torpedo. It consists in adjusting responses, so as to reach a goal situation of a type that is given once for all by certain internal arrangements of the net; these arrangements remain fixed throughout its life. A more complex type of learning is the self-modifying or *goal-changing* feedback. It allows for feedback readjustments of those internal arrangements that implied its original goal, so that the net will change its goal, or set for itself new goals that it will now have to reach if its internal disequilibrium is to be lessened. Goal-changing feedback contrasts, therefore, with Aristotelian teleology, in which each thing was supposed to be characterized by its unchanging *telos*, but it has parallels in Darwinian evolution.[20]

---

[18] Cf. John Dollard, "The Acquisition of New Social Habits," in Ralph Linton, ed., *The Science of Man in the World Crisis* (New York: Columbia Univ. Press, 1945), p. 442; with further references. "Drives . . . are 'rewarded,' that is, . . . they are reduced in intensity . . ."—A. Irving Hallowell, "Sociopsychological Aspects of Acculturation," in Linton, *op. cit.*, p. 183; cf., in the same volume, Clyde Kluckhohn and William H. Kelly, "The Concept of Culture," pp. 84-86; and E. R. Hilgard, *Theories of Learning* (New York: Appleton-Century-Crofts, 1948). Cf. also the references to Wiener and Ashby in footnote 6.

[19] Rosenblueth, Wiener, and Bigelow, *op. cit.*, p. 18. "By behavior is meant any change of an entity with respect to its surroundings. . . . Accordingly any modification of an object, detectable externally, may be denoted as behavior"—*Ibid.*

[20] The performance of a human goal seeker who strives for new goals on reaching each old one has been immortalized in Goethe's *Faust*:

Im Weiterschreiten find't er Qual und

We can now restate our earlier distinction as one between two kinds of goal-changing by internal rearrangement. Internal rearrangements that are still relevant to goal-seeking in the outside world we may call "learning." Internal rearrangements that reduce the net's goal-seeking effectiveness belong to the pathology of learning. Their eventual results are self-frustration and self-destruction. Pathological learning resembles what some moralists call "sin."

Perhaps the distinction could be carried further by thinking of several orders of purposes.

A first-order purpose in a feedback net would be the seeking of *immediate satisfaction,* that is, of an internal state in which internal disequilibrium would be less than in any alternative state, within the range of operations of the net. This first-order purpose would correspond to the concepts of "adjustment" and "reward" in studies of the learning process. Self-destructive purposes or rewards would be included in this class.

By a second-order purpose would be meant that internal and external state of the net that would seem to offer to the net the largest probability (or predictive value derived from past experience) for the net's continued ability to seek first-order purposes. This would imply *self-preservation* as a second-order purpose of the net, overriding the first-order purposes. It would require a far more complex net.

A third-order purpose might then mean a state of high probability for the continuation of the process of search for first- and second-order purposes by a group of nets beyond the "lifetime" of an individual net. This would include such purposes as the *preservation of the group* or "preservation of the species." Third-order purposes require several complex nets in interaction. Such interaction between several nets, sufficiently similar to make their experiences relevant test cases for one another, sufficiently different to permit division of labor, and sufficiently complex and readjustable to permit reliable communication between them—in short, such a *society* —is in turn essential for the higher levels of the learning process that could lead beyond third-order purposes.

Among fourth-order purposes we might include states offering high probabilities of the *preservation of a process* of purpose-seeking, even beyond the preservation of any particular group or species of nets. Such purposes as the preservation or growth of "life," "mind," "order in the universe," and all the other purposes envisaged in science, philosophy, or religion, could be included here.

The four orders overlap, their boundaries blur, and there seems to be no limit to the number of orders or purposes we may set up as aids to our thinking. Yet it may be worthwhile to order purposes in some such fashion, and to retain, as far as possible, the model of the feedback net that permits us to compare these purposes to some degree with physical arrangements and operations. The purpose of this procedure would not be to reduce intellectual and spiritual purposes to the level of neurophysiology or mechanics. Rather it would be to show that consistent elaboration of the simpler processes can elevate their results to higher levels.

---

Glueck
Er, unbefriedigt jeden Augenblick.

Analytical understanding of this process need not diminish its sublimity, and its emotional impact on us in our experience of recognition. *Faust* becomes no more trivial by our knowledge of goal-changing feedbacks than a sunrise becomes trivial by our knowledge of the laws of refraction.

### Values and the Capacity to Learn

The movements of messages through complex feedback networks may involve the problem of "value" or the "switchboard problem," that is, the problem of choice between different possibilities of routing different incoming messages through different channels or "associative trails"[21] within the network. If many alternative channels are available for few messages, the functioning of the network may be hampered by indecision; if many messages have to compete for few channels, it may be hampered by "jamming."

The efficient functioning of any complex switchboard requires, therefore, some relatively stable operating rules, explicit or implied in the arrangements of the channels. These rules must decide the relative preferences and priorities in the reception, screening, and routing of all signals entering the network from outside or originating within it.

There are many examples of such rules in practice: the priority given fire alarms in many telephone systems; or the rules determining the channels through which transcontinental telephone calls are routed at different loads of traffic; these last include even the "hunting" of an automatic switchboard for a free circuit when the routing channels are fully loaded. They illustrate the general need of any complex network to decide in some way on how to distribute its "attention" and its priorities in expediting competing messages, and how to choose between its large number of different possibilities for combination, association, and recombination for each message.

What operating rules accomplish in switchboards and calculating machines is accomplished to some extent by "emotional preference" in the nervous systems of animals and men, and by cultural or institutional preferences, obstacles, and "values" in groups or societies. Nowhere have investigators found any mind of that type that John Locke supposed "to be, as we say, white paper." Everywhere they have found structure and relative function.

In much of the communications machinery currently used, the operating rules are rigid in relation to the content of the information dealt with by the network. However, *these operating rules themselves may be made subject to some feedback process.* Just as human directors of a telephone company may react to a traffic count by changing some of their network's operating rules, we might imagine an automatic telephone exchange carrying out its own traffic counts and analyses, and modifying its operating rules accordingly. It might even modify the physical structure of some of its channels, perhaps adding or dropping additional microwave beams (which fulfill the function of telephone cables) in the light of the traffic or financial data "experienced" by the network.[22]

What seems a possibility in the case of man-made machinery seems to be a fact in living nerve systems, minds, and societies. The establishment and abolition of "conditioned reflexes" have long been studied in animals and men, and so have the results of in-

---

[21] Vannevar Bush, "As We May Think," *Atlantic Monthly*, CLXXVI (July, 1945), 101-8.

[22] An automatic telephone exchange capable of opening new channels in response to its own traffic counts was reported under construction by the Phillips Company of Eyndthove, Holland (*Science News Letter*, Washington, D.C., April 10, 1948, p. 233). A telephone exchange that would install such a channel control itself would represent one more extension of the same principle.

dividual and group learning. Such processes often include changes in the "operating rules" that determine how the organism treats subsequent items of information reaching it.

Any network whose operating rules can be modified by feedback processes is subject to *internal conflict* between its established working preferences and the impact of new information. The simpler the network, the more readily internal conflicts can be resolved by automatically assigning a clear preponderance to one or another of two competing "channels" or "reflexes" at any particular moment, swinging from one trend of behavior to another with least delay. The more complex, relatively, the switchboards and networks involved, the richer the possibilities of choice, the more prolonged may be the periods of indecision or internal conflict. Since the net acquires its preferences through a process of history, its "values" need not all be consistent with each other. They may form circular configurations of preference, which later may trap some of the impulses of the net in circular pathways of frustration. Since the human nervous network is complex, it remains subject to the possibilities of conflicts, indecision, jamming, and circular frustration. Whatever pattern or preferences or operating rules govern its behavior at any particular time can only reduce this affliction, but cannot abolish it.[23]

Since the network of the human mind behaves with some degree of plasticity, it can change many of its operating rules under the impact of experience. It can learn, not only superficially but fundamentally: with the aid of experience the human mind can change its own structure of preference, rejections, and associations. And what seems true of the general plasticity of the individual human mind applies even more to the plasticity of the channels that make up human cultures and social institutions and those particular individual habit patterns that go with them. Indeed, this cultural learning capacity seems to occur in some proportion to the ability of those cultures to survive and to spread.

Since all learning including changes in goals or values consists in physical internal rearrangements, it depends significantly on material resources. The *learning capacity* of any system or organization, that is, the range of its effective internal rearrangements, can thus be measured to some extent by the number and kinds of its *uncommitted resources*. Such resources need not be idle; but they must be reassignable from their current functions. There is a qualitative element in learning capacity, since it depends not only on the amount of uncommitted resources but also on their configurations. Yet, since learning capacity consists in an overall performance, a particular configuration of internal elements can be replaced, in many cases, by some functionally equivalent configuration of others. This is the more probable, the richer the range of available rearrangements, and thus, again, the greater the amount of uncommitted resources, and of facilities for their quick and varied recommitment.

Learning capacity can be tested by two independent sets of operations: first, by outside tests of a system's overall performance in a given situation, much as the learning capacity of rats is tested in a maze and that of armies is tested in battle; and second, by analysis of its inner structure. Thus the greater learning capacity of rats compared to frogs can be predicted from the greater size and complexity of the

---

23 "Man is the only organism normally and inevitably subject to psychological conflict" (J. S. Huxley, *Man Stands Alone* [New York: Harper & Row, Publishers, 1941], pp. 22-26, with examples).

rat's central nervous system, and the greater learning capacity or adaptability of one army relative to another can be predicted if, other things being equal, it has greater facilities of communication and transport and a greater "operational reserve" of uncommitted man power and equipment. Since overall performance tests are cheap in rats, but expensive in armies or in the defense of cities against atom bombs, the prediction of probable learning capacity from structural analysis and the suggestions for probable improvements by the same method may have considerable practical importance.

So far we have described two kinds of feedback: "goal-seeking," the feedback of new external data into a net whose operating channels remain unchanged; and "learning," the feedback of external data for the changing of these operating channels themselves. A third important type of possible feedback is the feedback and simultaneous scanning of highly selected internal data, analogous to the problem of what usually is called "consciousness."

# CONSCIOUSNESS AS PATTERNS OF COMMUNICATION FLOW

*Consciousness* may be defined, as a first approximation and for the purposes of this discussion, as a collection of internal feedbacks of secondary messages. *Secondary messages* are messages about changes in the state of parts of the system, that is, about primary messages. *Primary messages* are those that move through the system in consequence of its interaction with the outside world. Any secondary message or combination of messages, however, may in turn serve as a primary message, in that a further secondary message may be attached to any combination of primary messages or to other secondary messages or their combinations, up to any level of regress.

In all these cases, secondary messages function as symbols or internal labels for changes of state within the net itself. They are fed back into it as additional information, and they influence, together with all other feedback data, the net's subsequent behavior. "Consciousness" does not consist merely in these labels, but in the processes by which they are derived from the net and fed back into it, and in the processes by which two or more such secondary messages are brought to interact with each other.

## Consciousness in Social Organizations

Feedback messages about some of the net's internal states occur in simple form in electronic calculators where they serve important functions in recall. They may occur, in extremely complex patterns, in the human nervous system, where they are not easy to isolate for study. But they also occur, and can be studied with relative ease, in the division of labor of large human teams that process information and collectively fulfill certain functions of thought. We find such teams in industrial research laboratories, and in political or military intelligence organizations.

We can observe how guide cards and index tabs are added to the information moving through, or stored within, the filing systems, libraries, card catalogues, or "document control centers" of intelligence organizations (such as the State Department or, during World War II, the Office of Strategic Services), and how these secondary symbols influence the further treatment of the information. The heads, policy boards, or project committees of such organizations cannot deal with all the vast information in the original documents. They deal mostly with titles, description sheets, summaries, project requests, routing slips, and other secondary symbols, while a great deal of the material continues to be processed "below the level of the consciousness" of the guiding and policy-making parts of the organization. Only those feedback circuits and decisions that are "picked up" through the attachment and feedback of secondary symbols become directly "conscious" for the organization.

To be sure, the selective function of any network is by no means limited to this "conscious" zone of secondary symbols. On the contrary, what reaches that zone for separately labeled and recorded processing depends in turn on what has been selected or rejected, associated or disassociated, routed or blocked, recorded or misfiled or erased within the rest of the system. There is some automatic screening carried out by the reporter on the beat, and by the desk analyst in the intelligence organization; and we may suspect similar screening processes in the "nonconscious" remembering and forgetting, the "aversions" and "hunches" of the individual mind, as well as in many of the "unverbalized" conventions and assumptions, preferences or taboos of human societies and cultures.[24]

The powers of the "nonconscious," internally unlabeled processes within a network, can be positive as well. An experience may be built up into a perception and recorded in memory, two and two may be put together, new associations, discoveries and insights may

be put together "nonconsciously" without the intervention of secondary symbols, until secondary symbols are attached to the new combination, and suddenly the image of the new synthesis breaks through into the realm of consciousness, seeming all ready and armored, like Pallas Athene springing forth from the head of Zeus in the Greek legend.[25]

By attaching secondary symbols to some of our steps in a calculation or sequence of behavior we may change its outcome. For these secondary symbols are fed back into the net, and the message of which the net has become "conscious" may then appear in the net with greater frequency than its unlabeled alternatives, and it may remain more readily available for preferred treatment. This treatment may be preferred association, recording, transmission, blocking, or suppression, according to the current operating rules of the system.

If secondary symbols become attached to parts or connections in the net that embody these operating rules, then these rules themselves become "conscious" for the net. By being fed back into it, they become statistically reinforced for more effective application; and they may be changed more easily if this possibility is included in the net. The effects of such internal labeling may be thought of as to some extent comparable to the effect of dra-

---

[24] "By 'culture' we mean those historically created selective processes which channel men's reactions both to internal and to external stimuli"—Clyde Kluckhohn and William H. Kelly, "The Concept of Culture," in Linton, The Science of Man in the World Crisis, p. 84.

[25] For a description of this experience of "sudden insight," and of its unreliability, see Bertrand Russell, History of Western Philosophy (New York: Simon and Schuster, 1945), pp. 123-124 and 289-290. Cf. also W. B. Cannon, The Way of an Investigator (New York: Norton, 1945), pp. 57-67; G. Polya, How to Solve It, (Princeton, N.J.: Princeton Univ. Press, 1945), pp. 56-58; W. James, Varieties of Religious Experience (New York: Modern Library, n.d.), pp. 370-413; and J. Rosett, The Mechanism of Thought, Imagery and Hallucination (New York: Columbia Univ. Press, 1939), passim.

matic symbols or publicity devices in a society. Once attached to particular ideas, practices, or laws, they may lift them from their previous obscure existence into the crossfire of public attention.[26]

The ensemble of secondary symbols may easily misrepresent the net's actual content. Some primary symbols may be "overrepresented" by ample feedback, while others may not be made "conscious" at all. Consciousness, therefore, may be false consciousness, much as the actual personality of a man may be quite different from what he thinks it is. Similarly, by attaching suitable symbols and feedbacks to selected aspects of their behavior, groups or nations can be given highly misleading ideas about their own character.

## Confrontation for Simultaneous Inspection

Consciousness, however, involves not one operation but at least two. It requires first of all a high degree of selection and abstraction from the stream of primary or lower-order messages, and their highly condensed and abridged mapping into a much smaller number of higher-order messages. But it also implies, as a rule, the more or less simultaneous scanning or inspection of as much of this abridged second-order information as can be encompassed in the "focus of consciousness"—or the "span of attention" or "span of control"—of a person, or in the effective range of surveillance or control of an organization.

Physical examples of such condensed and concentrated arrangements of sec-

ondary symbols for their simultaneous —or nearly simultaneous—inspection are abundant. They include the nineteenth century military staff maps on which colored pins and other movable symbols represented troops; the underground plotting center in the Battle of Britain in 1940 where, on a large simplified map of southern England and the Channel, wooden counters were moved with rakes by army personnel, so as to represent the strength, position, direction, and speed of attacking and defending aircraft and to permit quick decisions about the best use of still disposable British fighter defenses; and the transparent plastic screen in the antiaircraft control center of post-World War II vessels in the premissile age, when the quickly changing reported numbers and movements of attacking enemy aircraft were chalked in color on one side of the plastic, so as to permit the officer on the other side to encompass at one glance the rapidly mounting attacks from many directions against his ship, and to decide on the best allocation of his own antiaircraft batteries, and perhaps fighter planes, for his defense; and the "situation room" of the early 1950's, where the President of the United States was reportedly briefed almost daily by his subordinates on the changing conditions and crises around the world, was similarly designed to facilitate simultaneous inspection. A current offspring of all these simpler devices could perhaps be seen in the vast warning and computing systems of the late 1950's and early 1960's—such as the SAGE system—that are designed to collect and compare a large number of highly abbreviated data, radar readings, and the like, so as to make or keep their operators aware of all actual or apparent movements of aircraft or missiles toward the territory of the United States.

·      ·      ·

---

[26] The importance of consciousness in the growth of nationalism is stressed, without defining consciousness itself, in Hans Kohn, *The Idea of Nationalism* (New York: Macmillan, 1944), pp. 6-16.

How does this feedback notion of consciousness compare with other approaches? In the behaviorist school of psychology, we are told that "consciousness" and conscious processes "are excluded as not subject to scientific investigation, or . . . reinterpreted as covert language responses."[27] In social science writings, consciousness is often stressed, and ascribed to groups, but usually this is done without definition or description in any but intuitive terms.[28] Two recent writers describe individual consciousness as follows:

[The] integrative (regnant) process in the brain . . . according to the findings and speculations of neurophysiologists . . . are capable of self-awareness (as if they had a mirror in which to see themselves). During the passage of one event many, but not all, of the regnant processes have the property of consciousness, at the moment of their occurrence or soon afterwards if recalled by retrospection. Thus the stream of consciousness is nothing more than the subjective (inner) awareness of some of the momentary forces operating at the regnant level of integration in the brain field.[29]

This is a suggestive description in the language of everyday life in which processes behave like small individuals who "reign," "see themselves as if they had a mirror," and "have the property of consciousness" that "is nothing more than . . . subjective (inner) awareness." But it is not very helpful as a concept from which we might derive new observations and experiments.

In contrast to this, what are the operational implications of our feedback model? First of all, if consciousness is a feedback process, then it requires material facilities and is carried on at some material cost in terms of facilities and time. Some of the facilities that are tied up, and some of the delay imposed on primary processes, should be capable of measurement.

Second, feedback processes have structures, circuits, channels, switching relationships, incompatibilities, and discontinuities that might be susceptible of mapping.

In the third place, if we cannot isolate the physical facilities involved, we might devise functional tests for possible patterns, limits, and discontinuities in the performance of the process of consciousness. If these tests should yield a map of discontinuities in performance, we might derive a basis for further inferences about the structure of the underlying facilities and processes themselves.[30]

Similar considerations might apply to the processes of "consciousness" in nations, classes, or other social groups.

[27] Gardner Murphy, *Personality* (New York: Harper & Row, Publishers, 1947), p. 981. "Consciousness" and "awareness" are referred to in the text, but do not appear in the elaborate glossary and subject index. A similar view is taken by W. Ross Ashby, *Design for a Brain* (London: Chapman & Hall, 1952), pp. 11-12.

[28] Kohn, *op. cit.*; Harold D. Lasswell, *The Analysis of Political Behaviour* (London: Oxford Univ. Press, 1949), pp. 22, 108, 116, 215, 240, 284, etc.

[29] Clyde Kluckhohn and Henry A. Murray, eds., *Personality in Nature, Society, and Culture* (New York: Knopf, 1948), p. 9; italics omitted.

[30] For a discussion of consciousness in physiological as well as psychological terms, see D. O. Hebb, *The Organization of Behavior* (New York: Wiley, 1949), pp. 144-46; and for a suggestive survey of much earlier literature on this topic, C. R. Noyes, *Economic Man in Relation to His Natural Environment* (New York: Columbia Univ. Press, 1948), I, 98 ff.; II, 1138 ff. Both works indicate a return of interest to a crucial topic, but they also show the difficulties of analyzing consciousness with none but physiological and psychological material that usually is hard to take apart or reassemble. Here the aid of structural data from the theory and practice of communications, as developed in engineering, mathematics, and the social sciences, might show its usefulness.

If there are such processes, how are they organized and patterned? What are the manpower, facilities, symbols, learning processes, and teamwork relations by which they are carried on? If consciousness resembles a feedback, does it also resemble the feedback's peculiar kinds of instability? A small change in a feedback circuit can bring about a large change in its over-all performance. Are there analogies for this in social life?

The feedback model of consciousness is more than a verbal explanation. It is a concept. For it suggests many questions that sooner or later should be answered, one way or another, by observation and experiment.

# unconscious processes in groups: on authority

## chapter five

The cybernetic model is incomplete as a model for human groups. As stated, it deals with the low-energy, high-control sector but not with the high-energy, low-control sector. Both operate in human groups. One must go beyond the model both to understand what drives or motivates the system and to discover not only the locus of human needs but also the channels through which emotions flow and the structures that attachments and animosities establish. Although future models of this second sector might conceivably complement the cybernetic model, leaving information processing undisturbed, it seems more likely that the individual and collective workings of such phenomena as love, fear, sex, anxiety, and aggression intrude into information processing, resulting in blocking, jamming, and short-circuiting the otherwise liberated and increasingly sophisticated intellectual capabilities featured in the cybernetic model. A number of later selections in this volume support the point that many groups fail to achieve "consciousness" for psychological and sociological reasons. (See Vogel and Bell, and Jaques.) One reason, suggested by Freud in the first selection that follows, is that modern man remains saddled with his primitive origins and, indeed, seems compelled to re-enact the social dramas of primitive man; another, suggested by Brown in the second selection, is that just as no man's mind is free from the physical body, no group is free from involvement in love's body, or from the unconscious processes of collective man.

In his *Group Psychology and the Analysis of the Ego*, Freud applied psychoanalytical concepts in an attempt to account for the origin and the development of human collectivities. If the individual is essentially irrational, our understanding of him is best enlarged by analysis of the structuring and dynamics of his unconscious. Similarly, the group can be seen as a structure of unconscious, emotional ties among members, the leader, and the collectivity. Group structure and culture is more than the purely rational, inevitable precipitates of external pressures and sociological "laws"; it is as well the responses to shared, unconscious needs of group members. Such needs center upon the issues of power and authority. Although the roots of these issues might be traced back to the "primal horde," it is important to recognize that for practical purposes Freud's argument rests less upon the historical accuracy of the "primal horde" than it does upon the broad applicability of his analogy. The significant point is that issues of the primal horde, and the fantasies that accompany them, reappear in one form or another in every group.

A clear implication of Freud's group psychology is that the group leader, whether present or not, will represent a focal point for unconscious feelings associated with the chief.

Freud's group psychology is not, of course, immutable. We expect advances to emerge from depth psychology that will have implications for a more comprehensive paradigm of groups. Although Freud's presentation is sketchy from this viewpoint, it remains as a significant example of how another dimension of analysis can be applied to increase our understanding of group dynamics.

## The Group and the Primal Horde

SIGMUND FREUD

In 1912 I took up a conjecture of Darwin's to the effect that the primitive form of human society was that of a horde ruled over despotically by a powerful male. I attempted to show that the fortunes of this horde have left indestructible traces upon the history of human descent; and, especially, that the development of totemism, which comprises in itself the beginnings of religion, morality, and social organization, is connected with the killing of the chief by violence and the transformation of the paternal horde into a community of brothers.[1] To be sure, this is only a hypothesis, like so many others with which archaeologists endeavor to lighten the darkness of prehistoric times—a "Just-So-Story," as it was amusingly called by a not unkind English critic[2]; but I think it is creditable to such a hypothesis if it proves able to bring coherence and understanding into more and more new regions.

Human groups exhibit once again

Reprinted from Sigmund Freud, Group Psychology and the Analysis of the Ego, in the Standard Edition of the Complete Psychological Works of Sigmund Freud, rev. and ed. by James Strachey (London: The Hogarth Press Ltd., 1955), Vol. 18, pp. 122-28, by permission of Sigmund Freud Copyrights Ltd., the Institute of Psycho-Analysis, The Hogarth Press Ltd., and the Liveright Publishing Corporation.

[1] Totem and Taboo, Standard Ed., 13 [Essay IV. Freud uses the term horde to signify a relatively small collection of people.]

[2] [In the first edition only, the name "Kroeger," appeared here. This was evidently a misprint for "Kroeber"—incidentally the name of the well-known American anthropologist.]

the familiar picture of an individual of superior strength among a troop of equal companions, a picture which is also contained in our idea of the primal horde. The psychology of such a group, as we know it from the descriptions to which we have so often referred—the dwindling of the conscious individual personality, the focusing of thoughts and feelings into a common direction, the predominance of the affective side of the mind and of unconscious psychical life, the tendency to the immediate carrying out of intentions as they emerge—all this corresponds to a state of regression to a primitive mental activity, of just such a sort as we should be inclined to ascribe to the primal horde.[3]

Thus the group appears to us as a revival of the primal horde. Just as primitive man survives potentially in every individual, so the primal horde may arise once more out of any random collection; in so far as men are habitually under the sway of group formation we recognize in it the survival of the primal horde. We must

conclude that the psychology of groups is the oldest human psychology; what we have isolated as individual psychology, by neglecting all traces of the group, has once since come into prominence out of the old group psychology, by a gradual process which may still, perhaps, be described as incomplete. We shall later venture upon an attempt at specifying the point of departure of this development.

Further reflection will show us in what respect this statement requires correction. Individual psychology must, on the contrary, be just as old as group psychology, for from the first there were two kinds of psychologies, that of the individual members of the group and that of the father, chief, or leader. The members of the group were subject to ties just as we see them today, but the father of the primal horde was free. His intellectual acts were strong and independent even in isolation, and his will needed no reinforcement from others. Consistency leads us to assume that his ego had few libidinal ties; he loved no one but himself, or other people only in so far as they served his needs. To objects his ego gave away no more than was barely necessary.

He, at the very beginning of the history of mankind, was the "superman" whom Nietzsche only expected from the future. Even today the members of a group stand in need of the illusion that they are equally and justly loved by their leader; but the leader himself need love no one else, he may be of a masterful nature, absolutely narcissistic, self-confident and independent. We know that love puts a check upon narcissism, and it would be possible to show how, by operating in this way, it became a factor of civilization.

The primal father of the horde was not yet immortal, as he later became by deification. If he died, he had to be replaced; his place was probably taken by a youngest son, who had up to then

---

[3] What we have just described in our general characterization of mankind must apply especially to the primal horde. The will of the individual was too weak; he did not venture upon action. No impulses whatever came into existence except collective ones; there was only a common will, there were no single ones. An idea did not dare to turn itself into an act of will unless it felt itself reinforced by a perception of its general diffusion. This weakness of the idea is to be explained by the strength of the emotional tie which is shared by all the members of the horde; but the similarity in the circumstances of their life and the absence of any private property assist in determining the uniformity of their individual mental acts. As we may observe with children and soldiers, common activity is not excluded even in the excretory functions. The one great exception is provided by the sexual act, in which a third person is at best superfluous and in the extreme case is condemned to a state of painful expectancy. . . .

been a member of the group like any other. There must therefore be a possibility of transforming group psychology into individual psychology; a condition must be discovered under which such a transformation is easily accomplished, just as it is possible for bees in case of necessity to turn a larva into a queen instead of into a worker. One can imagine only one possibility: the primal father had prevented his sons from satisfying their directly sexual impulsions; he forced them into abstinence and consequently into the emotional ties with him and with one another which could arise out of those of their impulsions that were inhibited in their sexual aim. He forced them, so to speak, into group psychology. His sexual jealousy and intolerance became in the last resort the causes of group psychology.[4]

Whoever became his successor was also given the possibility of sexual satisfaction, and was by that means offered a way out of the conditions of group psychology. The fixation of the libido to women and the possibility of satisfaction without any need for delay or accumulation made an end of the importance of those of his sexual impulsions that were inhibited in their aim, and allowed his narcissism always to rise to its full height. . . .

We may further emphasize, as being specially instructive, the relation that holds between the contrivance by means of which an artificial group is held together and the constitution of the primal horde. We have seen that with an army and a Church this contrivance is the illusion that the leader loves all of the individuals equally and justly. But this is simply an idealistic remodeling of the state of affairs in the primal horde, where all of the sons knew that they were equally *persecuted* by the primal father, and *feared* him equally. This same recasting upon which all social duties are built up is already presupposed by the next form of human society, the totemic clan. The indestructible strength of the family as a natural group formation rests upon the fact that this necessary presupposition of the father's equal love can have a real application in the family.

But we expect even more of this derivation of the group from the primal horde. It ought also to help us to understand what is still incomprehensible and mysterious in group formations— all that lies hidden behind the enigmatic words "hypnosis" and "suggestion." And I think it can succeed in this too. Let us recall that hypnosis has something positively uncanny about it; but the characteristic of uncanniness suggests something old and familiar that has undergone repression.[5] Let us consider how hypnosis is induced. The hypnotist asserts that he is in possession of a mysterious power that robs the subject of his own will; or, which is the same thing, the subject believes it of him. This mysterious power (which is even now often described popularly as "animal magnetism") must be the same power that is looked upon by primitive people as the source of taboo, the same that emanates from kings and chieftains and makes it dangerous to approach them (*mana*). The hypnotist, then, is supposed to be in possession of this power; and how does he manifest it? By telling the subject to look him in the eyes; his most typical method of hypnotizing is by his look. But it is precisely the

---

[4] It may perhaps also be assumed that the sons, when they were driven out and separated from their father, advanced from identification with one another to homosexual object-love, and in this way won freedom to kill their father. [See *Totem and Taboo*, Standard Ed., 13, 144.]

---

[5] Cf. "The 'Uncanny,' " Standard Ed., 17.

*sight* of the chieftain that is dangerous and unbearable for primitive people, just as later that of the Godhead is for mortals. Even Moses had to act as an intermediary between his people and Jehovah, since the people could not support the sight of God; and when he returned from the presence of God his face shone—some of the *mana* had been transferred on to him, just as happens with the intermediary among primitive people.[6]

It is true that hypnosis can also be evoked in other ways, for instance by fixing the eyes upon a bright object or by listening to a monotonous sound. This is misleading and has given occasion to inadequate physiological theories. In point of fact these procedures merely serve to divert conscious attention and to hold it riveted. The situation is the same as if the hypnotist had said to the subject: "Now concern yourself exclusively with my person; the rest of the world is quite uninteresting." It would of course be technically inexpedient for a hypnotist to make such a speech; it would tear the subject away from his unconscious attitude and stimulate him to conscious opposition. The hypnotist avoids directing the subject's conscious thoughts toward his own intentions, and makes the person upon whom he is experimenting sink into an activity in which the world is bound to seem uninteresting to him; but at the same time the subject is in reality unconsciously concentrating his whole attention upon the hypnotist, and is getting into an attitude of *rapport*, of transference on to him. Thus the indirect methods of hypnotizing, like many of the technical procedures used in making jokes,[7] have

the effect of checking certain distributions of mental energy which would interfere with the course of events in the unconscious, and they lead eventually to the same result as the direct methods of influence by means of staring or stroking.[8]

Ferenczi has made the true discovery that when a hypnotist gives the command to sleep, which is often done at the beginning of hypnosis, he is putting himself in the place of the subject's parents. He thinks that two sorts of hypnotism are to be distinguished: one coaxing and soothing, which he considers is modeled on the mother, and another threatening, which is derived from the father.[9] Now the com-

---

[6] See *Totem and Taboo* [second essay] and the sources there quoted.

[7] [The distracting of attention as part of the technique of joking is discussed at some length in the latter half of Chapter V of Freud's book on jokes, *Jokes and Their Relation to the Unconscious*, Standard Ed., 8. The possibility of this mechanism playing a part in "thought-transference" is mentioned in *Psycho-Analysis and Telepathy*, Standard Ed., 18 (1921), 175. But perhaps Freud's earliest allusion to the idea is to be found in his final chapter in *Studies on Hysteria*, Standard Ed., 2. Toward the beginning of the second section of that chapter Freud brings forward this same mechanism as a possible part explanation of the efficacy of his "pressure" procedure.]

[8] This situation, in which the subject's attitude is unconsciously directed toward the hypnotist, while he is consciously occupied with monotonous and uninteresting perceptions, finds a parallel among the events of psychoanalytic treatment, which deserves to be mentioned here. At least once in the course of every analysis a moment comes when the patient obstinately maintains that just now positively nothing whatever occurs to his mind. His free associations come to a stop and the usual incentives for putting them in motion fail in their effect. If the analyst insists, the patient is at last induced to admit that he is thinking of the view from the consulting-room window, of the wallpaper that he sees before him, or of the gas-lamp hanging from the ceiling. Then one knows at once that he has gone off into the transference and that he is engaged upon what are still unconscious thoughts relating to the physician; and one sees the stoppage in the patient's associations disappear, as soon as he has been given this explanation.

[9] S. Ferenczi, "Introjection and Transfer-

mand to sleep in hypnosis means nothing more nor less than an order to withdraw all interest from the world and to concentrate it on the person of the hypnotist. And it is so understood by the subject; for in this withdrawal of interest from the external world lies the psychological characteristic of sleep, and the kinship between sleep and the state of hypnosis is based on it.

By the measures that he takes, then, the hypnotist awakens in the subject a portion of his archaic heritage which had also made him compliant toward his parents and which had experienced an individual reanimation in his relation to his father; what is thus awakened is the idea of a paramount and dangerous personality, toward whom only a passive-masochistic attitude is possible, to whom one's will has to be surrendered—while to be alone with him, "to look him in the face," appears a hazardous enterprise. It is only in some such way as this that we can picture the relation of the individual member of the primal horde to the primal father. As we know from other reactions, individuals have preserved a variable degree of personal aptitude for reviving old situations of this kind. Some knowledge that in spite of everything hypnosis is only a game, a deceptive renewal of these old impressions, may, however, remain behind and take

care that there is a resistance against any too serious consequences of the suspension of the will in hypnosis.

The uncanny and coercive characteristics of group formations, which are shown in the phenomena of suggestion that accompany them, may therefore with justice be traced back to the fact of their origin from the primal horde. The leader of the group is still the dreaded primal father; the group still wishes to be governed by unrestricted force; it has an extreme passion for authority; in Le Bon's phrase, it has a thirst for obedience. The primal father is the group ideal, which governs the ego in the place of the ego ideal. Hypnosis has a good claim to being described as a group of two. There remains as a definition for suggestion: a conviction which is not based upon perception and reasoning but upon an erotic tie.[10]

---

[10] It seems to me worth emphasizing the fact that the discussions in this section have induced us to give up Bernheim's conception of hypnosis and go back to the *naïf* earlier one. According to Bernheim all hypnotic phenomena are to be traced to the factor of suggestion, which is not itself capable of further explanation. We have come to the conclusion that suggestion is a partial manifestation of the state of hypnosis, and that hypnosis is solidly founded upon a predisposition which has survived in the unconscious from the early history of the human family. [Freud had already expressed his skepticism about Bernheim's views on suggestion in the preface to his translation of Bernheim's book on the subject, Standard Ed., 1.]

---

ence," *First Contributions to Psycho-Analysis* (London, 1952), Chap. II.

# unconscious processes in groups: on peers

## chapter six

Just as Melanie Klein has modified and extended Freud's formulations on the level of individual psychology, so does Norman O. Brown extend the Freudian perspective in the analysis of social systems.

Like Freud, Brown locates the essential forces and meaning of social life in the primitive, unconscious processes in which all men participate. Far more important than cultural ideals, legal structures, transient technologies, and other more obvious features of social establishments are man's needs and his unconscious fantasies about his individual and collective existence. Such needs and fantasies both revert to man's social origin and encompass all groups on the globe. If group structures can be seen to have an underground terrain, Brown is attempting to map this area for us. Although the language in that territory is often obscure and the customs strange, the social and psychological issues are old and familiar: the prerogatives of the chief and the jealousy of his sons, the sexual union of the parents and the exclusion of the child, the separation of boys from girls and the ganging up of the boys against the elders, the wrestle for power, the struggle for access to women, the division of groups and societies into parts, the conflict between brotherhoods, and the fantasy of superiority over neighboring groups. These ancient issues underlie all organizations and groups. As new groups form, they reappear all over again. As both primitive and elemental they are alive within the unconscious whenever men meet to work together.

Our selection provides only a glimpse of Brown's exploration of this terrain. He begins with Freud, who, for obscure reasons, thought in strictly male terms and in whose view the unconscious processes are organized into a group through the identification of sons with the chief, or the father, or the leader. Following Melanie Klein, Brown realistically admits females into the basic structure. The *overthrow* of the chief as the original crime is translated into the *separation* of father from mother and the identification of the young with this partnership. The young identify with the duality of male and female in their sexual partnership, which symbolically represents the creative source of social existence.

# Liberty

NORMAN O. BROWN

Freud's myth of the rebellion of the sons against the father in the primal, prehistoric horde is not a historical explanation of origins, but a supra-historical archetype; eternally recurrent; a myth; an old, old story.

Freud seems to project into prehistoric times the constitutional crisis of seventeenth-century England. The primal father is *absolute monarch* of the horde; the females are his *property*. The sons form a *conspiracy* to *overthrow* the despot, and in the end substitute a *social contract* with *equal rights* for all. This anachronistic history directs us to look for the recurrence of the archetype in the seventeenth century.

Cf. Freud, *Moses and Monotheism*, pp. 130-33, 188.

In the *First Treatise of Civil Government*, Locke attacks Sir Robert Filmer's defense of absolute monarchy, entitled *Patriarcha*. Sir Robert Filmer, like Freud, identifies patriarchy and monarchy, political and paternal power. Filmer, like Freud, derives constitutional structure from a primal or prehistoric mythical family, from the paternal powers of our father Adam. Like Freud, Filmer attributes to the primal father unlimited power over his sons, including the power and propensity to castrate them.

Reprinted from Norman O. Brown, *Love's Body* (New York: Random House, 1966), pp. 3-6, 8-15, 17-26, 29-30, by permission of the author and Random House, Inc. Copyright © 1966 by Norman O. Brown.

Locke contradicts Filmer's primal fatherhood—a "strange kind of domineering phantom, called 'the fatherhood'" he says, a "gigantic form"—with the postulate of all men in the primal state of nature free and equal. To vindicate liberty is to vindicate the children, *liberi*, the sons, against paternal despotism. Locke kills Filmer's fatherhood, lays that phantom. The battle of books reenacts Freud's primal crime.

Locke, *Two Treatises of Civil Government*, pp. 6, 7.

Liberty means equality among the brothers (sons). Locke rejects Filmer's rule of primogeniture, which transmits the full power of father Adam to one of his sons, and makes one brother the father of his brethren. How can a man get power not only over his own children, but over his brethren, asks Locke. "Brother," he says, "is the name of friendship and equality, and not of jurisdiction and authority." Against Filmer's fatherhood Locke champions liberty, equality, fraternity. Locke has father Adam's property divided equally among all his sons. Liberty, equality: it is all a dispute over the inheritance of the paternal estate.

Locke, *Two Treatises of Civil Government*, p. 92.

But the equality of brotherhood is a leveling in the presence of a father; it is a way of dividing what belongs to a father—"the father's equal love." Locke's equality in the state of nature belongs to men as sons of God. Liberty means sonship. To make all men free and equal in the state of nature, Locke allows no man the status of father, and makes all men sons of the Heavenly Father. The phantom of fatherhood is banished from the earth, and elevated to the skies. "The state of Nature has a law to govern it, and reason, which is that law, teaches all mankind who will but consult it, that being equal and independent, no one ought to harm another in his life, health, liberty or possessions; for men being all the workmanship of one omnipotent and infinitely wise Maker, all the servants of one sovereign Master, sent into the world by His order and about His business; they are His property." Procreative power itself is transferred from the earthly to the heavenly father. The parents are only guardians of the children they had begotten, "not as their own workmanship, but the workmanship of their own Maker, the Almighty." God is the "author and giver of life." Parents are only the guardians of their children: fathers are not even fathers of their children. Filmer's sons were subject to castration; Locke castrates the earthly fathers. Thus the defense of sonship turns into the discovery of another father, the "real" father; and the real question in politics is Jesus' question, Who is my father?

Locke, *Two Treatises of Civil Government*, pp. 119-20, 143, 37; cf. p. 147. Cf. Freud, *Group Psychology*, pp. 89, 95.

Here is the inner contradiction in liberty, equality, and fraternity. Sonship and brotherhood are espoused against fatherhood: but without a father there can be no sons or brothers. Locke's sons, like Freud's, cannot free themselves from father psychology, and are crucified by the contradictory commands issuing from the Freudian super-ego, which says both "thou shalt be like the father," and "thou shalt not be like the father," that is, many things are his prerogative. Fraternal organization in the body politic corresponds to ego-organization in the body physical. As fraternal organization covertly assumes a father, ego-organization covertly assumes a super-ego.

Cf. Freud, *The Ego and the Id*, p. 44.

.    .    .

What is the division of labor? Durkheim in his book on the division of labor saw two distinct principles, antagonistic and complementary, as warp and woof of human social organization, which he called mechanical and organic solidarity. Mechanical solidarity is union based on likeness; and it finds its clearest expression in kinship. Organic solidarity is union based on differentiation and organic interdependence; its expression is the division of labor. Durkheim associates mechanical solidarity not only with the family but also with the collective conscience and with criminal law as a repressive system—in Freudian terms, the super-ego and the father. Organic solidarity on the other hand he associates with the civil law which sustains persons, properties and contracts on the basis of equity and equality.

Cf. Durkheim, *The Division of Labor*.

In *Group Psychology and the Analysis of the Ego* Freud adumbrated the distinction between two archetypes of social psychology: the individual psychology which in the primal horde belonged to the father alone, and the group psychology of the sons, or brothers. Fatherhood and brotherhood are the archetypes brooding in the background of such sociological abstractions as Durkheim's mechanical and organic solidarity; or Gierke's *Herrschaft* and *Genossenschaft*, the imperial and fraternal principles, which dialectically combine to weave the changing fabric of Western social corporate bodies. It is the specific gift of psychoanalysis to see behind these sociological abstractions the human face;

and their name is fatherhood and brotherhood.

Cf. Freud, *Group Psychology*, p. 92; Brophy, *Black Ship to Hell*, p. 73; Gierke, *Das deutsche Genossenschaftsrecht*, I, pp. 12-16.

Locke suggests that the fraternity is formed not by birth but by election, by contract; Plato's fraternity based on the division of labor excludes the family; Durkheim's organic solidarity is the opposite of kinship. This brotherhood is not made inside the family, nor by the father; is not born of the flesh, but of the spirit; is not natural, but artificial. Rousseau would say it is based on will; in the vocabulary of Freud's *Totem and Taboo* it is totemic brotherhood. In totemic brotherhood the bond which unites the brothers is not family relationship or blood kinship. The totem clan is defined by a peculiar relation to its particular totem animal, plant, or object; by virtue of which they are of one body, and have one common totem ancestor. The body is mystical, and the ancestor mythical.

Cf. Cornford, *From Religion to Philosophy*, pp. 56-57.

Only in the latest of his tellings of the story, in *Moses and Monotheism*, does Freud distinguish the brotherhood from the natural relation among the sons inside the family. In that version the brotherhood comes into being after the sons are expelled from the family, when they "club together" in the wilderness; the social contract perpetuates "the attachment that had grown up among them during the time of their exile." They club together in the fatherless wilderness; it is a fraternity of young men in college, away from home. The artifice that makes the brotherhood, the social contract, is initiation.

Freud, *Moses and Monotheism*, pp. 131-32.

If the story is to be told in the form of anthropology, then the sons and brothers are to be found not inside the family, but in the clubs or fraternities or secret societies, which are not merely outside the family but rather diametrically contradict it. In the family there is a natural symbiosis of those who have a natural need for each other: male and female; parent and child. The fraternity, or club, or secret society strives to put asunder what is joined in the family—male and female, parent and child. In primitive secret societies, in puberty rites, in *Altersklassen und Männerbünde*, the persistent tendency is to separate the sexes and the generations; to form homosexual and coeval groupings. Besides the natural union of the sexes in the family of which Aristotle speaks, there is also unconscious hostility between the sexes; "an archaic reaction of enmity"; taboos which prescribe sexual separation, mutual avoidance; the castration complex. Without an understanding of the seamy side of sexuality there is no understanding of politics.

Cf. Freud, "The Taboo of Virginity," p. 234; Reik, "Couvade," p. 50 and "The Puberty Rites of Savages," pp. 154-55; Crawley, *Mystic Rose* I, pp. 44-45, 54-55, 171; Blüher, *Die Rolle der Erotik in der männlichen Gesellschaft*; Webster, *Primitive Secret Societies*; Schurtz, *Altersklassen und Männerbünde*.

Conventional Anglo-Saxon political theory, dismissing Nazism as an irrelevant aberration, a lunatic episode, in the history of the West, is all patriarchal. In the Greek polis, where it all begins, historians and philosophers see only fatherhood and the family. The theory is Aristotle's, modernized by Fustel de Coulanges. The minority opposition to the orthodox line of patriarchal interpretation has clustered round the hypothesis of a contrary matriarchal factor. There is a connection between matriarchy and fraternity, even as there is an alliance between

Mother Earth and the band of brothers led by Cronus to castrate Father Sky. But Freud directs us to the idea that the true, the only contrary of patriarchy is not matriarchy but fraternity.

Cf. Bachofen, *Das Mutterrecht*, pp. 869-71.

Fraternity, which is the governing principle of Plato's ideal state, was the governing principle of one real state—Sparta. And Aristotle's emphasis on fatherhood and the family corresponds to the reality of Athens. Just as the antithesis of Aristotle and Plato incarnates the battle of fatherhood against brotherhood, so does the antithesis Athens vs. Sparta. And Sparta is a constellation in the horoscope of Western culture as fixed, as recurrent, as Athens.

According to the current patriarchal orthodoxy, Sparta is a "land-holding aristocracy," and then the great war is between progressive, democratic, and commercial Athens and reactionary, aristocratic, and agrarian Sparta. The truth is that the indispensable basis for a "land-holding aristocracy"—the house-and-land-holding patriarchal family—is lacking at Sparta. Fustel de Coulanges, with a candor and clarity not imitated by his followers, admits that his theoretical construction does not apply to Sparta. At the time of the Dorian invasion, he says, "the old rule of the gens had already disappeared. We no longer distinguish among them this ancient organization of the family; we no longer find traces of the patriarchal government, or vestiges of the religious nobility, or of hereditary clientship; we see only warriors, all equal, under a king."

Fustel de Coulanges, *The Ancient City*, Book IV, Chap. XIII, p. 459.

"Warriors, all equal" is fraternal organization. The Spartan educational system sent the boys away from home at the age of seven, into the wilderness, to be initiated in boy scout or wolf cub packs, in which each boy lived, ate, and slept together with his coevals. The adult military organization prolonged these groupings and the principle of being boys together (the "peers" or *homoioi*) into a total way of life. The mess halls, *syssitia*, where the Spartan warrior lived, ate, and slept together with his comrades, correspond to the primitive institution of the men's house. Spartan society was a hierarchy not based on either property or blood, but on graduated degrees of initiation—initiation into secret societies. Thucydides named secrecy as the distinctive principle of their polity.

Cf. Jeanmaire, *Couroi et Courètes*; Thucydides V, p. 68.

The men's house and the home are mutually antagonistic institutions; the Spartan bridegroom had to spend the night of his marriage in the men's house, and could visit his wife only if he could slip away from his comrades by stealth. One might expect the homosexual emphasis of fraternal organization to degrade the status of women; but it was at Sparta that women had freedom and dignity, while the women of the Athenian patriarchal family were degraded into nonentity. The fraternal style of sexual separation maintains a relation of mutuality, with equality and exchange, between the sexes. While the man spent his life in the men's house, the Spartan woman was mistress of the household: the fraternal style of sexual separation naturally results in a matriarchy of the household as well as a sexual morality free from patriarchal jealousies. It is in this sense that we should understand the claim that there was no adultery at Sparta.

Cf. Bachofen, *Das Mutterrecht*, pp. 255-60;

Nilsson, "Die Grundlage des spartanischen Lebens."

The energy which builds fraternal organization is in rebellion against the family and the father; it is youthful energy. Ortega y Gasset can see that the primeval political association is the secret society, not the gray-bearded senate, because he is willing to acknowledge the youthful, or sportive, or playful origin of the state. "It was not," he says, "the worker, the intellectual, the priest, properly speaking, or the businessman who started the great political process, but youth, preoccupied with women and resolved to fight—the lover, the warrior, the athlete." The ideology of utilitarianism which in the origin of the state and everywhere in life sees only obedience to necessity and the satisfaction of elementary vital needs, is senile, and in politics sees only senatorial activity. Youthful energy has that exuberance which overflows the confines of elementary necessity, and rises above labor into the higher, or is it lower, sphere of play.

Ortega y Gasset, "The Sportive Origin of the State," p. 32.

Academic orthodoxy, senile and senatorial, is against fraternities; against Sparta; against Plato; against athletics; against play; against sex; against youth. "The fate of the sons," says Freud, "was a hard one; if they excited the father's jealousy they were killed or castrated or driven out." *Virginibus puerisque canto.* The Voice of the Ancient Bard, saying,

Youth of delight, come hither,
And see the opening morn,
Image of truth new born.

Folly is an endless maze,
Tangled roots perplex her ways.
How many have fallen there!
They stumble all night over bones
of the dead,

And feel they know not what but
care,
And wish to lead others, when they
should be led.

Freud, *Moses and Monotheism*, p. 131; and Blake, "The Voice of the Ancient Bard," *Songs of Innocence.*

"Youth preoccupied with women and resolved to fight": politics as juvenile delinquency. Ortega is thinking, as Freud did also, of a connection between fraternal organization and exogamy, conceived as form of "marriage by capture." The band of brothers feel the incest taboo and the lure of strange women; and adopt military organization (gang organization) for purposes of rape. Politics as gang bang. The game is juvenile, or, as Freud would say, infantile; and deadly serious; it is the game of Eros and Thanatos; of sex and war.

.    .    .

Brotherhood is always a quarrel over the paternal inheritance. "After the killing of the father a time followed when the brothers quarrelled among themselves for the succession." Justice is the solution and the perpetuation of the quarrel; as Heraclitus said, justice is the strife. Equals are rivals; and the dear love of comrades is made out of mutual jealousy and hate. "Observation has directed my attention to several cases in which during early childhood feelings of jealousy derived from the mother-complex and of very great intensity arose against rivals, usually older brothers. This jealousy led to an exceedingly hostile aggressive attitude against brothers (or sisters) which might culminate in actual death-wishes, but which could not survive farther development. Under the influence of training—and certainly not uninfluenced also by their own constant powerlessness—these wishes yielded to repression and to a transformation, so that the rivals of the earlier period became the first homosexual love-objects." Brotherhood is an agonal relation between competing brothers.

Freud, *Moses and Monotheism*, p. 132; and "Certain Neurotic Mechanisms in Jealousy," p. 242.

The Rule of Law is the Rule of Force. Justice is Strife; and in the arbitrament of battle Ares is just. In the ordeal of battle is a divine judgment: Rome won world rule by ordeal, and hence by right; it was by divine will that the Romans prevailed in the athletic contest for world rule. Jehovah is a man of war; deeds of justice hath he loved. The question could only be decided by an appeal to heaven, that is, by war and violence. The violence vindicates (*vim dicare*).

Cf. Dante, *De Monarchia*, II, 8, 9; Goitein, *Primitive Ordeal and Modern Law*, p. 64. Hume, *Political Essays*, p. 57.

The fraternal principle of equality, the paternal principle of domination; division of power (federation) or monopoly; coordination or subordination; reciprocity (interdependence) or sovereign self-sufficiency. "Sinful man hates the equality of all men under God and, as though he were God, loves to impose his sovereignty on his fellow men." Fraternity was the relation between the elements in pre-Socratic philosophy—those antagonistic pairs, the hot and the cold, the moist and the dry; and then Anaxagoras brought back the paternal and monarchical principle of *nous*. And at the same time Anaxagoras' friend Pericles, *nous* in action, sought to establish a monarchy among the Greek cities. In the archaic age, the age of the pre-Socratic philosophers, the sixth century B.C., the century of Spartan hegemony, the relations between cities were fraternal and agonal; a *concordia discors*, out of opposites the fairest harmony. Like the balance of power in

the old brotherhood of nations, or "concert of Europe," in which, Ranke said, "The union of all must rest upon the independence of each single one. Out of separation and independent development will emerge true harmony."

Augustine, *De Civitate Dei*, XIX, 12; von Laue, *Leopold Ranke, The Formative Years*, p. 218.
Cf. Schaefer, *Staatsform und Politik*; Vlastos, "Equality and Justice in early Greek cosmologies."

The old agonal warfare was between brothers; conducted according to rules; limited in objectives, and limited in time, in a necessary alternation of peace and war; the brothers need each other in order to fight again another day. The new warfare is total: it seeks an end to war, an end to brotherhood.

The quarrel is over the paternal inheritance. Fraternities are moieties, or segments, into which the body of the world is divided; giving to each a property, a lot (Moira); a system of provinces marked off by boundaries, i.e., fenced by taboo. The myths represent totemism as what remains of a diminished totality, or what results from a separating out from each other of what was previously united. Here is the origin of the division of labor— something that Freud did not know. The division of labor is established by distributing the parts among the clans as their totems. " 'The plan, or order, which was carried out when all the people camped together, was that of a wide circle. This tribal circle was called Hu-dhu-ga, and typified the cosmos. . . . The circle was divided into two great divisions or halves' (the exogamous phratries). 'The one called In-shta-sun-da represented the Heavens; and the other, the Hun-ga-she-nu, denoted the Earth. . . . Each of the two great divisions was subdivided into clans, and each of the ten clans had its particular symbol' (totem) 'representing a cosmic force, one of the various forms of life on the Earth.'"

Cornford, *From Religion to Philosophy*, p. 69; cf. pp. 55-56. Cf. Lévi-Strauss, *Totemism*, p. 26.

That is why the body politic, for example in ancient Athens, Rome, or Israel, is composed of artificially symmetrical parts. According to Aristotle's scheme, rejected as "artificial" by the modern revisionists, the Athenians were distributed into four tribes, corresponding to seasons, each of the four tribes being divided into three parts so that there would be altogether twelve, corresponding to months, called trittyes or phratries; with thirty clans going to make up each phratry, as days make up the month. In Rome a mystic interplay between three and ten produced three tribes, thirty curies (the Roman equivalent of the Greek phratry), three hundred gentes, three thousand households each supplying one footsoldier. It is a military organization of *Quirites*; and when assembled, it consists of, and votes by, groups— *comitia curiata*—not individuals.

Cf. Aristotle, *Constitution of Athens*, pp. 208-9; Mommsen, *History of Rome*, I, pp. 101-2; Sinaiski, *La Cité quiritaire*; Brandon, *History, Time and Deity*, pp. 62, 73-74; Ortega y Gasset, "The Sportive Origin of the State," pp. 33-40.

The quarrel is over the paternal inheritance. But the paternal inheritance is the paternal body itself. "All partook of his body," says Freud. The body of the world which is broken into pieces is the body of the god. As the Christians say: others bequeath to their heirs their property, but he bequeathed himself, that is the flesh and blood of his body. The fall is the Fall into Division of the one universal man. Civil strife is dismemberment:

O let me teach you how to knit again
This scattered corn into one mutual
  sheaf,
These broken limbs again into one
  body.

Freud, *Moses and Monotheism*, p. 131; Shakespeare, *Titus Andronicus*, V, iii. Cf. Lubac, *Corpus Mysticum*, p. 77; Blake, *Night* I, 1. 21.

The body of the world which is broken into pieces is the body of the god. This is Freud's "cannibalistic act." "The 'native bear' when slain is thus divided. The slayer has the left ribs: the father the right hind leg, the mother the left hind leg, the elder brother the right fore-arm, the younger brother the left fore-arm, the elder sister the backbone, the younger the liver, the father's brother the right ribs, the mother's brother of the hunter a piece of the flank." "The various totems were only the name given to the different parts of Baiame's [the Great Spirit] body." The body is divided equally: no one came away from the feast without his fair share. A Thyestean banquet: "the fathers shall eat the sons in the midst of thee, and the sons shall eat their fathers."

Freud, *Moses and Monotheism*, p. 132; Harrison, *Themis*, p. 141, and *Epilegomena*, XXXI; Ezekiel V: 10.

Fraternities are moieties or segments of one body. But the segments are sexes; "the prototype of all opposition or contrariety is the contrariety of sex." Fraternal organization is a separating out of opposites which must forever seek each other out: contrary and complementary halves; sexes. "The two exogamous sections are opposed as male and female, since the male belonging to one phratry must marry a female from the other. This contrariety is reconciled in marriage—the union of opposites." The marriage combines

Eros and Thanatos, Love and Strife.
Cornford, *From Religion to Philosophy*, p. 65; cf. p. 68.

Division, duality, two sexes; in a sense there are always two brothers. "There is in every act a sociological dualism; two parties who exchange services and functions, each watching over the measure of fulfillment and the fairness of conduct of the other." Dual organization. There is something here that Freud did not know. There are always two fraternities, not one; and exogamy is not marriage by capture but part of the ritual of Eros and Thanatos in the dual organization. Totemism is not based on an analogy between man and animal, but on an analogy between the differentiation of men into fraternities and the differentiation of animals into species. Lévi-Strauss quotes Bergson: "When therefore they [the members of two clans] declare that they are two species of animals, it is not on the animality but on the duality that they place the stress." The resemblances presupposed by so-called totemic systems is between two systems of differences—animals as a kingdom divided into species, and men as a kind divided into segments which are each one a species.
Malinowski, *Crime and Custom*, pp. 25-26. Cf. Huizinga, *Homo Ludens*, p. 55; Hocart, *The Progress of Man*, pp. 238-42; Mac-Leod, *Origin and History of Politics*, pp. 213-14, 218-19; Roheim, *War, Crime and the Covenant*, pp. 99-100; Lévi-Strauss, *Totemism*, p. 95.

Dual organization is sexual organization. The structural principle is the union of opposites. "The most general model, and the most systematic application, is to be found perhaps in China, in the opposition of the two principles of Yang and Yin, as male and female, day and night, summer and winter, the union of which results in an organized

totality (*tao*) such as the conjugal pair, the day, or the year." The agon, contest, between winter and summer, night and day, is coitus. "The efficacy of the ceremonies seemed to depend upon the participants confronting each other face to face and performing alternate gestures. There must sit a party of hosts—here a party of guests. If some were supposed to represent the sun, heat, and summer, the principle *yang*, others embodied the moon, cold, winter, the principle *yin*. . . . The seasons were imagined as belonging to one or the other sex. Nevertheless the actors were all men."
Lévi-Strauss, *Totemism*, p. 89; Granet, *Chinese Civilization*, p. 169.

The prototype of all opposition or contrariety is sex. The prototype of the division into two sexes is the separation of earth and sky, Mother Earth and Father Sky, the primal parents. The primal one body that was divided among the brothers was parental and bisexual—the two become one flesh—the parents in coitus; in psychoanalytical jargon, the "combined object." The primal crime is also the crime of Cronus, the youngest of the brothers, severing the member that joined Father Sky and Mother Earth. The fraternity comes together, on a contract, or covenant, "when they cut the calf in twain and passed between the parts thereof." "It was an ancient custom for allies to pass between severed parts, that being enclosed within the sacrifice, they might be the more sacredly united in one body."
Jeremiah XXXIV: 18; Calvin on Genesis XV: 10. Cf. Roheim, "Covenant of Abraham," pp. 452-59; *War, Crime and the Covenant*, pp. 19-20; and "Some Aspects of Semitic Monotheism."

At this point we go beyond Freud,

with Melanie Klein: the body that the brothers partook of was not the body of the father, but the body of the father and mother combined. "In Peter's second hour my interpretation of the material he had brought had been that he and his brother practised mutual masturbation. Seven months later, when he was four years and four months old, he told me a long dream. . . . 'There were two pigs in a pigsty and in his bed too. They ate together in the pig-sty. There were also two boys in his bed in a boat; but they were quite big, like Uncle G——(a grown-up brother of his mother) and E——(a girl friend whom he thought almost grown-up).' Most of the associations I got for this dream were verbal ones. They showed that the pigs represented himself and his brother and that their eating meant mutual *fellatio*. But they also stood for his parents copulating together. It turned out that his sexual relations with his brother were based on an identification with his mother and father, in which Peter took the role of each in turn." Compare the case of two brothers, Franz and Günther, age five and six. "The brothers got on very badly together, but on the whole Günther seemed to give way to his younger brother. Analysis was able to trace back their mutual sexual acts as far as the age of about three and a half and two and a half respectively, but it is probable that they had begun even earlier. . . . An analysis of the phantasies accompanying the acts showed that they not only represented destructive onslaughts upon his younger brother, but that the latter stood for Günther's father and mother joined in sexual intercourse. Thus his behavior was in a sense an actual enactment, though in a mitigated form, of his sadistic masturbatory phantasies against his parents."

The material of the analysis; of *Finnegans Wake*; of World History.

Klein, *Psychoanalysis of Children*, pp. 49, 167.

The brothers introject the parents in coitus, in a new coitus, a new covenant or coming together. In dual organization, in exogamous phratries between whom there is intercourse and antagonism, the brothers perpetually reenact in their mutual relations what Freud calls the primal scene; their wrestling is sexual as well as aggressive, in imitation of the parental copulation.

Cf. Calif, "Justice and the Arbitrator."

Moieties in reciprocal exchange are to each other as male and female; and also as mother and child. "We are here in the midst of a society which overcomes its retribution anxiety by a kind of division of labor. . . . The fundamental idea common to all of the tribes is that the men of any totemic group are responsible for the maintenance of the supply of the animal or plant which gives its name to the group. . . . Each group by its ceremonial attitude serves as a guarantee for the permanent existence of 'good objects' for the other group." Each group is to the other a breast; but, as we know from Melanie Klein, the breast is equated with the penis. Thus copulation is always oral. One of Melanie Klein's discoveries in the world of the unconscious is the archetypal—primordial and universal—fantasy of (parental) coitus as a process of mutual devouring—oral copulation; or rather, cannibalistic; and therefore combining in one act the two Oedipal wishes, parental murder and incest; and including sexual inversion, since the male member is seen as a breast sucked. The contest or coitus is always a funeral feast (game) on or beside a grave; "A Christian Altar, by the requirements of Canon Law, should contain relics of the dead." It is always *Hamlet*, Act I, Scene ii:

> The funeral baked meats
> do coldly furnish forth the marriage tables.

Freud's vision and Melanie Klein's finally meet and merge into one. *Consummatum est.*

Roheim, *Eternal Ones of the Dream*, p. 150; and Jones, *Anathémata*, p. 51.
Cf. Klein, *Psychoanalysis of Children*, pp. 68, 188, 213, 269; and "The Early Development of Conscience," p. 273.

Like all good archetypes the story can also take the form of a comedy. As Karl Marx observed in the *Eighteenth Brumaire of Louis Bonaparte*, there is eternal recurrence in history; events and personalities reappear, "on the first occasion they appear as tragedy; on the second, as farce." Like the satyr play after the trilogy of tragedies; or the modern dual organization, the two-party system.

Marx, *Eighteenth Brumaire of Louis Bonaparte*, Chap. I, *ad init.*

Political parties are primitive secret societies: Tammany's Wigwam; caucus; mafia; cabal. The deals are still always secret, in a smoke-filled room. Political parties are conspiracies to usurp the power of the father, "a taking of the sword out of the hand of the Sovereign." Political parties are antagonistic fraternities, or moieties; a contest between Blues and Greens in the Hippodrome; an agon between Leather Seller and Sausage Seller to seduce and subvert Old Man Demos; an Eskimo drumming contest; organized not by agreement on principle, but by confusing the issues to win; in a primitive ordeal or lottery in which the strife is justice, might makes right, and the *major* is the *sanior pars*.

Hobbes, *Leviathan*, p. 202.
Cf. Heckethorn, *Secret Societies*; Schattschneider, *Party Government*, pp. 39-41, 44; Calhoun, *Athenian Clubs in Politics and Litigation*; Cornford, *Origins of Attic Comedy*; Ostrogorski, *Democracy and the Organization of Political Parties*; Headlam, *Election by Lot*, pp. 19, 26, 33; Washington, *Farewell Address. The Federalist*, Nos. 9 and 10; Huizinga, *Homo Ludens*, pp. 85, 65-67, 207.

It is the tale of Shem and Shaun in North Armorica. "Bostonians sometimes seemed to love violence for its own sake. Over the years there had developed a rivalry between the South End and the North End of the City. On Pope's Day, November 5, when parades were held to celebrate the defeat of Guy Fawkes' famous gunpowder plot, the rivalry between the two sections generally broke out into a free-for-all with stones and barrel staves the principal weapons. The two sides even developed a semimilitary organization with recognized leaders, and of late the fighting had become increasingly bloody. In 1764 a child was run over and killed by a wagon bearing an effigy of the pope, but even this had not stopped the battle. Despite the effort of the militia, the two sides had battered and bruised each other until the South End finally carried the day. When Boston had to face the problem of nullifying the Stamp Act, it was obvious that men who fought so energetically over the effigy of a pope might be employed in a more worthy cause" —to dress up as Indians and hold a Boston Tea Party, the *Finnegans Wake* of American History, the foundation legend.

Morgan, *The Stamp Act Crisis*, p. 121.
Cf. Forbes, *Paul Revere*, pp. 97-98.

The comic wearing of the Indian mask, in the Boston Tea Party, of Tammany's Wigwam, is the lighter side of a game, a ritual, the darker side of which is fraternal genocide. Indian are our Indian brothers; one of the ten lost tribes of Israel; the lost sheep we came to find; now unappeased ghosts in the unconscious of the white man. Cf. Lawrence, *Studies in Classic American Literature*, pp. 44-45; Allen, *The Legend of Noah*, Chap. VI.

## Bibliography

ALLEN, D. C., *The Legend of Noah*. Urbana, Ill.: Univ. of Illinois Press, 1949.

ARISTOTLE, *Politics and Athenian Constitution*, trans. J. Warrington. London: J. M. Dent; New York: Dutton, 1961.

AUGUSTINUS, A., *The City of God*, trans. M. Dods. New York: Modern Library, 1950.

BACHOFEN, J. J., in K. Meuli, ed., *Das Mutterrecht, Gesammelte Werke*, II-III. Basel: B. Schwabe, 1948.

BLAKE, W., in G. Keynes, ed., *The Complete Writings*. London: Nonesuch Press; New York: Random House, 1957.

BLÜHER, H., *Die Rolle der Erotik in der männlichen Gesellschaft*. Stuttgart: E. Klett, 1962.

BRANDON, S. G. F., *History, Time and Deity*. New York: Barnes & Noble, 1965.

BROPHY, B., *Black Ship to Hell*. New York: Harcourt, Brace & World, 1962.

CALHOUN, G. M., *Athenian Clubs in Politics and Litigation*. Austin: Univ. of Texas Press, 1913.

CALIF, V., "Justice and the Arbitrator," *American Imago*, VII (1950), 259-77.

CALVIN, J., *Commentaries on the First Book of Moses, Called Genesis*, trans. J. King. Grand Rapids, Mich.: W. B. Eerdmans Pub. Co., 1948.

CORNFORD, F. M., *From Religion to Philosophy: A Study in the Origins of Western Speculation*. New York: Harper & Row, Publishers, 1957.

———, in T. H. Gaster, ed., *The Origin of Attic Comedy*. Garden City, N.Y.: Doubleday Anchor Books, 1961.

CRAWLEY, A. E., *Mystic Rose: A Study of Primitive Marriage and of Primitive Thought in Its Bearing on Marriage*. New York: Boni & Liveright, 1927.

DANTE ALIGHIERI, *De Monarchia*, trans. H. W. Schneider. New York: Liberal Arts Press, 1957.

DE LUBAC, H., *Corpus Mysticum*. Paris: Aubier, 1949.

DURKHEIM, E., *The Division of Labor in Society*, trans. J. W. Swain. New York: The Free Press, 1947.

FORBES, E., *Paul Revere and the World He Lived In*. Boston: Houghton Mifflin Co., 1962.

FREUD, S., "Certain Neurotic Mechanisms in Jealousy, Paranoia, and Homosexuality," *Collected Papers*, II. London: International Psycho-Analytical Press, 1953, pp. 232-43.

———, *The Ego and the Id*, trans. J. Riviere. London: L. & Virginia Woolf at the Hogarth Press and the Institute of Psycho-Analysis, 1927.

———, *Group Psychology and the Analysis of the Ego*, trans. J. Strachey. London: International Psycho-Analytical Press, 1922.

———, *Moses and Monotheism*, trans. K. Jones. London: Hogarth Press, 1951.

———, "The Taboo of Virginity," *Collected Papers*, IV, pp. 217-35.

———, *Totem and Taboo*. New York: Vintage Books, 1961.

FUSTEL DE COULANGES, N. D., *The Ancient City: A Study on the Religion, Laws, and Institutions of Greece and Rome*, trans. W. Small. Boston: Lee & Shepard, 1882.

GIERKE, O., *Das deutsche Genossenschaftsrecht*. Berlin: Weidman, 1881.

GOITEIN, H., *Primitive Ordeal and Modern Law*. London: G. Allen & Unwin, Ltd., 1923.

GRANET, M., *Chinese Civilization*, trans. K. E. Innes and M. R. Brailsford. New York: Meridian Books, 1958.

HARRISON, J. E., *Epilegomena to the Study of Greek Religion; Themis: A Study of the Social Origins of Greek Religion*. New Hyde Park, N.Y.: University Books, 1962.

HEADLAM-MORLEY, J. W., *Election by Lot at Athens*, 2nd. ed., revised by D. C. Magregor. Cambridge: Cambridge Univ. Press, 1933.

HECKETHORN, C. W., *The Secret Soci-*

*eties of All Ages and Countries.* London: G. Redway, 1897.

HOBBES, T., *Leviathan.* New York: Dutton, Everyman ed., 1950.

HOCART, A. M., *The Progress of Man.* London: Methuen & Co., 1933.

HUIZINGA, J., *Homo Ludens: A Study of the Play Element in Culture.* Boston: Beacon Press, 1955.

HUME, D., in C. W. Hendel, ed., *Political Essays.* New York: Liberal Arts Press, 1953.

JEANMAIRE, H., *Couroi et Courètes.* Lille: Bibliothèque Universitaire, 1939.

JONES, D., *The Anathémata: Fragments of an Attempted Writing.* New York: Chilmark Press, 1963.

KLEIN, M., "The Early Development of Conscience in the Child," *Contributions to Psycho-Analysis 1921-1945.* London: Hogarth Press, 1950.

———, *The Psychoanalysis of Children.* New York: Grove Press, 1960.

LAWRENCE, D. H., *Studies in Classic American Literature.* New York: Viking Press, 1964.

LÉVI-STRAUSS, C., *Totemism*, trans. R. Needham. Boston: Beacon Press, 1963.

LOCKE, J., *Two Treatises of Civil Government.* London: Dent; New York: Dutton, Everyman ed., 1953.

MACLEOD, W. C., *The Origin and History of Politics.* London: Chapman & Hall, Ltd.; New York: Wiley, 1931.

MALINOWSKI, B., *Crime and Custom in Savage Society.* London: K. Paul, Trench, Trubner & Co., Ltd.; New York: Harcourt, Brace & World, 1926.

MARX, K., *Eighteenth Brumaire of Louis Bonaparte.* New York: International Publishers, 1963.

MOMMSEN, T., *History of Rome*, trans. W. P. Dickson. New York: C. Scribner, 1870.

MORGAN, E. S., and H. M. MORGAN, *The Stamp Act Crisis: Prologue to Revolution.* Chapel Hill, N.C.: Univ. of North Carolina Press, 1953.

NILSSON, M. P., "Die Grundlage des spartanischen Lebens," *Klio*, XII (1912), 308-40.

ORTEGA Y GASSET, J., "The Sportive Origin of the State," *Toward a Philosophy of History.* New York: W. W. Norton & Co., 1941, pp. 13-40.

OSTROGORSKI, M., *Democracy and the Organization of Political Parties.* New York: The Macmillan Co., 1922.

PLATO, *The Republic*, trans. B. Jowett. New York: Modern Library, 1941.

REIK, T., "Couvade and the Psychogenesis of the Fear of Retaliation," *Ritual: Psychoanalytical Studies.* New York: Farrar, Strauss & Giroux, 1946, pp. 27-90.

———, "The Puberty Rites of Savages," in *ibid.*, pp. 91-166.

ROHEIM, G., "Covenant of Abraham," *International Journal of Psychoanalysis*, XX (1939), 452-59.

———, *The Eternal Ones of the Dream.* New York: International Universities Press, 1945.

———, "Some Aspects of Semitic Monotheism," *Psychoanalysis and the Social Sciences*, IV (1955), 169-222.

———, *War, Crime and the Covenant.* Monticello, N.Y.: Medical Journal Press, 1945.

SCHAEFER, H., *Staatsform und Politik.* Leipzig: Dieterich'sche Verlagsbuchhandlung, 1932.

SCHATTSCHNEIDER, E. E., *Party Government.* New York: Holt, Rinehart & Winston, 1942.

SCHURTZ, H., *Altersklassen und Männerbünde.* Berlin: G. Reimer, 1902.

SINAISKI, V., *La Cité quirtaire.* Riga, 1923.

THUCYDIDES, *The Peloponnesian War*, trans. B. Jowett. New York: Bantam Books, 1960.

VON LAUE, T. H., *Leopold Ranke, The Formative Years.* Princeton, N.J.: Princeton Univ. Press, 1950.

WEBSTER, H., *Primitive Secret Societies.* New York: The Macmillan Co., 1908.

# Part 3

## observing and experimenting with groups

Any attempt to move from the level of theoretical formulation to the level of determining empirical truth raises crucial problems for the viability of a science. Because theory is endowed with meaning only through empirical applicability, and because research results are fed back into theoretical ventures, research strategy and technique must be seen as a crucial link in the entire enterprise of the study of groups. In this sense, methodological competence must precede the development of a valid paradigm of high explanatory power, and this is achieved only through constant, realistic assessment of our current and past techniques. Such an assessment may serve as a jumping-off point for improvement, as well as representing a base line by which to judge the validity of reported findings.

Aside from questions of accuracy of observations, validity of measures, efficiency of tests, and reasonableness of inferences, a critical methodological issue in the study of groups is how the investigator and group members orient and respond to each other and what effects that relationship has on both his readings and the integrity of the group. The investigator who wishes to study established groups in their natural setting must be able to gain their confidence and trust without losing his bearings as an objective scientist; and the investigator who wishes to test hypotheses in the laboratory must become aware of how he, the setting, his operations, and even his hypotheses can alter the group and influence his findings.

The first article in this section, written by two of the most productive researchers in the area of small groups, highlights some of the problems encountered in gaining access to adolescent gangs and reports the techniques that are used in the attempt to circumvent such problems.

The discussion of "The Experimenter Effect" by Kintz *et al.* gives us reason to stop and re-examine the mass of data that has been produced through the relatively recent proliferation of small group experimental studies. When the experimental technique first caught hold in the study of small groups, its proponents supported it as a great methodological advance, providing the researcher the possibility of much "purer" results than had been obtained previously. We believe this is still potentially true, yet a greater understanding of the dynamics of the experimental situation is required before the potential can be realized. Kintz *et al.* also illustrate how social science can utilize its imperfect techniques to bring about long-range progress. Using the social-psychological perspective to understand our research relationships can obviously lead to their improvement.

# chapter seven

## Studying Behavior in Groups

MUZAFER SHERIF                    CAROLYN W. SHERIF

Within the research design . . . , the focus of interest is on patterned sequences of behavior in small groups functioning in their natural habitats. We are concerned with the consequences of membership in groups to which individuals belong *of their own choosing*, and any characteristics of interaction in those groups which lead to such consequences. Therefore, we cannot ignore the spatial and sociocultural frameworks within which the individuals actually behave and interact. In fact, specification of the sociocultural setting and neighborhood is the logical and necessary first step in actual research operations.

In presenting the findings of a multifaceted investigation . . . , there is decided advantage in looking first at the groups and member behavior. In this way, we can be more specific about the domain of discourse, and the interplay between individual behavior, group, and setting can be made more explicit. Accordingly, . . . we shall de-

Reprinted from Muzafer Sherif and Carolyn W. Sherif, *Reference Groups: Exploration into Conformity and Deviation of Adolescents* (New York: Harper & Row, Publishers, 1964), pp. 107-21, by permission of the authors and Harper & Row, Publishers. Copyright © 1964 by Muzafer Sherif and Carolyn W. Sherif.

scribe in some detail how groups were selected for study and how they were studied. . . .

### The Domain of Groups Studied

Groups of six to a dozen or more boys, from 13 to 18 years of age, have been studied for periods of time ranging from five to seven months or longer. These groups were all "natural" formations, in the sense that they had evolved from the individual members' own choices of association, rather than from adult initiative and programming. Such informal patterns of association, developing through initiative of the participants, are particularly significant during the adolescent period. . . .

The groups were chosen for study on the basis of regularly observed interactions among the same individuals at specified locations. In other words, we looked for *regular* and *recurrent interactions*, leaving the issue of whether these associations were patterned and whether the participants shared any values or traditions as a question to be investigated. Our hypotheses predicted that clusters chosen on the basis of frequency of association would be patterned, but patterning was not the initial criterion of selection.

After the area or neighborhood of study was specified (high, middle, or low in social rank), the search began for recurrent associations among adolescent boys within that area. An observer assigned to the task began watching any or all locations where boys might congregate: for example, empty lots, drugstores, drive-in restaurants, pool halls, school and church grounds, parks, and recreation centers. During this phase of the study, he was instructed never to approach boys of this age directly and never to *question* them if they should approach him.

When he had observed a regular association of the same boys on several successive periods of observation—possibly at different times of day, in different activities, and at different locations in the neighborhood—it became the focus of his observation. This method of selection involved several calculated risks. In the mobile and changing scene of a modern city, the observer might witness coincidental associations of boys on two or more occasions. Or, after gathering at certain spots several times, some boys might not congregate again at these same locations for weeks because of changing weather or new interests.

It would have been much easier to have selected formally organized youth clubs or activity groups for study. Our more difficult method, however, insured that the associations were the kind developed through the initiative and choices of the individuals involved.

The criterion of observed frequency of interaction meant that the groups selected gathered frequently in public locations, as contrasted with exclusive contact in one another's homes. This limitation on the kind of groups studied can be turned to an advantage in investigating the interplay of individual, group, and their setting. "Visible"

groups both contribute to the character of their neighborhoods and are, like others, affected by it.

. . .

The next section takes up problems of research procedures and methods which are universally important in studying human groups and behavior of members. These are the problems which led to the development of the methods for study used in the present research.

## Methods in Studying the Human Individual

Even the physical sciences have become aware that the procedures and instruments used to study a phenomenon may affect the phenomenon itself.[1] In the social sciences and psychology, the seriousness of the problem is magnified many times because human beings not only act and react, but think about their actions and reactions. The sentient individual usually tries his best to behave in ways he considers appropriate to the situation, in ways he thinks he is *expected* to behave by those who count for him—including his friends, his employer, his cronies, and even a researcher whose profession he holds in high esteem.

There was a period after World War II when investigators of small groups and social influences collected data on group communications by tape recorder and through one-way screens as though the foregoing problems did not exist. They assured themselves and others that "people get used to the microphone after a few minutes and forget they are being observed."

---

[1] N. Wiener, *Cybernetics, or Control and Communication in the Animal and the Machine,* 2nd ed. (New York: M.I.T. Press, 1961).

People may lose their initial awareness of a piece of equipment or even of a live observer busily recording their words and deeds. But does reduction of initial self-awareness mean that they are behaving without regard to the very significant fact that they are being studied? It does not.

In recent years, there has been growing concern among researchers over the highly special character of social situations where one participant wears the halo of "scientific investigator" and the others the yoke of "subject." Thus, there has been both theoretical analysis and research into the "social psychology of psychological experiments." Exactly the same problems inhere in field studies relying on *direct* observation and interviews, as we shall see.

The critical feature of the research situation—as a social situation—is that the individual has allowed himself to become an object of investigation and that he is aware of being so. This overriding fact is indicated by his willingness to engage in tasks and discussions on topics which would seem nonsensical to him in any other setting, his concern to turn in a creditable performance, his questions about his behavior ("Did I do well?"), his wish to "see through" the procedures, and even his desire to contribute data which confirm the research hypotheses.[2] It is this fact that accounts for his unwitting sensitivity to signs in the situation which point to certain behaviors rather than others.[3] As McGuigan[4] indicates,

automation of research procedures for data collection cannot vitiate this overriding fact. Many years ago, Dashiell[5] demonstrated that the mere knowledge that one is participating in an experiment at the same time as others can produce behavioral effects ordinarily found in face-to-face competition. Even though each subject performed in a room *alone*, the sight of other individuals going to other cubicles made him sensitive to the fact that his performance would be compared with theirs.

In experiments on group formation and intergroup relations in 1949, 1953, and 1954,[6] we sought to eliminate the "investigator-subject" relationship which gives most research situations a distinctive, even unique character. The "subjects" were not informed that they were subjects in an experiment, but came to the scene as campers in a summer camp. Their words and deeds were never recorded in their view, nor were they informed of the arrangements of facilities and tasks prepared as part of the experimental conditions.

In the present research on groups in field situations, the same problems were considered and the same solution adopted. When people are carrying on the business of living, the fact of being observed is even more serious than in the laboratory—which is, after all, a spe-

[2] Cf. M. Orne, "On the Social Psychology of the Psychological Experiment: With Particular Reference to Demand Characteristics and Their Implications." Paper presented at American Psychological Association, annual meetings, New York, 1961 (mimeographed).

[3] R. Rosenthal, "On the Social Psychology of the Psychological Experiment: With Particular Reference to Experimenter Bias." Paper to symposium, American Psychological Association, annual meetings, New York, 1961 (mimeographed).

[4] F. J. McGuigan, "The Experimenter—A Neglected Problem." Paper presented at American Psychological Association, annual meetings, New York, 1961 (mimeographed).

[5] J. F. Dashiell, "An Experimental Analysis of Some Group Effects," *Journal of Social Psychology*, XXV (1961), 190-99; *idem* "Experimental Studies of the Influence of Social Situations on the Behavior of Individual Human Adults," in C. Murchison, ed., *Handbook of Social Psychology* (Worcester, Mass. Clark Univ. Press, 1935).

[6] M. Sherif, and Carolyn W. Sherif, *An Outline of Social Psychology*, rev. ed. (New York: Harper & Row, Publishers, 1956).

cial sort of place set apart from one's "real life."

In real life, groups develop among individuals whose emotional and motivational promptings (as well as sheer proximity at work or play) lead them into interaction with one another. In the course of their interactions, they become bound to one another through awareness of common problems, of being in the same boat, of mutual sympathy and understanding, of "belonging" together. Such groups do not form or maintain themselves for the whims of the researcher who wants to study them.

Most "participant observers" in field settings (neighborhood, factory, club) find this out. They are apt to receive protests against their presence and procedures which "invade our privacy."[7] Observers who do not try to "participate," but merely record frequencies of interaction, encounter similar protests when they try to get within earshot to record the content of those interactions.[8]

Therefore, in the present research, the individuals who were observed did not know that they were being studied. All methods of data collection were adapted to insure that they did not.

The fact that individuals were not behaving as "subjects" does not eliminate the importance of the observer's *presence* to them as another individual. But it does insure that the situations in which observer and group members interact are not perceived by them in terms of the highly special character of a "research situation"—

---

[7] H. W. Polsky, *Cottage Six—The Social System of Delinquent Boys in Residential Treatment* (New York: Russell Sage Foundation, 1962).

[8] F. B. Miller, " 'Resistentialism' in Applied Social Research," *Human Organization,* XII (1954), 5-8.

with all that means concerning one's personal worth, "normality," and the protection of one's "secrets" (especially if these secrets concern socially unacceptable behaviors).

## "Investigator Bias"

In research in field situations, the problem of "investigator bias" is even more aggravated than in laboratory research. Here we refer not to deliberate dishonesty, but to the all-too-human tendency to search for facts from the constant flow of interaction which support one's cherished hunches. In a sense, this problem is less serious than those of "subject-awareness," because, in the long run, science is not a one-shot, all-or-nothing affair. The scientific observer who specifies his methods and procedures leaves the way open for correction by others with different hunches.

Nevertheless, the problem of *selectivity* in observation cannot be avoided by the conscientious investigator. In the present research, we have met this problem by using a *combination of methods* to obtain data . . . , and by the use of independent observers who were not informed about the problem or the nature of the group under study. If the results of several independent procedures are congruent, we have an operational basis for claims to the validity and reliability of findings.

Perhaps the best control for observer bias in our research has been the search for invariant properties of group interaction and their behavioral consequences. When different observers of groups functioning in locations hundreds of miles apart and at times over a period of several years report similar behavioral events time after time, we may reasonably expect that their reports reflect recurring and significant processes.

The decision to eliminate the "investigator-subject" relationship and the resulting "awareness of being studied" meant that an observer had to be able to enter and move about a study area without attracting attention as a mysterious outsider. Consequently, the primary qualification of an observer was his "fit" into a neighborhood, in terms of the dominant characteristics of its population.

If the population of an area was predominantly white, native-stock American, on the one hand, or, on the other, Spanish-speaking American of Mexican descent, the observer represented those classifications in appearance and speech. As often as possible, the observer had had experience living or working in neighborhoods of the type he entered for study. This was particularly important in low rank neighborhoods with Spanish-speaking residents, since the dialect spoken is well-nigh unintelligible to other Spanish speakers, including native Mexicans. Even among English-speaking youngsters, however, an observer had to be sufficiently informed on youthful lingo to keep from sounding like a "square" to them.

In many instances, observers adapted their behavior to local customs as the study went along. Thus, one observer found himself gaining greater acceptance when he altered his "table manners" to conform with those of group members, who usually ate without knives or forks. Another found that "gunning" the motor of his car when starting brought him in closer touch with the "drag racing" buffs he was observing. A third found that he was expected to share a cigarette with others present.

Observers were all young male adults from about five to ten years older than the individuals they studied. Most were students at the time of the research; a few were working in allied fields, for which the problems and tasks of observation were pertinent. Each was instructed by the senior author in periodic personal conferences and by prepared written instructions before and during the entire period of observation. In each city, professional colleagues served as on-the-spot supervisors. . . .

While "good fit" with the neighborhood was an essential qualification of an observer, definite limitations upon this "fit" were necessary. Observers were somewhat older than the youths studied. This age gap was necessary in part because the tasks of observing required a higher educational level than those of the adolescent boys studied. In addition, however, the age differential was regarded as essential to avoid the observer becoming too closely identified, psychologically, with "his" group, and to preclude his involvement in their activities as a "member" competing for "standing" in the eyes of others. This possibility assumed more than methodological significance in those groups which did engage in socially unacceptable ("delinquent") behaviors. An observer who came to feel himself as *one* of a group which engaged in activities illegal for the adolescent age (e.g., drinking) or in general (e.g., theft) might not have been able to heed the unequivocal instruction to all observers not to engage in illegal activities (even though they might learn about them before or after they occurred).

Whenever necessary, authority figures in a neighborhood (e.g., police, recreation or welfare officials, businessmen) were informed of the purpose of the observer's presence in the neighborhood, both to protect the observer from any possible suspicion or rumors from adults and to assure their cooperation in establishing appropriate conditions of study, which invariably has been given generously.

## Methods of Selection

During the course of the research, procedures for selecting and observing groups have been developed, tried out, and elaborated. The information on procedures given throughout this chapter summarizes the detailed written instructions developed on this basis for observers and discussed with them at length.

The method for obtaining data about a group for potential study was the observer's concrete reports on the frequency of *interaction* among the same boys in specific locations in the neighborhood he was to concentrate upon. Direct questioning of the youths themselves, even of their names, was specifically forbidden at this point. Any information that came to the observer *without* direct inquiry was utilized, of course (e.g., an adult commenting, "Those kids are always hanging around here"). The selection of a group, however, hinged on the observer's reports on *frequency of association* in interaction episodes he had witnessed.

The observer was instructed to go about getting information on recurrent interaction episodes as follows:

Choose one or several locales in the area as the initial base of operations: for example, a park, soda fountain, empty lot, playground, "hangout," agency, or recreation center. Observe the interactions among boys between the ages of 13 and 18 years.

Investigate these locales at different times of the day, but regularly. While it is important to have several possible bases of observation, these should be within the area agreed upon for study. Do not move your base too frequently. By returning regularly at different times to a location where you have observed boys interacting, the probability is increased that the same boys will be observed again. Once a recurrent association is spotted in one place, it should be followed to other locations.

All observations at this phase of study are from "outside" or "at a distance." Your behavior should not attract the special attention of individuals you may eventually select for study. Until a particular cluster has been singled out for study, appear to be interested in the activities of others, as well, before you get close to the group more likely to be selected. If individuals approach you, you should respond, but not question them about each other or their activities.

When a number of boys, 13–18 years old, have been observed interacting together during at least four observation periods within approximately two weeks, this cluster is a potential group for study. Interaction includes arriving or departing together, conversing, playing, or "taking sides" with each other.

While *frequency of association* is the main criterion for selection, any *unsolicited* evidence of "sticking together," mutual secrecy, exclusiveness from others, or other manifestations of being part of a group should be carefully recorded in terms of *behavioral events* which you observed. These observations should be specific, not in the form of an "impression" on your part.

The aim of the selection procedure is to locate a pattern of regular association among at least six or seven individuals, possibly with a "fringe" of less frequent interaction with other boys.

## Methods of Observation

Observation is a basic procedure for data collection in most of the social sciences, even in experimentation. Too frequently it is regarded as an art whose success depends upon unique skills of the observer. There is no question that the experiences and interests of some individuals equip them better for observation than those of others, and that we know very little about what makes a person a "good observer." For example, we know very little about the experiences and skills which enable the "good observer" to see behavioral events in terms of sequences of actions, reactions, and interactions of all of the participants, instead of perceiving and evaluating them solely in terms of how they affected *him*.

Nevertheless, we can and have learned about *conditions* and *procedures* for observation which are optimal for any observer in order to collect relevant and significant data about behavior in groups as it actually occurs. The primary condition of observation, from which all others in this research stem, is that at no time should the individuals being observed be aware that they are *subjects* of study or that the observer is their *investigator*. As we have seen, the knowledge that one is being observed, even while performing a simple task, does influence behavior.

If we are interested in behavior in groups as it occurs in actual life and in the variables which affect it, the "investigator-subject relationship" is extraneous. So too are any procedures or techniques for data collection which clutter and interrupt the natural course of give-and-take among the individuals studied.

The interaction process as it occurs in a natural way among individuals who "count" to each other is essential data to explain the behaviors of a single participant. Lacking such data, a competent social worker characterized one of the boys we studied as "not only *anti*social, but completely *a*social." She had observed and interviewed him at a recreation center whose adult personnel was a special target for members of the boy's group. They took particular delight in outrageous behavior in the presence of these adults. This "asocial" boy happened to be the recognized leader of the group, and frequently displayed a strong sense of responsibility, loyalty, and protectiveness toward its members. Conversely, we have observed numerous instances in which "Sunday best" manners were adopted for the benefit of an adult "investigator" or a teacher. After this display of sweet reasonableness, the adult would be unable to understand how the boy could participate in some of the activities of his group.

In order that individuals not be aware of being "studied," observers were instructed *never* to take notes or write down observations in the boys' presence. If a specific situation called for writing something (for example, keeping score, making a list, taking "minutes") he could utilize the opportunity to jot down other symbols without being detected. As a general rule, however, observers were instructed to write all observations *as soon as possible* after leaving the group. Adherence to this rule was strongly emphasized, to minimize omissions and commissions of forgetting.

The foregoing procedural precaution necessarily resulted in loss of many details of the interaction process from the observer's reports. This sacrifice was made deliberately. It was our conviction that recurrent events in different groups reported by different observers, cross-checked through independent techniques for data collection, would provide more relevant data in the long run than detailed accounts or records of single interaction episodes under artificial conditions.

The loss of data from the observers' reports was reduced by another method: While it is clearly impossible for an observer to recall everything that happened, even immediately after the event, he has a much better opportunity of good recall if he focuses *on only one aspect* of the interaction process at a time.

Accordingly, the observation of a group was divided into successive phases, the observer being instructed on the *focus* of each forthcoming observation phase. The first of these, as we have seen, was simply *frequency of interaction* observed from a distance. Successive phases of observation then focused on (1) status differentiations among the individuals (organization), (2) normative or evaluative behaviors, including reactions to deviation, and (3) specification of each member's behavior relative to the group's organization and norms. Data on relations with other peer groups and with adult authorities in the setting were obtained throughout these phases, usually being so striking that they were not difficult to recall. Only when the phases of observation were complete did the observer begin to interview the boys themselves and other people in the neighborhood to reconstruct a "natural history" of the group, using public records, private reports, and case history materials.

## The Observer's Role

The condition that the observer never appear to the group members as an "investigator" of their behavior required that some credible pretext for his presence be established and that he develop his own role in the interaction situations in harmony with this pretext. The pretext and the role further had to be such that the observer's presence would appear natural, while interfering as little as possible with the ordinary flow of interaction among members. In brief, the aim was for the observer to gain admittance and eventually to be welcomed into group discussions and activities as a participant *without* becoming an adult leader or a member competing for attention and prestige with others.

Such a role is not as difficult to establish as it may sound, nor is it an unusual relationship, as we found in the course of the research. Most of the groups we studied had contacts with one or more young adults toward whom they turned for advice, special skills, or small favors. Many times these outside contacts were with older brothers, relatives of members, friendly neighbors, or recreation workers who took an interest in them.

The observers were told to try to develop pretexts for being around which made them appear "harmless" in the boys' eyes and which could be developed into "big brother" relationships through doing small favors and helping out when asked. The observer was *not* to give unsolicited advice or push himself into their affairs to "help."

Since neighborhoods, observers, and groups differed, the pretexts used varied also. The desired consequence of a pretext was always the same, however: to *bring* the boys *to the observer*, instead of the observer intruding upon the boys. One rather well-padded observer began working out at a play area in a poor neighborhood with a brand new ball. When, as he had hoped, the boys asked him to let them play with the ball too, he told them he would be working out fairly regularly in an attempt to lose weight. Another in a well-to-do neighborhood became a devotee of the charcoal-broiled hamburgers at a drive-in restaurant and of folk music at a popular "beatnik" coffee house patronized regularly by the boys he observed. The youths came to him out of admiration for his new and expensive car, whereupon he obliged by letting some of them drive it, by driving past the homes of girls they wanted to impress, and so on.

A more common pretext at parks or recreational facilities was to tell the boys (after they came to investigate the observers' sports equipment or car, or ask him to fill in on a team) that he was receiving school credit for experience in some recreation or sports activities. He was required to have actual experience with boys their age so that *eventually, in the future,* he would be prepared to have a job working with youth. This pretext required the cooperation and active sympathy of officials in the park or recreation area. It was essential that they understood his role and reinforced the fact that he had *no authority* in that location over the boys or anyone else. Observers using this pretext were also cautioned to demonstrate to adult authorities that their function in the research in no way implied an evaluation of the authorities' program or agency, as indeed it did not.

## Establishing Rapport with the Group

Observers were instructed from the beginning to report any efforts they made toward gaining entry to and establishing rapport with the group. Any behavioral evidence of *resistance, suspicion, secrecy,* and *deliberately misleading statements* on the part of members was noted, as well as any evidence of acceptance by the group. The criterion for judging acceptance by the group was that the more the observer was welcomed by members at places and in activities they considered as exclusively group affairs, the more he had succeeded in establishing good rapport.

One of the major findings of the research is that every observer reported evidence of curiosity, suspicion, or mistrust from group members during the

initial period of the study, before his role was clearly established by his own consistent behavior. The degree of such suspicion, its manifestations, and duration differed. Its significance in the present context is that even with a clear and acceptable reason (pretext) for the observer's presence, the boys required specific demonstration of his helpful and harmless intent through his own behavior before accepting him into their circle.

In other words, we found that some degree of "privacy" and of secrecy is characteristic of groups to which individuals belong of their own choosing. In general, the degree and extent of such secrecy in the dozen groups studied have varied with the frequency with which the members engaged in activities which would have been appraised as socially unacceptable by adults if they had known about them. In view of these invariant findings of "secrecy," one wonders at the validity of pronouncements about the character of relationships and interaction in youth groups or gangs from those who have viewed them only from outside the bounds of the group's privacy, or only through interviews and "tests" of individual members.

Signs of the reduction of secrecy and increased rapport with the group included such dramatic incidents as members telling the observer their real names after cooperating in a hoax of pseudonyms. Many boys came to trust their observer to the point of telling him about escapades that they would not have revealed to their parents or authorities. A few even asked the observer to join in such activities (which he was instructed not to do), promising him protection and their testimony of his innocence if they were caught.

The observer was instructed to gain acceptance and develop good rapport in the following ways:

1. To insure by word and deed that group members are aware of his lack of authority in the situations where they were together.
2. To appear in word and deed as a "bigger brother" who is interested in them, wishes them well, and may be helpful on occasions.
3. To avoid any signs of dislike or disapproval of any member, on the one hand, or signs of "favoritism," on the other.
4. To avoid suggesting or initiating activities for the group *unless* such activities are deliberately planned as a part of the research design.
5. To be helpful in activities initiated by group members without display of skills which put the observer in a rivalry situation for status with group members.

On the basis of experience, we found that the greatest difficulty for the young adults who served as observers was to temper their efforts to be helpful, their efforts to be accepted, and their cautiousness in following instructions in a way that all three could be accomplished. Therefore, it was emphasized that too aggressive attempts to be accepted might be seen as "meddling," and too effective help or skills be viewed by high-status members as a "challenge" to their positions. On the other hand, complete passivity could be interpreted as indifference or disapproval, and lack of skills would result in loss of interest by the boys. For example, when members started an activity, such as a game, the observer was to show interest in it and sufficient skill to appear a "regular" guy, without competing or "stealing the show" from group members.

# chapter eight

## The Experimenter Effect

B. L. KINTZ *et al.*

It is significant that a problem which perplexed some of the most influential scientists of Germany in 1904 was resolved at that time, yet should con-

Reprinted from B. L. Kintz, D. J. Delprato, D. R. Mettee, C. E. Persons, and R. H. Schappe, "The Experimenter Effect," *Psychological Bulletin*, LXIII, No. 4 (April, 1965), 223-32, by permission of the authors and the American Psychological Association. Copyright © 1965 by the American Psychological Association.

taminate psychological investigations of the present day, that is, the experimenter's influence on his subjects. The amazing horse of Mr. von Osten caused an uproar throughout all of Germany which Professor Stumpf and his co-workers, through meticulous investigation, demonstrated to be the result of the questioners' unintentional, involuntary cues utilized by the animal. This incident dramatically emphasized the stimulus value of "unconscious" cues emitted by an experimenter to his animal subjects. Even though questioners of "Hans" were aware that this might be the explanation for his feats and were most careful in attempting to refrain from allowing him this advantage, the unconscious cues were still emitted until the situation was carefully analyzed and the specific variables controlled (21).

McGuigan states:

While we have traditionally recognized that the characteristics of an experimenter may indeed influence behavior, it is important to observe that we have not seriously attempted to study him as an independent variable [18, p. 421].

However, Stumpf with his careful, detailed measurements of questioners' cues began the study of the experimenter as an independent variable in 1904, but not until recently has this problem been considered by experimental psychologists for study (5, 18, 29). Clinical psychologists have long led the way in this aspect of investigation. The personal effect of examiners upon patients' performance in clinical tests was initiated as an object of study 35 years ago (19). Yet, psychologists working in the laboratory have not been completely unaware of the implications of experimenter influence upon subjects.

Ebbinghaus in discussing the effects of early data returns upon psychological research stated:

It is unavoidable that, after the observation of the numerical results, suppositions should arise as to general principles which are concealed in them and which occasionally give hints as to their presence. As the investigations are carried further, these suppositions, as well as those present at the beginning, constitute a complicating factor which probably has a definite influence upon the subsequent results [6, pp. 28-29].

Pavlov, noting the apparent increase in learning ability of successive generations of mice in experiments on the inheritance of acquired characteristics, suggested that an increase in the teaching ability of experimenters may have, in fact, constituted the critical variable (12, p. 327).

The foregoing yields some indication of the scope inherent in this phenomenon. However, response-induced bias is not the only data-affected result. A study in which experimenters $(Es)$ recorded the frequency of contractions and head turns of planaria demonstrated that $E$'s expectancy can dramatically influence the data obtained in this type of situation (5). In this case subject's $(S$'s) responses were not affected, but highly statistically significant differences in number of reported responses were obtained for $E$'s expecting a low frequency of response and for $E$'s expecting a high frequency of response. In other words, $Es$ saw (reported) what they expected to see.

Thus far we have seen that $E$ may not only bias $S$'s responses but also that this interpretation of $S$'s responses may be biased. Because these effects are dependent upon $E$'s knowledge of the hypothesis to be tested or his expectancy, one can readily propose that the solution to this problem would be, as is often the case, a simple matter of having research assistants $(As)$ who are unaware of the hypothesis collect the data for $E$. In testing this suggestion, it was found that "a subtle transfer of cognitive events" existed, resulting in response bias (34, p. 313). The authors state:

Our finding of a subtle transmission of $E$'s bias to their $As$ forces us to retract an earlier suggestion for the reduction of $E$ bias [25]. Our recommendation had been to have $E$ employ a surrogate data collector who was to be kept ignorant of the hypothesis under test. The implication of the suggestion was simply not to have $E$ tell $A$ the hypothesis. It now appears that $E$'s simply not telling $A$ the hypothesis may not insure *A*'s ignorance of that hypothesis [34, pp. 332-33].

It is the present authors' contention that wherever an experimenter-subject relationship exists, the possibility also exists for *E* to contaminate his data by one or more of a multitude of conveyances. It appears that experimental psychology has too long neglected the experimenter as an independent variable. By relating some of the findings of clinical and social psychologists, as well as the few experimental studies to date, it is hoped that experimental psychologists will no longer accept on faith that the experimenter is necessary but harmless. Implications for experimental, counseling, and testing psychology will also be considered.

## Research Findings

### Nondifferentiated Effects

Research studies have been, on the whole, minimal in reporting differential results with regard to individual *E*s. In particular, this is true concerning careful discussion of the possible reasons for the differing data. It is, however, illustrative of the pervasiveness of experimenter effect to examine several of the studies which have shown a nondifferentiated experimenter influence.

Lord (16) was interested in examining Rorschach responses in three different types of situations. Thirty-six *S*s took the Rorschach three times—once from each of three different female examiners. Of the Rorschach responses being considered for differences within *S*s. Lord found 48 to yield *t* tests significant at the .10 level. Of these, 27 were due to examiner differences.

In an interesting study on learning without awareness (22), 30 different *E*s—all students in advanced experimental psychology classes—were employed. The *S*s responded to 240 stimulus words with another word which came to mind. Half the *S*s were instructed to guess, and half were told, the "correct" principle of answering which was to give common associations as found in speaking and writing. Differences among *E*s were highly significant sources of data variance. Postman and Jarrett suggest that since complete universal uniformity of experimenter behavior is apparently impossible, the difficulty experienced in attempting to replicate results of other investigators is to be expected.

Using a verbal conditioning paradigm, Kanfer (15) reinforced verb responses with a flashing light, under three different reinforcement schedules. Two *E*s were employed, with apparently little difference between them. In reinforcing *S*s, *E* simply was required to distinguish between verbs and nonverbs. A significant interaction was found between *E* and method. There was more frequent reinforcement of words for one schedule than for the others, the frequency varying with the *E*. Apparently, even the ability of an *E* to perform such a relatively elementary, objective task as judging whether a word is, or is not, a verb, is highly subject to individual differences.

A recent experiment (37) investigated different patterns of digit grouping. An incidental finding from this study is pertinent here. In analyzing the variance of perfect memorizing, an *E* effect was found, significant at the .01 level. Further, this effect was largely due to only one of the four *E*s, since repetition of the analysis without this *E*'s data yielded no significant *E* difference.

An avoidance study using rats (14) was primarily concerned with the effects of alcohol on learning the avoidance response in a Miller-Mowrer shuttle box. Two teams, of two *E*s each, were employed. The alcohol did not produce differential results, but the different E teams did. It is likely that this outcome is due to differences in the handling of the animals by Es.

## Personality

In discussing the differential effect of E upon S, Masling (20) was writing with particular attention to projective testing. However, it seems logical to postulate that if sex and aspects of the examiner's personality (such as warmth or coldness) are causative of differential results in projective testing, the influence of these personal variables may also be felt in other, even objective, situations.

In attempting to assess effects of personality factors of experimenters in the experimental situation, McGuigan (17) compared trait scores of Es on personality tests with dependent variable scores of Ss. He did not obtain any significant correlations, but noted several quite high ones that may indicate directional influences. For example, the more neurotic (Bl-N scale of the Bernreuter) the E, the poorer the performance of S.

The effect of E's personality upon Ss' performances had been investigated earlier (35) using projective techniques. Nine Es took the Rorschach, which was scored blindly by two experienced clinical psychologists. The Es were then trained in administering the Rorschach, and each E gave it to 30 Ss. An attempt was made to deliberately standardize the questioning procedures used. After taking the Rorschach, each S filled out a questionnaire designed to elicit his attitudes about the particular E. Sanders and Cleveland found that overtly anxious Es (as indicated by their own Rorschach responses) tended to elicit more subject flexibility and responsiveness, while overtly hostile Es (again measured by their Rorschach responses)

drew more passive and stereotyped responses and less of the hostile responses. The Ss' questionnaires indicated that Es who were most liked were those who had been rated low on anxiety and hostility.

The research just mentioned has been primarily interested in the effect of the personality of E, per se, on Ss' performances. One further study is especially interesting, as it tries to answer the pertinent question of whether E's personality and personal bias can interact. Rosenthal, Persinger, and Fode (32) used 10 naive Es, who were biased to expect certain results. They found that agreement of final data and E bias were related to Es' scores on the MMPI scales, L, K, and Pt, but not to age or grade-point average.

The S-E personality interaction is dependent, of course, not only on the personality of E, but also to some degree on that of S. In one of the few studies designed to investigate this interaction, Spires (39; cited in 18) used a 2 × 2 design in a verbal conditioning paradigm, reinforcing a particular class of pronouns with the word "good." The Ss were divided into two groups, one of which had scored high on the Hy scale of the MMPI and one of which had scored high on the Pt scale. Each group was subdivided in half, receiving either a positive or a negative "set" ("this experimenter is warm and friendly" or "this experimenter is cold and unfriendly"). The high Hy-positive set group far surpassed the other three groups. The high Hy-negative set group performed the poorest. Thus, not only E's personality, but Ss' perception of this personality, can contribute to the E effect.

Investigation of Ss' perception of E has been undertaken by two related studies (28, 31). In the first experiment, Ss were asked to rate E on a number of variables. In the second study, the experiment was not actually conducted, but only described, and Ss were requested to imaginatively rate their imaginary E. Yet a correlation which was calculated between the ratings of the first and second studies yielded an $r$ of .81. This would appear to support the hypothesis that naive Ss, in particular, may have a kind of predetermined "set" about what a "typical" E is like—scientific, intelligent, etc.

## Experience

Investigators with widely variant amounts of experience are busily conducting studies every day. Cantril (4) stated that interviewers who are highly experienced show as much bias as those who are less experienced. In an experimental investigation, however, Brogden (3) came to a different conclusion. Four Es each trained a group of rabbits and recorded the acquisition speed of a conditioned shock-avoidance response. The rabbits of the three experienced Es reached the learning criterion faster than the naive E's rabbits. To further study this result, the naive E was required to run another group of rabbits to see whether his practice would produce more rapid conditioning in the second group. Another experienced E trained another group of Ss to serve as a control measure. The data show both a significant E practice effect (for the naive E only) and a significant difference between Es.

## Sex

Several studies have been concerned with investigating the manner in which results are influenced by E differences in sex. In a verbal conditioning study (1), Ss were reinforced for saying hostile words. Two clearly distinguishable Es were employed: one—a young, petite feminine girl; the other—a mature,

large masculine male. Significantly more hostile words were emitted in the presence of the female E. It is conceivable that Ss perceived the male E as being more hostile than the female E, in which case the results confirm Sanders and Cleveland's (35) findings that hostile Es elicit fewer hostile responses from their Ss than do other Es.

Sarason and Minard (36) also found that sex and hostility significantly influenced Ss' performances. Degree of contact between S and E and E's prestige value (as perceived by S) also contributed significant effects. Sarason and Minard warn that ignoring these situational variables is hazardous research methodology.

In a very recent experiment investigating the sex variable, Stevenson and Allen (40) show what is perhaps the most clear-cut demonstration of S-E interaction. Eight male and eight female Es each tested eight male and eight female Ss in a simple sorting task. The mean number of responses was recorded at 30-second intervals. With either male or female Es, female Ss made more responses than did male Ss. However, all Ss performed relatively better under an opposite-sexed E.

## Expectancy Effect

Perhaps the component of experimenter effect which is the cause of greatest concern is that by which the E in some way influences his Ss to perform as he has hypothesized. The reasons for concern about expectancy effect are that so little is known about it and so little research has been devoted to it. Only recently have systematic studies been conducted in this area.

Rosenthal and Fode (26) demonstrated the problem clearly in an experiment with two groups of randomly assigned animals. One group of six Es was instructed that its group of rats was "maze-bright" and a second group of six Es was instructed that its group of rats was "maze-dull." In a simple T maze, the maze-bright rats performed significantly better than the maze-dull rats.

In a similar study (30) investigators divided 38 Es into 14 research teams, each 'of which had one rat randomly assigned to it. Six of the teams were told that their rats were bred for dullness and the other eight were told that their rats had been bred for brightness. Seven experiments, including such tasks as operant acquisition, stimulus discrimination, and chaining of responses, were conducted. In seven out of eight comparisons (overall $p = .02$), difference in performance again favored Es who believed their Ss to be bred for brightness. A factor which may have prompted the difference was that Es who believed their rats were bred for brightness handled them more than Es who believed their rats were bred for dullness.

In both experiments cited, the question arises as to the sensitivity of the animal to attitudinal differences in Es transmitted through the tactual and sensory modalities. Further research is required to clarify the issue.

## Modeling Effect

Modeling effect is defined (24) as a significant correlation between E's performance and the performance of randomly assigned Ss on the same task.

Graham (9) divided 10 psychotherapists into two groups on the basis of their perception of movement in Rorschach inkblots. In the ensuing psychotherapeutic sessions, patients of the group of psychotherapists that perceived more movement in the inkblots saw a significantly greater amount of movement than the patients of the group of psychotherapists that had perceived less movement.

In the area of survey research the phenomenon of modeling has been reported in studies by Cantril (4) and Blankenship (2), who have found that interviewers elicit from their interviewees, at a probability greater than chance, responses which reflect the interviewers' own beliefs.

Rosenthal (24) reported eight experiments conducted to assess the existence and magnitude of experimenter modeling effect by employing the task of Ss' rating a series of photographs of people on a scale of apparent successfulness and unsuccessfulness ranging from $-10$ to $+10$. Prior to each experiment, Es had rated the photos which were selected because in earlier ratings on the same scale they had yielded a mean value of zero. The resulting eight rank-order correlations between Es' ratings and their Ss' ratings ranged from $-.49$ to $+.65$. Only the rho of $+.65$ was significantly different from 0 ($p < .001$), but the hypothesis of equality among the eight rhos was rejected using a chi-square test ($p < .005$).

Hammer and Piotrowski (13) had three clinical psychologists and three interns rate 400 House-Tree-Person drawings on a 3-point scale of aggression. The degree of hostility which clinicians saw in the drawings correlated .94 with the evaluations of their personal hostility made by one of the investigators.

## Early Data Returns Effect

Early data returns effect is the problem of the experimenter who is receiving feedback from his experiment through early data returns and who contaminates the subsequent data. The reasons why this occurs are unclear but some suggestions are that E's mood may change if the data are contrary to his expectations, or if the data are in agreement with his expectations, there is the possibility of heightening an existing bias. There is evidence (33) that this mood change in $E$, brought about by "good results," may lead him to be perceived by the Ss as more "likable," "personal," and more "interested" in their work and thereby influence their performance.

In the study by Rosenthal, Persinger, Vikan-Kline, and Fode (33), three groups of four $E$s each had three groups of four Ss rate the apparent success of people in photographs on a scale ranging from $-10$ to $+10$. The $E$s were instructed that Ss' mean rating would be about $+5$. In each of two experimental groups, two Ss were confederates of the investigator while in a control group all of the Ss were naive. One of the confederate pairs was instructed to give "good data" (in accord with $E$'s expectations) and the other pair was instructed to give "bad data" (contrary to $E$'s expectations). Ratings of all Ss were learned after several trials. It was hypothesized that the experience of having obtained good data would lead those $E$s to obtain "better" subsequent data, while the experience of having obtained bad data would lead those $E$s to obtain "worse" data in relation to the control. Although neither experimental group differed significantly from the control group, the experimental groups were significantly different from each other. There was a further tendency for the effect of early returns to become more pronounced in the later stages of data gathering.

Griffith (11) states clearly the effect of early data returns in an autobiographical documentary:

Each record declared itself for or against . . . (me) . . . (and) . . . (my) . . . spirit rose and fell almost as wildly as does the gambler whose luck supposedly expresses to him a higher love or reflection [11, p. 309].

## Overview of Cues and Their Transmission

After discussing at some length the various experimenter effects, the question must certainly arise as to how the experimenter contaminates his data. What are these cues and how are they transmitted? Some suggestions have been made but it is necessary to look at evidence dealing directly with the problem. It was suggested earlier that in the case of laboratory animals it might be due to tactual and kinesthetic cues, but probably also involved are all of the sensory processes of the organism so that $E$ inadvertently transmits cues by nearly everything that he does.

In dealing with humans, because of the probable lack of bodily contact, cues are transmitted verbally and/or visually. But "verbally" implies not only the words, but also the inflectional and dynamic processes of speaking.

The transmission of verbal cues was first dramatically demonstrated by Greenspoon (10) who, by reinforcing plural nouns with "mmm-hmmm," was able to increase the frequency of emission of such words.

In a similar experiment, Verplanck (41) was able to control the content of Ss' conversation by agreeing with some opinions and disagreeing with others. The results showed that every $S$ increased in his rate of speaking opinions with reinforcement by agreement, and 21 out of the 24 Ss decreased their rate of opinion statements with nonreinforcement.

Rosenthal and Fode (27) conducted two experiments specifically designed to investigate the transmission of cues from $E$ to his human Ss. The Ss were to rate the apparent success or failure of persons in photographs on a scale ranging from $-10$ to $+10$. All $E$s received identical instructions except that five of them were told that their Ss would probably rate the pictures at about +5 while the remaining Es were told their Ss would probably rate the pictures at about −5. Further, prior to the experiment, each E rated the pictures on the same scale as the Ss. Results showed that Ss for high-biased (+5) Es obtained significantly higher mean ratings than Ss of low-biased (−5) Es. Since Es were not permitted to say anything to Ss other than what was on the instruction sheet, the communication of bias must have been done by tone, manner, gesture, or facial expression. The second experiment designed to investigate this nonverbal transmission of cues was conducted in the same manner as the first with the exception that now, instead of E showing each photo to his Ss, each set of 10 photos was mounted on cardboard and labeled so that S could give his rating without Es' handling the photos. The results showed that elimination of visual cues from E to S did significantly reduce the effect of E's bias. It can be hypothesized then that visual cues play an important part in the phenomenon of E bias, but probably to a lesser degree than verbal cues.

Wickes (42) also showed the import of visual cues by effectively using nodding, smiling, and leaning forward in his chair as reinforcement for certain responses given to inkblots by clients in psychotherapy sessions.

Considerable research is required to learn what the cues are, how they are transmitted and how they can be controlled.

**Implications of the Experimenter Effect**

The preceding survey of the literature has revealed the existence of the experimenter effect in all aspects of psychology. Although the experimenter effect is generally recognized and perhaps paid lip service, it tends to be a forgotten skeleton in the research psychologist's closet. Comparison of a study by Postman and Jarrett (22) with one by Spence (38) provides an example.

Postman and Jarrett commented:

We have paid too little attention to the contributions made by variations in Es' behavior to the experimental results. The difficulty which many psychologists experience in repeating the results of other investigators may be due to our failure to attack systematically the role of differences among Es [22, p. 253].

Spence (38), after examining various aspects of variability occurring in experiments using the Taylor Manifest Anxiety scale, says the following in concluding his discussion of the experimenter-subject interaction:

This is, nevertheless, a potentially important variable and should be investigated further, possibly by deliberately manipulating the behavior of E [38, p. 136].

It is clear from a comparison of these two statements that during the past 12 years the progress in examining and controlling the experimenter effect has been something less than spectacular. Thus, the objective of this portion of the present paper is to attempt to alter further research procedure by emphasizing the implications of the experimenter effect as it relates to the individual psychologist engaged in his varied activities.

*Clinical Implications*

Clinicians have long recognized the influence of the experimenter (therapist) upon the behavior of a subject (client). In fact, the differing view existing in the clinical realm as to the most effective therapeutic procedure to utilize seem to have their origin in the clinician's conception of the role of the therapist in the therapeutic situation. For example, the psychoanalyst believes transference is essential if the client is to be led to adjustment, whereas the nondirective therapist strives to accompany the patient along the road to adjustment rather than to lead.

Even though clinicians not only recognize but argue over the implementation of the experimenter influence, they are not exempt from a thorough evaluation of the implications (some of which are discussed below) that the experimenter variable holds for the clinical field.

Perhaps a reevaluation of the experimenter variable will reveal that pseudodifferences exist among the effects of various psychotherapeutic techniques. Goldstein (8) showed that clients who are rehabilitated by a particular technique may be more products of perceived therapist expectancies than of therapeutic techniques. An essentially different technique employed by a therapist expecting good results with his procedure can rehabilitate the client just as completely.

Considering the present state of sophistication in the clinical realm, it is not unreasonable to assume that therapist expectancies are likely to play a large part in client rehabilitation. Thus, the pseudoproblem may tend to thwart intensive searches for valid, operationally defined therapeutic procedures.

Other more specific clinical areas affected by *E-S* interaction would include the effect upon patients' Rorschach scores as a function of experimenter differences (16), the once-removed influence of the experienced clinician's effect upon a neophyte therapist's prognosis of a patient (25), the possibility that the therapist may be a contributing factor to the patient's failure to recover as the result of perceived negative therapist expectancy (35), and the not-so-alluring possibility that patients receiving the stamp of rehabilitation have only adjusted to the wishes of the therapist and not necessarily to the emotional problems which brought them to the therapist originally (41).

These are important problems for practicing clinicians, and it is to their credit that they have recognized this, as evidenced by the increasing use of the team approach in diagnosing clients. Utilization of the team approach may be extended to therapy in order to reduce the negative aspects of the clinician-client interaction.

Such a team approach might involve the objective assignment of patients to therapists by means of a large-scale correlational determination of what therapist-patient "personality types" interact most effectively in the therapeutic situation. Of course, the determination of personality types still leaves us with all the previously mentioned *E-S* interaction problems, but nonetheless attempts at improvement can be made even if imperfect tools must be used.

## Implications for the Field of Testing

The general field of testing, which would include IQ tests, placement tests, reading readiness tests, aptitude tests, etc., is also beset with the problem of the experimenter variable. Even though there have been rigorous attempts at standardization of test items and procedures in this area, E or administrator of the test still influences the test taker in other subtle ways (15, 23).

The implications of the experimenter effect in the testing area have many ramifications. It is questionable whether many tests have been proven sufficiently reliable and valid in their own right, and this problem is further complicated by the experimenter variable. Judgment of an individual's score on special abilities and IQ tests, etc., must not only be viewed in light of which test was used, but must also take into consideration the previously ignored variable of the specific administrator. In addition to knowing that a person achieved an IQ score of 105 on the Stanford-Binet and not the Wechsler, it is also necessary to know whether or not $E$ was threatening, docile, friendly, anxious, or expected the test taker to be smart, dumb, score well, etc. (1, 18, 23).

The administrator contamination problem may eventually be resolved by the application of machines to the administration of tests. At this time a more judicious selection of the hundreds of available tests on the part of administrators, using test results to guide their decision-making process, is essential. In addition, test results should be viewed with a more sophisticated, critical eye, with IQ and aptitude scores being considered as but some of many indices of performance. All persons using test scores must recognize the strong influence of $E$ and make decisions accordingly.

### Experimental Implications

The psychologist engaged in controlled experimentation should realize that he has failed to provide a control for himself. That this variable is disregarded is evidenced by Woods' (43) investigation of 1,737 published experiments, of which 42–45 per cent involved multiple authorship. None of these ran an analysis of experimenter interaction.

One particular aspect of controlled experimental endeavor which has neglected the experimenter effect is learning theory research. Much energy is expended on "crucial" experiments which ostensibly attempt to determine which of the conflicting theories of Hull, Tolmon, Guthrie, and others are correct. At the present time these crucial experiments have produced results which are generally inconclusive, except for establishing a high correlation between the theory an $E$'s results support and his theoretical position.

The experiments already reviewed provide a speculative base for partially explaining the conflicting results obtained by the supporters of various learning theories. As Rosenthal (25) has shown, experimenter bias is a powerful influence in the experimental situation. The $E$ has many opportunities to influence, unintentionally, Ss who have been brought into a very strange, highly structured situation. In view of this, it is not surprising—it should be expected—that $E$s favoring a particular learning theory would tend to obtain results favoring this same theory.

Results reported recently (5, 26, 29) indicate that $E$s also affect the results of studies using nonhuman Ss. These findings further emphasize the possibility that the overlooked experimenter variable may have contaminated many crucial learning experiments.

This is not to suggest that being able to replicate studies and/or controlling the experimenter variable is the panacea for psychology's problems. But it can not be overemphasized that at the present time $E$ is a powerful, yet much ignored, variable. It is a strange paradox that even many of the most adamantly scientific of psychologists have failed to control for the experimenter variable.

### Conclusions

Future experimentation might prove more profitable if more rigorous communication could be established between researchers of differing points of view and theoretical orientations so that a system of research exchange might be established. This suggestion admittedly presents a multitude of problems, not the least of which would be that of authorship credit. Although this and many other problems would arise, they would not be insurmountable.

If research exchange were implemented it might prove an effective means of controlling the experimenter effect and, in addition, bring scientific communication into the prepublication stage of research. This in itself might prove to be the most important contribution of all.

Other suggestions for control of the experimenter variable have been given previously by Rosenthal (25) and McGuigan (18). These suggestions included counterbalancing of Es and the use of factorial designs which include the experimenter as a major independent variable. Fode (7), as reported by Rosenthal (25), found that both visual and auditory cues influenced the behavior of Ss. Thus, another suggestion involves the elimination of verbal and visual cues, including inflections of the voice, speaking peculiarities, gestures, etc., as transmitted to Ss during the reading of instructions.

This paper, which began with a discussion of a horse and the subtlety of experimenter cues, has ranged far afield. We have seen that the experimenter effect exerts an insidious influence upon the relationship between counselor and client. Indeed, the more objective and nondirective the counselor, the greater the potential hidden effect. To be unaware of the relationship between counselor and client expectations is to lose much of the control that a counselor must maintain over the counseling situation. In the same way teachers must be aware that objective appraisal by their students is affected by the goals which the students believe their teachers have. And finally, but probably most important at this time, directors of laboratory research who use student Es, must be aware of the extremely great effect of their personal biases, which can be perceived by the student Es and translated into practically any significant experimental effect.

## Bibliography

1. BINDER, A., D. McCONNELL, and N. A. SJOHOLM, "Verbal Conditioning as a Function of Experimenter Characteristics," *Journal of Abnormal and Social Psychology*, LV (1957), 309-14.
2. BLANKENSHIP, A. B., "The Effect of the Interviewer upon the Response in a Public Opinion Poll," *Journal of Consulting Psychology*, IV (1940), 134-36.
3. BRODGEN, W. J., "The Experimenter as a Factor in Animal Conditioning," *Psychological Reports*, XI (1962), 239-42.
4. CANTRIL, H., *et al.*, *Gauging Public Opinion*. Princeton, N.J.: Princeton Univ. Press, 1944.
5. CORDARO, L., and J. R. ISON, "Psychology of the Scientist: X. Observer Bias in Classical Conditioning of the Planarian," *Psychological Reports*. XIII (1963), 787-89.
6. EBBINGHAUS, H., *Memory: A Contribution to Experimental Psychology* (orig. pub. 1885; trans. H. A. Ruger and Clara E. Bussenius). New York: Teachers College, Columbia Univ., 1913.
7. FODE, K. L., "The Effect of Nonvisual and Non-verbal Interaction on Experimenter Bias" (Master's thesis, University of North Dakota, 1960).
8. GOLDSTEIN, A. P., *Therapist-Patient Expectancies in Psychotherapy*. New York: Pergamon Press, 1962.
9. GRAHAM, S. R., "The Influence of Therapist Character Structure upon Rorschach Changes in the Course

of Psychotherapy," *American Psychologist*, XV (1960), 415.

10. GREENSPOON, J., "The Reinforcing Effect of Two Spoken Sounds on the Frequency of Two Responses," *American Journal of Psychology*, LXVIII (1955), 409-16.

11. GRIFFITH, R. M., "Rorschach Water Precepts: A Study in Conflicting Results," *American Psychologist*, XVI (1961), 307-11.

12. GRUENBERG, B. C., *The Story of Evolution*. Princeton, N.J.: D. Van Nostrand, 1929.

13. HAMMER, E. F., and Z. A. PIOTROWSKI, "Hostility as a Factor in the Clinician's Personality as It Affects His Interpretation of Projective Drawings," *Journal of Projective Techniques*, XVII (1953), 210-16.

14. HARRIS, H. E., E. B. PICCOLINO, H. B. ROBACK, and D. K. SOMMER, "The Effects of Alcohol on Counter Conditioning of an Avoidance Response," *Quarterly Journal of Alcoholic Studies*, XXV (1964), 490-97.

15. KANFER, F. H., "Verbal Conditioning: Reinforcement Schedules and Experimental Influence," *Psychological Reports*, IV (1958), 443-52.

16. LORD, E., "Experimentally Induced Variations in Rorschach Performance," *Psychological Monographs*, LXIV (1950), Whole No. 316.

17. McGUIGAN, F. J., "Variation of Whole-Part Methods of Learning," *Journal of Educational Psychology*, LI (1960), 213-16.

18. ———, "The Experimenter: A Neglected Stimulus Object," *Psychological Bulletin*, LX (1963), 421-28.

19. MARINE, EDITH L., "The Effect of Familiarity with the Examiner upon Stanford-Binet Test Performance," *Teachers College Contributions in Education*, CCCLXXXI (1929), 42.

20. MASLING, J., "The Influence of Situational and Interpersonal Variables in Projective Testing," *Psychological Bulletin*, LVII (1960), 65-85.

21. PFUNGST, O., *Der Kluge Hans* (orig. pub. 1905; trans. C. L. Rahn). New York: Holt, 1911.

22. POSTMAN, L., and R. F. JARRETT, "An Experimental Analysis of Learning without Awareness," *American Journal of Psychology*, LXV (1952), 244-55.

23. ROSENTHAL, R. "Experimenter Attributes as Determinants of Subjects' Responses," *Journal of Projective Techniques*, XXVII (1963), 324-31.

24. ———, "Experimenter Modeling Effects as Determinants of Subjects' Responses," *Journal of Projective Techniques*, XXVII (1963), 467-71.

25. ———, "On the Social Psychology of the Psychological Experiment: The Experimenter's Hypothesis as Unintended Determinant of Experimental Results," *American Scientist*, LI (1963), 268-83.

26. ———, and K. L. FODE, "The Effect of Experimenter Bias on the Performance of the Albino Rat," *Behavioral Science*, VIII (1963), 183-89.

27. ———, "Psychology of the Scientist: V. Three Experiments in Experimenter Bias," *Psychological Reports*, XII (1963), 491-511.

28. ———, C. J. FRIEDMAN, and L. L. VIKAN-KLINE, "Subjects' Perception of Their Experimenter under Conditions of Experimenter Bias," *Perceptual and Motor Skills*, XI (1960), 325-31.

29. ROSENTHAL, R., and E. S. HALAS, "Experimenter Effect in the Study of Invertebrate Behavior," *Psychological Reports*, XI (1962), 251-56.

30. ROSENTHAL, R., and R. LAWSON, "A Longitudinal Study of Experimenter Bias on the Operant Learning of Laboratory Rats," *Journal of Psychiatric Research*, II (1964), 61-72.

31. ROSENTHAL, R., and G. W. PERSINGER, "Let's Pretend: Subjects' Perception of Imaginary Experimenters," *Perceptual and Motor Skills*, XIV (1962), 407-9.

32. ———, and K. L. FODE, "Experimenter Bias, Anxiety, and Social Desirability," *Perceptual and Motor Skills*, XV (1962), 73-74.

33. ROSENTHAL, R., G. W. PERSINGER, LINDA L. VIKAN-KLINE, and K. L. FODE, "The Effect of Early Data Returns on Data Subsequently Obtained by Outcome-Biased Experi-

menters," *Sociometry*, IV (1963), 487-98.

34. ROSENTHAL, R., G. W. PERSINGER, LINDA L. VIKAN-KLINE, and R. C. MULRAY, "The Role of the Research Assistant in the Mediation of Experimenter Bias," *Journal of Personality*, XXXI (1963), 313-35.

35. SANDERS, R., and S. E. CLEVELAND, "The Relation between Certain Experimenter Personality Variables and Subjects' Rorschach Scores," *Journal of Projective Techniques*, XVII (1953), 34-50.

36. SARASON, I. G., and J. MINARD, "Interrelationships among Subjects, Experimenters, and Situational Variables," *Journal of Abnormal and Social Psychology*, LXVII (1963), 87-91.

37. SEVERIN, F. T., and M. K. RIGBY, "Influences of Digit Grouping on Memory for Telephone Numbers," *Journal of Applied Psychology*, XLVII (1963), 117-19.

38. SPENCE, K. W., "Anxiety (drive) Level and Performance in Eyelid Conditioning," *Psychological Bulletin*, LXI (1964), 129-40.

39. SPIRES, A. M., "Subject-Experimenter Interaction in Verbal Conditioning" (Doctoral thesis, New York University, 1960).

40. STEVENSON, H. W., and SARA ALLEN, "Adult Performance as a Function of Sex of Experimenter and Sex of Subject," *Journal of Abnormal and Social Psychology*, LXVIII (1964), 214-16.

41. VERPLANCK, W. S., "The Control of the Content of Conversation," *Journal of Abnormal and Social Psychology*, LI (1955), 668-76.

42. WICKES, T. H., "Examiner Difference in a Test Situation," *Journal of Consulting Psychology*, XX (1956), 23-26.

43. WOODS, P. J., "Some Characteristics of Journals and Authors," *American Psychologist*, XVI (1961), 699-701.

# Part 4
## the empirical study of structure and dynamics

As expected in a young branch of science, the empirical study of groups proceeds on a number of fronts simultaneously: from rigorous training in systematic data-collecting techniques to highly intuitive interpretations of symbolic process in therapy groups; from sophisticated, controlled experiments in the laboratory to the comparison of rituals in primitive and modern secret societies. Our selections in this section present at least part of the range of approaches. One describes observational methods, two report laboratory experiments testing specific hypotheses, and others present analyses of groups in their natural settings, ranging from street-corner gangs to administrative committees in industry. These last selections are concerned with one aspect or another of the broader problem of the dynamic interplay among personality, the group's social system, and its culture—the problem referred to in the preceding theoretical section. Most deal with this interplay at the complex level of preconscious processes, and each interprets the dynamics by one or more major hypotheses, which we think will not only excite the student but also encourage the social scientist to expand the range of both his models and methods to take them into account.

As introduction, the first article compares three observational approaches developed in the laboratory, in therapy, and in training groups. Any observational technique does more than permit quantification of data in a regularized way (although this may be highly important); it establishes a particular perspective, among several available, from which group process is to be observed. Although "simplifying" the process by abstracting a single facet often makes it more comprehensible, there is simultaneously a temptation to treat the abstracted datum as somehow representative of the whole. For this reason an awareness of what any observational system does or does not actually yield is crucial to its proper use.

The second selection is from Whyte's classic study of a street-corner gang, where he shows both how the gang's values are expressed through the social ranking of its members and how they are maintained by subtle influences on individual performances. One result is that bowling scores are an objective reflection of that ranking.

To what extent do findings about ad hoc groups (such as strangers assembled to work on an experimenter's task) apply to more established, "real life" groups in society? The next selection addresses that question. Through an experimental test, Leik compares the role structures that appear in groups of strangers with those in families. Whereas on the one hand his test indicates general progress in stating the functional problems of groups, on the other hand his conclusion that the dynamic relationships are different in the two types of groups warns us that a major gap has to be bridged before we can confidently generalize from one set of groups to another.

How groups react to the stranger (and he to them) is the topic in the selection reporting the Norwegian experiment. Under what conditions do groups allow their boundaries to be crossed by outsiders? Under what conditions does the outsider both feel welcome and want to join? The experimental results bring into question our traditional beliefs about the exclusiveness of the tightly knit group.

The response to the disturbing member within the group is the topic in the next two selections. In the first, Dentler and Erikson call for a balanced functional analysis of deviance. Fully recognizing that the deviant is often dysfunctional to the group, they look at the other side of the coin, as it were, asking if the deviant also serves useful functions. They note that the ethos, values, and norms of most groups do not simply exist but instead must be worked out through actual experience. It is chiefly through members' reactions to concrete acts that they learn which ones are and are not deviant, and it is through interaction with the deviant that they discover and eventually define the boundaries of acceptability. In this sense, the presence of the deviant helps the group define its boundaries, and, in this sense, the *not-us* within the group helps members learn both what *us* is and what *us* should be. In their investigations of families with a mentally ill child, Vogel and Bell find that the child tends to be used unconsciously as a scapegoat for the unresolved conflicts between the parents. In spite of the cost of personality impairment of the child, this mechanism affords an uneasy, yet effective, means for the family to hold itself together.

Contrary to the popular belief that training and self-analytic groups are "unnatural" and "unlifelike," Slater points out that it is precisely because these settings present an unprogrammed existence that elemental issues of personal and social life are brought out where they can be confronted. In his selection, Slater describes the profound sense of loss members experience when the leader neither nurtures them nor guides them but instead sets their task and places responsibility upon them. Their initial defense against this deprivation is to deify the leader. Slater draws a parallel between this phenomenon and the origin of primitive religion. In his view, the dynamics he observes in the small group is one instance of the dynamics that operates in societies in general.

In this section's final selection, Jaques adds a new dimension to the relationship between personality and the social system of the group. His central idea is that members (unconsciously, yet in collusion) create and share certain illusions about their relationships that serve to defend all parties against depressive anxiety. A familiar example is when the "normal" differences between boys and girls are amplified by both boys and girls as a means of defending each party against the anxiety associated with close contact with the other. For similar reasons, the differences between generations, races, classes, and, of course, nations may be amplified. When such collective illusions become a new basis for interaction, they effectively alter the original relationships. Thus the participants not only *use* the original system but through that use create a modified system. Whereas the original system might be explicable in terms of responses to the basic functional problems of adaptation and integration, the newly modified system can best be understood as a product of collusive and therefore collective defenses against anxiety. One implication of this position is that regardless of the realities of the original system, members will resist correcting their distorted definition of it, for to do so would undermine their defense against the anxiety it arouses. Another is that such a collective definition, serving a pervasive need, represents a massive resistance to the development of just the quality of system consciousness Deutsch suggests in his cybernetic model. Whether social science or other disciplines can advance the understanding of group dynamics enough to reassure group members to the extent that they are able to forego their collective defenses is one of the challenges for both theorists and practitioners in the field.

# chapter nine

## Group Observation

WARREN G. BENNIS                    HERBERT A. SHEPARD

This paper is an introduction to the subtle art of observing group process. Perhaps "subtle" is the wrong word: the major subtleties lie in making one's already shrewd observations explicit to oneself, and in deciding which of them to communicate to others. For we are all great process observers at heart.

Reprinted from Warren G. Bennis and Herbert Shepard, "Group Observation," in *The Planning of Change: Readings in the Applied Behavioral Sciences*, eds. Warren G. Bennis, Kenneth D. Benne, and Robert Chin (New York: Holt, Rinehart & Winston, Inc., 1961), pp. 743-56, by permission of the authors and Holt, Rinehart & Winston, Inc. Copyright © 1961 by Holt, Rinehart & Winston, Inc.

When Arthur Godfrey is playing his ukelele on TV and glowers at his pianist, we forget the song he's playing long enough to wonder about Mr. Godfrey's relations with his staff. And when a teacher is asked a perceptibly hostile question by an aggressive student, we lose interest in what the question was about and observe how the professor handles the situation and the student.

When any ordinary mortal enters a strange group he tries to size up the situation, perhaps cautiously by quiet scrutinization, perhaps aggressively by sticking his neck out to see how far he can go. He learns who the leaders are, how the other members are lined up, what the rules of the game are. His methods of learning these things and of getting into the group are peculiarly his own; they are part of his personality. He has his characteristic means of getting his own way, of keeping out of trouble—or of getting into trouble—of competing, and of gaining approval. He usually does not talk about them or think about them; most of the time he is hardly aware of the enormous skill he demonstrates in using them.

"I don't know what I've said until I've heard the response to it" is one of Professor Norbert Wiener's aphorisms. This is especially true in an unfamiliar social setting, where communication is strange and strained. Every statement is a sort of trial balloon in which the speaker ascends only a little way—in order not to be badly hurt by the fall should the balloon fail. The little "feelers" people put out in such a situation are extraordinarily delicate and sensitive antennae—superbly constructed for detecting the signs of approval and disapproval, of warmth and hostility, of submission and domination. Everybody has a pretty good set of instruments for group observation.

In fact, the ordinary mortal's instruments of group observation are so well-constructed that they are taken for granted. He is usually content to use them at about 10 per cent of capacity, and he neglects their maintenance and repair. He may not even recalibrate them as his experience widens and his values change. But since they were mostly developed in early youth, in a family group quite different from groups he encounters later in life, he may well be missing something.

Renovating the antennae is not an easy job. The principal method recommended in this book is first, making a rigorous effort to observe what is going on, and second, comparing one's observations with observations made by other members of the group. Easier said than done! Before a person can share his interpretations of what is going on, of how he feels, he has to be in a situation where he is not likely to get hurt for his courage. He has to be anchored in a group that shares his sentiments, beliefs, and feelings about many important matters; a group in which he is received with warmth and understanding. Yet process observations are themselves means to greater understanding. So he is in a dilemma: should he demand understanding as a condition for making process observations, or should he demand process observations as a means for better understanding?

Observations based on systematic collection and analysis of obvious data are easy to communicate, easy to understand. Hence, one way out of the dilemma is to start with observations which are based on straightforward methods of data collection. The rest of this chapter describes four such methods.

The following excerpt from a group discussion will be useful in illustrating the four methods of observation.

BILL: I'm beginning to gather that the subjects we speak on are relatively unimportant. The trend of the group is sort of beginning to fascinate me. In other words, what we have, if anyone follows me, but what we have is a group-centered sort of deal. I believe that at the first meeting that we needed leadership, which Jim and other people still both admire. I believe now though that the group is becoming sufficiently adjusted so that we want to have a diffused leadership. In other words, we all want to share in leadership and that is what Gordon, for instance, thinks is the most efficient way that a group can act. In other words, it's real unanimous approval rather than an authoritarian mind. It seems to me that we have been destroying leadership that we needed in the past, that is for the last three or four meetings we have been doing that. And I wonder if that is really what is happening, if we are trying to accomplish this diffused leadership.

JIM: This diffused leadership, I don't think it's a question of efficiency. I think it's a question of satisfaction. As far as efficiency, if someone says "You do this, that, and the other thing," that gets things done faster, and it gets more things done, but as far as people in the group feeling that they are part of a decision . . .

BILL: If something doesn't last, it's not efficient, that's the only way I look at it. In other words, unless it's a real approval . . .

JIM: In other words, efficiency . . .

BILL: or participation. I don't consider it to be efficient.

JIM: You mean efficiency doesn't mean getting things done and the quantity . . .

BILL: Yeah, well, I didn't mean that, that's a good point.

JIM: You had the idea of satisfaction.

BILL: Right. That's probably a better way of putting that.

VIC: Are the same people bored week in and week out?

BILL: Hmm?

VIC: Are the same . . . ?

JOE: I think we've exhibited something in the last three weeks which is very characteristic of a so-called group of leaders, and that's the selfishness on the part of every individual. I think the initiator of the topic, Jim last week and Vic this week, and Ed this week, has, I think, felt this a little subconsciously or maybe consciously when they've asked for group approval of their subject, because they realized that they couldn't get it done or that they couldn't get the topic of conversation without everybody in the group approving it wholeheartedly and this selfishness has manifested itself in quite . . . well I thought, three different ways to the point where everybody wants to be a part of the original idea.

Carrying on with Vic's point, I have tried to observe since the "boredom" discussion came up a few weeks ago, just which people are bored and how fre-

quently, and I've found that the same people are bored every week and only to the point where they will talk or be excited about a topic if they themselves are the initiator of this topic. Otherwise they have sat back and looked bored. Another way of not approving of a topic or not having felt that it was theirs was the extreme pessimism expressed as to the outcome of any discussion. The third way, people avoid topics completely. That's what happened with Jim last week. Until the point where, until, back to last week again, we ended up discussing the topic. Only it was this time instead of Jim's idea it was everybody's idea. Everybody came in on the discussion. I think it's very characteristic of a group like this, because everybody wants to be . . . it's the same thing, going back to fighting, what we talked about at the beginning, when we talked about this leadership discussion: whether we should have a formal leader appointed or would one grow out of the group. The people that didn't want to appoint a formal leader I think were afraid to. Because they felt they had their chance to be leader, why shouldn't I be able to fight for it?

ART: Is that true of you, Joe, because you were one of the great fighters?

JOE: I think it's partly true, yes. I can see it, I can see it very easily now. I think that it's happened continuously from one leader to the next—if we want to modify our definition of leader a little bit, each initiator . . . has been thought of as a leader. And everybody else has knocked them down. And I think it's all part of our own selfishness in something like this.

BERT: I agree in a large percentage with what Bill has had to say. It's something that you, at least in my case, you don't confirm too easily with evidence but you sort of sense it when you're speaking. You're not speaking with ideas, but you're speaking with weapons more or less. It's your status which is involved in everything you have to say. You're either saying something to make yourself stand out or knocking someone else down. It's a very difficult atmosphere in which to express yourself. It makes you very insecure. If you wanted evidence, about the only thing I could dig up I guess would be the fact that, first, it's terribly difficult to enter any conversation, and second, it's very difficult for the group to reach a decision on anything, and third, probably is that subgroups have been marked by a tremendous amount of disregard for the rest of the group and the conversation has been carried on among themselves.

I'm not sure whether any group ever achieves a state where everyone's status is accepted to a certain extent and what they say isn't a reflection on themselves personally, but I should think it would be something which the group would like to strive for possibly if you were trying to get something done. And it's one of the things I would like to learn out of a group of this sort—how something like that could be accomplished. Maybe it can be and maybe it can't, I don't know.

The above excerpt might be summarized in the minutes of the meeting as follows, "Leadership problems were discussed." Perhaps if one were describing the meeting to an absent member, a little more might be said: "Bill and Joe and Bert talked about how people have been acting in the group, and pointed out that people who try to get the group to do something never succeed. Joe showed his usual tendency to monopolize the conversation but the group was interested in what he was saying, though some of them may have resented it."

In this case the observer said a little bit about the participants' feelings, their roles in the group, and how the interaction among them proceeded. There were undoubtedly some more process factors that the observer either did not see or refrained from reporting. But the observer cannot watch everything. There is a lot of activity going on in most groups, and what the observer perceives depends on what he attends to, as well as on the acuity of his perception. If he tries to attend to everything at once, he will be so distracted that he is likely to report a simple handshake as an utterly chaotic social situation. (Sometimes it is, of course.) Hence, the observer has to start by being sensitive only to certain aspects of the situation, and peacefully oblivious of others.

This adjustment may sometimes make the observer sound blind rather than perceptive when he reports his observations, since he may seem to have missed the whole point of the meeting, while watching very carefully some aspect that was of little consequence. However, the seeming blindness lasts only through a period of experimenting with different ways of looking at the situation, or frames of reference for observing it. After that, he can decide which one is appropriate for a particular meeting, or use several at once.

### The Interactionists

The observer might begin by concentrating on one aspect of the situation that is basic to any kind of group activity: who interacts with whom. The interactionists say: "Group life is the outcome of interaction among organisms."[1] The most extreme interactionists undertake to observe *only* the patterns of interaction, without reference to the content of communication. From the interaction patterns, whether of a two-person relationship, a small group, a large organization, or a whole society, it is possible to make predictions about other aspects of the group —its power structure, for example. There are some areas of disagreement

---

[1] C. Arensberg, "Behavior and Organization: Industrial Studies," in J. H. Rohrer and M. Sherif, eds., *Social Psychology at the Crossroads* (New York: Harper & Row, Publishers, 1951).

among the various authors who use interaction analysis. For example, Whyte and Homans introduce "sentiments" as important items to observe.[2] However, all interactionists share the view that much can be inferred from habitual patterns and changes in patterns in the interaction of members of a group.

When we chart the interaction of a group we are not interested in who hates whom and who loves whom, we are interested primarily in who interacts with whom. An interactionist observing a group is not concerned with what people are saying or how they are saying it. He is concerned only with the frequency of interaction, the participants in interaction, the initiation of interaction, the ordering of interaction, the duration of actions, and the interruption of actions.

Studies using interaction-analysis methods range from studies of decision-making in small groups to studies of the communication systems of large industrial organizations.[3] Strodtbeck, in his study of the family as a three-person group, found that "the most-speaking person wins the largest share of decisions and in all cases the least-speaking person wins least."[4] In his study of clerical workers engaged in repetitive work, Homans showed that high interaction was closely correlated with personal popularity and productivity.[5]

. . .

## Interaction Process Analysis

As a social scientist, the interactionist is interested in predicting behavior and in correlating interaction patterns with other aspects of the situation. As an observer, however, he is interested only in systematically recording an aspect of the situation that is obvious and unambiguous.

Some of the interactionists are interested in observing more than interaction patterns, however, and place enough emphasis on feelings, intentions, and meanings for them to earn consideration as a separate group. R. F. Bales has developed a system for categorizing behavior known as interaction process analysis. This is an ingenious method for analysing not only the interactions among group members, but also the sentiments accompanying interaction. It is "a way of classifying direct, face-to-face interaction as it takes place, act-by-act, and a series of ways of summarizing and analysing the result data so that they yield useful information."[6]

. . .

Profile No. 1 on the chart of the figure shows the pattern of interaction of a children's play group. Profile No. 2 is the average profile of interaction for five married couples. Profile No.

---

[2] William F. Whyte, *Patterns for Industrial Peace* (New York: Harper & Row, Publishers, 1951), pp. 162-63; George Homans, *The Human Group* (New York: Harcourt, Brace & World, 1951).

[3] F. L. W. Richardson and C. R. Walker, *Human Relations in an Expanding Company* (New Haven: Yale Univ. Labor and Management Center, 1948). See also E. D. Chapple (with the collaboration of C. M. Arensberg), "Measuring Human Relations: An Introduction to the Study of the Interaction of Individuals," *Genetic Psychology Monograph*, XXII (1949), 3-147.

[4] F. L. Strodtbeck, "The Family as a Three-Person Group," *American Sociological Review*, XIX (1954), 23-29.

[5] George Homans, "The Cash Posters: A Study of a Group of Working Girls," *American Sociological Review*, XIX, No. 6 (1954) 724-33.

[6] R. F. Bales, *Interaction Process Analysis: A Method for the Study of Small Group* (Reading, Mass.: Addison-Wesley, 1950) pp. 5-6.

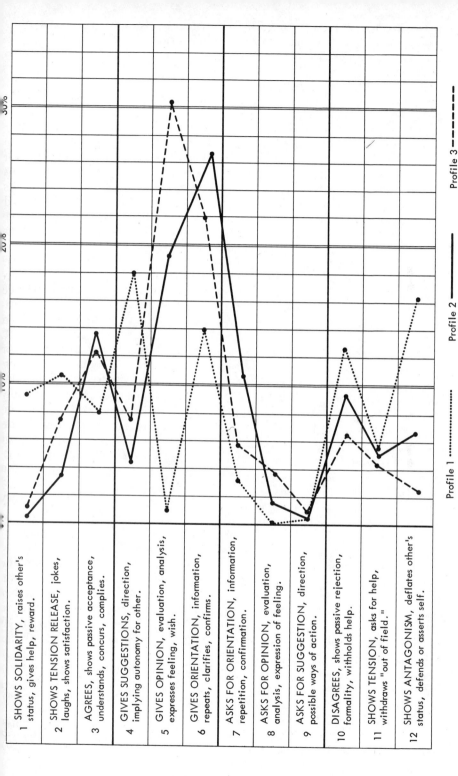

| | | 10% | 20% | 30% |
|---|---|---|---|---|
| 1 | SHOWS SOLIDARITY, raises other's status, gives help, reward. | | | |
| 2 | SHOWS TENSION RELEASE, jokes, laughs, shows satisfaction. | | | |
| 3 | AGREES, shows passive acceptance, understands, concurs, complies. | | | |
| 4 | GIVES SUGGESTIONS, direction, implying autonomy for other. | | | |
| 5 | GIVES OPINION, evaluation, analysis, expresses feeling, wish. | | | |
| 6 | GIVES ORIENTATION, information, repeats, clarifies, confirms. | | | |
| 7 | ASKS FOR ORIENTATION, information, repetition, confirmation. | | | |
| 8 | ASKS FOR OPINION, evaluation, analysis, expression of feeling. | | | |
| 9 | ASKS FOR SUGGESTION, direction, possible ways of action. | | | |
| 10 | DISAGREES, shows passive rejection, formality, withholds help. | | | |
| 11 | SHOWS TENSION, asks for help, withdraws "out of field." | | | |
| 12 | SHOWS ANTAGONISM, deflates other's status, defends or asserts self. | | | |

Profile 1 ··············    Profile 2 ———    Profile 3 – – – –

123

is the average profile of some 23,000 scores derived from a variety of discussion groups. Note the difference between the children's profile and Profile No. 3 in the social-emotional categories. Note also the relatively high degree of antagonistic social-emotional interaction in the husband-wife profiles. How would you account for these variations?

The completed interaction graph can tell us a good deal about group process. In it we can see the fluctuations of the group as it moves from hostile to friendly reactions, from problems of communication to problems of evaluation. Bales' studies indicate that in small discussion groups, where the group has a problem to solve, the process typically tends to follow a sequence of four phases. First, there is the "adaptive" phase of pooling information and other resources, and seeing how they can be used to accomplish the task. Second is the "goal-attainment" phase of actually working out the decisions and taking the action that completes the task. Third, there is an "integrative" phase of re-establishing group solidarity, which may have been disturbed in the second phase. The fourth phase, which overlaps the third, is a period of "tension-release," which consists of joking, laughter, and other expressions of relief that the job has been accomplished.

But how can acts, gestures, statements, and looks by a group be reliably deposited into twelve compartments by several different observers? How can one decide what constitutes a "unit" of interaction? Applying Bales' observation system requires more skill than that of merely counting interactions. Hence his observers are carefully trained in the details of scoring method so that their records agree. A detailed treatment of the criteria and conventions of scoring is given in the first two chapters and Appendix of *Interaction Process Analysis*.[7]

. . .

## Analysis of Group Mentality

It is a short step from common sense to Bales' category system. But it is a transatlantic hop from Bales to W. R. Bion,[8] a British psychiatrist who has formulated group process in quite different terms. Bion takes seriously the statement that a group is more than the sum of its members—that it has a life of its own.

In Bion's view, groups are essential to man's mental-emotional life. Participating in group mental life is essential to a full life for the individual; man seeks his fulfillment through group membership. To the group he brings his private needs and desires, and attempts to derive corresponding satisfactions from the group. Picture now the several members, each attempting to exploit the group for the fulfillment of his desires. The resultant product of this tangle of desires Bion calls the *group mentality*. The group mentality is a potpourri of individual needs contributed to by each individual in ways of which he is unaware, influencing him disagreeably when he is at variance with the prevailing emotional forces within the group.

The process is somewhat analogous to the working of a price system: one individual, in a competitive system, cannot autonomously set the price. Yet the eventual equilibrium price is the result of the activities of all the individuals, each of whom contributes to this result. As in an economic system

[7] *Ibid.*
[8] W. R. Bion, "Experiences in Groups I–VII," *Human Relations*, V, Nos. 1 (1948).

there is a disparity between what the individual wants from the group, and how much of the emotional pie the group is going to accord him. The group's method of organization for settling this dispute Bion calls the *group culture*: "I employ the phrase 'culture of the group' in an extremely loose manner: I include in it the structure which the group achieves at any given moment, the occupations it pursues, and the organization it adopts."[9]

Herbert A. Thelen and his associates have formalized Bion's ideas into a set of categories for recording group behavior.[10] In their version, the group mentality is differentiated into three emotional modalities, or recurring patterns of expressive behavior. These are "fight-flight," "pairing," and "dependency." *Fight-flight* represents the desires of the group to escape the task that faces the group, either by fighting it (or one another) or by running away from the task. *Pairing* represents the desire of the group to seek security by establishing pair relationships between members of the group. This is manifested in a number of ways: friendly smiles and winks, mutually supportive statements, and so on. *Dependency* represents the group's need to remain dependent on the leader, to retain him as protector, judge, and commander.

A fourth category of the group mentality, called, of all things, *work*, represents the desire of the group to engage in problem-solving activity. The work needs are frequently in conflict with the other needs of the group, and every member is caught in this struggle. A person who tends to support one of the other modalities is said to have a high *valency* for the modality. Persons who lead the group from one modality to another are called *barometric*. For purposes of categorizing, the work modality can be differentiated into four classes. *One-level work* is personally need-oriented. One-level statements may be triggered off by what is happening in the group, but they are expressions of personal need, and are not group-oriented. An observer watching one-level work feels that it interrupts the flow of the group, and is an expression of purely personal need. *Two-level work* involves maintaining or following through on the task the group is working on. An observer watching two-level work feels that it is group-oriented and necessary, but routine. *Three-level work* is group-focused work that usually has some new ingredient. It includes suggestions of new methods of attack on a problem, the visualization of goals, reality-testing of ideas. An observer watching three-level work feels that it is group-oriented, focused, and energetic, and that it has direction and meaning for the group. *Four-level work* is creative, insightful, and integrative. It usually involves an appropriate and insightful interpretation that brings together for the group a whole series of experiences and infuses meaning into them, and at the same time has immediate relevance to present problems. An observer watching four-level work feels that it is creative and exciting.

The relations between work achievement and activity in the other modalities of group mentality is an important matter for students of group dynamics. The definition of work levels helps in reaching an assessment of the achievement of discussion groups. Examples of statements representing the various categories of emotionality and work are given below.[11] Content is, of course,

[9] W. R. Bion, "Experiences in Groups: II," *Human Relations*, V, No. 1 (1948).

[10] H. Thelen *et al.*, *Methods for Studying Work and Emotionality in Group Operation* (Chicago: Univ. of Chicago Press, 1954).

[11] Adapted from *ibid.*, pp. 23-30.

important in determining how to classify any statement made in a group, but the examples given below are more or less self-explanatory.

## I. RATINGS OF EMOTIONALITY

### A. FIGHT STATEMENTS (f)

1. Attacking, deprecating the group; aggressive impatience with the group.
   *ex.* "You say you're satisfied and yet people feel withdrawn. I question the effectiveness of a group in which people don't feel involved."
   *ex.* "Aren't we ready to go? We've wasted enough time."
2. Attacking specific members.
   *ex.* "I question his motives."
   *ex.* "You feel you're just an average person, don't you?"
3. Blocking the group.
   *ex.* "Do you ever get any expression in role-playing that means anything? I wonder about the validity of the whole idea."
   *ex.* "I have not understood any of this."
4. Self-aggrandizement at the expense of others.
   *ex.* "I feel a responsibility to the group. I just can't sit back and let the group flounder."
   *ex.* "I resisted that idea every time it came up."
5. Projected hostility.
   *ex.* "I will volunteer to be the scapegoat."
   *ex.* "I don't mind being used by the group this way."

### B. FLIGHT STATEMENTS (fl)

1. Withdrawal or lessened involvement.
   *ex.* Silence
   *ex.* Doodling
2. Humor, fantasy, facetiousness, tension-releasing laughter.
   *ex.* (The dog barks, in response to a general tension in the group.) "He's our alter-ego." (Group laughs.) "He wants coffee." "He's smarter than we are." (Group leaves room.)
3. Inappropriate, overintellectualized, overgeneralized statements.

*ex.* "Any correlation between emotional tension and productivity is inverse . . ." (etc. etc.)
4. Total irrelevancy.
   *ex.* "I suggest coffee."
   *ex.* "We went to the best restaurant in Quebec."

### C. PAIRING (p)

1. Expressions of intimacy, warmth, and supportiveness.
   *ex.* "We all missed you yesterday."
   *ex.* "I felt a lot better when you said that."
2. Support of another person's idea.
   *ex.* "I believe we missed Bob's idea —that observation or process is a good starting-point."
   *ex.* "I agree very much with what Bill has been saying."
3. Expressions of commitment and warmth directed toward the whole group.
   *ex.* "We've come a long way since the first few days."
   *ex.* "We were really on the ball today."

### D. DEPENDENCY (d)

1. Appeals for support or direction.
   *ex.* "I'd feel better if the instructor would tell us just what he expects of the group."
   *ex.* "I don't know—what is the correct way?"
2. Reliance on a definite structure, procedure, or tradition.
   *ex.* "Why don't we appoint a chairman?"
   *ex.* "I think we should have some way of starting off each day. Maybe the observer should read his report from the previous meeting."
3. Reliance on outside authority.
   *ex.* "Is this the sort of thing that happens in other groups?"
   *ex.* "Why don't we get a speaker to talk about personality?"
4. Expressions of weakness or inadequacy.
   *ex.* "I'm all confused. Where do we go from here?"
   *ex.* "We *are* disorganized. Can't someone tell us what to do next?"

## II. RATINGS OF WORK

ONE-LEVEL WORK

*ex.* "I was amazed when the group laughed at what I said. I didn't think it was funny."

*ex.* "I'm used to dealing with people who express things more directly."

Two-Level Work

*ex.* "When should the observer start?"

*ex.* "What will we get out of having an observer?"

*ex.* "Does Joe really want to be the observer?"

*ex.* "Let's ask him."

Three-Level Work

*ex.* "So far we've covered three parts of this plan, is there anything left to do?" "Well, we ought to get into the question of what we're going to do with this information after we get it."

Four-Level Work

*ex.* "Permissiveness can be a trap. When you have something to fight, you might get a lot more involvement. And then there are hazards along with that—things may get destructive. The question is how to get involvement along with permissiveness."

### Role Analysis

In formally organized clubs and associations, some of the members hold special "offices"—chairman, secretary, etc. In connection with their offices, the chairman and secretary have certain duties—they have special roles in the organization. For example, the chairman chairs the meeting; the secretary reads the minutes.

In any group, whether formally organized or not, there are a number of roles played that are not dignified by a title, but that affect the way the group as a whole operates. If there is one member who habitually opposes all suggestions made by other group members, one cannot assume that he has recently been elected to the office of Group Opposer—it is simply the role that he characteristically takes in the group. Some persons are skilled in playing a number of group roles, but

most of us have only a few at our disposal and can be pigeonholed more easily.

The role that a person plays in a group sometimes surprises those who know him well apart from the group. The way a friend of yours behaves when he is a member of a group of several people may be quite different from the way he behaves in the two-person group consisting of him and you. In the larger group you see only one side of his personality—his group or membership role.

Membership roles have received a good deal of study. There are four main questions that can be asked about a membership role. First, what are its consequences for the person playing the role—what needs of his does it satisfy and what problems does it create for him? Second, what are its consequences for the other members of the group—what needs of theirs does it satisfy, what needs does it arouse? Third, what are its consequences for the integration of the group—does it increase or decrease cohesiveness, solidarity, mutual respect, etc.? Fourth, what are its consequences for the performance of the group's task—does it contribute towards the solution of the group's problem, or does it interfere with solving the problem?

A number of systems have been worked out to describe the variety of roles that occur in a group. Any one of these systems may be useful for assessing the potentialities of a group or understanding some of the difficulties the group has in working together. Two systems are presented below. Both of these, one developed by Benne and Sheats and one other by the Gibbs,[12]

---

[12] K. D. Benne and P. Sheats, "Functional Roles of Group Members," *Journal of Social Issues*, II (1948), 42-47; J. R. Gibb and L. M. Gibb, *Applied Group Dynamics* (Boulder, Colo.: Univ. of Colorado Press, 1956).

have been arrived at by asking the four questions listed above. Thus both systems have a set of roles—the Group Task roles—which are primarily useful for contributing toward problem solution (Question 4). The second set, Group Building and Maintenance Roles, are primarily useful for satisfying the needs of other members and contributing to group integration (Questions 2 and 3). The third set, Individual Roles, are expressions of personal, as opposed to group, needs. They are antithetical or irrelevant to achievement of the Group Task or Group Building and Maintenance. The Gibbs distinguish a fourth set of roles which are simultaneously task- and group-oriented.

I. *Task Roles*
Initiating activity; Seeking information; Seeking opinion; Giving information; Giving opinion; Elaborating; Coordinating; Summarizing; Testing feasibility.

II. *Group Maintenance Roles*
Encouraging; Gate keeping; Standard setting; Following; Expressing group feeling.

III. *Task and Group Roles*
Evaluating; Diagnosing; Testing for consensus; Mediating; Relieving tension.

IV. *Individual Roles*
Being aggressive; Blocking; Self-confessing; Competing; Seeking sympathy; Special pleading; Horsing around; Seeking recognition; Withdrawing.

# chapter ten

## Doc and His Boys

**WILLIAM F. WHYTE**

Besides Mike's crowd and Nutsy's boys, there were three other men who went to make up the Nortons as I knew them. Angelo Cucci, Fred Mackey (Macaluso), and Lou Danaro were all closely attached to Doc. Some years earlier, Fred's uncle had opened

Reprinted from William F. Whyte, *Street Corner Society* (Chicago: The Univ. of Chicago Press, 1955), pp. 11-24, by permission of The University of Chicago Press. Copyright © 1955 by The University of Chicago Press.

a grocery store on Norton Street and had placed Fred in charge part of the time. One day Danny got the boys to play a practical joke on him. They lined up in front of the counter and demanded protection money. Fred was panic-stricken until Doc took pity on him and explained the situation. Fred was so relieved that he looked upon Doc as his benefactor and frequently sought his company, even after the store had been sold.

For several years Lou Danaro had worked for Mr. Bacon, the headworker of the Norton Street Settlement, and had even lived in the house. The corner boys thought that he considered himself above them, and they would have nothing to do with him. Doc knew Lou's cousin very well. The cousins did not get along; Doc thought that was too bad, so, when he went out with Lou's cousin, he insisted that they get Lou to join them. In that way he struck up a friendship with Lou. When Lou finally broke with Mr. Bacon and moved out of the settlement, his friendship with Doc made it possible for him to be accepted on the street corner.

Fred and Lou both lived in the suburbs, but they drove into Eastern City for their part-time jobs and into Cornerville to join Doc and his friends.

When Doc first met him, Angelo was exceedingly shy and had no friends. He spent most of his time at home practicing the violin, which he hoped some day to play in a concert orchestra. When Doc accepted him as a friend, it was possible for Angelo to join the corner boys.

Close friendship ties already existed between certain of the men, but the Nortons, as an organization, did not begin to function until the early spring of 1937. It was at that time that Doc returned to the corner. Nutsy, Frank, Joe, Alec, Carl, and Tommy had a great respect for Doc and gathered around him. Angelo, Fred, and Lou followed Doc in making the corner their headquarters. Danny and Mike were drawn to Norton Street by their friendship for Doc and by the location of their crap game, right next to "the corner." Long John followed Danny and Mike.

The men became accustomed to acting together. They were also tied to one another by mutual obligations. In their experiences together there were innumerable occasions when one man would feel called upon to help another, and the man who was aided would want to return the favor. Strong group loyalties were supported by these reciprocal activities.

There were distinctions in rank among the Nortons. Doc, Danny, and Mike held the top positions. They were older than any others except Nutsy. They possessed a greater capacity for social movement. While the followers were restricted to the narrow sphere of one corner, Doc, Danny, and Mike had friends in many other groups and were well known and respected throughout a large part of Cornerville. It was one of their functions to accompany the follower when he had to move outside of his customary social sphere and needed such support. The leadership three were also respected for their intelligence and powers of self-expression. Doc in particular was noted for his skill in argument. On the infrequent occasions when he did become involved, he was usually able to outmaneuver his opponent without humiliating him. I never saw the leadership three exert their authority through physical force, but their past fighting reputations tended to support their positions.

Doc was the leader of the gang. The Nortons had been Doc's gang when they had been boys, and, although the membership had changed, they were still thought to be Doc's gang. The crap game and its social obligations prevented Danny and Mike from spending as much time with the Nortons as did Doc. They were not so intimate with the followers, and they expected him to lead.

Long John was in an anomalous position. Though he was five years younger than Doc, his friendship with the three top men gave him a superior standing. As Doc explained:

It's because we've always catered to Long John. When we go somewhere, we ask Long John to go with us. We come up to him and slap him on the back. We give him so much attention that the rest of the fellows have to respect him.

Nevertheless, he had little authority over the followers. At this time he was accustomed to gamble away his week's earnings in the crap game, and this was thrown up against him.

There is an important social distinction between those who hold crap games and those who play in them. The game-holders enjoy something of the standing of businessmen; the "shooters" are thought to be suckers. The Nortons as a group considered themselves above the crap-shooters' level, and at this time Long John was trying unsuccessfully to break away from the game.

In the spring of 1937 Nutsy was recognized informally as the superior of Frank, Joe, and Alec, but his relations with a girl had already begun to damage his standing. A corner boy is not expected to be chaste, but it is beneath him to marry a girl who is "no good." Nutsy was going so steadily with this girl that marriage seemed a distinct possibility, and, reacting to the criticism of his friends, he gradually withdrew from the gang. He did not again play a prominent role in the Nortons

until toward the end of my stay in Cornerville, but in the spring and summer of 1937 he was still a man of moderate importance.

As the story gets under way, Doc was twenty-nine; Mike, twenty-nine; Danny, twenty-seven; Long John, twenty-four; Nutsy, twenty-nine; Frank, twenty-three; Joe, twenty-four; Alec, twenty-one; Angelo, twenty-five; Fred, twenty-five; Lou, twenty-four; Carl, twenty-one; and Tommy, twenty. The accompanying chart presents a picture of the relations between the men as they appeared at this time. For purposes of shorthand designation, I shall refer to the top four men as the "leaders" and to the others as the "followers." If the special characteristics of Long John are borne in mind, this should not be confusing.

### Bowling and Social Ranking

One evening in October, 1937, Doc scheduled a bowling match against the Italian Community Club, which was composed largely of college men who held their meetings every two weeks in the Norton Street Settlement House. The club was designed to be an or-

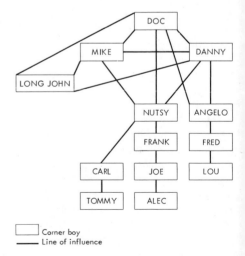

The Nortons: spring and summer 1937. Positions of boxes indicate relative status.

ganization of well-educated and superior men, although Doc was a member, and Angelo, Lou, and Fred of the Nortons had been voted in upon his recommendation. The other Nortons felt that the club was "high-toned," and around the corner it was known as the "Boys' Junior League." They were a little flattered that members of their group could mix with such a club, but their opinion was formed largely from the personalities of Chick Morelli, the president, and Tony Cardio, another prominent member, both of whom they considered snobbish and conceited. Consequently, the Nortons took this match very seriously.

Doc was captain of the Nortons. He selected Long John, Frank, Joe, and Tommy for his team. Danny and Mike were not bowling in this period. Chick and Tony led the Community Club team.

Feeling ran high. The Nortons shouted at the club bowlers and made all sorts of noises to upset their concentration. The club members were in high spirits when they gained an early lead but had little to say as the Nortons pulled ahead to win by a wide margin.

After the match I asked Frank and Joe if there was any team that they would have been more eager to beat. They said that if they could pick out their favorite victims, they would choose Chick Morelli, Tony Cardio, Joe Cardio (Tony's brother), Mario Testa, and Hector Marto. These last three had all belonged to the Sunset Dramatic Club.

Frank and Joe said that they had nothing against the other three men on the Community Club team but that the boys had been anxious to beat that team in order to put Chick and Tony "in their places." Significantly, Frank and Joe did not select their favorite victims on the basis of bowling ability. The five were good bowlers,

but that was not the deciding factor in the choice. It was their social positions and ambitions that were the objects of attack, and it was that which made victory over the Community Club so satisfying.

Lou Danaro and Fred Mackey had cheered for the club. Although they were club members, the boys felt that this did not excuse them. Danny said: "You're a couple of traitors—Benedict Arnolds. . . . You're with the boys—and then you go against them. . . . Go on, I don't want your support."

Fred and Lou fell between the two groups and therefore had to face this problem of divided allegiance. Doc's position on the corner was so definitely established that no one even considered the possibility of his choosing to bowl for the Community Club against the Nortons.

This was the only match between the two teams that ever took place. The corner boys were satisfied with their victory, and the club did not seek a return match. Tony Cardio objected to the way in which the Nortons had tried to upset the concentration of his team and said it was no fun to bowl against such poor sports. There were, however, clashes with individual members of the club. One night in November, Doc, Frank Bonelli, Joe Dodge, and I were bowling when Chick Morelli and Lou Danaro came in together. We agreed to have two three-man teams, and Chick and Doc chose sides. Chick chose Lou and me. The match was fairly even at first, but Doc put his team far ahead with a brilliant third string. Toward the end of this string, Chick was sitting next to Joe Dodge and mumbling at him, "You're a lousy bum. . . . You're a no-good bowler."

Joe said nothing until Chick had repeated his remarks several times. Then Joe got up and fired back at Chick, "You're a conceited ——! I feel like taking a wallop at you. I never knew anybody was as conceited as you. . . . You're a conceited ——!"

Doc stood between them to prevent a fight. Chick said nothing, and Doc managed to get the six of us quietly into the elevator. Joe was not satisfied, and he said to me in a loud voice: "Somebody is going to straighten him out some day. Somebody will have to wallop him to knock some of that conceit out of him."

When we were outside the building, Lou walked away with Chick, and the rest of us went into Jennings' Cafeteria for "coffee-ands." We discussed Chick:

Doc: It's lucky you didn't hit him. They'd be after you for manslaughter. You're too strong for the kid.

Joe: All right. But when somebody's too tough for me, I don't fool around. . . . He shouldn't fool around me. . . . If he's gonna say them things, he should smile when he says them. But I think he really meant it.

Doc: The poor guy, so many fellows want to wallop him—and he knows it.

Frank: I liked him all right until the other night. We went to the Metropolitan Ballroom. . . . He didn't mingle in at all. He just lay down on a couch like he wanted to be petted. He wasn't sociable at all.

After driving Chick home, Lou joined us in Jennings'. He said that Chick felt very bad about the incident and didn't know what it was that made people want to hit him. Lou added: "I know he didn't mean it that way. He's really a swell kid when you get to know him. There's only one thing I don't like about him." Then he told about a time when Chick had started an argument with a dance-hall attendant on some technicality involved in the regulations of the hall. Lou commented: "He was just trying to show how intelligent he was."

A few days later, when Joe's anger had subsided, Doc persuaded him to apologize.

Doc did not defend Chick for friendship's sake. Nor was it because they worked together in the Community Club. In the club Doc led a faction generally hostile to Chick, and he himself was often critical of the manner in which Chick sought to run the organization. But Doc had friends in both groups. He did not like to see the groups at odds with each other. Though friendship between the Nortons and Chick was impossible, it was Doc's function to see that diplomatic relations were maintained.

The Community Club match served to arouse enthusiasm for bowling among the Nortons. Previously the boys had bowled sporadically and often in other groups, but now for the first time bowling became a regular part of their social routine. Long John, Alec, Joe Dodge, and Frank Bonelli bowled several nights a week throughout the winter. Others bowled on frequent occasions, and all the bowlers appeared at the alleys at least one night a week.

A high score at candlepins requires several spares or strikes. Since a strike rarely occurs except when the first ball hits the kingpin properly within a fraction of an inch, and none of the boys had such precise aim, strikes were considered matters of luck, although a good bowler was expected to score them more often than a poor one. A bowler was judged according to his ability to get spares, to "pick" the pins that remained on the alley after his first ball.

There are many mental hazards connected with bowling. In any sport there are critical moments when a player needs the steadiest nerves if he is to "come through"; but, in those that involve team play and fairly continuous action, the player can sometimes lose himself in the heat of the contest and get by the critical points before he has a chance to "tighten up." If he is competing on a five-man team, the bowler must wait a long time for his turn at the alleys, and he has plenty of time to brood over his mistakes. When a man is facing ten pins, he can throw the ball quite casually. But when only one pin remains standing, and his opponents are shouting, "He can't pick it," the pressure is on, and there is a tendency to "tighten up" and lose control.

When a bowler is confident that he can make a difficult shot, the chances are that he will make it or come exceedingly close. When he is not confident, he will miss. A bowler is confident because he has made similar shots in the past and is accustomed to making good scores. But that is not all. He is also confident because his fellows, whether for him or against him, believe that he can make the shot. If they do not believe in him, the bowler has their adverse opinion as well as his own uncertainty to fight against. When that is said, it becomes necessary to consider a man's relation to his fellows in examining his bowling record.

In the winter and spring of 1937-38 bowling was the most significant social activity for the Nortons. Saturday night's intraclique and individual matches became the climax of the week's events. During the week the boys discussed what had happened the previous Saturday night and what would happen on the coming Saturday night. A man's performance was subject to continual evaluation and criticism. There was, therefore, a close connection between a man's bowling and his position in the group.

The team used against the Community Club had consisted of two men (Doc and Long John) who ranked high and three men (Joe Dodge, Frank Bonelli, and Tommy) who had a low standing. When bowling became a fixed group activity, the Nortons' team evolved along different lines. Danny joined the Saturday-night crowd and rapidly made a place for himself. He performed very well and picked Doc as his favorite opponent. There was a good-natured rivalry between them. In individual competition Danny usually won, although his average in the group matches was no better than that of Doc's. After the Community Club match, when Doc selected a team to represent the Nortons against other corner gangs and clubs, he chose Danny, Long John, and himself, leaving two vacancies on the five-man team. At this time, Mike, who had never been a good bowler, was just beginning to bowl regularly and had not established his reputation. Significantly enough, the vacancies were not filled from the ranks of the clique. On Saturday nights the boys had been bowling with Chris Teludo, Nutsy's older cousin, and Mark Ciampa, a man who associated with them only at the bowling alleys. Both men were popular and were first-class bowlers. They were chosen by Doc, with the agreement of Danny and Long John, to bowl for the Nortons. It was only when a member of the regular team was absent that one of the followers in the clique was called in, and on such occasions he never distinguished himself.

The followers were not content with being substitutes. They claimed that they had not been given an opportunity to prove their ability. One Saturday night in February, 1938, Mike organized an intraclique match. His team was made up of Chris Teludo, Doc, Long John, himself, and me. Danny was sick at the time, and I was put in to substitute for him. Frank, Alec, Joe, Lou, and Tommy made up the other team. Interest in this match was more intense than in the ordinary "choose-up" matches, but the followers bowled poorly and never had a chance. After this one encounter the followers were recognized as the second team and never again challenged the team of Doc, Danny, Long John, Mark, and Chris. Instead, they took to individual efforts to better their positions.

On his athletic ability alone, Frank should have been an excellent bowler. His ball-playing had won him positions on semiprofessional teams and a promise—though unfulfilled—of a job on a minor-league team. And it was not lack of practice that held him back, for, along with Alec and Joe Dodge, he bowled more frequently than Doc, Danny, or Mike. During the winter of 1937-38 Frank occupied a particularly subordinate position in the group. He spent his time with Alec in the pastry shop owned by Alec's uncle, and, since he had little employment throughout the winter, he became dependent upon Alec for a large part of the expenses of his participation in group activities. Frank fell to the bottom of the group. His financial dependence preyed upon his mind. While he sometimes bowled well, he was never a serious threat to break into the first team.

Some events of June, 1937, cast additional light upon Frank's position. Mike organized a baseball team of some of the Nortons to play against a younger group of Norton Street corner boys. On the basis of his record, Frank was considered the best player on either team, yet he made a miserable showing. He said to me: "I can't seem to play ball when I'm playing with fellows I know, like that bunch. I do much better when I'm playing for the Stanley A.C. against some team in Dexter, Westland, or out of town." Accustomed to filling an inferior position, Frank was unable to star even in his favorite sport when he was competing against members of his own group.

One evening I heard Alec boasting to Long John that the way he was bowling he could take on every man on the first team and lick them all.

Long John dismissed the challenge with these words: "You think you could beat us, but, under pressure, you die!"

Alec objected vehemently, yet he recognized the prevailing group opinion of his bowling. He made the highest single score of the season, and he frequently excelled during the week when he bowled with Frank, Long John, Joe Dodge, and me, but on Saturday nights, when the group was all assembled, his performance was quite different. Shortly after this conversation Alec had several chances to prove himself, but each time it was "an off night," and he failed.

Carl, Joe, Lou, and Fred were never good enough to gain any recognition. Tommy was recognized as a first-class bowler, but he did most of his bowling with a younger group.

One of the best guides to the bowling standing of the members was furnished by a match held toward the end of April, 1938. Doc had an idea that we should climax the season with an individual competition among the members of the clique. He persuaded the owner of the alleys to contribute ten dollars in prize money to be divided among the three highest scorers. It was decided that only those who had bowled regularly should be eligible, and on this basis Lou, Fred, and Tommy were eliminated.

Interest in this contest ran high. The probable performances of the various bowlers were widely discussed. Doc, Danny, and Long John each listed his predictions. They were unanimous in conceding the first five places to themselves, Mark Ciampa, and Chris Teludo, although they differed in predicting the order among the first five. The next two positions were generally conceded to Mike and to me. All the ratings gave Joe Dodge last position, and Alec, Frank, and Carl were ranked close to the bottom.

The followers made no such lists, but Alec let it be known that he intended to show the boys something. Joe Dodge was annoyed to discover that he was the unanimous choice to finish last and argued that he was going to win.

When Chris Teludo did not appear for the match, the field was narrowed to ten. After the first four boxes, Alec was leading by several pins. He turned to Doc and said, "I'm out to get you boys tonight." But then he began to miss, and, as mistake followed mistake, he stopped trying. Between turns, he went out for drinks, so that he became flushed and unsteady on his feet. He threw the ball carelessly, pretending that he was not interested in the competition. His collapse was sudden and complete; in the space of a few boxes he dropped from first to last place.

The bowlers finished in the following order:

| | |
|---|---|
| 1. Whyte | 6. Joe |
| 2. Danny | 7. Mark |
| 3. Doc | 8. Carl |
| 4. Long John | 9. Frank |
| 5. Mike | 10. Alec |

There were only two upsets in the contest, according to the predictions made by Doc, Danny, and Long John: Mark bowled very poorly and I won. However, it is important to note that neither Mark nor I fitted neatly into either part of the clique. Mark associated with the boys only at the bowling alleys and had no recognized status in the group. Although I was on good terms with all the boys, I was closer to the leaders than to the followers, since Doc was my particular friend. If Mark and I are left out of consideration, the performances were almost exactly what the leaders expected and the followers feared they would be. Danny, Doc, Long John, and Mike were bunched together at the top. Joe Dodge did better than was expected of him, but even

he could not break through the solid ranks of the leadership.

Several days later Doc and Long John discussed the match with me.

LONG JOHN: I only wanted to be sure that Alec or Joe Dodge didn't win. That wouldn't have been right.

Doc: That's right. We didn't want to make it tough for you, because we all liked you, and the other fellows did too. If somebody had tried to make it tough for you, we would have protected you. . . . If Joe Dodge or Alec had been out in front, it would have been different. We would have talked them out of it. We would have made plenty of noise. We would have been really vicious. . . .

I asked Doc what would have happened if Alec or Joe had won.

They wouldn't have known how to take it. That's why we were out to beat them. If they had won, there would have been a lot of noise. Plenty of arguments. We would have called it lucky—things like that. We would have tried to get them in another match and then ruin them. We would have to put them in their places.

Every corner boy expects to be heckled as he bowls, but the heckling can take various forms. While I had moved ahead as early as the end of the second string, I was subjected only to good-natured kidding. The leaders watched me with mingled surprise and amusement; in a very real sense, I was permitted to win.

Even so, my victory required certain adjustments. I was hailed jocularly as "the Champ" or even as "the Cheese Champ." Rather than accept this designation, I pressed my claim for recognition. Doc arranged to have me bowl a match against Long John. If I won, I should have the right to challenge Doc or Danny. The four of us went to the alleys together. Urged on by Doc and Danny, Long John won a decisive victory. I made no further challenges.

Alec was only temporarily crushed by his defeat. For a few days he was not seen on the corner, but then he returned and sought to re-establish himself. When the boys went bowling, he challenged Long John to an individual match and defeated him. Alec began to talk once more. Again he challenged Long John to a match, and again he defeated him. When bowling was resumed in the fall, Long John became Alec's favorite opponent, and for some time Alec nearly always came out ahead. He gloated. Long John explained: "He seems to have the Indian sign on me." And that is the way these incidents were interpreted by others—simply as a queer quirk of the game.

It is significant that, in making his challenge, Alec selected Long John instead of Doc, Danny, or Mike. It was not that Long John's bowling ability was uncertain. His average was about the same as that of Doc or Danny and better than that of Mike. As a member of the top group but not a leader in his own right, it was his social position that was vulnerable.

When Long John and Alec acted outside the group situation, it became possible for Alec to win. Long John was still considered the dependable man in a team match, and that was more important in relation to a man's standing in the group. Nevertheless, the leaders felt that Alec should not be defeating Long John and tried to reverse the situation. As Doc told me:

Alec isn't so aggressive these days. I steamed up at the way he was going after Long John, and I blasted him. . . . Then I talked to Long John. John is an introvert. He broods over things, and sometimes he feels inferior. He can't be aggressive like Alec, and when Alec tells him how he can always beat him, Long John gets to think that Alec is the better bowler. . . . I talked to him. I made him see that he should bowl better than Alec. I persuaded him that he was really the

better bowler. . . . Now you watch them the next time out. I'll bet Long John will ruin him.

The next time Long John did defeat Alec. He was not able to do it every time, but they became so evenly matched that Alec lost interest in such competition.

The records of the season 1937-38 show a very close correspondence between social position and bowling performance. This developed because bowling became the primary social activity of the group. It became the main vehicle whereby the individual could maintain, gain, or lose prestige.

Bowling scores did not fall automatically into this pattern. There were certain customary ways of behaving which exerted pressure upon the individuals. Chief among these were the manner of choosing sides and the verbal attacks the members directed against one another.

Generally, two men chose sides in order to divide the group into two five-man teams. The choosers were often, but not always, among the best bowlers. If they were evenly matched, two poor bowlers frequently did the choosing, but in all cases the process was essentially the same. Each one tried to select the best bowler among those who were still unchosen. When more than ten men were present, choice was limited to the first ten to arrive, so that even a poor bowler would be chosen if he came early. It was the order of choice which was important. Sides were chosen several times each Saturday night, and in this way a man was constantly reminded of the value placed upon his ability by his fellows and of the sort of performance expected of him.

Of course, personal preference entered into the selection of bowlers, but if a man chose a team of poor bowlers just because they were his closest friends, he pleased no one, least of all his team mates. It was the custom among the Nortons to have the losing team pay for the string bowled by the winners. As a rule, this small stake did not play an important role in the bowling, but no one liked to pay without the compensating enjoyment of a closely contested string. For this reason the selections by good bowlers or by poor bowlers coincided very closely. It became generally understood which men should be among the first chosen in order to make for an interesting match.

When Doc, Danny, Long John, or Mike bowled on opposing sides, they kidded one another good-naturedly. Good scores were expected of them, and bad scores were accounted for by bad luck or temporary lapses of form. When a follower threatened to better his position, the remarks took quite a different form. The boys shouted at him that he was lucky, that he was "bowling over his head." The effort was made to persuade him that he should not be bowling as well as he was, that

a good performance was abnormal for him. This type of verbal attack was very important in keeping the members "in their places." It was used particularly by the followers so that, in effect, they were trying to keep one another down. While Long John, one of the most frequent targets for such attacks, responded in kind, Doc, Danny, and Mike seldom used this weapon. However, the leaders would have met a real threat on the part of Alec or Joe by such psychological pressures.

The origination of group action is another factor in the situation. The Community Club match really inaugurated bowling as a group activity, and that match was arranged by Doc. Group activities are originated by the men with highest standing in the group, and it is natural for a man to encourage an activity in which he excels and discourage one in which he does not excel. However, this cannot explain Mike's performance, for he had never bowled well before Saturday night at the alleys became a fixture for the Nortons.

# chapter eleven

## Instrumentality and Emotionality in Family Interaction

ROBERT K. LEIK

Attempts to formulate theoretical principles which underlie family inter-

action pose problems which have not been adequately resolved. It is usually assumed by investigators of a "small groups" orientation that the structure

Reprinted from Robert K. Leik, "Instrumentality and Emotionality in Family Interaction," *Sociometry*, XXVI, No. 2 (1963), 131-45, by permission of the author and the American Sociological Association. Copyright © 1963 by the American Sociological Association.

and consequent interaction within the nuclear family follow principles applicable to small groups in general. A specific instance is the task versus social-emotional differentiation of leadership, first suggested by Slater and by Bales and Slater, which now appears in increasing frequency in discussions of family interaction.[1]

It is apparent from the research literature, however, that relatively little data exist in direct support of the equivalence of families and other small groups. For example, studies of coalition relationships in family interaction do not show the same results that are obtained from ad hoc experimental groups.[2] Similarly, a recent attempt to test "some widely held beliefs about marital interaction" showed little support for nine propositions derived from general small group research.[3] Although there may be valid reasons for the discrepancies, results do not show overwhelming evidence that family interaction coincides with theoretical expectations derived from non-family research.

The present paper will deal with one aspect of the comparability of family and non-family interaction. The particular problem to be studied is the importance of instrumentality, or task-oriented behavior, and of emotionality, in two respects. First, are the male role (instrumental, non-emotional) and female role (emotional, non-instrumental), which parallel the task leader and social-emotional leader, applicable to the actual interaction process within the family? Or are they merely a summary consequence of family division of labor?[4] Second, in what way do instrumentality and emotionality affect the process of reaching consensus?

[1] Philip E. Slater, "Role Differentiation in Small Groups," *American Sociological Review*, XX (June, 1955), 300-310, and Robert F. Bales and Philip E. Slater, "Role Differentiation in Small Decision Making Groups," Chapter V in Talcott Parsons and Robert F. Bales, eds., *Family, Socialization, and Interaction Process* (New York: The Free Press, 1955). Further use of this distinction between male and female roles occurs in the following: Morris Zelditch, Jr., "Role Differentiation in the Nuclear Family: A Comparative Study," Chapter VI in Parsons and Bales, *op. cit.*; Fred L. Strodtbeck and Richard D. Mann, "Sex Role Differentiation in Jury Deliberations," *Sociometry*, XIX (March, 1956), 3-11; William F. Kenkel, "Influence Differentiation in Family Decision Making," *Sociology and Social Research*, XLII (September-October, 1957), 18-25; and Jerold S. Heiss, "Degree of Intimacy and Male-Female Interaction," *Sociometry*, XXV (June, 1962), 197-208.

[2] Fred L. Strodtbeck, "The Family as a Three Person Group," *American Sociological Review*, XIX (February, 1954), 23-29.

[3] J. R. Udry, H. A. Nelson, and R. Nelson, "An Empirical Investigation of Some Widely Held Beliefs about Marital Interaction," *Marriage and Family Living*, XXIII (November, 1961), 388-90.

## Convergence in Interaction Patterns

Although the sex roles may differ in the emphasis placed on instrumentality and emotionality, it appears reasonable to suggest that for any particular interaction sequence involving both sexes, some compromise or convergence will have to take place. In a male-female dyad, for the man to concentrate heavily on a task while the woman is primarily concerned with expressive acts would be both inefficient and frustrating. The man will have no aid on the task; the woman no return for her emotional investment. Rather, it seems more probable that for certain purposes the woman will

[4] Although sex-role differentiation traditionally rests upon family division of labor, such as job versus child rearing, the attempt to relate this differentiation to instrumental and emotional behavior is based upon inferences from interaction data obtained in small group research, as noted above.

shift to a more instrumental frame of reference, and for other purposes, the man to a more emotional frame of reference. The standard role differentiation is more a consequence of interaction *outside* the dyad. Here the male is more apt to have responsibilities calling for instrumentality, while the female is more apt to need expressive behaviors.

The family context is particularly conducive to convergence in interaction due to the relative freedom from surveillance of that interaction by other people.[5] While the family members may well be aware of and profess agreement with standard sex role differentiation, they may just as readily behave quite differently behind the closed doors of their home. Thus a man may express traditional masculine values to his fellow workers, concomitantly insisting that his wife is, and should be, properly feminine. Nevertheless he may be quite willing to show considerable emotion privately to his wife and expect her at times to be businesslike.

Once a convergent pattern is established between family members, it is reasonable to assume that that pattern will influence the behavior of the members toward each other even when under third-party surveillance. Rather than displaying "public" behavior completely in accord with a standard role, the members will compromise between their private convergence and the standard public role, retaining some of the advantages of each.

Assuming, then, a "public" acceptance of the traditional sex role differentiation, the following patterns are predicted.

1. Interaction in groups of strangers will show differentiation by sex; males will display greater instrumentality and less emotionality than will females.
2. Interaction in family groups will show little or no differentiation by sex.
3. Interaction in family groups when under surveillance of others, such as personnel conducting an experiment, will show a compromise between 1 and 2 above.

## Effects of Instrumentality and Emotionality on Consensus

The effects of emotionality and instrumentality on the consensus seeking process depend upon the context of the interaction. If the concept of primary group is valid, family interaction occurs in a context of emotional solidarity. Members presumably are used to, and comfortable with, considerable emotionality in their interaction with each other. A comparable emotional tone among strangers, however, is apt to be embarrassing and uncomfortable, suggesting that it would not be conducive to satisfactory interaction.

Based on the above argument, it is expected that emotionality in family interaction will enhance member satisfaction, but will decrease satisfaction in stranger interaction. Because emotionality and instrumentality are in a sense complementary behaviors, the reverse relationships should hold for the effects of instrumentality on satisfaction in the two types of groups.

The relationships of degree of agreement to emotion and task orientation are less easily hypothesized. If, as has been indicated by previous small group research, efficiency in problem solving is in some degree antithetical to personal satisfaction,[6] then predictions in-

---

[5] See William J. Goode, "A Theory of Role Strain," *American Sociological Review*, XXV (August, 1960), 483-96, for a discussion of "third party" restraints on role bargaining.

---

[6] Small group research suggests that task emphasis brings about a reduced popularity, implying less member satisfaction. See, for

volving agreement will be the reverse of those for satisfaction. That is, agreement in family groups should show positive relationship to instrumentality and negative relationship to emotionality, the opposite predictions being made for stranger interaction. On the other hand, if the total consensus process, involving both agreement and satisfaction, rests upon common interaction factors, then predictions for agreement should parallel those for satisfaction.

Specific hypotheses, assuming a consensus-seeking context, are:

4. Emotionality will be *positively* related to personal satisfaction in family groups and *negatively* related to personal satisfaction in stranger groups;
5. Instrumentality will be *negatively* related to personal satisfaction in family groups and *positively* related to personal satisfaction in stranger groups.

If satisfaction and agreement are antithetical, then:

6a. Emotionality will be *negatively* related to agreement in family groups and *positively* related to agreement in stranger groups;
7a. Instrumentality will be *positively* related to agreement in family groups and *negatively* related to agreement in stranger groups.

However, if satisfaction and agreement are common products of the same underlying factors, then:

6b. Emotionality will be *positively* related to agreement in family groups

and *negatively* related to agreement in stranger groups;
7b. Instrumentality will be *negatively* related to agreement in family groups and *positively* related to agreement in stranger groups.

One further consideration is relevant. If interaction is appropriate to the context, as outlined above, then perception by each participant of the satisfaction gained by others from the interaction should be more accurate. This assertion rests upon the assumption that more appropriate interaction requires less concern on the part of the participants with the interaction itself, hence allows greater opportunity for observing the reactions of others present. As a final hypothesis, then:

8. Perception of the satisfaction of other participants is *positively* related to emotionality in family interaction and to instrumentality in nonfamily interaction.

It should be apparent that, by definition, private family interaction cannot be observed. Thus Hypothesis 2 cannot be subjected to experimental test. The remainder of the paper will report a test of the other hypotheses presented above.

**Experimental Procedure**

Nine families, consisting of father, mother, and college-aged daughter participated in 27 experimental group discussions. All groups were triadic and all were given the problem of reaching consensus on issues of some relevance to family values or goals.[7] The first set

---

example, Slater, *op. cit.*, and Bales and Slater, *op. cit.* Also, communication channel studies indicate that maximum efficiency and maximum member satisfaction are associated with contradictory systems. See Harold J. Leavitt, "Some Effects of Certain Communication Patterns on Group Performance," *The Journal of Abnormal and Social Psychology,* XLVI (January, 1951), 38-50.

[7] One of the problems used was: "Two students marry while still in college, but want to complete their college education. Some persons feel the parents' financial responsibility ceases when the child marries, while others feel the parents should continue financial sup-

of nine triads were homogeneous regarding both age and sex; all fathers, all mothers, or all daughters. These will be called the "ad hoc" groups. The second set of groups were composed of a father, a mother, and a daughter, but not of the same family. Thus the age-sex structure of a family was present, but members were not united by bonds of affection or familial history. These will be called "structured" groups. Finally, the nine families met as families. Each of the 27 subjects experienced the three types of group in the same order; i.e., ad hoc, then structured, then family. Although there may be some learning involved in successive experimental sessions, there is no reason to assume that it would occur differently between the three age-sex categories.

Data were obtained by observers behind a one-way screen who recorded the source, direction, and nature of each act, and by post experimental questionnaires. Categories of acts were derived from the Bales system, with simplification for the purposes of the specific study. Because emotion and task orientation were the major foci of this research, only these two aspects of the interaction were recorded. However, from previous use of such recording procedures, it was felt that the absolute disjunction of emotion and task orientation which is a necessary consequence of the Bales system was unrealistic and posed difficult decisions for observers. To avoid this problem, the task-nontask dichotomy was cross classified with the trichotomy of positive,

neutral, or negative emotion, resulting in the following six categories[8]:

1. Positive emotion, Task-oriented
2. Positive emotion, Non-task-oriented
3. Neutral emotion, Task-oriented
4. Neutral emotion, Non-task-oriented
5. Negative emotion, Task-oriented
6. Negative emotion, Non-task-oriented

Six variables will be discussed in this paper, two of which are definable in terms of the six categories of acts. These are:

*Instrumentality.* The ratio of task-oriented acts to total acts initiated.
Operationally, using $n_i$ to indicate the frequency of acts in category $i$, instrumentality $= (n_1 + n_3 + n_5)/\sum_1^6 n_i$

*Emotionality.* The ratio of emotional acts, either positive or negative, to all acts initiated.
Operationally, emotionality $=$

$$(n_1 + n_2 + n_5 + n_6)/\sum_1^6 n_i$$

Two observers recorded each session. Reliability was measured by product-moment correlations between measurements obtained by the two observers at each session. As defined above, instrumentality showed .95 reliability. Observer correlation for emotionality, however, was .78. The percentage distribution of instrumental or emotional acts among the participants in a given session showed similar reliability: .95 for instrumentality and .77 for emotionality. For all data reported, the average of the two observer scores was used, decreasing the error implied by

---

port. How would you solve this situation?" By careful scheduling of problems, it was possible to ensure that (1) each subject discussed each problem once and only once, and (2) problems were equally distributed among treatments to avoid contamination of results. Analysis showed no interaction between problem and either treatment or the age-sex category of the subject.

---

[8] Although the data show a tendency for task oriented acts to be neutral and for non-task acts to have a positive emotional content, categories 1, 4, and 5, not available in Bales' system, account for approximately one-third of the observed acts.

the rather low reliability of the emotional categories.

Three of the other four variables are definable in terms of the post-experimental questionnaire. Question 1 asked: "You may or may not have agreed with the group's decision regarding the best solution for the problem you were given. Please indicate by a check mark the degree to which you agreed or disagreed: (1) Complete agreement, (2) Agreed more than disagreed, (3) Neutral, open question, undecided, (4) Disagreed more than agreed, (5) Complete disagreement." The same question was repeated with reference to each of the other two participants in turn. Question 4 dealt with satisfaction: "You may or may not have enjoyed the group's discussion. Please indicate by a check mark the degree to which you enjoyed or were dissatisfied with the discussion: (1) Enjoyed very much, (2) Enjoyed somewhat, (3) Neutral, (4) Somewhat dissatisfied or uncomfortable, (5) Very dissatisfied or uncomfortable." As with agreement, this question was repeated with reference to the other two participants. All responses were scored inversely; i.e., "complete agreement" was scored 5, "complete disagreement" was scored 1.

Agreement. The extent to which the members of a group agreed with the decision reached. Operationally this variable consists of the sum of scores on Question 1 for the group participants.

Satisfaction. The extent to which the members of a group enjoyed the group's discussion. Operationally satisfaction consists of the sum of the scores on Question 4 for the group participants.

Accuracy of Perception; Satisfaction. The extent to which group members accurately perceived other participants' satisfaction. Absolute differences were computed between a subject's own satisfaction score and that imputed to

him by each of the others. The sum of these differences constitutes perceptual error with respect to satisfaction within the group. Correlations between this sum and other variables have been reversed in sign so that the inverse of perceptual error, i.e., perceptual accuracy, will be reported.[9]

A measure equivalent to accuracy of perception of satisfaction was computed for agreement, but showed such a close relationship with agreement itself that no additional information was obtained. Therefore this variable has been omitted from the data to be presented.

Time to Consensus. The length of time, in minutes, which each group required to reach consensus.

## Results

### Interaction

The ad hoc groups provide an initial check on the first hypothesis, that men will play a more instrumental, less emotional role than will women when they are interacting with strangers. Measures of instrumentality and emotionality, as defined earlier, were obtained for each session. Averages of these measures are reported in Table 1 for the three types of ad hoc sessions. Although the differences are not gross,[10] they are in the

---

[9] Note that perceptual accuracy is not necessarily the same as empathy. As has been recognized by investigators of empathy, there is a confounding tendency for persons to attribute to the other a similarity to self, then predict for self rather than really empathize. The concern of this study was only to determine whether the prediction of other's satisfaction, regardless of its basis in empathy or in assumed similarity, was related to the conditions of interaction.

[10] By computing instrumentality and emotionality as averages of group measurements, then using a t-test, only the difference between fathers' and mothers' emotionality at

TABLE 1 Interaction in Ad Hoc Groups: Mean Instrumentality and Emotionality by Type of Group[a]

| Type of session | Instrumentality | Emotionality |
|---|---|---|
| Father sessions | 70 | 22 |
| Mother sessions | 61 | 31 |
| Daughter sessions | 65 | 28 |

[a] Acts classified as either positively or negatively emotional are represented in the "Emotional" column. The classification scheme does not make task behavior and emotional behavior mutually exclusive nor are they exhaustive. Thus the rows do not sum to 100%.

expected direction. Males, when interacting with strangers, are both more instrumental and less emotional than are either set of females.

In the structured sessions, if the stereotypic sex role is considered appropriate for family interaction, but no convergence has occurred because "real" families are not involved, the men should account for more than one third of the task behavior while each of the women provides more than one third of the emotion present. Table 2 shows that the expectation is in general fulfilled. Note that mothers tend to play an intermediate role, providing approximately their share of task-oriented behavior (not significantly less than fathers) as well as a significantly high proportion of emotion. Daughters show significantly less task behavior and more emotion, as predicted. Both the ad hoc and the structured groups, then, display behavior essentially in accordance with Hypothesis 1.

tains statistical significance at the .05 level. This results largely from the fact of only three father, three mother, and three daughter sessions to contribute to the means shown. If all acts initiated in all groups of a given type are combined, providing one percentage for each age-sex category, denominators exceed 1,000 acts, and the differences between types of sessions are highly significant. Combining of groups in this manner seems inappropriate, however, since considerable variation between groups of a given type occurred. Data in Table 1, then, are suggestive, but not conclusive.

Subjects in a laboratory are, of course, aware of some surveillance. According to Hypothesis 3, interaction of the family groups should be a compromise between the ad hoc pattern and an essentially equal sharing of task and emotion. Again, Table 2 shows that, regarding instrumental behavior, Hypothesis 3 is substantiated. The divergence between fathers and daughters has been cut in half, while mothers retained their "equal share" position. Although fathers had displayed significantly greater task emphasis than daughters in structured groups, no significant differences appear in family task distribution.

In the emotion sphere, results are less clear. Fathers do show a slight increase in emotion but there is a switch between mothers and daughters, the latter remaining significantly higher than fathers in this sphere. While this switch is not directly relevant to Hypothesis 3, it implies a somewhat more complex problem concerning expressiveness in the family.

One possible difficulty with the data of Table 2 is the fact that the proportion of total group task behavior or emotional behavior initiated by an individual is partially dependent upon his overall rate of initiation. Thus a high initiator who is 50 per cent task oriented may contribute more instrumentality than a low initiator who is 75 per cent task oriented. In order to explore role differentiation further, the

TABLE 2 Mean Percentage Distribution of Task and Emotional Behavior[a]

| Family member | Structured groups | | Family groups | |
| --- | --- | --- | --- | --- |
| | Task behavior | Emotional behavior | Task behavior | Emotional behavior |
| Fathers | 40 | 24 | 36 | 26 |
| Mothers | 34 | 41 | 34 | 32 |
| Daughters | 26 | 35 | 30 | 42 |
| | 100 | 100 | 100 | 100 |

| Hypothesis: | Decision at .05 level: | Hypothesis: | Decision at .05 level: |
| --- | --- | --- | --- |
| Task | | Task | |
| F > M | reject | F = M | accept |
| F > D | accept | F = D | accept |
| Emotional | | Emotional | |
| F < M | accept | F = M | accept |
| F < D | accept | F = D | reject |

[a] The percentages in this table cannot be compared with those in Table 1, since Table 1 shows the proportion of all acts which were of a given type, whereas Table 2 shows the distribution of a given type of act among subjects. With each individual's proportion of the instrumental or emotional behavior in a given session treated as a single observation, means were computed across the nine fathers, nine mothers, and nine daughters. Because the scores derived from a given session must sum to unity, these means are dependent in a somewhat complex manner. To avoid three way dependency, t-tests were computed between pairs of means. Inferences drawn therefrom are subject to some qualification.

overall rate of initiation of each individual was used as a base line to determine whether he overemphasized or underemphasized a particular type of behavior. Two sets of ratios were computed. The numerators were, respectively, the proportion of total group task behavior initiated by the individual and the proportion of total group positive emotion[11] initiated by the individual. The denominator in both cases was the proportion of total group behavior initiated by the individual. A ratio in excess of 1.00 indicates overemphasis on the specified type of behavior, whereas a ratio less than 1.00

---

[11] Only positive emotion has been used here for two reasons. First, it comprises the major portion of emotion, and is more reliable than total emotion. Secondly, the role differentiation being tested is meaningful only if the woman emphasizes positive emotion, not just emotion in general.

indicates underemphasis. All ratios have been multiplied by 100 for convenience.

As Table 3 indicates, structured sessions show consistent and, for emotion, significant differentiation by sex, with no difference between mothers and daughters either in the task or the emotional area. Family sessions, on the other hand, show a somewhat different picture. Father's ratios indicate, as before, a clear task emphasis. Daughters emphasize task even less than before, with no change in emotional emphasis. Mothers provide the most interesting difference from structured sessions: in five out of nine times their ratios *exceed* 100 for both task and emotion. It appears that mothers and daughters play comparable roles with strangers. But when interaction takes place within the family, mothers "take over" a greater share of the task area

TABLE 3    Task and Emotion Rates Based on Initiation Rate[a]

| Family Member | Number of sessions | | | |
| --- | --- | --- | --- | --- |
| | Task rate | | Emotion rate | |
| | > 100 | ≤ 100 | > 100 | ≤ 100 |
| **Structured groups** | | | | |
| Father | 6 | 3 | 1 | 8 |
| Mother | 3 | 6 | 7 | 2 |
| Daughter | 3 | 6 | 7 | 2 |
| | $\chi^2 = 2.7, p > .05$ | | $\chi^2 = 10.8, p < .01$ | |
| **Family groups** | | | | |
| | Task rate | | Emotion rate | |
| | > 100 | ≤ 100 | > 100 | ≤ 100 |
| Father | 6 | 3 | 1 | 8 |
| Mother | 5 | 4 | 5 | 4 |
| Daughter | 1 | 8 | 7 | 2 |
| | $\chi^2 = 6.3, p < .05$ | | $\chi^2 = 8.3, p < .05$ | |

[a] The ratios obtained for any three group members are interdependent only to the extent that any dichotomizing procedure requires algebraic balance around a cutting line; in this case, a ratio of 100. Thus any two members can be said to be independent, with the third dependent upon them and the relevant totals. This is precisely the "degrees of freedom" concept incorporated into $\chi^2$.

with a somewhat lessened (but still important) emotional emphasis. Concomitantly, daughters "back out" of the task sphere even more than they did in role playing sessions, producing a significant age differentiation in contrast to the sex differentiation of structured groups.

Another way of demonstrating the relationship being emphasized is to combine data in Table 3 alternately by sex or by age so as to produce sets of 2 × 2 tables which indicate the relative importance of sex and age in the distribution of task and emotional behavior. If $Q$ is used as an index, the association between sex and, respectively, task and emotional behavior in structured groups is .60 and .93. Age, however, is associated with type of behavior to a considerably lesser degree, the indices being .33 and .63 respectively for task and emotion. Thus sex is a notably more important variable of differentiation for structured groups.

When the same analysis is applied to family data, the association of sex with task and emotion is .60 and .80, respectively. This is similar to associations found in the structured data. Age, however, shows associations of .85 for task and .75 for emotion. Age in family sessions is a more important variable than sex for the distribution of task behavior, and nearly as important as sex for the distribution of emotion. Thus the switch in emotion between mothers and daughters shown in Table 2 becomes clearer.

In the family, apparently, mothers attempt a dual role, sharing the task sphere with their husbands, and the emotional sphere with their daughters. It can be suggested from the data presented that bridging the gap between the traditional role emphases of male and female is acceptable when the female shares the task orientation of her husband. However, at least where daughters are present, the husband does not move equally in the direction of female emotionality.

In general the present data give reason to doubt that the task leader *vs.* emotional leader sex differentiation provides an accurate description of the actual *interaction* of family members.

*Consensus.* The remaining analysis concerns the effects of instrumentality and emotionality on the consensus process. The six variables were factor analyzed for the three types of session. For each type of group, an initial centroid solution was obtained, then orthogonally rotated so that the three major factors were as nearly comparable as possible from group to group.[12] Factor I has been labeled "Agreement" to reflect the fact that agreement has the highest loading on this factor for all groups. For a similar reason, Factor II is labelled "Satisfaction." Factor III is difficult to name because loadings for no single variable or set of variables are consistent across groups. Therefore the label "Residual" is applied to indicate that the groups vary in what remains after the first two factors are extracted. Table 4 shows the loadings of the variables by type of session for each of the three factors.

Several aspects of the factor analysis are worth noting. *First,* simultaneous maximization of agreement and satisfaction poses a contradiction in all three types of group. In family groups,

if the interaction is highly task oriented, agreement is greater but satisfaction diminishes somewhat. As interaction becomes more emotional (presumably subject to a point of diminishing returns) satisfaction increases greatly, but at the expense of agreement. Although this particular contradiction disappears for non-family groups, a parallel problem exists concerning the time taken to reach consensus. Whereas a short discussion is associated with agreement, a longer one is associated with satisfaction. Thus a common problem exists for each of these types of group, but for somewhat different reasons. In accordance with the earlier discussion, the first form of hypotheses 6 and 7 should be used; i.e., hypotheses 6a and 7a are implied by the contradiction of satisfaction and consensus.

*Second,* the effects of instrumentality and emotionality on family agreement and satisfaction are, as expected, quite different from the effects of those variables in ad hoc and structured groups. Considering satisfaction first, specific findings are as follows:

1. Emotionality is moderately *positively* related to satisfaction in ad hoc groups and *not* related to satisfaction in structured groups, but is *strongly positively* related to family satisfaction. This finding supports the hypothesized effect of emotionality on family satisfaction, but does not support the expectation for stranger groups. Hypothesis 4 is thus partially validated.

2. Instrumentality is *not* related to satisfaction in ad hoc groups, is moderately *positively* related to satisfaction in structured groups, and is moderately *negatively* related to family satisfaction. This finding in general supports Hypothesis 5.

3. With regard to agreement, the factor analysis indicates that: Emotionality is *positively* related to agreement in non-family groups but *negatively* related to agreement in family groups.

---

[12] For centroid and rotation procedures, see any standard reference on factor analysis, such as Karl J. Holzinger and Harry H. Harman, *Factor Analysis* (Chicago: Univ. of Chicago Press, 1941).

TABLE 4    Combined Factor Solutions for Three Types of Groups[a]

| | Factors | | | | | | | | |
| | I: "Agreement" | | | II: "Satisfaction" | | | III: "Residual" | | |
| Variables | Ad hoc groups | Structured groups | Family groups | Ad hoc groups | Structured groups | Family groups | Ad hoc groups | Structured groups | Family groups |
|---|---|---|---|---|---|---|---|---|---|
| Agreement | .93 | 1.00 | 1.00 | — | — | — | — | — | — |
| Consensus time | −.69 | −.39 | −.82 | .21 | .30 | — | −.57 | −.40 | −.25 |
| Satisfaction | — | .21 | .53 | .69 | .95 | .80 | .22 | — | — |
| Emotionality | .36 | .43 | −.46 | .33 | — | .82 | .72 | .38 | .24 |
| Instrumentality | — | — | .50 | — | .28 | −.26 | −.27 | .69 | −.67 |
| Perception of satisfaction | — | .66 | .50 | — | .63 | — | .71 | .33 | .69 |

[a] Loadings of less than .20 have been omitted.

This finding directly supports Hypothesis 6a.

4. Instrumentality is *not* related to agreement in non-family groups, but is *positively* related to family agreement. This finding in part supports Hypothesis 7a.

Clearly, both task orientation and emotion have different implications for non-family groups than they have for the family.

It should be noted that family loadings on Factor I are of considerable magnitude for all six variables. On the other hand, structure groups show little or no relationship between agreement and either satisfaction or instrumentality, and ad hoc groups display these two zero relationships and a further lack of relationship between agreement and perception of satisfaction. It appears that the process of reaching agreement is relatively explicit in stranger groups and, conversely, relatively inclusive in family groups. If this is generally valid, family consensus involves more than those facets which would be found in the laboratory study of ad hoc groups. The consensus process in family interaction, then, is a special case deserving research attention.

The implications of the time it takes to reach consensus seem to be similar for all three types of group. In each case, time is negatively related to agreement, although to varying degrees, is moderately related to satisfaction except in the family, and is negatively related to Factor III. Perhaps the strong relationship between emotion and satisfaction in family groups accounts for the reduced importance of discussion time in this instance.

The factor matrix is less useful for testing Hypothesis 8 than are the simple correlations between perception of satisfaction and instrumentality and emotionality. These correlations show that perception of satisfaction is, as hypothesized, negatively related to instrumentality in the family ($-.31$) and positively related to instrumentality in structured groups ($+.40$). Contrary to expectation, there is a small negative relationship with instrumentality in ad hoc groups ($-.13$). Findings regarding emotionality are essentially the reverse of those predicted. For family, structured, and ad hoc groups, respectively, the correlations are $-.07$, $+.47$, and $+.55$. The family correlation is sufficiently low to suggest no relationship, but this is still an unexpected result for which no adequate explanation can be offered from the present data. In all three types of group, accurate perception appears to require adequate time; the correlations with consensus time are $-.81$, $-.40$, and $-.61$.

## Summary

Eight hypotheses have been stated, seven of which were subjected to an exploratory test. As a consequence of the data reported, the following tentative conclusions are reached.

1. The traditional male role (instrumental, non-emotional behavior) as well as the traditional female role (emotional, non-task behavior) appear when interaction takes place among strangers. These emphases tend to disappear when subjects interact with their own families. Particularly is this true for instrumentality, because of a dual role for mothers.

2. The satisfaction of family members is positively related to emotionality and negatively related to instrumentality as hypothesized. Conversely, instrumentality is either negatively related to or irrelevant for satisfaction in stranger interaction. Contrary to prediction, however, emotionality is, in ad hoc groups, at least, positively related to satisfaction.

3. For all types of group, agreement and

satisfaction appear somewhat contradictory. Consequently, agreement in family interaction is negatively related to emotionality and positively related to instrumentality. For non-family sessions, agreement is positively related to emotionality but unrelated to instrumentality.

In general, the relevance of instrumentality and emotionality is quite different for family interaction than for interaction among strangers. This major finding poses new problems for the theoretical integration of family research with that based on ad hoc experimental groups. Such integration is possible only through a recognition of the fact that the context of interaction with strangers places a meaning on particular acts which is different from the meaning of those acts within the family group.

# hapter twelve

## Group Structure and the Newcomer

THEODORE M. MILLS et al.

What determines how the newcomer ecomes related to the group? In this aper we report results of an experimental test of some factors and suggest heir implication for the sociology of mall groups.

The occurrence of the newcomer is requent and familiar: the new neighor, the recruit, the immigrant, the reshman, the trainee, the new executive, etc. When we include the new-

Reprinted from Theodore M. Mills in collaboration with Anders Gauslaa, Yngvar ,øchen, Thomas Mathiesen, Guttorm Nør-tebø, Odd Ramsøy, Sigurd Skirbekk, Olav kårdal, Liv Torgersen, Birger Tysnes, and )rjar Øyen, *Group Structure and the New-omer: An Experimental Study of Group Ex-ansion* (Oslo: Universitetsforlaget, 1957), by ermission of Universitetsforlaget. Copyright ⊇ 1957 by The Norwegian Research Council or Science and the Humanities. The project nd the report are the joint effort of a semiar in the study of small groups, at the nstitut for Sosiologi, University of Oslo, Norway, during 1955-56.

born, it is clear that continued social existence is impossible without newcomers, and without effective processes of amalgamation. The arrival of an outsider changes the situation both for him and for the group, setting in motion reactions to the change and processes of mutual adjustment which may or may not be satisfactory in their outcome. In any concrete case these processes are probably complex, being subject to the interaction of a number of variables, such as age of the group, its function in the larger society, its relation to other groups, its organization, how members in the initial group feel about one another, what the new person seems like, or is like, why he comes, etc. One aim in studying these processes is to reduce the problem to simpler terms. Another is to explore group properties. Often, through analysis of reactions to change, properties inherent but not evident in the group—and in this case in the newcomer—may be brought to light.

Some discussions of the question

emphasize the point of view of the newcomer, such as Simmel's description of the stranger[1] and Schuetz's analysis of strains as the stranger becomes more or less integrated in a society.[2] In another context Simmel identifies chiefly with members of the group as he describes the likely reactions of an intimate pair to the appearance of a third party[3]; and von Wiese takes essentially the same point of view in his analysis of the expansion of the triad.[4] Freud and subsequent psychoanalytic writers write from within the group when they trace the impact of the newborn child upon the older child and upon the father.[5] We take the theoretical position—possibly shared by these writers—that the process is the result of interaction between factors associated with the group and factors associated with the newcomer. However, in our experiment we test only one set of factors—those associated with the structure of the original group.

Our questions are: How does the structure of relationships in the initial group affect the relationship that develops between the newcomer and group members? And how does the position of a given member in the structure affect his relationship with the newcomer? Actually, our experimental question is even more limited than this. Since we vary group structure and a given person's place in it by using two role-players interacting with a "naive" subject, our dependent variable is the newcomer's relationship with the single "naive" subject rather than with all group members. Moreover, we select only one characteristic of group structure (but we believe a basically important one); namely, the degree to which each of the three members accepts, and feels accepted by, the others. This characteristic we call emotional integration, or, for brevity, integration. The single characteristic of a person's position is the degree to which he feels accepted or rejected by other group members. As we test these variables, other important factors mentioned above are held as nearly constant from group to group as possible.

## The First Hypothesis

The first hypothesis and its alternative are extrapolations from Freud, and from Simmel and von Wiese, respectively. From their discussions of the family and two and three person groups, we derive hypotheses which may hold for a wider variety of situations, including small groups in a laboratory. Needless to say, since we do not test their propositions in their settings we intend neither to prove nor to disprove them. Instead, we test how well the generalizations, rooted in their discussions but made by us, hold in the laboratory.

Freud and subsequent psychoanalytical investigators have found that one of the more significant events in the life cycle is the arrival of a new brother or sister. Hostility toward the infant and a wish to throw him out is often found in the older child. Hostility on this occasion may be a universal reaction,[6] though its intensity and the way

---

[1] G. Simmel, "Der Fremde," in *Soziolgie*, 2nd printing (München and Leipzig: Verlag von Dunker und Humblot, 1922), pp. 509-12. See also K. H. Wolff, ed., *The Sociology of Georg Simmel* (New York: The Free Press, 1950), pp. 402-8.

[2] A. Schuetz, "The Stranger," *The American Journal of Sociology*, XLIX, No. 6 (May, 1944), 499-507.

[3] *Op. cit.*, Chaps. 2, 3, and 4.

[4] Leopold von Wiese and Howard Becker, *Systematic Sociology; on the Basis of the Beziehungsiehre and Gebildelehre of Leopold von Wiese* (New York: Wiley, 1932), pp. 525-27.

[5] Sigmund Freud, *The Complete Psychological Works of Sigmund Freud*, ed. James Strachey, Vol. XVII (London: Hogarth, 1955).

---

[6] The connection between this phenom-

it is handled probably vary considerably. Adding the assumption, which we believe is consistent with psychoanalytical tradition, that the child who feels relatively secure in his emotional attachments to father and mother will feel less hostility than one who feels less secure, our first hypothesis is:

**A member of the initial group who feels accepted by others is more likely to develop a congenial relationship with a newcomer than a member who feels isolated from and rejected by the others.**

The alternative to this hypothesis derives from Simmel's and von Wiese's discussions of the expansion of the dyad and triad. Simmel argues that two people who have an intimate and warm relationship will, when confronted with a newcomer, feel and express hostility toward him and that he will reciprocate. In this case, contrary to the first hypothesis, rejection is from secure members. Presumably, rejection is more likely than had the pair been in conflict.

Von Wiese utilizes Simmel's principle in his discussion of the expansion of the triad: "What is really normal (in terms of frequency distribution) [for the triad] is that two of the members are more intimate with each other than they are with the third, and . . . frequently . . . two members become allies . . . and . . . relegate the third to an inferior rank." "In many instances the underprivileged member seeks to strengthen his position by forming alliances outside the triad. He . . . finds a new partner, so that *a new pair is formed*. The triadic group

has been transmuted into a double pair. . . ."[7]

If a genuine interacting unit of four persons is formed by this expansion, the double pair pattern forms only because the accepted members have rejected the newcomer, the isolated member has welcomed him and in each case the new member has reciprocated. This view is based on Simmel's and von Wiese's principles, and it constitutes our alternative to the first hypothesis.

## The Second Hypothesis

The second hypothesis (and its alternative) concerns the total patterns of emotional ties in the group. It is based upon the premise that a fully integrated group—where emotional ties between all members are positive—has richer resources for handling successfully the problem of integration entailed in assimilating a new member than do groups which already have within them negative relationships, or from one point of view, unresolved problems of integration.[8] Our hypothesis is that:

**The degree of integration in the initial group—the proportion of emotional ties that are congenial—increases the probability that a positive relationship will be established with the newcomer.**

The alternative to this hypothesis derives from the common observation that a close "in-group" resents an intruder—like Simmel's intimate pair, and like Becker's folk society which he says has ". . . self-imposed mental and

---

enon and Miller and Dollard's frustration-aggression hypothesis depends, of course, upon the nature of the attachment of older child to the mother. See J. Dollard *et al.*, *Frustration and Aggression* (New Haven: Yale Univ. Press, 1939).

[7] Von Wiese and Becker, *op. cit.*, pp. 525-27.

[8] Though this proposition is not made in Talcott Parsons, Robert F. Bales, and Edward Shils' *Working Papers in the Theory of Action* (New York: The Free Press, 1935), it is based upon their argument.

social isolation vis-à-vis the stranger; there is a deep dislike of the person who concretely represents the forces of change."[9] This alternative, then, is that full integration decreases the probability that a positive relationship will be developed with the newcomer; partial integration—where at least one member is isolated—increases it.

In summary, according to the first and second hypotheses, we expect the warmest relationship to develop when the original members are friendly, the coolest when they are in conflict. In partially integrated groups, we expect a warm relationship to develop between the newcomer and those who already have friends in the group, and a cool relationship to develop in respect to those who are initially rejected. According to the alternative hypotheses, on the other hand, we expect the warmest relationship to develop with a rejected member and the coolest to occur when the initial members are friendly.

In the next section we describe how the newcomer is introduced into the group, how we use role-playing to vary systematically feelings of acceptance and group integration, and how we match the first subject and the newcomer on certain characteristics. We report the effectiveness of the role-playing, present our measures and our experimental design and show how we test the hypotheses.

**Procedures**

*Introducing the New Member*

A visitor arriving before a typical experimental session would find six members of the research team assembled in a small observation room. Two are sitting close to a one-way screen preparing sheets for scoring behavior according to Bales' technique,[10] one tests the tape recorder, one—the experimenter—readies instructions, questionnaires, etc., and the other two check each other on details, for they have just changed from civilian clothes to military uniforms. When all is ready, these, the role-players, leave by the back door and are followed later by the experimenter. Lights are dimmed; visible through the screen is a larger room with a table, four chairs, several cabinets and a microphone in the center of the table.

The experimenter enters with three soldiers—the disguised role-players and a naive subject. He explains the aim of investigating how groups solve problems, explains the one-way screen, the observers, the tape-recorder, the microphone and what is expected of them. There will be two tasks, each lasting 25 minutes; for the first there will be three members of the group and for the second, four. The task is to tell a single dramatic story weaving together three pictures,[11] which will be shown for 20 seconds. The group is to work together on the story. An award will be given to the group producing the best drama. After questions and clarification the discussion begins.

In observing the group processes carefully, the visitor would become aware of the gradual appearance and the eventual crystallization of a definite pattern of relationships between the three men. He may find the subject and one role-player interpreting

[9] Howard Becker, *Through Values to Social Interpretation* (Durham, N.C.: Duke Univ. Press, 1950), p. 50.

[10] Robert F. Bales, *Interaction Process Analysis* (Reading, Mass.: Addison-Wesley, 1950).

[11] H. A. Murray, *Thematic Apperception Test* (Cambridge, Mass.: Harvard Univ. Press, 1943).

the pictures in very much the same way, developing a dramatic theme which seems satisfying to both. The other role-player sees something else in the pictures, wanting some other hero, some other ending. By the time the task is over and the members have had a five-minute break for informal talk, the visitor would see that what was agreement on the story has deepened to personal warmth and that disagreement has grown to dislike. In this the visitor finds the end-product of our attempt to establish, artificially but convincingly, a particular group structure in which the naive subject has a given degree of acceptance and the group as a whole is integrated at a specified level. As explained below, the visitor would find other structures on other occasions.

Following the five-minute break, the men fill out questionnaires. From the subject's answers we learn whether his perceptions and feelings correspond to the desired pattern and we learn how he feels about a new member joining the group. In the meantime, the newcomer, having been introduced to the others, reports in writing how he feels about entering an established group.

The second task session begins. Explanations and instructions are repeated and the group starts working on the second story about another set of pictures. For about five minutes the role-players maintain attitudes and types of behavior that re-affirm the relationships of the first session. Gradually they withdraw so that whatever relationship seems natural between the first subject and the newcomer may develop. Withdrawal is only partial, for they return act for act, agreement for agreements, etc.

When time is up, the experimenter asks the role-players to retire to another room—the withdrawal of the two role-players is of course made to appear incidental—and gives the subjects questionnaires much like those filled out earlier by the first subject.

Although the experimental run is over, there remains the critically important "cooling-out" period, during which the subjects are made fully aware of the experimental procedures and are encouraged to release whatever tension this new view generates. Calling in the role-players, the experimenter explains the precise purpose and methods of the study. Role-players identify themselves, explain their roles, how their behavior fits the design of the experiment and how on other occasions they act different roles. They encourage the subjects to re-live with them from this new viewpoint the important events in the discussions. The "cooling-out" process differs from subject to subject and may take from 15 to 45 minutes. The subjects are paid and asked not to discuss their experience with anyone. Our brief report cannot go into the complications and functions of "cooling-out"—functions for the role-players, the research team as a whole, as well as for the subjects—we simply note that one of our chief aims is to make perfectly clear why deception is used and to show precisely where it is and is not used. The other is to permit catharsis, especially for the subjects.

*Establishing Differences beween Groups in Personal Acceptance and in Group Integration*

Our visitor found one pattern in the first session. It is through the use of four patterns that we control the two independent variables.

In Pattern I, which we call the *all positive*, the role-players create as nearly as possible a feeling of complete acceptance between all three. How the subject feels about the pictures, what he wants and needs the story to be, becomes the baseline for their reactions, their comments and their suggestions.

From the indications he gives, they build up the group's culture so that it mirrors his attitudes, values and preferences. They move from this level to personal warmth, regardless of what is being talked about. The subject is fully accepted in a well-integrated group.

In Pattern II—the *all negative*—the role-players develop a disorganized group, where no two are in agreement and where in time there is antipathy between all. Natural idiosyncrasies in projections are amplified; whatever baseline for agreement there might have been is erased; and compromise or submission is discouraged. From this state of confusion and failure in the task they shift to deeper hostility in the subsequent informal period. The subject, like the others, is rejected in a disintegrated group.

In the other two patterns, two members are in coalition against the third. In Pattern III the subject is *out* of the coalition (rejected); in IV he is *in* the coalition (accepted). Both patterns are partially integrated. Our hypothetical visitor saw Pattern IV.

To summarize, role-players create four types of patterns in the first session: Two in which the subject is *accepted*; two in which he is *rejected*. One is *fully* integrated, one *malintegrated* and two are *partially* integrated.

### Effectiveness of Role-Playing

The role-players were effective in almost three-fourths of their attempts (27 out of 38). They trained for two and a half months. They practiced upon themselves and upon preliminary subjects, each player taking all roles in all patterns, learning to work with partners, learning the behavior that strengthens or weakens a pattern and gaining skill in adapting quickly to different types of subjects. In spite of training, however, one-fourth of the attempts were failures—a proportion we have come to expect. When the role-playing is beyond the superficial level, actor's feelings are directly involved. Disturbances of the day or session before may press to be played out during the session, altering or destroying the desired pattern. The actor may really like the subject to whom he must be hostile, or vice versa. Basically compatible partners may on occasions be unable to make "hostility" convincing, or players with unresolved problems between them may find cooperation even in being hostile too much to achieve. Moreover, feelings of guilt associated with deception and fear of omnipotence associated with success, when out of perspective, often press against effective assumption of the role. These and other problems lead us to expect a number of failures in any long series of runs.

They also make it advisable to decide before the analysis of results what constitutes a satisfactory run. For inclusion as an experimental case, we require that the desired pattern be unquestionably apparent in *both* the observers' records of supportive and non-supportive behavior during the session and in the subject's picture of the emotional ties between the three members.

The observers' records are summarized by calculating the *rate of support* from each member to the others. Based upon the interaction process analysis scores, it is defined and calculated as follows:

The rate at which member 1 supports member 2, for example, is given by the equation:

$$\text{Rate}_{12} = \frac{A_{12} - D_{12}}{B_2 + C_2}$$

Where $A_{12}$ is the frequency of supportive acts (Bales' categories 1, 2 and 3) initiated by member 1 and directed to member 2.

$D_{12}$ is the frequency of non-support ive acts (categories 10, 11 and 12) initiated by member 1 and directed to member 2.

$B_2$ and $C_2$ combined is the frequency of instrumental acts (categories 4 through 9) initiated by member 2 regardless of their recipients.

As an illustration, the rates for one of the experimental groups are as follows (case no. 44, the subject-*in*-coalition pattern):

|   | Support to | | |
|---|---|---|---|
| Support from | Subject | Ally | Isolate |
| Subject | — | .38 | −.16 |
| Ally | .36 | — | −.42 |
| Isolate | −.34 | −.39 | — |

The second basis for assessing the role-playing is, as we have said, the subject's picture of the emotional ties between members which is obtained from his answer to this question[12]:

Sometimes people agree with each other but at the same time they may not like each other. In other cases people may disagree, yet like each other. We would like to know how the members of your group liked each other.

You will be given detailed instructions by the experimenter. He will tell you how to use the following scale:
−3 disliked him strongly
−2 disliked him somewhat
−1 disliked him more than liked him
1 liked him more than disliked him
2 liked him somewhat
3 liked him very much.

(The experimenter explains how to use the scale in completing the following matrix):

---

[12] The question is a modification of Tagiuri's relational analysis; see R. Tagiuri, "Relational Analysis: An Extension of Sociometric Method with Emphasis upon Social Perception," *Sociometry*, XV (1952), 91-104.

|   | A | B | C |
|---|---|---|---|
| Person A[a] likes/dislikes | — | 3 | −2 |
| Person B likes/dislikes | 3 | — | −3 |
| Person C likes/dislikes | −3 | −3 | — |

[a] A is subject, B is ally, and C is isolate in this particular case.

The subject's answers from case no. 44 are inserted for illustration. From the support rates described above and the subject's assessment of who likes whom it is apparent that case no. 44 is fully acceptable. Overt interaction shows the two-against-one pattern; the subject's feelings toward others and his perceptions of how they feel, reflect it perfectly.

A total of 38 sessions were run. Our design has 8 cells; four patterns times two sets of role-players. Though 27 of the 38 sessions met our criteria, their distribution was uneven so that one cell had only two satisfactory cases. Since our supply of subjects was exhausted, we accepted one case that failed to meet all the criteria in order to have three cases in each cell, or a total of 24 experimental cases. The average support rates for these are shown in Table 1; and, the average "liking" ratings are shown in Table 2. Examination of the support rates shows that the desired patterns are evident in all sets of cases. The same is true for "liking." We believe we have four distinctly different types of structures which vary in the degree to which the subject is accepted and in the degree of group integration. Moreover, we are convinced that the subjects perceive and act according to the desired patterns.

## How First Subject and Newcomer Are Matched

In our design the purpose in matching subjects is to reduce the between-persons and between-groups error due

TABLE 1 Average Support Rates during First Sessions:
Best Six Sessions in Each Pattern

| | | Who supports whom[a] | | | | | |
|---|---|---|---|---|---|---|---|
| Pattern | | $S–R_1$ | $S–R_2$ | $R_1–S$ | $R_1–R_2$ | $R_2–S$ | $R_2–R_1$ |
| I | All Positive | .24 | .21 | **.30** | **.25** | **.26** | .16 |
| II | All Negative | —.02 | —.16 | —.28 | —.35 | —.35 | —.45 |
| III | S *Out of* Coalition | —.03 | —.06 | —.19 | **.37** | —.45 | **.33** |
| IV | S *In* Coalition | **.32** | —.11 | **.39** | —.30 | —.31 | —.24 |

[a] S is subject; $R_1$ is first role-player, and $R_2$ is second role-player. Where the support rate should be high, the figure is in boldface.

TABLE 2 Average Ratings by the Subject of Who Likes Whom:
Best Six Sessions in Each Pattern

| | | Who likes whom[a] | | | | | |
|---|---|---|---|---|---|---|---|
| Pattern | | $S–R_1$ | $S–R_2$ | $R_1–S$ | $R_1–R_2$ | $R_2–S$ | $R_2–R_1$ |
| I | All Positive | **2.3** | **2.7** | **2.0** | **2.0** | **2.2** | **2.5** |
| II | All Negative | —1.3 | —0.2 | —1.8 | —1.8 | —1.7 | —1.2 |
| III | S *Out of* Coalition | **1.3** | **1.2** | —1.0 | **2.8** | —0.2 | **2.8** |
| IV | S *In* Coalition | **2.5** | —0.3 | **1.8** | —1.5 | —0.8 | —1.7 |

[a] For meanings of S and R, see Table 1. When ratings should be high, the figure is in boldface.

to personality and social factors. First subject and newcomer are matched on sex, age, current role in the Norwegian society and on basic tendencies in interacting with others, as measured by Schutz's FIRO test.[13]

Schutz's test was given to 539 Norwegian army recruits who had been in the service from one to four months. Using scores from five Guttman scales, Schutz classifies a respondent as *personal, counter-personal* or *over-personal*. Using scores from three other scales, he classifies him as *counter-dependent* or *dependent*. By personal he means that the person has no deep-seated anxiety about being accepted by others; by counter-personal, that he does and that he handles it by keeping others enough at a distance so that they have little opportunity for rejecting him; by over-personal he means that the person has anxiety and that he manages it by closely engaging others. By independent he means that the person has no basic conflict concerning authority figures or in assuming an authority role; by counter-dependent, that he does and that he tends to attack authority or authorized rules; by dependent, that he has conflict and that he handles it by being overly submissive to authority and to rules, depending more upon them than upon himself. Schutz's test also classifies individuals on *assertiveness*, from low to high.

On personal-ness and on dependence, the sample of 539 subjects are classed as shown in Table 3. Only those individuals classed as personal and dependent were used as experimental subjects (figure in italics). Par

---

[13] William C. Schutz, *FIRO: A Three-Dimensional Theory of Interpersonal Behavior* (New York: Holt, Rinehart & Winston, 1958).

TABLE 3    Selected Results of FIRO Test: 539 Subjects

| Dependence | Personal-ness | | | | |
| --- | --- | --- | --- | --- | --- |
| | Counter-personal | Personal | Over-personal | Uncertain | Total |
| Counter-dependent | 25 | 29 | 17 | 33 | 104 |
| Dependent | 45 | 101 | 35 | 146 | 327 |
| Uncertain | 19 | 31 | 16 | 42 | 108 |
| Total | 89 | 161 | 68 | 221 | 539 |

ticular pairs of subjects were, in addition, matched on assertiveness. Later in the experimental run, but not systematically, pairs were also matched on the linguistic region of their home residence, and subjects very low on assertiveness and intelligence (data from army records) were eliminated. Members in a given pair were stationed at different training camps, there being two widely separated ones in the Oslo area.

## Measures of the Dependent Variable

The relationship between first subject and newcomer is considered to approach full congeniality when there is positive anticipation by the first subject, active and supportive behavior while working together and while being "free" together, and, finally, mutual liking of one another. We shall describe our measures of these characteristics in detail.

*Anticipated Value.* Immediately after being introduced to the newcomer the first subject is asked to reply to the following question:

"Another member joins the group. How will his arrival alter the possibility of your ideas and opinions being incorporated into the final group decision?
1. Greatly decrease the chances
2. Decrease them somewhat
3. Increase them somewhat
4. Greatly increase the chances"

From number one through number four, the answers are scored: −2, −1, +1 and +2.

*Behavior in a Working Group.* For this we take two measures during the second session: a) the rate of interaction between subjects (as the inverse of avoidance) and b) mutual support between them. Both are derived from interaction process analysis scores. The first is the average number of acts directed toward one another divided by the average initiations by all members.[14] The second is the average support rate between the two subjects which is explained above.[15]

---

[14] This ratio is used to offset any pace-setting tendencies the role-players might have had.

[15] Two reliability tests were made between interaction process analysis observers. The first was done on the raw frequency of acts of a given category originating from a given member and directed toward another given member during the discussion period. Scores were plotted on Mosteller-Tukey binomial probability paper. For 10 sessions selected at random we found that agreement between scorers could be entirely due to chance. This poor reliability on raw scores is due chiefly to the fact that one observer tallied more scores in all categories than the other.

In the second test we correlated the support rates. Since the rate is a ratio of several sets of a single observer's scores it is less affected by total number of scores. The product-moment correlation coefficient for 96 support rates from 10 sessions selected at random is +.69. With this degree of agreement, we consider the average between the rates of the two observers a good estimate of supportive behavior in the groups.

TABLE 4    Experimental Design

| Pattern during first session | Teams of role-players | |
| | A | B |
| --- | --- | --- |
| I  All Positive | case  1 | case  4 |
|    Subject accepted; | 2 | 5 |
|    group fully integrated | 3 | 6 |
| II  All Negative | 7 | 10 |
|    Subjects rejected; | 8 | 11 |
|    group malintegrated | 9 | 12 |
| III  Subject *Out* of Coalition | 13 | 16 |
|    Subject rejected; | 14 | 17 |
|    group partially integrated | 15 | 18 |
| IV  Subject *In* Coalition | 19 | 22 |
|    Subject accepted; | 20 | 23 |
|    group partially integrated | 21 | 24 |

*Behavior While Alone.* In the "free period," when the role-players have been withdrawn and the subjects are left with nothing to do, we again measure their rate of activity and their supportive behavior. Interaction is calculated this time by counting the number of seconds of overt behavior and dividing by the total time they are left together.

*Liking of One Another.* As stated above, at the end of the second session subjects fill in a liking matrix which, except for the additional row and column for the newcomer, is the same as the one presented earlier to the first subject and illustrated above. To estimate from their ratings the degree of mutual liking, we use the following ratio:

$$\frac{1 \text{ plus first's rating of second plus second's rating of first}}{1 \text{ plus the difference between their ratings of one another}}$$

## The Experimental Design

Our experimental design, shown in Table 4, is set up for analysis of vari-

ance, the two principle sources of variance we are interested in being (a) the characteristics of the pattern in the initial group and (b) the role-playing teams. Cases have been re-numbered for the reader's convenience.

## Testing the Hypotheses

A note about how we test the hypotheses is necessary. If personal acceptance in the previous group does in fact lead to a more congenial relationship, we should expect more positive readings in Pattern IV than in Pattern III. This comparison affords a clean test, for in other characteristics, such as degree of integration, sufficient agreement to reach a decision, heterogeneity of relationships (some positive, some negative) the two patterns are identical. Testing the second hypothesis, on group integration, is less straightforward. We cannot, for example, conclude from a comparison of fully integrated and malintegrated patterns how the variable operates because some of the other properties just mentioned, including personal acceptance, also dif-

| Structural characteristics | Patterns | | | |
|---|---|---|---|---|
| | I | II | III | IV |
| 1. To what extent is there full, *positive integration?* | full | none | partly | partly |
| 2. Is there sufficient agreement for *successful* completion of tasks? | yes | no | yes | yes |
| 3. Are relationships *heterogeneous*—some positive, some negative? | no | no | yes | yes |
| 4. Is the subject *accepted* by someone else? | yes | no | no | yes |

fer. To see how a test is possible in spite of this interdependence we first examine the characteristics of all four patterns as shown above.

Though there is interdependence, it is evident that no two patterns are alike in all characteristics. This means that we may infer which variables or simple combinations of variables account for any observed rank order in congeniality. For example, if the relationship in Pattern IV is more positive than in Pattern III (indicating the predicted effect of acceptance) but if in addition we find that Pattern I is still more positive than IV and that Pattern II is more negative than III, we can conclude that personal acceptance and group integration interact to produce the greatest likelihood of a positive relationship. In fact, this is what is predicted by the first and second hypotheses. No other set of differences will enable us to reject the null hypotheses, and this set cannot be accounted for by the effects of the other structural characteristics listed above. Therefore, providing the first hypothesis holds, we test the second hypothesis by testing specifically for the following rank order in congeniality of relationship between first subject and newcomer:

| Pattern | Rank order |
|---|---|
| I | 1 |
| II | 4 |
| III | 3 |
| IV | 2 |

Correspondingly, the alternative hypotheses are tested in terms of given rank orders. Since the hypotheses do not contend that complete interaction exists between acceptance and group integration, there are a greater number of rank orders, which if observed enable us to reject the null hypotheses. The principal ones are:

| Pattern | Rank orders | | |
|---|---|---|---|
| I | 4 | 3 | 4 |
| II | 3 | 4 | 2 |
| III | 1 | 1 | 1 |
| IV | 2 | 2 | 3 |

**Results**

We now follow in chronological order the development of the relationship between a member of the initial group and the newcomer. As we come to each measure we present the means for the four patterns, the relevant results from the analysis of variance and our conclusions regarding the two hypotheses and their alternatives. We do not report the breakdown of means by role-playing teams because in no case were teams a significant source of variance.

*Anticipated Value.* We find that the subject *out of* the coalition values the newcomer the most; the subject in a fully integrated group the least. From Pattern I through IV, the rank order is 4, 3, 1, 2, differences between the four means being significant at the .05 level.

The results, we see, are contrary to the first and second hypotheses and in line with the alternative hypotheses. Being accepted by someone in the initial group lessens the value of the newcomer and this is accentuated when all members accept each other. In this instance, before the two persons interact, and from the point of view only of the first subject, the evidence supports the principle derived from Simmel and von Wiese.

*The Working Relationship.* Actually working together is a different matter. Results show that having an ally in the previous group leads to a *better* working relationship. In itself, the state of integration of the group makes no difference. Instead, another group characteristic mentioned above, namely, heterogeneity of ties, interacting with acceptance, constitutes the second important factor. This means that one works best with the newcomer when one has had, and has, an ally and some other member of the group has been, or is, rejected. One works least well when the group has been disorganized—when all members reject one another. From Pattern I through IV, the average activity rates are .28, .16, .21, and .38; the average support rates are .14, −.18, .01, and .28, the differences between the latter means being significant at the .01 level. Since the two measures are associated we take the more definite set of differences (support rates) as an estimate of the relationship. Pattern IV is more positive than Pattern III, which means that while other variables are constant, personal acceptance leads to a more congenial working relationship.

What is the effect of group integration? It cannot be a positive factor because support is lower when there is complete integration (Pattern I) than when there is only partial integration (Pattern IV). On the other hand, it cannot be a negative factor because support is lower when there is malintegration (Pattern II) than when it is partial (Pattern III). Our conclusion is that it makes no important difference. Do any of the other structural properties mentioned above? Group success does not, because even though Pattern II is unsuccessful and significantly lower in support than the others, there is a significant difference between two successful patterns (I and IV).

We suggest that *heterogeneity of relationships* along with *personal acceptance* accounts for the major observed differences. Results show that the most positive relationship exists when there are both positive and negative ties and the first subject is accepted (IV). The least positive relationship exists when ties are homogeneous and the subject is rejected (II).

Conclusion: For the first hypothesis, which involves personal acceptance, we reject both the null and alternative hypotheses. For the second, involving group integration, we do not reject the null hypothesis. Integration is indeterminate. We conclude that a) personal acceptance/rejection and b) heterogeneity/homogeneity of the emotional ties are the two important variables. It is perhaps of interest that relativity of acceptance is not symmetrical: being relatively better off than others induces a positive relationship, but being relatively deprived does not induce the most unsatisfactory one.

*How Subject and Newcomer Interact When Alone.* As we might expect, when the role-players are withdrawn and when there is no task before them, the subjects interact differently. From Pattern I through IV, the average activity rates are 73.5, 66.8, 87.5, and 88.4; the average support rates are .23, .31, .29, and .40, the differences between these latter means being significant at the .05 level, except between Patterns II and III. We see, first, that activity and support are not associated as they were in the working group. The subjects in the homogeneous patterns (I and II) are relatively passive; while those in the heterogeneous groups are more active. Neither this nor the observed rank order in support is expected from either set of hypotheses. It is true that support is higher in Pattern IV than in III, indicating (in line with the first hypothesis) that acceptance leads to a positive relationship, but the effect is not general, for support is lower in Pattern I (where there is acceptance) than in two patterns where there is rejection. Analysis shows that neither personal acceptance, nor integration, nor heterogeneity, nor group success determine the difference. . . .

*How Subjects Feel about Each Other.* Using the sociometric rating and the ratio described in the previous section, an analysis of variance test shows no significant differences between pairs of subjects in the four patterns. For this measure we reject no null hypotheses.

*How Satisfied the Subjects Are with Their Group Experience.* Since items in the satisfaction questionnaire we used[16] refer to what happened in the group as a whole rather than specifically to the relationship between subjects, we do not use the data as a test of our hypotheses. We simply present the scores to give a fuller picture of how the subjects feel in the working group. From Pattern I through IV, average scores for the first subject are 58, 40, 41 and 54; average scores for the newcomer are 52, 43, 56 and 53, with differences in the first set significant at the .05 level, except for Patterns II and III, and differences in the second set also significant at the .05 level, except for Patterns I and IV. In three of the patterns the scores follow the support rates fairly closely: satisfaction is high and mutual in Patterns I and IV and low and mutual in Pattern II. In Pattern III the subject is dissatisfied while the newcomer is more satisfied than in any other type of group. This difference is probably due to the fact, which we shall refer to later, that the newcomer rejects the subject out of the coalition (just as the others do), joining their coalition.

*Conclusion.* The general conclusion from our results is that, with expansion of a group, the emotional ties between members of the initial group help determine how the new person will fit in. The obvious note in this should not cover up several important implications. The first is that the organization of the whole group, as well as the particular place a member has in it, makes a difference. How you work with a new member is determined as much by how others react to *each other* as it is influenced by how they feel toward you. The second is that, at least in shifting from three to four persons, there apparently exists no structural tendency associated with the foursome (two-against-two, for example) that erases the effects of the ties in the previous threesome.

In more detail, what can be concluded about the effect of the two independent variables in our hypotheses? In respect to personal acceptance, our results show that, in anticipation of the newcomer, it *decreases* his expected value; that, in the actual working

---

[16] Sample items taken from the Bales' Satisfaction Questionnaire (unpublished): "Some of the participants were too aggressive," "I felt like a guinea pig." The subject is asked to check one of six responses from strongly agreed to strongly disagreed. Responses are weighted arbitrarily and the sum of checked responses constitutes the satisfaction score. A high score indicates high satisfaction.

group, it *increases* the probability of a positive relationship; and, finally, it *increases* this probability when they are alone, providing ties in the original group were heterogeneous. Group integration *reduces* the anticipated value of the newcomer, but it has no important effect one way or another in the working group or in the "free" period. The variable either plays a tertiary role or no significant role at all. In its place as an important group characteristic is *heterogeneity*. It interacts with personal acceptance, *increasing* the probability of a positive working relationship. Neither these three variables, nor any other that we have tested, affects significantly our measure of the mutuality of liking between old member and newcomer.

If we take the working relationship as an estimate of how old member and newcomer get along in a group—as an estimate superior to anticipations alone and to interaction when the role-players are not present—the results show, to repeat, that a) the *acceptance* of a given member by others and b) the *heterogeneity* of the emotional ties in the initial group interact to produce a higher probability of a congenial relationship. In our experiment this case is represented by Pattern IV. Here the first subject is a member of a coalition against a third person; on arrival the newcomer is welcomed into and joins the coalition, rejecting the isolate.

### Discussion

As noted above, Simmel's proposition that acceptance in the pair increases the probability of a negative relationship with the newcomer is, in effect, applied by von Wiese to the expansion of the triad. His application is under a special set of conditions which we do not duplicate experimentally. For one thing, the isolate in our experiment is not free to "seek out" a partner. Secondly, the experimental group is a single working unit, whereas it is not clear whether von Wiese has in mind this kind of group—or whether he refers to semi-detached pairs with no more than three persons interacting at any one time. With these differences in conditions making a direct test of his argument impossible, we can only say that in our setting we find no evidence whatever that the group separates into two pairs. On the contrary, when the situation is most ripe —when the threesome is split two-against-one and when the isolate says he would *value* a partner—the newcomer makes the simple choice of joining the *others*, who (we find from the reactions in Pattern IV) welcome him, if for no other reason than to avoid a two-two split which might jeopardize their positions. Our evidence is that the coalition pattern in the threesome develops into the three-against-one split. Moreover, we believe that in a working group, even in the relatively unusual case where the isolate is given the prerogative of choosing the new group member, it would take a strong positive relationship indeed to stand up against the contrary forces which tend to keep the isolate an isolate.

Our evidence is that we cannot generalize from Simmel's proposition to the expansion of the triad. We do not know if the proposition holds for the expansion of the dyad, but if it does we must ask whether the dynamics of expansion in the two cases might not be fundamentally different, or, in some respects, even opposite. Is the tendency in one case according to Simmel's proposition and in the other case according to the contrary principle derived from Freud?

With this question in mind, let us examine more closely such expansion of the triad as involves the variable of heterogeneity, a variable that neither

Simmel nor Freud discusses. First, let us assume that acceptance and heterogeneity operate for all group members of the triad as they do for the experimental subject; second, let us assume, for the moment, that the way one member relates to the newcomer does not materially affect how another will relate to him. Noting that from the present point of view Patterns III and IV are identical, and applying our findings, the structures develop into the four-person patterns shown in the accompanying figure.

In each case the prior pattern is visible in the subsequent structure. Moreover, other structural characteristics mentioned above remain essentially the same; homogeneity/heterogeneity, degree of integration, potential for success, etc. These facts suggest a simple but general principle of expansion; namely, *given a clear group organization and the addition of a new member, a set of forces operates which tends to preserve, with the minimum alteration, the essentials of the state of organization before the addition.*[17] Within "organization" should be in-

cluded both the pattern of internal ties and the relationship of the group to the external situation. Acceptance of the newcomer in the first pattern maintains the group's homogeneity and its integration; rejection in the disorganized group maintains disorganization; and absorption of the newcomer into the coalition maintains the balance of power within a coalition and keeps the isolate an isolate.

Now it is just this principle that apparently does not operate when the third member is added to the dyad. True, the congeniality of the pair is still visible in the new coalition pattern, but the group property of homogeneity changes to heterogeneity and full integration to partial. Some obvious but unique properties of the dyad become relevant. Heterogeneity cannot exist in the dyad. In our use of the term, even if positive cathexis exists but is not reciprocated, we consider the relationship incongenial, negative, and therefore homogeneous. Groups of all other sizes can be either heterogeneous or homogeneous. The second obvious point is that the quality of the relationship defines the nature of the group as a whole. If rejecting the newcomer is the way to maintain the former positive tie, the very

---

[17] See Parsons, Bales and Shils, *op. cit.*, pp. 99-103, for the related question of the conditions of equilibrium.

Tendencies in the structural development from three- to four-person groups. Strongest positive is indicated by shaded double lines; strongest negative by solid single line, and moderate negative by dotted line.

process of maintenance undermines the integrative and homogeneous character of the group. If Simmel is right, the preservation principle does not operate. Were it operating the new group would be "all positive."

For these reasons, we suggest that if Simmel is correct, the principles of ex-

pansion for the dyad are basically different from those of the triad. Moreover, it appears that the lower limit for the operation of the preservation principle is the increase from three to four members. We see no compelling reason at this time to suggest an upper limit.

# chapter thirteen

## The Functions of Deviance in Groups

ROBERT A. DENTLER                    KAI T. ERIKSON

Although sociologists have repeatedly noted that close similarities exist between various forms of social marginality, research directed at these forms has only begun to mark the path toward a social theory of deviance. This slow pace may in part result from the fact that deviant behavior is too frequently visualized as a product of organizational failure rather than as a facet of organization itself.

Albert Cohen has recently attempted to specify some of the assumptions and definitions necessary for a sociology of deviant behavior (3). He has urged the importance of erecting clearly defined

concepts, devising a homogeneous class of phenomena explainable by a unified system of theory, and developing a sociological rather than a psychological framework—as would be the case, for example, in a central problem which was stated: "What is it about the structure of social systems that determines the kinds of criminal acts that occur in these systems and the way in which such acts are distributed within the systems?" (3, p. 462). Cohen has also suggested that a theory of deviant behavior should account simultaneously for deviance and conformity; that is, the explanation of one should serve as the explanation of the other.

In this paper we hope to contribute to these objectives by presenting some propositions about the sources and functions of deviant behavior in small groups. Although we suspect that the same general processes may well characterize larger social systems, this paper will be limited to small groups, and more particularly to enduring task and

Reprinted from Robert A. Dentler and Kai T. Erikson, "The Functions of Deviance in Groups," Social Problems, VII, No. 2 (Fall, 1959), 98-107, by permission of the authors and The Society for the Study of Social Problems. Copyright © 1959 by The Society for the Study of Social Problems. See Kai T. Erikson, Wayward Puritans: A Study in the Sociology of Deviance (New York: Wiley, 1966).

primary groups. Any set of propositions about the functions of deviance would have to be shaped to fit the scope of the social unit chosen for analysis, and we have elected to use the small group unit in this exploratory paper primarily because a large body of empirical material dealing with deviance in groups has accumulated which offers important leads into the study of deviance in general.

With Cohen, we define deviance as "behavior which violates institutionalized expectations, that is, expectations which are shared and recognized as legitimate within a social system" (3, p. 462). Our guiding assumption is that deviant behavior is a reflection not only of the personality of the actor, but the structure of the group in which the behavior was enacted. The violations of expectation which the group experiences, as well as the norms which it observes, express both cultural and structural aspects of the group. While we shall attend to cultural elements in later illustrations, our propositions are addressed primarily to the structure of groups and the functions that deviant behavior serves in maintaining this structure.

## Proposition One

Our first proposition is that *groups tend to induce, sustain, and permit deviant behavior*. To say that a group *induces* deviant behavior, here, is to say that as it goes through the early stages of development and structures the range of behavior among its members, a group will tend to define the behavior of certain members as deviant. A group *sustains* or *permits* this newly defined deviance in the sense that it tends to institutionalize and absorb this behavior into its structure rather than eliminate it. As group structure emerges and role specialization takes place, one or more role categories will be differentiated to accommodate individuals whose behavior is occasionally or regularly expected to be deviant. It is essential to the argument that this process be viewed not only as a simple group adjustment to individual differences, but also as a requirement of group formation, analogous to the requirement of leadership.

The process of role differentiation and specialization which takes place in groups has been illuminated by studies which use concepts of sociometric rank. Riecken and Homans conclude from this evidence: "The higher the rank of a member the closer his activities come to realizing the norms of the group . . . and there is a tendency toward 'equilibration of rank'" (11, p. 794). Thus the rankings that take place on a scale of social preference serve to identify the activities that members are expected to carry out: Each general rank represents or contains an equivalent role which defines that member's special relationship to the group and its norms. To the extent that a group ranks its members preferentially, it distributes functions differentially. The proposition, then, simply notes that group members who violate norms will be given low sociometric rank; that this designation carries with it an appropriate differentiation of the functions that such members are expected to perform in respect to the group; and that the roles contained in these low-rank positions become institutionalized and are retained in the structure of the group.

The most difficult aspect of this proposition is the concept of *induction* of deviance. We do not mean to suggest that the group creates the motives for an individual's deviant behavior or compels it from persons not otherwise disposed toward this form of expression. When a person encounters a new group, two different historical continuities meet. The individual brings to the group a background of private experience which disposes him to certain patterns of conduct; the group, on the other hand, is organized around a network of role priorities to which each member is required to conform. While the individual brings new resources into the group and alters its potential for change and innovation, the group certainly operates to rephrase each member's private experience into a new self-formula, a new sense of his own needs.

Thus any encounter between a group and a new member is an event which is novel to the experience of both. In the trial-and-error behavior which issues, both the functional requirements of the group and the individual needs of the person will undergo certain revisions, and in the process the group plays an important part in determining whether those already disposed toward deviant behavior will actually express it overtly, or whether those who are lightly disposed toward deviating styles will be encouraged to develop that potential. *Inducing* deviance, then, is meant to be a process by which the group channels and organizes the deviant possibilities contained in its membership.

The proposition argues that groups induce deviant behavior in the same sense that they induce other group qualities like leadership, fellowship, and so on. These qualities emerge early and clearly in the formation of new groups, even in traditionless laboratory groups, and while they may be diffusely distributed among the membership initially they tend toward specificity and equilibrium over time. In giving definition to the end points in the range of behavior which is brought to a group by its membership, the group establishes its boundaries and gives dimen-

sion to its structure. In this process, the designation of low-ranking deviants emerges as surely as the designation of high-ranking task leaders.

**Proposition Two**

Bales has written:

The displacement of hostilities on a scapegoat at the bottom of the status structure is one mechanism, apparently, by which the ambivalent attitudes toward the . . . "top man" . . . can be diverted and drained off. These patterns, culturally elaborated and various in form, can be viewed as particular cases of mechanisms relevant to the much more general problem of equilibrium [2, p. 454].

This comment provides a bridge between our first and second propositions by suggesting that deviant behavior may serve important functions for groups—thereby contributing to, rather than disrupting, equilibrium in the group. Our second proposition, accordingly, is that *deviant behavior functions in enduring groups to help maintain group equilibrium.* In the following discussion we would like to consider some of the ways this function operates.

*Group Performance*

The proposition implies that deviant behavior contributes to the maintenance of optimum levels of performance, and we add at this point that this will particularly obtain where a group's achievement depends upon the contributions of all its members.

McCurdy and Lambert devised a laboratory task which required full group participation in finding a solution to a given problem (7). They found that the performance of their groups compared unfavorably with that of individual problem-solvers, and explained this by noting the high likelihood that a group would contain at least one member who failed to attend to instructions. The group, they observed, may prove no stronger than its weakest member. The implication here, as in the old adage, seems to be that the group would have become correspondingly stronger if its weakest link were removed. Yet this implication requires some consideration: to what extent can we say that the inattentive member was acting in the name of the group, performing a function which is valuable to the group over time? To what extent can we call this behavior a product of group structure rather than a product of individual eccentricity?

As roles and their equivalent ranks become differentiated in a group, some members will be expected to perform more capably than others; and in turn the structure of the group will certainly be organized to take advantage of the relative capabilities of its members—as it demonstrably does in leadership choice. These differentials require testing and experimentation: the norms about performance in a group cannot emerge until clues appear as to how much the present membership can accomplish, how wide the range of variation in performance is likely to be, and so on. To the extent that group structure becomes an elaboration and organization of these differentials, certainly the "weak link" becomes as essential to this process as the high-producer. Both are outside links in the communication system which feeds back information about the range of group performance and the limits of the differentiated structure.

As this basis for differentiation becomes established, then, the group moves from a state in which pressure is exerted equally on all members to conform to performance norms, and moves toward a state in which these norms become a kind of anchor which locates the center of wide variations in behavior. The performance "mean" of a group is of course expected to be set at a level dictated by "norms"; and this mean is not only achieved by the most conforming members but by a balance of high and low producers as well. It is a simple calculation that the loss of a weak-link, the low producer, would raise the mean output of the group to a point where it no longer corresponded to original norms unless the entire structure of the group shifted as compensation. In this sense we can argue that neither role differentiation nor norm formation could occur and be maintained without the "aid" of regular deviations.

*Rewards*

Stated briefly, we would argue that the process of distributing incentives to members of the group is similarly dependent upon the recurrence of deviant behavior. This is an instance where, as Cohen has urged, an explanation of conformity may lead to an explanation of deviance. Customarily, conformance is rewarded while deviance is either unrewarded or actively punished. The rewards of conformity, however, are seen as "rewarding" in comparison to other possible outcomes, and obviously the presence of a deviant in the group would provide the continual contrast without which the reward structure would have little meaning. The problem, then, becomes complex: the reward structure is set up as an incentive for conformity, but depends upon the outcome that differentials in conformity will occur. As shall be pointed out later, the deviant is rewarded in another sense for his role in the group, which makes it "profitable" for him to serve as a contrast in the conventional reward structure. Generally speaking, comparison is as essential in the maintenance of norms as is conformity: a norm becomes most evident in its occasional violation, and in this sense a group maintains "equilibrium" by a controlled balance of the relations which provide comparison and those which assure conformity.

## Boundaries

Implicit in the foregoing is the argument that the presence of deviance in a group is a boundary-maintaining function. The comparisons which deviance makes possible help establish the range in which the group operates, the extent of its jurisdiction over behavior, the variety of styles it contains, and these are among the essential dimensions which give a group identity and distinctiveness. In Quaker work camps, Riecken found that members prided themselves on their acceptance of deviations, and rejected such controls as ridicule and rejection (10, pp. 57–67). Homans has noted that men in the Bank Wiring Group employed certain sanctions against deviant behavior which were felt to be peculiar to the structure of the group (5). A group is distinguished in part by the norms it creates for handling deviance and by the forms of deviance it is able to absorb and contain. In helping, then, to give members a sense of their group's distinctiveness, deviant behavior on the group's margins provides an important boundary-maintaining function.

**Proposition Three**

Kelley and Thibault have asserted:

It is common knowledge that when a member deviates markedly from a group standard, the remaining members of the group bring pressures to bear on the deviate to return to conformity. If pressure is of no avail, the deviate is rejected and cast out of the group. The research

on this point is consistent with common sense [6, p. 768].

Apparently a deviating member who was *not* rejected after repeated violations would be defined as one who did not deviate markedly enough. While there is considerable justification to support this common-sense notion, we suggest that it overattends to rejection and neglects the range of alternatives short of rejection. The same focus is evident in the following statement by Rossi and Merton:

What the individual experiences as estrangement from a group tends to be experienced by his associates as repudiation of the group, and this ordinarily evokes a hostile response. As social relations between the individual and the rest of the group deteriorate, the norms of the group become less binding for him. For since he is progressively seceding from the group and being penalized by it, he is less likely to experience rewards for adherence to . . . norms. Once initiated, this process seems to move toward a cumulative detachment from the group [8, p. 270].

While both of the above quotations reflect current research concerns in their attention to the group's rejection of the individual and his alienation from the group, our third proposition focuses on the common situation in which the group works to prevent elimination of a deviant member. *Groups will resist any trend toward alienation of a member whose behavior is deviant.* From the point of view of the group majority, deviants will be retained in the group up to a point where the deviant expression becomes critically dangerous to group solidarity. This accords with Kelley and Thibault's general statement, if not with its implication; but we would add that the point at which deviation becomes "markedly" extreme—and dangerous to the group—cannot be well-defined in advance. This point is located by the group as a result of recurrent interaction between conforming members who respect the central norms of the group and deviating members who test its boundaries. This is the context from which the group derives a conception of what constitutes "danger," or what variations from the norm shall be viewed as "marked."

From the point of view of the deviant, then, the testing of limits is an exercise of his role in the group; from the point of view of the group, pressures are set into motion which secure the deviant in his "testing" role, yet try to assure that his deviation will not become pronounced enough to make rejection necessary. Obviously this is a delicate balance to maintain, and failures are continually visible. Yet there are a great many conditions under which it is worth while for the group to retain its deviant members and resist any trend which might lead the majority membership and other deviant members to progressive estrangement.

**Illustrations of Propositions**

Each of the authors of this paper has recently completed field research which illuminates the propositions set forth here. Dentler studied the relative effectiveness of ten Quaker work projects in influencing conformity with norms of tolerance, pacifism, democratic group relations, and related social attitudes (4). One interesting sidelight in this study was the finding that while all ten groups were highly solidary, those with relatively higher numbers of sociometric isolates exhibited higher degrees of favorable increased conformity.

Case study of five of the ten groups, using interviews and participant observation, revealed that the two groups achieving the greatest favorable changes in tolerance, democratism, pacifism, and associated attitudes not only had the highest proportions of social isolates, but some of the isolates were low-ranking deviants. Of course none of the groups was without at least one isolate and one deviant, and these roles were not always occupied by the same member. But in the two high-change groups low-rank deviants were present.

In one group, one of these members came from a background that differed radically from those of other members. Although these were cooperative living and work projects, this member insisted upon separately prepared special food and complained loudly about its quality. Where three-fourths of the group members came from professional and managerial families, and dressed and acted in conformity with upper-middle-class standards, this deviant refused to wear a shirt to Sunday dinner and often came to meals without his shoes. He could not hold a job and lost two provided by the group leader during the first two weeks of the program.

His social and political attitudes also differed radically from group norms, and he was often belligerently assertive of his minority perspectives. He had no allies for his views. In an interview one of the group leaders described the group's response to this deviant:

At first we didn't know how to cope with him though we were determined to do just that. After he came to Sunday dinner in his undershirt, and after he smashed a bowl of food that had been fixed specially for him—as usual—we figured out a way to set down certain firm manners for him. There were some rules, we decided, that no one was going to violate. We knew he was very new to this kind of life and so we sought to understand him. We never rejected him. Finally, he began to come to terms; he adapted, at least enough so that we can live with him. He has begun to conform on the surface to some of our ways. It's been very hard to take that he is really proud of having lost his first two jobs and is not quiet about it. Things have gone better since we made a birthday cake for him, and I feel proud of the way our group has managed to handle this internal problem.

The same group sustained another deviant and even worked hard to retain him when he decided to leave the group. Here a group leader discusses group relations with this member:

X left our group after the first four weeks of the eight-week program. He had never been away from home before although he was about 21 years old. He couldn't seem to adjust to his job at the day camp, and he just couldn't stand doing his share of the housework and cooking. This lack of doing his share was especially hard on us, and we often discussed privately whether it would be good for him to relieve him of any household chores. We decided that wouldn't be right, but we still couldn't get him to work. Funny, but this sort of made housework the center of our group life. We are proud that no one else has shirked his chores; there is no quibbling now. . . . Anyway, X kept being pressured by his mother and brother to come home, but we gave him tremendous support. We talked it all out with him. We let him know we really wanted him to stay. This seemed to unify our group. It was working out the problem of X that seemed to unify our group. It was working out the problem of X that seemed to help us build some group standards. He began to follow some of our standards but he also stayed free to dissent. His mother finally forced him to come home.

In the second high-change group, there were also two extreme deviants. Here a group leader comments on one of them:

I've never got over feeling strongly antagonistic toward K. K has been a real troublemaker and we never really came to terms with him or controlled him significantly. He is simply a highly neurotic, conflicted person as far as life in our group goes. Personally, I've resented the fact that he has monopolized Z, who without him would have been a real contributor but who has become nothing more than a sort of poor imitation of K. After we had been here about half the summer, incidentally, a professional came out from staff headquarters and after observing our meetings he asked why K hadn't been dismissed or asked to leave the group early in the summer. But K didn't leave, of course, and most of us wouldn't want him to leave.

Finally a group leader described the reaction to the departure of its second deviant, who was repeatedly described in interviews as "kind of obnoxious":

On the night N was upstairs talking with your interviewer, the group got together downstairs suddenly to talk about getting up a quick party, a farewell party for him. In 15 minutes, like a whirlwind, we decorated the house and some of the fellows wrote a special song of farewell for N. We also wrote a last-minute appeal asking him to stay with the group and people ran about asking, "What are you doing for N?" There seemed to be a lot of guilt among us about his leaving. We felt that maybe we hadn't done enough to get him more involved in the life of our group. I think there was some hidden envy too. After he had left, a joke began to spread around that went like this: If you leave now maybe we'll have a party for you.

The group with the lowest amount of change during the summer contained two low-ranking members, one of whom deviated from the group's norms occasionally, but no evidence came to light to indicate that this group achieved the same intensity in social relationships or the same degree of role differentiation as did groups with more extremely deviant members. Members of this low-change group reflected almost without exception the views expressed in this typical quotation:

Objectively, this is a good, congenial group of individuals. Personally they leave me a little cold. I've been in other project groups, and this is the most congenial one I've been in; yet, I don't think there will be any lasting friendships.

All these quotations reflect strong impressions embodied in our observational reports. Taken as a whole they illustrate aspects of our three postulates. While this material does not reveal the sense in which a group may induce deviance—and this is perhaps the most critical proposition of all—it does show how groups will make great efforts to keep deviant members attached to the group, to prevent full alienation. By referring to our findings about attitude change we have hoped to suggest the relevance of deviance to increasing conformity, a functional relationship of action and reaction.

In 1955–56, Erikson participated in a study of schizophrenia among basic trainees in the U.S. Army, portions of which have been published elsewhere (1). Through various interview and questionnaire techniques, a large body of data was collected which enabled the investigators to reconstruct short histories of the group life shared by the future schizophrenic and his squad prior to the former's hospitalization. There were eleven subjects in the data under consideration. The bulk of the evidence used for this short report comes from loosely structured interviews which were conducted with the entire squad in attendance, shortly after it had lost one of its members to the psychiatric hospital.

The eleven young men whose breakdown was the subject of the interviews all came from the north-eastern corner of the United States, most of them from rural or small-town communities. Typically, these men had accumulated long records of deviation in civilian life: while few of them had attracted psychiatric attention, they had left behind them fairly consistent records of job failure, school truancy, and other minor difficulties in the community. Persons in the community took notice of this behavior, of course, but they tended to be gently puzzled by it rather than attributing distinct deviant motives to it.

When such a person enters the service, vaguely aware that his past performance did not entirely live up to expectations current in his community, he is likely to start negotiating with his squad mates about the conditions of his membership in the group. He sees himself as warranting special group consideration, as a consequence of a deviant style which he himself is unable to define; yet the group has clearcut obligations which require a high degree of responsibility and coordination from everyone. The negotiation seems to go through several successive stages, during which a reversal of original positions takes place and the individual is fitted for a role which is clearly deviant.

The first stage is characteristic of the recruit's first days in camp. His initial reaction is likely to be an abrupt attempt to discard his entire "civilian" repertoire to free himself for adoption of new styles and new ways. His new uniform for daily wear seems to become for him a symbolic uniform for his sense of identity: he is, in short, overconforming. He is likely to interpret any gesture of command as a literal moral mandate, sometimes suffering injury when told to scrub the floor until his fingers bleed, or trying to consciously repress thoughts of home when told to get everything out of his head but the military exercise of the moment.

The second stage begins shortly thereafter as he fails to recognize that "regulation" reality is different from the reality of group life, and that the circuits which carry useful information are contained within the more informal source. The pre-psychotic is, to begin with, a person for whom contacts with peers are not easy to establish, and as he tries to find his way into these circuits, looking for cues to the rhythm of group life, he sees that a fairly standard set of interaction techniques is in use. There are ways to initiate conversation, ways to impose demands, and so on. Out of this cultural lore, then, he chooses different gambits to test. He may learn to ask for matches to start discussion, be ready with a supply of cigarettes for others to "bum," or he may pick up a local joke or expression and repeat it continually. Too often, however, he misses the context in which these interaction cues are appropriate, so that his behavior, in its over-literal simplicity, becomes almost a caricature of the sociability rule he is trying to follow. We may cite the "specialist" in giving away cigarettes:

I was out of cigarettes and he had a whole pack. I said, "Joe, you got a smoke?" He says "yes," and Jesus, he gave me about twelve of them. At other times he used to offer me two or three packs of cigarettes at a time when I was out.

Or the "specialist" in greetings:

He'd go by you in the barracks and say, "What do you say, Jake?" I'd say, "Hi, George, how are you?" and he'd walk into the latrine. And he'd come by not a minute later, and it's the same thing all over again, "What do you say, Jake?" It seemed to me he was always saying "hi" to someone. You could be sitting right beside him for ten minutes and he would keep on saying it.

These clumsy overtures lead the individual and the group into the third stage. Here the recruit, almost hidden from group view in his earlier over-conformity, has become a highly visible group object: his behavior is clearly "off beat," anomalous; he has made a presentation of himself to the squad, and the squad has had either to make provisions for him in the group structure or begin the process of eliminating him. The pre-psychotic is clearly a low producer, and in this sense he is potentially a handicap. Yet the group neither exerts strong pressures on him to conform nor attempts to expel him from the squad. Instead, he is typically given a wide license to deviate from both the performance and behavior norms of the group, and the group in turn forms a hard protective shell around him which hides him from exposure to outside authorities.

His duties are performed by others, and in response the squad only seems to ask of him that he be at least consistent in his deviation—that he be consistently helpless and consistently anomalous. In a sense, he becomes the ward of the group, hidden from outside view but the object of friendly ridicule within. He is referred to as "our teddy bear," "our pet," "mascot," "little brother," "toy," and so on. In a setting where having buddies is highly valued, he is unlikely to receive any sociometric choices at all. But it would be quite unfortunate to assume that he is therefore isolated from the group or repudiated by it: an accurate sociogram would have the deviant individual encircled by the interlocking sociometric preferences, sheltered by the group structure, and an important point of reference for it.

The examples just presented are weak in that they include only failures of the process described. The shell which protected the deviant from visibility leaked, outside medical authorities were notified, and he was eventually hospitalized. But as a final note it is interesting to observe that the shell remained even after the person for whom it was erected had withdrawn. Large portions of every squad interview were devoted to arguments, directed at a psychiatrist, that the departed member was not ill and should never have been hospitalized.

### Discussion

The most widely cited social theories of deviant behavior which have appeared in recent years—notably those of Merton and Parsons (8, 9)—have helped turn sociologists' attention from earlier models of social pathology in which deviance was seen as direct evidence of disorganization. These newer models have attended to the problem of how social structures exert pressure on certain individuals rather than others toward the expression of deviance. Yet the break with the older social disorganization tradition is only partial, since these theories still regard deviance from the point of view of its value as a "symptom" of dysfunctional structures. One aim of this paper is to encourage a functional approach to deviance, to consider the contributions deviant behavior may make toward the development of organizational structures, rather than focusing on the implicit assumption that structures must be somehow in a state of disrepair if they produce deviant behavior.

Any group attempts to locate its position in social space by defining its symbolic boundaries, and this process of self-location takes place not only in reference to the central norms which the group develops but in reference to the *range* of possibilities which the culture makes available. Specialized statuses which are located on the margins of the group, chiefly high-rank leaders and low-rank deviants, become critical referents for establishing the end points of this range, the group boundaries.

As both the Quaker and Army illustrations suggest, deviant members are important targets toward which group concerns become focused. Not only do they symbolize the group's activities, but they help give other members a sense of group size, its range and extent, by marking where the group begins and ends in space. In general, the deviant seems to help give the group structure a visible "shape." The deviant is someone about whom something should be done, and the group, in expressing this concern, is able to reaffirm its essential cohesion and indicate what the group is and what it can do. Of course the character of the deviant behavior in each group would vary with the group's general objectives, its relationship to the larger culture, and so on. In both the Quaker groups and Army squads, nurturance was a strong element of the other members' reaction to their deviant fellow. More specifically in the Army material it is fairly sure that the degree of helplessness and softness supplied by the pre-psychotic introduced emotional qualities which the population—lacking women and younger persons—could not otherwise afford.

These have been short and necessarily limited illustrations of the propositions advanced. In a brief final note we would like to point out how this crude theory could articulate with the small group research tradition by suggesting one relatively ideal laboratory procedure that might be used. Groups composed of extremely homogeneous members should be assigned tasks which require group solution but which impose a high similarity of activity upon all members. If role differentiation occurs, then, it would be less a product of individual differences or the specific requirements of the task than a product of group formation. We would hypothesize that such differentiation would take place, and that one or more roles thus differentiated would be reserved for deviants. The occupants of these deviant roles should be removed from the group. If the propositions have substance, the group—and this is the critical hypothesis—would realign its members so that these roles would become occupied by other members. While no single experiment could address all the implications of our paradigm, this one would confront its main point.

This paper, of course, has deliberately neglected those group conditions in which deviant behavior becomes dysfunctional: it is a frequent group experience that deviant behavior fails to provide a valued function for the structure and helps reduce performance standards or lower levels of interaction. We have attempted here to present a side of the coin which we felt was often neglected, and in our turn we are equally—if intentionally—guilty of neglect.

## Summary

This paper has proposed the following interpretations of deviant behavior in enduring primary and task groups:

1. Deviant behavior tends to be induced, permitted, and sustained by a given group.
2. Deviant behavior functions to help maintain group equilibrium.
3. Groups will resist any trend toward alienation of a member whose behavior is deviant.

The substance of each proposition was discussed heuristically and illustrated by reference to field studies of deviant behavior in Quaker work projects and Army basic training squads. A laboratory test was suggested as one kind of critical test of the paradigm. The aim of the presentation was to direct attention to the functional interdependence of deviance and organization.

## Bibliography

1. ARTISS, KENNETH L., ed., *The Symptom as Communication in Schizophrenia*. New York: Grune & Stratton, 1959.
2. BALES, ROBERT F., "The Equilibrium Problem in Small Groups," in A. Paul Hare *et al.*, eds., *Small Groups*. New York: Knopf, 1955, pp. 424-56.
3. COHEN, ALBERT K., "The Study of Social Disorganization and Deviant Behavior," in Robert K. Merton *et al.*, eds., *Sociology Today*. New York: Basic Books, 1959, pp. 461-84.
4. DENTLER, ROBERT, *The Young Volunteers*. Chicago: National Opinion Research Center Report, 1959.
5. HOMANS, GEORGE W., *The Human Group*. New York: Harcourt, Brace, 1950.
6. KELLEY, HAROLD H., and JOHN W. THIBAULT, "Experimental Studies of Group Problem Solving and Process," in Gardner Lindzey, ed., *Handbook of Social Psychology*, Vol. II. Reading, Mass.: Addison-Wesley, 1954, pp. 759-68.
7. McCURDY, HAROLD G., and WALLACE E. LAMBERT, "The Efficiency of Small Human Groups in the Solution of Problems Requiring Genuine Cooperation," *Journal of Personality*, XX (June, 1952), 478-94.
8. MERTON, ROBERT K., *Social Theory and Social Structure*, rev. ed. New York: The Free Press, 1957.
9. PARSONS, TALCOTT, *The Social System*. New York: The Free Press, 1951, pp. 256-67, 321-25; and TALCOTT PARSONS, ROBERT F. BALES, and EDWARD A. SHILS, *Working Papers in the Theory of Action*. New York: The Free Press, pp. 67-78.
10. RIECKEN, HENRY, *Volunteer Work Camp*. Reading, Mass.: Addison-Wesley, 1952, pp. 57-67.
11. ———, and GEORGE W. HOMANS, "Psychological Aspects of Social Structure," in Gardner Lindzey, ed., *Handbook of Social Psychology*, Vol. II. Reading, Mass.: Addison-Wesley, 1954, pp. 786-832.

# chapter fourteen

## The Emotionally Disturbed Child as the Family Scapegoat

**EZRA F. VOGEL**                    **NORMAN W. BELL**

The phenomenon of scapegoating is as old as human society. Sir James Frazer records, in *The Golden Bough*,[1] numerous instances, reaching back to antiquity, of public scapegoats, human and other. He views the process of scapegoating as one in which ". . . the evil influences are embodied in a visible form or are at least supposed to be loaded upon a material medium, which acts as a vehicle to draw them off from the people, village, or town."[2] The scapegoat's function ". . . is simply to effect a total clearance of all the ills that have been infesting a people."[3] Frazer was dealing with the phenomenon at the level of a society, tribe, village, or town. It is the purpose of this paper to examine the same phenomenon within families, by viewing an emotionally disturbed child as an embodiment of certain types of conflicts between parents. This pattern is a special case of a common phenomenon, the achievement of group unity through

the scapegoating of a particular member. It is, perhaps, more widely known that a group may achieve unity through projection of hostilities to the outside,[4] but there are also a large number of cases where members of a particular group are able to achieve unity through scapegoating a particular member of that group. Thus, the deviant within the group may perform a valuable function for the group, by channeling group tensions and providing a basis for solidarity.

The notion that the family is in large part responsible for the emotional health of the child is a compelling one

Reprinted from Norman W. Bell and Ezra F. Vogel, eds., *The Family* (New York: The Free Press, 1960), pp. 382-97, by permission of the editors and The Macmillan Company. Copyright © 1960 by The Free Press.

[1] Sir James Frazer, *The Golden Bough*, abridged ed. (New York: Macmillan, 1927).

[2] *Ibid.*, p. 562.

[3] *Ibid.*, p. 575.

[4] In addition to Frazer, *op. cit.*, see also Emile Durkheim, "Deux lois de l'évolution pénale," *L'Année Sociologique*, IV (1899), 55-95; Henri Hubert and Marcel Mauss, "Essai sur la nature et la fonction du sacrifice," *L'Année Sociologique*, II (1897), 29-138; William Robertson Smith, *The Religion of the Semites* (London: A. and C. Black, 1927); Roger Money-Kyrle, *The Meaning of Sacrifice* (London: Hogarth, 1930); George Herbert Mead, "The Psychology of Punitive Justice," *American Journal of Sociology*, XXIII (1918), 577-620; Ruth S. Eissler, "Scapegoats of Society," in Kurt R. Eissler, ed., *Searchlights on Delinquency* (New York: International Universities Press, 1949), 288-305; and Clyde Kluckhohn, "Navaho Witchcraft," *Papers of the Peabody Museum of American Archaeology and Ethnology*, Harvard University, XXII (1944).

in contemporary behavioral science. By and large, however, the research has focused largely on the mother-child relationship, and the independent variable by which the mother-child relationship and the child-rearing practices are usually explained is the personality and developmental history of the mother. Recently, an attempt has also been made to treat the father-child relationship, again largely in terms of the personality and developmental history of the father. While in clinical practice there is some awareness of family dynamics, in the literature, the family has largely been treated simply as a collection of personalities, and the child's personality development has been seen almost exclusively as a direct result of the separate personalities of his parents.[5] Rarely is the interaction of parents treated as a significant independent variable influencing childhood development. Even the broader cultural patterns have been considered, childhood development has been related to child-rearing practices and socialization into the culture, with little consideration of the family as the mediating unit.

Data for this paper are derived from the intensive study[6] of a small group of "disturbed" families, each with an emotionally disturbed child, and a matched group of "well" families without clinically manifest disturbance in any child. Of the nine families in each group, three were Irish-American, three Italian-American, and three old-American. The families were seen by a team including psychiatrists, social workers, psychologists, and social scientists. The disturbed families, on which this paper is based, were seen weekly in the offices of a psychiatric clinic and in their homes over periods ranging from one to four years. Detailed information was gathered about the members' developmental histories and character structure, but even more specific data were obtained about current processes.

The present paper is concerned with how a child in the family, the emotionally disturbed child, was used as a scapegoat for the conflicts between parents and what the functions and dysfunctions of this scapegoating are for the family.

In all the disturbed families it was found that a particular child had become involved in tensions existing between the parents.[7] In the "well" families used for control purposes, either the tensions between the parents were not so severe or else the tensions were handled in such a way that the children did not become pathologically involved. In general, both parents of the emotionally disturbed child had many of the same underlying conflicts, but in relationship to each other, they felt themselves to be at opposite poles, so that one spouse would act out one side of the conflict and the other would act out the other side of the conflict. They had developed an equilibrium in which

---

[5] This is not to deny relevance of psychological aspects. The same facts can be related to a number of different theoretical systems, but here focus is on the group dynamics.

[6] For other reports of this research, see John P. Spiegel, "The Resolution of Role Conflict within the Family," *Psychiatry*, XX (1957), 1-16; Florence Rockwood Kluckhohn, "Family Diagnosis: Variations in the Basic Values of Family Systems," *Social Casework*, XXXIX (1958), 1-11; and John P. Spiegel, "Some Cultural Aspects of Transference and Countertransference," in Jules H. Massermann, ed., *Individual and Family Dynamics* (New York: Grune & Stratton, 1959).

---

[7] It should be noted that only families which had never been separated or divorced were included in the present sample. Of course, there are also cases of emotionally disturbed children where only one parent is living with the children and cases in which one parent is living with other relatives. Hence, tensions between parents cannot be the universal cause of emotional disturbance. A more general hypothesis would be that the emotionally disturbed child is always the focus of primary-group tension.

they minimized contact with each other and minimized expressions of affect, particularly hostility, which they strongly felt for each other, and this made it possible for them to live with each other.[8] But this equilibrium had many difficulties, the most serious of which was the scapegoating of a child.

## Sources of Tension That Lead to Scapegoating

It is our contention that scapegoating is produced by the existence of tensions between parents which have not been satisfactorily resolved in other ways. The spouses in the disturbed families had deep fears about their marital relationship and about the partner's behavior. They did not feel they could predict accurately how the other would respond to their own behavior. Yet, the other's response was of very great importance and was thought to be potentially very damaging. The partners did not feel they could deal with the situation by direct communication, because this might be too dangerous, and they resorted to manipulations of masking, evading, and the like. This atmosphere of tension has several sources. One of the sources was the personality problems of each spouse, but in the present analysis the focus will be on the group sources of the tension. These tensions usually have several sources. At a very general level, one of the main sources of tension was conflict in cultural value orientations.[9] Value orientations are abstract, general conceptions of the

nature of human nature and man's relationship to it, of man's relation to man, of the most significant time dimension, and of the most valued type of activity. All societies have preferences and alternative preferences to these basic dimensions; these preferences are expressed within a wide range of phenomena. In complex ways, they are related to personality and social structure and to more specific values. When people are in the process of acculturation, as was the case with the families of Irish and Italian backgrounds, many possibilities for value-orientation conflict arise. Any one individual may have been socialized into conflicting or confused patterns, and be unsuccessful in bridging the gap. Marriage partners may have been socialized into different patterns and be working on different assumptions. All our disturbed families had problems of these sorts. Some were trying to shift quickly to a set of orientations they had not thoroughly internalized, and without having neutralized previous orientations. Others were trying to live by conflicting orientations.[10]

A common example of the cultural value conflicts was the conflict centered around the problems of individual performance. There were considerable pulls toward the American middle-class achievement patterns. In families which had partially internalized both sets of value orientations, it was impossible to live up to both sets of values, and whichever the family chose, this meant that certain conflicts would result.

Another source of tension was the relations of the family and the larger community. Disturbed families usually

---

[8] This is spelled out in more detail in Ezra F. Vogel, "The Marital Relationship of Parents and the Emotionally Disturbed Child" (unpublished Ph.D. thesis, Harvard University, 1958).

[9] See Florence R. Kluckhohn, *loc. cit.*; and F. Kluckhohn, Fred L. Strodtbeck *et al.*, *Variations in Value Orientations* (New York: Harper & Row, Publishers. 1961).

[10] Well families, by contrast, had bridged the gap between the orientations of different ethnic or class groups. They had succeeded in neutralizing old orientations before taking on new ones. Usually such families were changing in a slower and more orderly fashion.

had problems in this area, rejecting and/or being rejected by the community. In some cases, a family had very severe disapproval of a very close-knit ethnic neighborhood directed at them. In other cases, families had moved from ethnic neighborhoods to more fashionable suburbs and suffered in their own eyes by comparison to their new neighbors. Consequently, their social relationships with these neighbors were often minimal; when they did exist, they were usually strained or else one spouse had fairly good relationships with some friends and the partner had poor relationships with these friends. All families, to a greater or lesser extent, had problems in their relationships with families of orientation. Typically, the wife was strongly attached to her parents and antagonistic towards her husband's family, while the husband was attached to his parents and antagonistic to his wife's family. If either spouse was critical of his in-laws, the partner typically defended his own parents and became more critical of his in-laws. If one spouse was critical of his own parents, the partner was often friendly to them. The unbalanced attachments to parents and parents-in-law was not resolved. Changes usually produced more tension, but the basic sources of strain remained unchanged.[11]

### The Selection of the Scapegoat

The tensions produced by unresolved conflicts were so severe that they could not be contained without some discharge. It is not surprising that some appropriate object was chosen to symbolize the conflicts and

draw off the tension. Conceivably, some person or group outside the family could serve in this capacity. However, in these disturbed families, the parents had by and large internalized the standards of the surrounding community sufficiently so that they had great difficulty in finding a legitimate basis for scapegoating outsiders. In addition, most of these families had very tenuous ties with the community, and since they were very concerned about being accepted, they could not afford to antagonize their associates. While some of the families did, at times, have strong feelings of antagonism toward various members of the community in which they lived, they could rarely express this antagonism directly. Even if at times they were able to manifest their antagonism, this usually led to many additional complications, and the family preferred to scapegoat its own child.[12]

Channeling the tensions within the family did not lead to difficulties with the outside, but usually the latent hostilities between the husband and wife made it very difficult to deal with problems openly between them. There was always danger the partner might become too angry, which would lead to severe and immediate difficulties. A number of factors made a child the

---

[11] Discussed at length in Norman W. Bell, "The Impact of Psychotherapy Upon Family Relationships" (unpublished Ph.D. thesis, Harvard University, 1959).

[12] The one family which did occasionally express antagonism directly to outsiders was the most disturbed family in the sample. The expression of hostility to neighbors was filled with such conflicts and added complications that it inevitably proved inadequate and the family returned to the scapegoating of their child.

While many members of these families did express prejudice towards minority groups, this prejudice did little to drain the severe tensions within the family. Perhaps the minority group was not symbolically appropriate for the handling of any of the family conflicts, or perhaps they were not sufficiently available to serve as a continual focus of family tensions.

most appropriate object through which to deal with family tensions. First of all, the child was in a relatively powerless position compared to the parents. While he was dependent on the parents and could not leave the family, he was not able effectively to counter the parents' superior power. Although the parents' defenses were fairly brittle in comparison with those of well parents, still their defenses were much stronger than those of their children. Because the child's personality is still very flexible, he can be molded to adopt the particular role which the family assigns to him. When the child does take on many of the characteristics which the parents dislike in themselves and each other, he becomes a symbolically appropriate object on which to focus their own anxieties. Since the person scapegoated often develops such severe tensions that he is unable to perform his usual task roles, it is important that those family members performing essential, irreplaceable functions for the family not be scapegoated. The child has relatively few tasks to perform in the family, compared to the parents or other elders, and his disturbance does not ordinarily interfere with the successful performance of the necessary family tasks. The "cost" in dysfunction of the child is low relative to the functional gains for the whole family.

In all cases, with partial exception of one family, a particular child was chosen as the scapegoat, while other children were relatively free of pathology. The selecting of a particular child is not a random matter; one child is the best symbol. Just as a dream condenses a variety of past and present experiences and a variety of emotional feelings, the scapegoat condenses a variety of social and psychological problems impinging on the family.

Who is selected as the scapegoat is intimately related to the sources of tension. Where value-orientation conflicts existed, the child chosen was the one who best symbolized these conflicts. For example, if the conflicts revolved about achievement, a child who failed to achieve according to expectations could become the symbol of failure. Alternatively, a child might be an appropriate object because he was achieving independently and thus violating norms of loyalty to the group.

The position of the child in the sibling group frequently became a focus for the unresolved childhood problems of the parents. If the parents' most serious unresolved problems were with male figures, the child chosen to represent the family conflict was usually a male child. Similarly, sibling order could be a strong factor. If one or both parents had difficulties with older brothers, an older boy in the family might become the scapegoat.

In two cases, the sex or sibling position of the child seemed to be particularly important in the selection of a particular child as the family scapegoat. In one of these cases, the mother was the oldest of three siblings and had considerable feelings of rivalry with her next younger sister which had never been effectively resolved. Although the father had two older siblings, they were so much older that to him they were a separate family. In his effective family environment, he was the older of two children and had considerable feelings of rivalry toward a younger brother who displaced him and for whom he subsequently had to care. This couple has three children, and there was an unusual amount of rivalry between the oldest and the second sibling. Both the parents sided very strongly with the oldest child. They were continuously conscious of the middle child bothering the older, for which they severely criticized this middle child. There are many striking parallels, even to small details, in the relationship between the parents and their next younger siblings and the relationship between their oldest child and the next younger sibling.

Another pattern revolved about the identification of a child with a parent whom he resembled. This was found in all families, sick and well, in one form or another; but in the disturbed families, the child was seen as possessing very undesirable traits, and although the parent actually possessed the same traits, the focus of attention was the child and not the parent. In one family, in particular, this pattern was striking. The father and the eldest son had very similar physical characteristics; not only did they have the same first name but both were called by the same diminutive name by the mother. At times, the social worker seeing the mother was not certain whether the mother was talking about her husband or her son. The wife's concerns about the husband's occupational adequacy were not dealt with directly, but the focus for her affect was the child and his school performance. In fact, the son was criticized by his mother for all the characteristics which she disliked in her husband, but she was unable to criticize her husband directly for these characteristics. She channeled all her feelings, especially anxiety and hostility, to the child, although her husband had similar problems. Furthermore, in order to control her feelings toward her husband, she remained very aloof and distant and was not able to express to him her positive or negative feelings. While she channeled many criticisms and anxieties through the child, she also expressed many of her positive feelings to the child, thereby leading to severe Oedipal conflicts. The husband was not happy about his wife being so aloof from him, but on the other hand he found that by co-operating with his wife in criticizing the child, he was able to keep the burden of problems away from himself. He thus joined with the wife in projecting his own difficulties and problems onto the child and in dealing with them as the child's problems rather than as his own.

In three of the families, the scapegoat had considerably lower intelligence than did the other children in the family. In all these families, there were serious conflicts about the value of achievement, and the parents had great difficulty themselves in living up to their own achievement aspirations. In all these three cases, the parents were unable to accept the fact that their children had limited abilities, and they continually held up impossible standards for these children. Although all three children had I.Q.'s in the 80's or below and had failed one grade or more, all three mothers stated that they intended that their children should go to college. At the beginning of therapy, one of the mothers hoped her son would attend medical school and become a doctor; another had begun to put away a small amount of money from a very tight budget for her daughter's college education, even though the daughter's intelligence was that of a moron. At the beginning of therapy, none of the parents was able to deal directly with his own difficulties in achievement. In contrast, in one of the families, there were two children in the family who had very low intelligence, one of whom had failed a grade in school, but the family scapegoat was a boy who had normal intelligence. In this case, the parents, who had average intelligence, had resolved their conflicts about achievement by denying that they were interested in achievement and accepting their social position. This child of slightly higher intelligence and greater physical activity was seen by them as a very aggressive child who was always doing too much, and the parents were continually worried that he was "too smart."[13]

In a number of cases, the disturbed child either had a serious physical disease when he was young or a striking physical abnormality such as a hare lip, bald spots in the hair, or unusually unattractive facial features. The mere existence of some such abnormality seemed to draw attention to one particular child, so that if there were some sorts of anxieties or problems in the family at all, the child with the physical peculiarities seemed to become the focus of the family problems. Here again, however, it was not the mere existence of a physical defect but its meaning[14] in the life of the family which gave it its significance. For example, in some families there was a feeling that they had committed certain sins by not living up to their ideals, for instance by using contraceptives. This was a very common problem, since many families could not possibly live up to the two opposing sets of ideals which they had at least partially internalized. The child's physical abnormality became a symbol of the family's sin of not having lived up to some partially internalized values, and the malformed child was seen as a sinful child who was not living up to the standards of the group. Since the family's relationship with the community was often tenuous, the fact that one of their children had physical abnormalities that made the child the focus of neighborhood ridicule, served to make the parents increasingly ashamed of the child's physical characteristics and to focus increasingly more attention on this child. For example, one of the main concerns of the family with the unusually ugly child was that other children were continually teasing her about her appearance. However, the concern was less for the child herself, and more for the whole family. Her problems symbolized the parents' past and present problems with the neighborhood; rather than sympathize with the child, they abused her all the more. In another case in which a female child's physical illness became a focus of the family's problems, the parents were extremely concerned about her safety, which was again related in part to the potential dangers in social relationships with the outside world. As a result of the girl's illness, the family became much more cautious than was necessary, and on some occasions they were even reluctant to accept medical advice that she could participate in certain activities without danger to her health. The continual contacts that the child had with middle-class professional personnel through hospitalization and clinic visits led her to accept certain middle-class American values more than did the rest of the family, and the family was continually expressing the feeling that she had different attitudes after hospitalization and contact with hospital personnel. The disliked attitudes ascribed to the child were in general those of

13 While in virtually all these families, there were considerable problems about achievement, another family seen by one of the authors as part of another investigation was very closely tied to the traditional ethnic patterns and had not yet seriously begun to incorporate American achievement values. In this family, there was one child, seriously substandard in intelligence, with very ugly physical features, who had epileptic seizures. There were also some children who were above average in intelligence. This family had no serious conflicts about achievement, and none of the children were scapegoated.

14 Alfred Adler, Understanding Human Nature (New York: Greenberg, 1927), and Alfred Adler, "The Cause and Prevention of Neurosis," Journal of Abnormal and Social Psychology, XXIII (1928), 4-11.

middle-class American culture.[15] Not only abnormalities but general body type could become the symbol to call forth scapegoating. In two families, the spouses had many problems in their sexual life. Rather than face these maladjustments directly, the problems were expressed through concern about the masculinity and normality of a slender, graceful son.

While the general process of symbolization of a scapegoat is very similar to the dream symbolization, there is one problem in the family selection of a scapegoat which is not met in the selection of a dream symbol, and that is the problem of availability. While in dreams, any symbolic representation is open to the dreamer, in the family only a very small number of children are available as the potential scapegoats. Hence, when there is a serious family problem and no child is an appropriate symbol of the problem, there must be considerable cognitive distortion in order to permit the most appropriate one available to be used as a scapegoat. For example, in one family which was very concerned about the problems of achievement, the focus of the family's problems was the eldest son. Although he was receiving passing grades in school, whereas the parents had had very poor school records, the parents were very critical of his school performance. Because of this pressure, the child worked hard and was able to get somewhat better marks on his next report card. However, the mother stoutly maintained that her son didn't deserve those grades, that he must have cheated, and she continued to criticize him for his school performance.

The other aspect of the problem of availability resulted from the fact that the parents apparently have had tensions since early in marriage. As nearly as it was possible to reconstruct the marital history, it appeared that the spouses had selected each other partly on the basis of the fact that they shared many of the same conflicts and understood each other quite well. Not long after marriage, however, they seemed to have become polarized in their conflicts, so that one parent represented one side of the conflict and the other represented the other side. This seems to have given each of the spouses a way of handling his own conflicts and allowed each to remain fairly consistent and well integrated by projecting difficulties onto the partner. However, it also led to very severe difficulties in the marital relationship and created many tensions which were quickly displaced onto the first available and appropriate object, very often the first child. Since the eldest child was the first one available for scapegoating, he often seems to have been assigned this role and, once assigned, has continued in it. Perhaps because of his prior availability and his closer involvement in the adult world, he is a more appropriate object for the scapegoating.[16] In

---

[15] In the well families, there were cases of comparable physical illness which did not result in the same type of anxieties in the family.

[16] No adequate large-scale studies are available to provide an estimate of the proportion of emotional disturbances found in the eldest child. Many small-scale studies have been made, but they are inconsistent and contradictory. See John P. Spiegel and Norman W. Bell, "The Family of the Psychiatric Patient," in Silvano Arieti, ed., *American Handbook of Psychiatry* (New York: Basic Books, 1959). In the present study, slightly more than half were eldest children, a finding similar to that in another small sample of emotionally disturbed children: Sydney Croog, "The Social Backgrounds of Emotionally Disturbed Children and their Siblings" (unpublished Ph.D. thesis, Yale University, 1954). It has also been noted that eldest sons are more likely to be involved in problems of inheritance and rivalry, and are more likely to be adult-oriented. See such

the one case in which a child was able to escape the scapegoat role by decreasing his attachment to the home, the next most appropriate child was used in the scapegoat role.

## Induction of the Child into the Scapegoat Role

If the child is to be a "satisfactory" scapegoat, he must carry out his role as a "problem child." The problem behavior must be reinforced strongly enough so that it will continue in spite of the hostility and anxiety it produces in the child. This delicate balance is possible only because the parents have superior sanction power over the child, can define what he should or should not do, and control what he does or does not do. This balance necessarily requires a large amount of inconsistency in the ways parents handle the child.

The most common inconsistency was between the implicit (or unconscious) and the explicit role induction.[17] In all cases, certain behavior of the child violated recognized social norms. In some instances stealing, firesetting, expressions of hostility, or unco-operativeness affected the child's relationships with people outside the family. In other instances, bed-wetting, resistance to parental orders, or expression of aggression to siblings affected relationships in the family. But in all instances, while the parents explicitly criticized the child and at times even punished him, they supported in some way, usually implicitly, the persistence of the very behavior which they criticized. This permission took various forms: failure to follow through on threats, delayed punishment, indifference to and acceptance of the symptom, unusual interest in the child's symptom, or considerable secondary gratification offered to the child because of his symptom. The secondary gratification usually took the form of special attention and exemption from certain responsibilities. While the parents had internalized social norms sufficiently to refrain from violating the norms themselves, they had not sufficiently internalized them to prevent giving encouragement to their children for acting out their own repressed wishes. The wish to violate these norms was transferred to the child, but the defenses against this wish were never as strong in the child.[18]

Another type of inconsistency seen was that one parent would encourage one type of behavior, but the other parent would encourage an opposing type of behavior. The result again was

---

diverse studies as George Peter Murdock, *Social Structure* (New York: Macmillan, 1949); Sigmund Freud, *Moses and Monotheism* (New York: Knopf, 1939); and Charles McArthur, "Personalities of First and Second Children," *Psychiatry*, XIX (1956), 47-54.

[17] The way the parent gives the child implicit approval to act out his own unconscious wishes has already been well described for the relationship between a single parent and a single child. Adelaide M. Johnson, "Sanctions for Superego Lacunae of Adolescents," in Kurt R. Eissler, ed., *Searchlights on Delinquency* (New York: International Universities Press, 1949); Melitta Sperling, "The Neurotic Child and his Mother: A Psychoanalytic Study," *American Journal of Orthopsychiatry*, XXI (1951), 351-64. For a more detailed account of family role-induction methods, see Speigel, "The Resolution of Role Conflict within the Family," in N. W. Bell and E. F. Vogel, eds., *op. cit.*, pp. 361-81.

---

[18] Here again, the analogy to the individual personality system is instructive. Just as Freud's hysteric patients expressed a *belle indifference* to their symptoms and a surprising reluctance to change them, so did these parents have a *belle indifference* to the symptoms of their children. Just as the individual's symptom represents an expression of his own unconscious wish, so does the child's symptom represent an expression of his parents' unconscious wishes.

that the child was caught in the conflict. This also permitted one spouse to express annoyance to the other indirectly without endangering the marital relationship. For example, in one case, the father objected to the son's leaving toys lying around and would violently explode at the child for such behavior, implying that the mother was wrong in permitting him to do this. The mother realized that the father exploded at such behavior and did not stop the father since she "knew he was right." Nevertheless, she often indicated that the child need not bother picking up the toys, since she felt that he was too young to have to do such things by himself and that the father was too strict. If the mother's encouragement of the behavior annoying to the father was explicit, there would be danger that the father's hostility would be directed at the mother rather than the child. By keeping the encouragement implicit the mother was able to deny that she had encouraged the child. The father was usually willing to accept this denial, even if he did not believe it, rather than risk an explosion with his wife. In some instances, however, the other spouse was angered or felt compelled to criticize the other for not handling the child properly. Then the encouragement of the child to behave in a certain way would have to become more subtle to avoid criticism of the other spouse, another delicate balance to maintain. A parent had to give sufficient encouragement to the child to perform the act, without making it so obvious that his spouse felt obliged to criticize him.

In addition to the inconsistent pressures resulting from the difference between explicit and implicit expectations and from the differences between the expectations of the two parents, the child also had to deal with changes in each parent's expectations. From the parent's conscious point of view,

this inconsistency resulted from an attempt to reconcile two conflicting desires: teaching the child to behave properly and not being "too hard on the child." When a parent was consciously attempting to teach the child proper behavior, he was extremely aggressive and critical.[19] At other times, the parent felt he had been too critical of the child and permitted him to behave in the same way without punishment, and would be extremely affectionate and supportive. While the explanation given for this inconsistency was that he wanted to teach the desired behavior without being "too hard on the child," its latent function was to prevent the child from consistently living up to the ostensibly desired behavior and to preserve the disliked behavior. The period of not being "too hard on the child" served to reinforce the disapproved behavior and the period of "being firm" permitted the parents to express their anxieties and hostility. This balance was also very delicate since it was always possible that negative sanctions would become so severe that the child would refuse to behave in such a way that parents felt he could legitimately be punished.

The delicacy of this balance was perhaps best exemplified by the problem of bed-wetting. Parents complained about bed-wetting, but at the same time they could not bring themselves to do anything to alter the child's be-

---

[19] While the control imposed by parents in well families sometimes appeared to be extremely aggressive and punitive, this aggression was not such a massive critical attack on the child and did not carry the threat of such severe sanctions as did the aggression by the disturbed parents. In the well families, the punishment of the child was not regarded by the child as so damaging, and there was ordinarily the possibility of escaping further punishment by behaving in a different, desired way. There were few possibilities for the child to escape this hostility in the disturbed family.

havior. If the therapists could get both parents to be firm at the same time, the child would usually stop bed-wetting. Very soon, however, by putting a rubber sheet on the bed, or buying special night clothes "just in case he wets," the child was encouraged again to wet. One mother succeeded several times in finding methods to stop her son's wetting, but immediately stopped using them "since he's stopped now." In several cases, the parents would alternate in being concerned and trying to be firm and being unconcerned and implicitly encouraging the behavior, at all times remaining inconsistent, one with the other. It seemed clear that whether or not the child wet his bed was a relatively sensitive index of just where the balance of rewards from the parents lay. In general, however, the implicit demands carried the greater sanction power and the child continued with the behavior of which the parents unconsciously approved and consciously disapproved. Presumably, the sanctions of the parents against bed-wetting would increase as the child grew older, and the balance would become delicate only at that later time.

Since these conflicting expectations existed over a long period of time, it is not surprising that the child internalized these conflicts. Once a child was selected as a deviant, there was a circular reaction which tended to perpetuate this role assignment. Once he had responded to his parents' implicit wishes and acted in a somewhat disturbed manner, the parents could treat him as if he really were a problem. The child would respond to these expectations and the vicious cycle was set in motion. Both the child and the parents, then, had complementary expectations. The particular role assigned to the child was appropriately rewarded. It is difficult, if not impossible, to distinguish just at what point the parents

began treating the child as if he were a problem and at what point the child actually did have internalized problems. There does not seem to be any sudden development of the child's problems; rather, it is a process occurring over a period of time. By the time the family was seen in the clinic, the vicious cycle was well established, and the child had internalized his disturbed role to such an extent that it was difficult to effect change only by removing external pressures. This was, of course, particularly true for older and more disturbed children. The fact that the child becomes disturbed adds stability to the role system, so that once set in motion, scapegoating did not easily pass from one child to another. In the well families, when scapegoating did take place, it was less severe and did not become stabilized with one child as a continual scapegoat.

## The Rationalization of Scapegoating

When a scapegoating situation was established, a relatively stable equilibrium of the family was achieved. However, there were difficulties in maintaining the equilibrium. Parents had considerable guilt about the way they treated the child, and when the child was identified as disturbed by neighbors, teachers, doctors, or other outside agencies, pressure was brought to bear for some action to be taken. When called upon to explain, parents did not have much difficulty in explaining why they were so concerned about the child, but they did have great difficulty in rationalizing their aggressive and libidinal expressions to the children.

One way in which the parents rationalized their behavior was to define themselves, rather than the children, as victims. They stressed how much difficulty there was coping with all the problems posed by their child. For example, mothers of bed-wetters complained about the problems of keeping sheets clean and the impossibility of the child staying overnight at friends' or relatives' homes. Such rationalizations seemed to relieve some of the guilt for victimizing the children and served as a justification for continued expressions of annoyance toward the children.

Another way was to emphasize how fortunate their children really were. For most of these parents, the standard of living provided for their children was much higher than the standard of living they enjoyed when they were children. One of the central complaints of these parents, particularly the fathers, was that the children wanted too much and got much more than the parents ever got when they were children. This was seen by the parents as a legitimate excuse for depriving their children of the toys, privileges, and other things they wanted, and for refusing to recognize the children's complaints that they were not getting things. A closely related type of rationalization stems from the change of child-rearing practices over the past generation. The parents felt that their parents were much stricter than they were with their children and that children nowadays "get away with murder." Many of the parents had acute conflicts about how strict to be with children, and when the parents did express aggression to the children, they often defined it as beneficial strictness and "giving the child a lesson." Since their own parents were much more severe with them, their own children don't realize "how good they have it."

The parents also used various specific norms to justify their behavior. Even though the parents may be giving implicit encouragement to break these norms, the fact that these social norms are explicitly recognized gives the parents a legitimate basis for punishing the children. As long as the permission for disobeying the sanctions is implicit, it is always possible for the parents to deny that they are really giving it. In general, these parents were reluctant to admit that their child had an emotionl disturbance or that he was behaving the way he was because of certain inner problems. They generally interpreted the disturbed child's behavior as willful badness. They felt that the child could behave differently if he really wanted to. Hence, what was needed, in their view, was not consideration, advice, and help, but a "lesson" in how to behave, i.e., severe reprimands and punishment; but even this they could not give. At times, the parents attempted to deny completely that they were scapegoating this particular child. They insisted very rigidly that "we treat all the children just the same." At other times, the parents insisted that this one particular child was just different from all others, implying that this child deserved punishment and that they were good parents since their other children have turned out so well.

Frequently, the mothers expressed, although inconsistently, unusually strong affection for a son. They justified this almost invariably in the same way: the child had problems and difficulties and thus needed more help and care than the other children. However, what they considered care and protection far exceeded the usual limits. This can be seen for example, in the mother who carried her twelve-year-old son from the bed to the bathroom so that he could avoid bed-wetting, in the mother who continually fondled her adolescent son and called him "lovie," and in the frequent slips of the tongues by a variety of family members which identified the mother and son as spouses. Fathers, on the other hand, often had special attachments to, and fondness for, daughters.

All these attempts of the parents to

rationalize their behavior had a very defensive quality and showed the difficulty these parents had in reconciling their own behavior with general social norms about child-rearing. In the more severely disturbed families, the pressing nature of their problems required serious distortion of social norms, but in the mildly disturbed families, more attention was given to the social norms, and attempts were made to express emotions in more acceptable ways. In any event, much energy was required to keep the balance stable, a state which required co-ordination of many subtle and inconsistent feelings and behaviors. It was, in effect, an "armed truce," and the danger of an explosion was constantly present.

## Functions and Dysfunctions of Scapegoating

### Functions

Although the present paper has been concerned with the dynamics of the family as a group in relation to an emotionally disturbed child, some comments should be made on the functions that scapegoating serves for the parents individually and for external social systems. For the parents, scapegoating served as a personality-stabilizing process. While the parents of these children did have serious internal conflicts, the projection of these difficulties onto the children served to minimize and control them. Thus, in spite of their personality difficulties, the parents were able to live up to their commitments to the wider society, expressing a minimum of their difficulties in the external economic and political systems. Most of the parents were able to maintain positions as steady workers and relatively respectable community members.

While the scapegoating of the child

helped the parents live up to their obligations to the community, often they did not live up to their obligations as adequately as other families, and the whole family became a scapegoat for the community. Then the same mechanisms existed between the outer community and the family as between parents and child. The families, like their children, seldom fought back effectively; instead they channeled their additional frustrations and tensions through the child. Once established, many forces may play into the scapegoating situation. Though the child suffered additional burdens, through the medium of the family, he helped drain off the tension of the broader community in relation to a particular family.

From the point of view of the family, the primary function of scapegoating is that it permits the family to maintain its solidarity. In all the disturbed families, there were very severe strains which continually threatened to disrupt the family.[20] In all the disturbed families, very serious dissatisfactions between spouses came to light during the course of therapy, which were much more severe than those found in the well families. In the two families with the most severely disturbed children, when the scapegoating of the child eased up during therapy, the explosions between parents became so severe that there was serious fear that the family might break up. In the one case in which the problems between spouses remained relatively latent throughout therapy, marital problems emerged more clearly after the termination of therapy, and this led to serious anxiety attacks of the father. Yet, considering these internal strains, all

---

[20] In one well family, when there was considerable marital tension it was handled in a very overt fashion, and marital problems were not dealt with through the child.

of these families have shown surprising stability. Only in one family had there been a brief period of voluntary separation between the parents, and it had occurred before their first child was born. By focusing on one particular child, the families were able to encapsulate problems and anxieties which could potentially disrupt various family processes. There seemed to be an added solidarity between the parents who stood united against the problem child. The fact that it is a child who is disturbed permits the parents to continue to perform the tasks necessary for household maintenance with relative stability. Since the child is in a dependent position and contributes relatively little to family task activities, his malfunctioning does not seriously interfere with family stability.

## Dysfunctions

While the scapegoating of a child is effective in controlling major sources of tensions within the family, when a child becomes emotionally disturbed, this leads to disturbing secondary complications which are, however, generally less severe than the original tensions. One dysfunction is that certain realistic problems and extra tasks are created for the family. The child does require special care and attention. If, for example, the child is a bed-wetter, then the family must either wake him up regularly, or wash many sheets and take other precautions. This becomes particularly acute when traveling, visiting, or attending camp. Often the child cannot be left alone, and someone must continually look after him. If the child is to receive treatment, then the parents must expend time and money in providing this.

In addition, while the child is responsive to the implicit sanctions of his parents, he, too, may develop mechanisms of fighting back and punishing his parents for the way they treat him. Often the child becomes very skilled in arousing his parents' anxieties or in consciously bungling something his parents want him to do. Of course, the mother, being present during most of the day, experiences more of this counteraggression, and this in part accounts for her readiness to bring the child in for treatment. In most of these families it was the mother who took the initiative in seeking treatment. It would appear that as long as she can carefully control the amount of hostility the child expresses to her, she can tolerate this dysfunction, but when hostility rises above a certain point she is willing to seek outside help.

While the functions of the scapegoat within the nuclear family clearly outweigh his dysfunctions, this is typically not the case with the child's relationship outside the nuclear family. While the family gives the child sufficient support to maintain his role in the family, the use of him as a scapegoat is often incompatible with equipping him to maintain an adjustment outside the nuclear family. This problem becomes particularly acute when the child begins important associations outside the nuclear family in relationship with peers and his teachers at school.[21] It is at this time that many

21 At adolescence, the time when more demands for independent existence are made, a large number of acute disturbances appear. Many who were adequately adjusted to the roles they were assigned within the family, were unable to meet the new adjustment outside the family. See, for example, Nicholas J. Demerath, "Adolescent Status and the Individual" (unpublished Ph.D. thesis, Harvard University, 1942). A large number of acute psychoses also occur as soon as the army recruit leaves home and enters military service. Under ordinary circumstances, the socialization of the child prepares him for the social demands of external society. See, for example, Talcott Parsons, "The Incest Taboo in Relation to Social Structure and the Socialization of the Child," *British Journal of Sociology*,

referrals to psychiatric clinics are made.[22] While the child's behavior was perfectly tolerable to the parents before, his behavior suddenly becomes intolerable. While he may still be performing the role the family wants him to play in order to be a scapegoat, this comes into conflict with his role as a representative of the family. The family is thus in conflict between using the child as a scapegoat and identifying with the child because of his role as family representative to the outside. Both sides of this conflict are revealed most clearly in the one family which carried on a feud with the outside and alternated between punishing the daughter for her poor school behavior and criticizing the teachers and children in school for causing problems for their daughter. In nearly all of these disturbed families, school difficulty was a crucial factor in the decision to refer the child for psychiatric treatment. While the child's behavior was rewarded at home, it was not rewarded at school, and while the family could tolerate the child's maladaptive behavior at home, when the school took special note of the child's behavior, this proved embarrassing and troubling to the parents.

This problem in relation to the outside world is perhaps most striking in the case of the school, but it is also true, for example, in relationships with neighbors and relatives. Neighbors and relatives are likely to be very critical of the family for the child's disturbed behavior, and it is often at such times that the family makes the greatest effort to get rid of the child's maladaptive behavior. In those families which alternated between punishing and rewarding the child's behavior, difficulty with the outside was often a cue to the family to move into the stage of punishing and criticizing the child's behavior.

While, as a whole, the child's disturbance served to relieve family tensions, it often led to further family tensions. To the extent that outside norms or standards, by which the child does not abide, are considered legitimate, inevitable frustrations arise. While the parents made strenuous efforts to interpret this as a result of the child's behavior and not of their own behavior, this effort was never completely successful. In accordance with modern child rearing theory to which they are at least exposed, they consider themselves at least partly responsible for the disturbance of the child, and this seems to have been particularly true at the time of therapy. Thus, the child's disturbance feeds back into the problems which must be faced by the parents, and the marital pair often project the responsibility for the child's disturbance onto each other. The mother will say, for example, that the father doesn't spend enough time with the children, and the father will say that the mother doesn't manage the children properly. While this was thus dysfunctional to the marital relationship, it never became so prominent that the parents ceased using the child as a scapegoat. The predominant direction of aggression was still toward the badly behaved child rather than toward the other spouse.

While the disturbed behavior leads to some dysfunctions for the family, it is the personality of the child which

V (1954), 101-17; and David Aberle and Kaspar Naegele, "Middle-Class Fathers' Occupational Roles and Attitudes toward Children," *American Journal of Orthopsychiatry*, XXII (1952), 566-78.

[22] The importance of difficulties with the associations outside the nuclear family in directing the family for psychiatric treatment has long been recognized by clinicians. See, for example, Anna Freud, "Indications for Child Analysis," in *The Psychoanalytic Study of the Child*, Vol. I (New York: International Universities Press, 1945).

suffers most as a result of the scape-goating. Any deviant or scapegoat within a group feels strong group pressure which creates considerable conflicts for him.[23] While other groups may also maintain their integration at the expense of the deviant, in the nuclear family this can be stabilized for a long period of time and result in far more serious personality impairment of the child assigned to the deviant role. The development of the emotional disturbance is simply part of the process of internalizing the conflicting demands placed upon him by his parents. While in the short run the child receives more rewards from the family for playing this role than for not playing this role, in the long run this leads to serious personality impairment. In short, the scapegoating mechanism is functional for the family as a group but dysfunctional for the emotional health of the child and for his adjustment outside the family of orientation.

[23] See, for example, the analysis of the case of Long John's nightmares in William F. Whyte, *Street Corner Society* (Chicago: Univ. of Chicago Press, 1943); and a report of Asch's experiments in Solomon E. Asch, *Social Psychology* (Englewood Cliffs, N.J.: Prentice-Hall, 1952).

# chapter fifteen

## Deification as an Antidote to Deprivation

PHILIP E. SLATER

A commonplace occurrence in training and therapy groups is the metaphorical or derisive reference to the leader as some sort of deity. This typically arises very early in the life of the group, although it may continue in some form for a considerable period.

I.[1] Ezriel quotes the following exchange from the opening minutes of the first session of a therapy group:

Reprinted from Philip E. Slater, *Microcosm: Structural, Psychological and Religious Evolution in Groups* (New York: John Wiley & Sons, Inc., 1966), pp. 7-23, by permission of the author. Copyright © 1966 by Philip E. Slater.

F2: . . . I am inclined to agree with Dr. Ezriel. There is a slight resentment against him. I feel you [Ezriel] should have been talking to us for a little longer.

F4: I think we all agree that we have been rather left in the lurch, in the open.

M2: It may arise from the fact that Dr. Ezriel sits there and says nothing. As if we were all gathered in front of an altar.[2]

Note the rapid shift here from feelings of abandonment, to hostility toward the one who abandons, to deification of this abandoning one. Note also the direct relationship between the leader's silence and the religious metaphor. It is this passivity which perhaps makes "Buddha" a particularly favored designation for the leader.

[1] See Appendix II [of the original volume] for a discussion of the sources and significance of examples.

[2] H. Ezriel, "A Psycho-analytic Approach to Group Treatment," *British Journal of Medical Psychology*, XXIII (1950), 65.

The anxiety generated by the leader's passive role is acute, even in sophisticated groups where it is anticipated. Some members may have been in similar groups before, or may have undergone psychoanalysis or a comparable experience. Yet the knowledge gained in such situations fades before the fantasies aroused by a new group leader, especially when he first appears in the garb of one of those archetypal autocrats, the doctor or the teacher. His violation of these fantasies is experienced as abandonment, and produces feelings of helplessness and bewilderment.

IIc. A student reported to an observer, "I feel like a mosquito trying to bite an iron ball."

IId. A student reported: "During the first several discussions I was filled with anxiety. A half hour before class my stomach would get tight and when class was over I felt very relaxed and relieved."

IIe. A member of this group said, after several meetings, that he experienced a feeling of emotional starvation every time he entered the room where the group was held. A second member reported a dream in which the group leader gave him an exam with three questions. He answered the first but had difficulty reading the second, and before he could make it out, the examination was over.[3] A few meetings later, a third member reported a dream in which he waved his arms and castigated the group for not doing its job, but when they asked him what he wanted to say he couldn't think of anything. A fourth reported a dream in which he came to the group meeting and the room was empty.

IIf. In an early meeting of another group several members reported coming to the session "empty," i.e., with "nothing particular" on their minds. They suggested holding the session out of doors, and when this movement lost impetus, began a discussion of nursery schools, of observing children through one-way mirrors, and of the difficulty of managing interaction in a group of twelve people. Several people were eating during this discussion and food was mentioned a good deal. The first meeting of this group had begun with a ten minute silence.

. . . We will deal in more detail with oral manifestations in groups, but the following illustration is noteworthy in its fusion of hunger and deification.

XII. One woman had brought some chocolate, which she diffidently invited her . . . neighbor . . . to share. One man was eating a sandwich. A graduate in philosophy, who had in earlier sessions told the group he had no belief in God, and no religion, sat silent, as indeed he often did, until one of the women with a touch of acerbity in her tone, remarked that he had asked no questions. He replied, "I do not need to talk because I know that I only have to come here long enough and all my questions will be answered without my having to do anything."
I then said that I had become a kind of group deity; that the questions were directed to me as one who knew the answers without need to resort to work . . . and that the philosopher's reply indicated a disbelief in the efficacy of prayer but seemed otherwise to belie earlier statements he had made about his disbelief in God. . . . By the time I had finished speaking I felt I had committed some kind of gaffe. . . . In me a conviction began to harden that I had been guilty of blasphemy in a group of true believers.[4]

This process of loss and deification

---

[3] Among other things this is a rather beautiful representation of conscious, preconscious, and unconscious material. The first is understood, the second can scarcely be made out, and the third is utterly unavailable.

[4] W. R. Bion, "Group Dynamics: A Review." In Melanie Klein, Paula Heimann, and R. E. Money-Kyrle, eds., *New Directions in Psycho-Analysis* (New York: Basic Books, 1957), p. 445.

is described most dramatically by Bennis in a paper on "depressive anxiety" in groups. Of particular relevance to deification is the following exchange which occurred in a group whose leader was actually absent for several meetings.

III. During a skittish part of that meeting the group talked about "a sort of spontaneous fountain that will bring forth and all we have to do is sit and drink."

"I think you are referring to the rock pile."

"I think the 'rock pile' is interesting since rocks were the original god figures when people used to worship gods all the time."

"This is too deep."

"Rock of Ages, Rock of my Fathers. "[5]

Here the feeling of oral deprivation is combined with the fantasy of nurturant abundance, and a supernatural solidity and permanence is substituted for realistic loss and uncertainty. The concept of the stone deity is an ambivalent fusion, for although stone is on the one hand reliable and everlasting, unlike the elusive and forsaking leader, it is also ungiving and comfortless, just as he is, and epitomizes the loneliness and desolation the members feel in response to his lack of nurturance.

The "rock pile" response is more than a sophisticated metaphor, however, and goes to the root of all religious phenomena. It is found even at the animal level, considerably developed among primates but observable in the simplest of herd animals. Thus Brody gives the following account, drawn from Guthrie-Smith, of the behavior of baby lambs when the mother dies:

The orphaned one then stands for long intervals by the mother's body, bleating, cold, hungry. When compelled to nibble at the grass, she does not venture far, and if perchance shepherds pass near she runs to the spot where the mother lies. She continues to do so for days and weeks, always camping by the store of wool and bones at night, even when they have sunk putrefied into the ground. *Eventually the feelings originally called forth by the ewe appear to be transferred to the prominent object near which the ewe died. This "foster mother rock" then is put in the role of parent, protector and companion* [italics mine].[6]

This process is vital to an understanding of primeval religion (i.e., those forms of which modern primitive religions are highly elaborated offshoots). It bears a relatively transparent relationship, for example, to such later phenomena as ancestor worship, totemism, and the early worship of trees in Europe and stones, stone piles, or stone pillars in the Eastern Mediterranean countries. In the latter cases it is often explicit that the landmark denotes either a grave or at least the dwelling of an ancestral spirit. Neumann argues that stones "are among the oldest symbols of the Great Mother Goddess, from Cybele and the stone of Pessinus . . . to the Islamic Kaaba and the stone of the temple in Jerusalem, not to mention the *omphaloi*, the navel stones, which we find in so many parts of the world."[7]

The importance of permanence in

---

[5] W. G. Bennis, "Defenses Against 'Depressive Anxiety' in Groups: The Case of the Absent Leader," *Merrill-Palmer Quarterly*, VII (1961), 11.

[6] Sylvia Brody, *Patterns of Mothering* (New York: International Universities Press, 1956), p. 95. Compare the use of stone in connection with burials in our own society. For a fascinating fictional rendering of this process see V. Gloag, *Our Mother's House* (New York: Simon & Schuster, 1963). Readers familiar with this novel will appreciate its relevance to many of the phenomena discussed here.

[7] E. Neumann, *The Great Mother* (New York: Pantheon, 1955), p. 260.

this worship of stones is underlined by the Tsimshian myth of Stone and Elderberry Bush, who quarrel as to who will give birth first. Txämsem assists Elderberry Bush: "For that reason people do not live many years. . . . If Stone had given birth first to her child, it would not be so."[8]

Jane Harrison also emphasizes the concept of permanence in early religions. She quotes Pausanias' statement that "in the olden time all the Greeks worshipped unwrought stones instead of images" and points out that the Herm was both tomb and boundary marker (a survival of which she finds in the fact that the Russian word *tchur* means both boundary and grandfather). "Into that pillar the mourner outpours, 'projects' all his sorrow for the dead protector, all his passionate hope that the ghost will protect him still." She suggests that the use of the Herm as an oracle simply extends the practice of going to the living elders for advice.[9]

But it is the combination of permanence and silence or motionlessness which gives the stone its religious utility and poignance. The dreaded aloneness and the fantasy devised to forfend it are fused in this symbol, for although indifferent, the stone nonetheless endureth forever.

To thee, O Lord, I call; my rock, be not deaf to me, lest, if thou be silent to me, I become like those who go down to the pit. (*Psalms 28:1*)

Be thou to me a rock of refuge. (*Psalms 71:3*)

Totemism reflects a translation of this basic idea of "not-alone-ness" into the more symbolic and sophisticated terms of relatedness to a species, partly because of the greater salience of these kinds of objects in the environments of totemistic cultures.

That the relationship is more basic than these specific connections is argued most vigorously by Freud, who sees all religious manifestations as an effort to recapture the blissful dependency of childhood.

When a human being has himself grown up, he knows, to be sure, that he is in possession of greater strength, but his insight into the perils of life has also grown greater, and he rightly concludes that fundamentally he still remains just as helpless and unprotected as he was in his childhood, that faced by the world he is still a child. Even now, therefore, he cannot do without the protection which he enjoyed as a child. But he has long since recognized, too, that his father is a being of narrowly restricted power, and not equipped with every excellence. He therefore harks back to the mnemic image of the father whom in his childhood he so greatly overvalued. He exalts the image into a deity and makes it into something contemporary and real. The effective strength of this mnemic image and the persistence of his need for protection jointly sustain his belief in God.[10]

In much of Western religion the key factor in this process is (in psychoanalytic terms) the transfer of many ego functions to the superego. One need not be strong, or intelligent, or able, or realistic—one need only be good. The world is transformed from an un-

[8] F. Boas, "Tsimshian Mythology," *Thirty-first Annual Report of the U.S. Bureau of Ethnology, 1909-1910* (1916), p. 62.

[9] Jane Ellen Harrison, *Mythology* (London: Longmans, 1924), pp. 5-10.

[10] S. Freud, "New Introductory Lectures in Psychoanalysis," in *The Standard Edition of the Complete Psychological Works of Sigmund Freud*, Vol. 22 (London: Hogarth, 1964), p. 163. Piaget seems to hold a similar view (J. Piaget, *The Moral Judgment of the Child* [London: Kegan Paul, 1932], p. 88). We need not, of course, include Freud's patriarchal bias in our acceptance of this basic idea.

certain, chaotic, and indifferent environment in which the pathways to success, happiness, or even survival are unknown and unpredictable to one which is ordered, controlled, and planned, with simple rules (either ethical or ritual) of behavior which all can follow.[11]

In most nonwestern religions this "good behavior" approach is absent or far less marked, but the substitution of order for chaos, prescription for ambiguity, and deity for isolation is present wherever the separateness of man from his environment is clearly perceived.[12]

From this viewpoint the oft heard accusation that the training group situation is an "artificial" one is not only absurd but ironic, for in fact it is a rather precise analogue of life itself. What differentiates training groups from "natural" task groups is their mortality, their confusion, and their leadership structure. Most groups formed to accomplish some purpose are potentially immortal, have a more

or less clear goal or at least a plan of action or an agenda, and a clearly defined leadership. Training groups are born knowing they must die; they do not know, aside from some ill-formulated notions about self-understanding, growth, and knowledge of group processes, why they are there or what they are going to do; and struggle perpetually with the fact that the object whom they fantasy to be powerful and omniscient in fact does nothing, fails to protect them or tell them what to do, and hardly seems to be there at all. Is this unlifelike? Is the most persistent theme of the training group situation, the plaintive "what are we supposed to be doing; what is the purpose and meaning of it all?" a query that is never heard outside of the esoteric confines of an unnatural "laboratory" setting? On the contrary, it issues from the central dilemma of life itself—that which human beings have always been most unable to face, taking refuge instead in collective fantasies of a planned and preordained universe, or in the artificial imperatives of a daily routine and personal or institutional obligation.

Training groups have similar difficulty in accepting the idea of an unprogrammed existence. They react with dread to the realization that nothing will happen unless they make it happen—that they are literally being left to their own devices, that there are no rules, no plan, no restraints, no explicit goals.[13] They, too, construct myths which serve to deny the frightening responsibility and aloneness which this state of affairs confers upon them.

---

[11] We might therefore be justified in positing a "morality principle" intermediate to the pleasure and reality principles. Parental love induces the child to adopt the latter. Fear of losing this love causes regression to the morality principle. Absence of such love causes inability to abandon the pleasure principle. The aesthetic stance is a primitive form of this morality principle.

[12] I am indebted to a student, William Bauer, for developing the connection between this line of thought and Huizinga's analysis of the pleasure derived from play (cf. J. Huizinga, Homo Ludens [Boston: Beacon Press, 1950]). For play, religion, and indeed all of culture may be seen as an attempt to create an improved little world, ordered and manageable, intellectually imaginable, with fixed rules and a finite set of outcomes, as an escape from and an insulation against the accidental, uncertain, infinite, chaotic, ambiguous, and inexorably indifferent and insensitive character of nature. Choice seems to frighten humans, and when religious fantasies decay men employ clocks and other machines to regulate their movements.

---

[13] This is, of course, a highly exaggerated picture of the freedom of the situation. It is surprising how many requirements, explicitly stated goals, and structural limits can be added to the setting without altering in the slightest this feeling about it or perception of it.

These myths and individual fantasies, furthermore, tend to confirm Fromm's thesis that even a sadomasochistic relationship in which one is used, abused, and exploited is often preferred to a state of "moral aloneness,"[14] for they are often sinister and macabre in the extreme.

The most common, the most pervasive, the most elaborated of these myths is the notion that the entire group experience is some kind of complicated scientific experiment. This takes many forms—sometimes it is seen as a stress experiment, sometimes as a stealthy personality test, or more often simply as a laboratory study of group development—but all varieties have two themes in common: (1) that the goal of the group leader is acquisitive and inquisitive rather than didactic or therapeutic, and (2) that the situation is not under the members' control—that they are helpless pawns in an unknown and unknowable game. Every occurrence is seen as a calculated experimental intervention. A visitor is a "plant," a leader's illness is a "test," objects left behind, chairs disarranged by previous occupants of the room, external noises, disturbances, or intrusions are all "gimmicks" to "see how we would react." These interpretations are thus comparable to religious visions and other paranoid "insights."

Often conjoined with the experiment myth, but sometimes occurring independently, is the myth of Inevitable Evolution or Universal Utility: the idea that everything taking place in the group, no matter how trivial, frivolous, tedious, and repetitive may seem, is an essential and anticipated aspect of the group's development. This myth is equivalent to religious explanations of "evil." Since group lead-

ers usually perceive more order and meaning in the interaction than do other members, they contribute heavily to the formation of this myth.

IIb. It was the fourth meeting, and Monty was expressing some discomfort with the lack of "niches" and "limits" in the course. John agreed, saying, ". . . actually, we're—guinea pigs, kind of. We're the experiment, where we think we're discussing the situation and deciding it, and actually we're all revealing to ourselves our psychological makeup and so on and so forth, and we're putting ourselves on display, whereas in other courses it's exactly the reverse. I mean it's kind of like a science fiction story, where we think we're in control of everything and actually we're looking up to something." Monty then quoted a joke told in another course about conditioning experiments: ". . . every time the rat presses a bar the man drops in—the experimenter drops in a piece of food, and the rat goes over and presses this bar when he's hungry, and when he's filled he stops, and the man says, 'look how well I have this rat trained,' and then you look at the rat and the rat says, 'well, look how well I have *him* trained. Every time I push the bar he drops food in'" (laughter).

Note the conjunction of the religious theme ("looking up to something") and the theme of oral plenty, both arising from the anxiety produced by the lack of structure in the group situation. John effectively denies that the members are free to make what they want of the group ("we *think* we're in control . . ."). Yet in the joke about the rat we can see the first seeds of the idea (later to blossom) that they might one day turn the tables on this "experimenter."

IIg. A difficult session a few weeks after the group began was characterized by depression, inaudibility, and long silences. Unhappiness was expressed over the absence of rules of order, which serve, it was said, to keep people from getting "cut up." Experiences in tutoring chil-

---

[14] E. Fromm, *Escape from Freedom* (New York: Holt, Rinehart and Winston, 1941).

dren were described. It was remarked that in a similar course at another university tape recorders were used to help "make sense" out of the interaction. Someone then told of an experiment in which tape recordings of the remarks of psychotic patients were edited in such a way as to "make sense," following which they were played back to the patient. A little later Debby described a movie, *The Fly*, in which a mad scientist attempted to re-compose the scattered atoms of a cat.[15] There were fantasies of observing the group from the ceiling, with the notion that perhaps more could be seen from there, or from some vantage point outside of it. Penny then confessed that a recent change in her own seating position had been a premeditated attempt to prove a theory of the group leader's about which she had read.

Three weeks later, during a difficult period surrounding the writing of a term paper, there was a long discussion of a "chance music" concert, "happenings," and other "planned-random" experiences.

Here we have examples both of obliquely stated experiment myths and of the myth of universal meaning. The desire for protection and the feeling of abandonment are reflected in the "rules of order" discussion. The regressed feeling of helplessness appears in the association to the tutoring of children. The dependent stance is beautifully depicted in the blissful passivity of the fantasy of the experimenter who "makes sense" out of psychotic utterances and feeds them back. Yet the experiment myth backfires because their helplessness makes them totally dependent on a possibly incompetent authority, who may not be able to "make sense" out of it at all and hence may leave them utterly atomized and psychotic—fragmenting not only the collectivity but individual egos.[16] Oc-

casionally we see a striving towards active initiative, primarily through identification with the group leader; that is, by finding some detached viewpoint similar to the leader's from which to view the proceedings. Yet along with this exaggerated magical respect for the leader's interpretive skills goes a comparable doubt about his competence (the "mad scientist"), which must be exorcised by devices such as Penny's. In the "chance music" discussion we find the same ambivalence: a desire to remove the group from authoritarian direction combined with a desire to have meaning and significance somehow emerge spontaneously and effortlessly from the proceedings without any activity, initiative, or interpretation on the part of the members.

IIb. At the end of this group members were asked on an exam to cite any group myths that had emerged during the course of the year, and to interpret their function for the group. While a great variety of "myths," fantasies, beliefs, and truths were offered in response to this question, the experiment myth was the overwhelming favorite (this was also true in three other groups, with different leaders, who took the same exam). It also seemed to have the greatest potency, for several of those who volunteered it as a myth and explained most brilliantly its motivational sources, also confessed that they still believed in it. The following are actual quotes from the responses to the exam question, consisting first of the various versions of the myths, then of some of the interpretations offered.

"This course was a large scale experiment."

"He was using us for his books as a live experiment."[17]

---

[15] Philip E. Slater, *Microcosm* (New York: Wiley, 1966), pp. 207-8.
[16] *Ibid.*, pp. 207 ff.

[17] It might be expected that knowledge of actual scientific interest in the group, such as is exhibited by this book, would increase the frequency of such fantasies, but the contrary seems to be the case. Groups conducted in laboratory observation rooms, knowing they are being observed, recorded, categorized, sub-

". . . the idea, to which I still cling, that the course was a proving ground for the young science of human relations, and that the members of the class were white rats."

"The course was an experiment in anxiety, similar to the conflicting Pavlov reflex experiments designed to make cats or white mice neurotic."

"The Department was selecting each individual's utterance from each session and was making a composite picture of each person, lifting his utterances out of context and splicing them on one after the other."

"It helped counteract our desire not to be too helpful to one another, because we were competing for grades and the favor of the authority figure. . . ."

". . . it would . . . suggest that there were ends we weren't being told . . . responsibility is taken from the group and placed in the hands of a directing authority. . . . The fact that it remains in my mind indicates that it is not yet cleared up. . . . It is an expression of a desire for a stronger authority, for outright direction."

"Fearing the knowledge of Dr. Slater we often said we believed we were being used as an experiment, thus invalidating the possible experiment."

". . . I think it is a truthful one. . . . It provides justification for Dr. S.'s avoidance of the position of leadership and guidance that we were so accustomed to in other courses. Dr. S. must be silent for some reason. . . . It could justify Dr. S.'s strange role."

". . . an aetiological myth, providing a reason for the existence of the class, where none seemed to exist—*it seemed better to think that there was a purpose, however hostile, behind the class than to remain in a group without any limits*" [italics mine].

IIf. The day before a meeting at which the group leader was to be absent, the group discussed teaching machines, Skinner boxes, and self-teaching physics books, and the alleged ill effects of such devices on the learning and mental health of the young. When this complaint was interpreted by the group leader, they launched into a full-fledged exposition of the experiment myth, complete with white rats and all.

Some weeks later a member remarked on an examination: "that the group felt the presence of a mother was evidenced in its most pronounced fantasy, i.e., the idea that the group was an experiment controlled from above."

The experiment myth is thus a religious one. It states, "We are not alone. All of this is part of a master plan which will only be revealed to us at the end. God is testing us, but if we are good and brave and true all will be well." It says that what seems like an uncontrolled and frightening chaos to ignorant mortals is really an orderly game. It is thus identical with the notion of a universe created by a quasi-omniscient deity, either as a testing-ground to separate sheep from goats or for some other abstruse purpose.[18]

jected to regular questionnaires and interviews, seem far less inclined to interpret events in this manner than those run under normal circumstances. Authorship of books on groups is often attributed to those who have written none, as part of the general tendency to aggrandize the group leader. The reader should perhaps be assured, however, that at the time this exam was given the present book was not contemplated nor was the significance of the experiment myth recognized. It was only because of a university regulation that exam books be kept a year that these data were still available when their significance was appreciated.

[18] The survival and hardy persistence of Judaism results in part from the timely introduction of an experiment myth. In biblical times warlike tribes who lost battles assigned the cause to the impotence of their god-of-battles. If conquered they assumed the enemy god to be more powerful and shifted some of their allegiance. The people of Israel, however, concluded that their god was not impotent but angry and bent on punishing them. This enabled them still to retain their belief in his omnipotence and to preserve their group identity intact.

deification as an antidote to deprivation     **197**

This is not the place to engage in a comparative study of religions, because although I think that most religions . . . both primitive and modern, can be shown to contain aspects of the experiment myth, such a task is beyond the scope of this work. For the moment I shall merely present as an example of a limiting case an unusual religious myth in which we can observe a kind of "return of the repressed." In this myth much of the sense of isolation, abandonment, and uncertainty against which religion is directed is retained, although an explanation for it is provided. It thus holds more firmly to that piece of reality which it seeks to overcome than perhaps any other religious myth in the world, and although it comes from a primitive society, it has a strangely modern, Kafka-like ring to it[19]:

Once upon a time Ndriananahary (God) sent down to earth his son Ataokoloinona . . . to look into everything and advise on the possibility of creating living beings. . . . But, they say, it was so insufferably hot everywhere that Ataokoloinona could not live there, and plunged into the depths of the earth to find a little coolness. He never appeared again.

Ndriananahary waited a long time for his son to return. Extremely uneasy . . . he sent servants to look for Ataokoloinona. They were men, who came down to earth, and each of them went a different way to try to find the missing person. But all their searching was fruitless. . . .

Seeing the uselessness of their efforts, men from time to time sent one of their number to inform Ndriananahary of the failure of their search, and to ask for fresh instructions.

Numbers of them were thus despatched to the Creator, but unluckily not one returned to earth. They are the Dead. To this day messengers are still sent to Heaven since Ataokoloinona has not yet been found, and no reply from Ndriananahary has yet reached the earth, where the first men settled down and have multiplied. They don't know what to do—should they go on looking or should they give up? Alas, not one of the messengers has returned to give us information on this point. And yet we still keep sending them, and the unsuccessful search continues.[20]

Whereas in macrocosmic mythmaking it is the perpetual silence of deities which must somehow be explained (or denied), in the training group it is the more immediate and concrete silence

---

[19] It need hardly be pointed out that a number of modern plays reflect the kinds of concerns we have been discussing in this section, e.g., Beckett's *Waiting for Godot* (which I have more than once heard used as a self-characterization by groups) and Pinter's *The Dumbwaiter*. Perhaps another expression of the same issue is the popularity in American films and television dramas of what I have called the "democratic pathos": the opposition of a strong, efficient, despotic, attractive, but villainous figure to either a young and powerless hero or an older, bumbling, kindly figure, with the villain being overcome only at the last moment by essentially implausible means. The villain may be a cattle baron, a captain of industry, a crime lord, a Hollywood producer, or, as in the film *Seven Days in May* (which epitomizes the theme), a military leader, but the essential conflict is the same. It is the American catharsis for ambivalence about democracy: the attractive tyrant is rejected in the end for the ineffectual, easy-going father who holds the proper values. Normally, these two images are kept sharply apart (cf. Martha Wolfenstein and N. Leites, *Movies: A Psychological Study* [New York: The Free Press, 1950]), but one could easily detect a tendency toward fusion in the public image of the late President Kennedy, who while maintaining the value emphasis, nonetheless communicated

certain qualities of toughness, efficiency, and invincibility that seemed to tap the more latent fantasy. This fusion may have contributed some of the intensity which characterized the grief reaction to his sudden death.

[20] M. Fauconnet, "Mythology of Black Africa," in *Larousse Encyclopedia of Mythology* (New York: Prometheus Press, 1959), pp. 480-81.

of the group leader. For it is this silence which activates the entire process. As soon as the members begin fully to realize that they have no one to lean on but each other, religious themes begin to creep into the discussion, and tend to recur whenever the members feel particularly abandoned and unprotected. Usually the remarks are highly tinged with sarcasm, that traditional measuring-rod of the gap between fantasy and reality. The group leader may be referred to as "the great stone face" (see the previous discussion about the "rock pile"), a "brooding inscrutable deity," a "metaphysical entity," or "The Impersonal Objective Being," and his interpretive function sardonically labelled "the Delphic Oracle" or "Zeus hurling thunderbolts."

IIc. During a prolonged period of great tension and confusion several group members one morning greeted the group leader as he entered with a blow-by-blow narration of his preliminary rituals: ". . . now he takes off his coat, now he starts the tape recorder, adjusts his chair . . ." etc., etc., concluding, as he seated himself, with the remark, ". . . and now God's in his Heaven and all's right with the world."

Here the hostile ridicule masks an intense yearning for order and control —a palpable pleasure was taken in this one bit of regularity (however functionless) in the situation. There is a particularly delicious irony in the closing remark, since all knew that although the leader's act of settling himself in his chair might in other situations signal the group's "coming to order," what seemed to them like utter chaos was about to ensue, and that "God in his Heaven" would simply look on with interest.

XI. During the first meeting of a group of adolescent females with a male leader, the members reacted to the lack of structure with some anxiety. They asked the leader what he wanted of them, and when he declined to provide an agenda they decided to discuss dreams, one member wondering if the leader would "psychoanalyze" them and report his conclusions at the end of the year. Another suggested he would help them do it themselves. After some further discussion of what their "assignment" was and another vain effort to obtain direction from the leader, there were several complaints that they "weren't getting anywhere." A discussion of dreams (it is entirely possible that the members knew this was a topic in which the leader had a special interest and competence) then began, but very rapidly led to the topic of religion, and whether beliefs in reincarnation or spiritualism were incompatible with a belief in God.

Toward the end of the year the question of religion again came up, again following a discussion of the leader's refusal to help. One member suggested that "maybe we're fighting for Mr. J. to give the answers to prove that we don't have any answers ourselves, but we really do!" After some discussion of the possibility of punishing the leader with a "silence strike," one girl argued that "maybe we don't want to be members of a mass; just female blobs. Maybe we want to be us; individuals; ourselves." To which another member replied, "A person can be himself and still be a part of something else. It's like being one with God." There ensued a long discussion of free will and determinism.[21]

These two religious discussions are analogous, since both involve conflict over dependency needs. The first is aroused by the initial shock of lack of structure, while the second appears when the members are taking tentative steps toward actively accepting independence.

The following example, although it contains no explicit religious references,

---

21 R. M. Jones, *An Application of Psychoanalysis to Education* (Springfield, Ill.: Charles C Thomas, 1960), pp. 31-33, 72-73.

is rather typical in its ambivalence about the freedom afforded by the leader's passive role.

IVc. In the fourth meeting of the group one girl made the following summary statement, directed to the group leader: "In the three days we've been together in the group I think everybody's loosened up a little bit, and intentionally you've deliberately—you haven't said anything at first—I think it's hard for people to— when they do speak—you start out with an artificial—or with a very academic approach and we don't know where we're going and we don't know exactly what we're trying to get at in this case—and you won't answer anything, so—we've got to do everything on our own—and just looking around at how we've come to do anything—certain people have come out, more or less leaders of the group, you've seen people—instead of addressing you, addressing members of the group in particular, raising their hands to that person, and other people at first afraid to say anything, and one by one I think almost everyone has contributed a little bit, and as we continue the group has developed a structure on its own, and I think it's almost your intention that we should be able to work on our own, so that perhaps some day if you didn't even come to class the discussion ought to run—with its own directions, and we could continue to think on our own so that perhaps (laughter) when we've left the context of the class we should be able to do the same as we've done in here on our own."[22]

On one level this statement is a reasonable summary not only of what takes place in the early meetings of groups, but also of some of the explicit goals of group leaders. At the same time we detect in it a rather plaintive note ("it's hard," "you won't answer," "we've got to do everything on our own") and mixed with group pride a touch of anxious and pious resentment ("cer-

tain people have come out," "instead of addressing you"), capped with a stubborn faith ("I think it's almost your intention"). This mixture of total acceptance of the leader's wisdom and resentment of his inactivity is fused in the remarks about the group's growing independence, as if to say, "I am a faithful believer, but look what's happening here: other people are taking over. I hope you know what you're doing." This aspect of her complex statement is reminiscent of a less ambivalent voice from the distant past:

Arise, O Lord! Let not man prevail.
  (*Psalms 9:19*)

Why dost thou stand afar off, O Lord?
Why dost thou hide thyself in times of trouble? (*Psalms 10:1-2*)

Rouse thyself! Why sleepest thou, O Lord?
Awake! Do not cast us off forever!
Why dost thou hide Thy face?
Why dost thou forget our affliction and oppression? (*Psalms 44:23-4*)

. . . their tongue struts through the earth.
Therefore the people turn and praise them. (*Psalms 73:9-10*)

Thy foes have roared in the midst of thy holy place;
they set up their own signs for signs. (*Psalms 74:4*)

Put not your trust in princes. (*Psalms 146:3*)

Be still before the Lord, and wait patiently for him;
fret not yourself over him who prospers in his way. (*Psalms 37:7*)

How great are thy works, O Lord!
Thy thoughts are very deep!
The dull man cannot know,
the stupid man cannot understand.
  (*Psalms 92:5-6*)

In groups, as in life, the ambiguity of the situation creates uncertainty

---

[22] T. M. Mills, transcript.

about the relative efficacy of conformity to the imagined authoritarianism of a silent figurehead or active striving toward the successes of the world. Mixed with pious acceptance of his wishes, we find doubt as to whether he prefers docile submission or "those who help themselves."

IIe. In the first three weeks of this group, in which the group leader was generally referred to rather casually as "God," the members were very concerned with how they were doing, and how this compared with the leader's expectations. One member had the fantasy that each person was receiving a tiny grade for every remark made. Another suggested that they were really like a primal group starting from scratch, and would have to develop their own god, cosmogony, polity, etc., after the manner of *Lord of the Flies*.[23] This led to some discussion of the group leader, after which they concluded that if they had come in at the beginning and he had not been there at all, they would still have required (*a*) an unknown, and (*b*) an authority, and would have fantasied a hidden tape recorder or one-way mirror, or that one of their number was really a spy.

In this fantasy they are simply describing in a more extreme form what has actually taken place.

Let us now summarize this early phase. We have suggested that the problems posed by death, loss, abandonment, and isolation generate religious ideas and sentiments. Dead parents become *Manes;* a dead leader becomes a hero or a god.[24] An attitude of reverence develops out of dependent

longings and the removal of the real object. Similarly, in training groups the passive role played by the leader is experienced as a death or loss, and reverent fantasies are produced by precisely the same two factors: (1) the withdrawal of authoritarian direction, which aggravates dependency needs, and (2) the minimization of personality cues through silence, which like physical absence facilitates transference responses. Frightened by the freedom and responsibility given to them, afraid that the shadowy and passive figure cannot fulfill their childlike longing, they begin to mold from early parental images a fantasy of an omniscient and omnipotent protector, who one day will step forward and lead them out of their labyrinthine confusion or give them the key or the secret formula which will reveal the master design behind the apparent disorder and chaos. The anarchic nature of the discussions will be shown to be an essential part of this larger predetermined order, which will all be understood at the "latter day," when the group comes to an end. The "experiment" myth is the most concrete version of this belief—a perfect example of a religious cosmogony in microcosm. We are reminded of Bacon's remark regarding Solomon: ". . . for so he saith expressly, 'The glory of God is to conceal a thing, but the glory of the King is to find it out'; as if, according to the innocent play of children, the Divine Majesty took delight to hide His works, to the end to have them found out; and as if kings could not obtain a greater honour than to be God's playfellows in that game. . . ."[25]

Before considering the revolt itself let us examine a group in which the experiment myth, had it arisen, would

[23] W. Golding, *Lord of the Flies* (New York: Putnam, 1955).

[24] If honored through a sufficient number of generations by a sufficiently prolific family, an ancestor may even become a god, somewhat after the fashion of a winner in a pyramid club (cf. N. D. Fustel de Coulanges, *The Ancient City* [Garden City, N.Y.: Doubleday, 1956], pp. 35-36).

[25] Quoted in H. M. McLuhan, *The Gutenberg Galaxy* (Toronto: Univ. of Toronto Press, 1962), p. 190.

have been unusually veridical, since the group was explicitly formed as part of a social psychological experiment. Volunteers were paid for their participation in the group and in addition to the group sessions were interviewed and tested individually for several hours. The group exemplifies rather clearly the transition from passivity and deification to a more active definition of their own role in the proceedings.[26]

XIII. The group met four times. During the first session the discussion turned briefly to the observers behind a one-way mirror and to the group leader, of whom it was remarked that "every once in a while he interjects—sort of like God." A little later George argued that "it would defeat the purpose if we analyzed what we were saying. That's their job. We're just supposed to talk." But Patty objected that "this is supposed to be for us, too. It's not just for them." Toward the end of the session the question of luncheon arrangements arose (there was to be an afternoon session also), since Patty, who was wearing a cast, did not want to go a long distance. Henry joked about intravenous feeding, and little pellets provided by the experimenters. A few minutes later George "wondered about the significance of J. B." (the group leader). The connection with MacLeish's play was quickly made, and Henry suggested that he was "having his dialogue with the devil and god," and Jane that he was "like a god or something." A little later they discussed "testimonies," which they quickly associated to the "brainwashing" techniques of the Chinese, noting that the groups used there also had a leader.

The second and third sessions brought more expanded definitions of the role of the members, beginning as defiant expressions of flight, such as a suggestion in the second session that "we can all put our heads down on the desk and go to sleep if we want to," and a fantasy of all leaving and going to the beach in the third.[27] But more and more they became interested in becoming closer to one another and learning about group process.

During the fourth and last meeting, when considerable attention was being paid to thoughts of separation and fantasies of reunion, the issue of what each person would take with them arose. Patty made the following statements: ". . . I know all of you, and . . . you mean something to me, that you didn't mean two Saturdays ago. But more than that we've made a thing here. See, we've made it. It wasn't here and now it's here, and we did it, and that's—and so, the trouble is, we have a responsibility to this thing we've made and I don't know whether this responsibility ends after we walk out of the door at five o'clock. . . ."

Later, amidst talk of whether they and the experimenters had learned anything she said: "But you're still treating it like it was, like what it was to begin with. You're saying, 'Here is an experiment, and you will participate and gain a lot for yourself.' But we made something more than that—more than what it was at the beginning, you see."[28]

This is a reasonably definitive statement of what the revolt signifies.

---

[26] For a fuller description of part of this process, see Philip E. Slater, *Microcosm*, p. 127.

[27] *Ibid.*

[28] R. D. Mann, transcript.

# chapter sixteen

## Social Systems as a Defense against
## Persecutory and Depressive Anxiety

It has often been noted that many social phenomena show a strikingly close correspondence with psychotic processes in individuals. Melitta Schmideberg[1] for instance, has pointed to the psychotic content of many primitive ceremonies and rites. And Bion[2] has suggested that the emotional life of the group is only understandable in terms of psychotic mechanisms. My own recent experience[3] has impressed upon me how much institutions are used by their individual members to reinforce individual mechanisms of defense against anxiety, and in particular against recurrence of the early para-

noid and depressive anxieties first described by Melanie Klein.[4] In connecting social behavior with defense against psychotic anxiety, I do not wish in any way to suggest that social relationships serve none other than a defensive function of this kind. Instances of other functions include the equally important expression and gratification of libidinal impulses in constructive social activities, as well as social cooperation in institutions providing creative, sublimatory opportunities. In the present paper, however, I propose to limit myself to a consideration of certain defensive functions, and in so doing I hope to illustrate and define how the mechanisms of projective and introjective identification operate in linking individual and social behavior.

The specific hypothesis I shall consider is that *one* of the primary cohesive elements binding individuals into institutionalized human association is that of defense against psychotic anxiety. In this sense individuals may be

Reprinted from Elliot Jaques, "Social Systems as a Defense against Persecutory and Depressive Anxiety," in Melanie Klein, Paula Heimann, and R. E. Money-Kyrle, eds., *New Directions in Psycho-Analysis: The Significance of Infant Conflict in the Pattern of Adult Behavior* (New York: Basic Books, Inc., 1955), Chap. 10, pp. 478-98, by permission of Basic Books, Inc. Copyright © 1955 by Basic Books, Inc.

[1] "The Role of Psychotic Mechanisms in Cultural Development," *International Journal of Psycho-Analysis*, XI (1930), 387-418.
[2] "Group Dynamics: A Re-view," in M. Klein et al., eds., *New Directions in Psycho-Analysis*, pp. 440-77.
[3] *The Changing Culture of a Factory* (London: Tavistock, 1951).

[4] The views of Mrs. Klein drawn upon in this paper are described in her two books, *The Psycho-Analysis of Children* (London: L. & Virginia Woolf at the Hogarth Press and the Institute of Psycho-Analysis, 1932), and *Contributions to Psycho-Analysis, 1921-45* (London: Hogarth Press, 1948), and in papers recently published in J. Riviere, ed., *Developments in Psycho-Analysis* (London: Hogarth Press and the Institute of Psycho-Analysis, 1952).

thought of as externalizing those impulses and internal objects that would otherwise give rise to psychotic anxiety and pooling them in the life of the social institutions in which they associate. This is not to say that the institutions so used thereby become "psychotic." But it does imply that we would expect to find in group relationships manifestations of unreality, splitting, hostility, suspicion, and other forms of maladaptive behavior. These would be the social counterpart of—although not identical with—what would appear as psychotic symptoms in individuals who have not developed the ability to use the mechanism of association in social groups to avoid psychotic anxiety.

If the above hypothesis holds true, then observation of social process is likely to provide a magnified view of the psychotic mechanisms observable in individuals, while also providing a setting in which more than one observer can share. Moreover, many social problems—economic and political —which are often laid at the door of human ignorance, stupidity, wrong attitudes, selfishness, or power seeking, may become more understandable if seen as containing unconsciously motivated attempts by human beings to defend themselves in the best way available at the moment against the experience of anxieties whose sources could not be consciously controlled. And the reasons for the intractability to change of many social stresses and group tensions may be more clearly appreciated if seen as the "resistances" of groups of people unconsciously clinging to the institutions that they have, because changes in social relationships threaten to disturb existing social defenses against psychotic anxiety.

Social institutions, as I shall here use the term, are social structures with the cultural mechanisms governing relationships within them. Social structures are systems of roles, or positions, which may be taken up and occupied by persons. Cultural mechanisms are conventions, customs, taboos, rules, etc., which are used in regulating the relations among members of a society. For purposes of analysis, institutions can be defined independently of the particular individuals occupying roles and operating a culture. But the actual working of institutions takes place through real people using cultural mechanisms within a social structure; and the unconscious or implicit functions of an institution are specifically determined by the particular individuals associated in the institution, occupying roles within a structure and operating the culture. Changes may occur in the unconscious functions of an institution through change in personnel, without there necessarily being any apparent change in manifest structure or functions. And conversely, as is so often noted, the imposition of a change in manifest structure or culture for the purpose of resolving a problem, may often leave the problem unsolved because the unconscious relationships remain unchanged.

## Projection, Introjection, and Identification in Social Relationships

In *Group Psychology and the Analysis of the Ego*, Freud takes as his starting point in group psychology the relationship between the group and its leader. The essence of this relationship he sees in the mechanisms of identifications of the members of the group with the leader and with each other.[5]

---

[5] S. Freud, *Group Psychology and the Analysis of the Ego* (London: International Psycho-Analytical Press, 1922), p. 80: He states, "A primary group . . . is a number of individuals who have substituted one and the

Group processes in this sense can be linked to earlier forms of behavior, since "identification is known to psycho-analysis as the earliest expression of an emotional tie with another person."[6] But Freud did not explicitly develop the concept of identification beyond that of identification by introjection, a conception deriving from his work on the retention of lost objects through introjection.[7] In his analysis of group life, he does, however, differentiate between identification of the ego with an object (or identification by introjection) and what he terms replacement of the ego ideal by an external object.[8] Thus, in the two cases he describes, the Army and the Church, he points out that the soldier replaces his ego ideal by the leader who becomes his ideal, whereas the Christian takes Christ into himself as his ideal and identifies himself with Him.

Like Freud, Melanie Klein sees introjection as one of the primary processes whereby the infant makes emotional relationships with its objects. But she considers that introjection interacts with the process of projection in the making of these relationships.[9] Such a formulation seems to me to be consistent with, although not explicit

in, the views of Freud expressed above. That is to say, identification of the ego with an object is identification by introjection; this is explicit in Freud. But replacement of the ego ideal by an external object seems to me implicitly to contain the conception of identification by projection. Thus, the soldiers who take their leader for their ego ideal are in effect projectively identifying with him or putting part of themselves into him. It is this common or shared projective identification which enables the soldiers to identify with each other. In the extreme form of projective identification of this kind, the followers become totally dependent on the leader, because each has given up a part of himself to the leader.[10] Indeed, it is just such an extreme of projective identification which might explain the case of panic described by Freud,[11] where the Assyrians take to flight on learning that Holofernes, their leader, has had his head cut off by Judith. For not only has the commonly shared external object (the figure-head) binding them all together been lost, but the leader having lost his head, every soldier has lost his head through being inside the leader by projective identification.

I shall take as the basis of my analysis of group processes the conception of identification in group formation, as described by Freud, but with particu-

---

same object for their ego ideal and have consequently identified themselves with one another in their ego."

[6] *Ibid.*, p. 60.

[7] "Mourning and Melancholia," *Collected Papers*, Vol. IV (London: Hogarth Press, 1925).

[8] *Group Psychology* . . . , p. 110.

[9] Cf. "Notes on some Schizoid Mechanisms," in J. Riviere, ed., *Developments in Psycho-Analysis*, p. 293: "I have often expressed my view that object relations exist from the beginning of life. . . . I have further suggested that the relation to the first object implies its introjection and projection, and that from the beginning object relations are moulded by an interaction between introjection and projection, between internal and external objects and situations."

[10] Cf. *Ibid.*, p. 301: "The projection of good feelings and good parts of the self into the mother is essential for the infant's ability to develop good object relations and to integrate his ego. However, if this projective process is carried out excessively, good parts of the personality are felt to be lost, and in this way the mother becomes the ego ideal; this process too results in weakening and impoverishing the ego. Very soon such processes extend to other people, and the result may be an over strong dependence on these external representatives of one's own good parts."

[11] *Group Psychology* . . . , p. 49.

lar reference to the processes of intro-jective and projective identification, as elaborated by Melanie Klein. Such a form of analysis has been suggested in another context by Paula Heimann,[12] who puts forward the notion that introjection and projection may be at the bottom of even the most complex social processes. I shall try to show how individuals make unconscious use of institutions by associating in these institutions and unconsciously cooperating to reinforce internal defenses against anxiety and guilt. These social defenses bear a reciprocal relationship with the internal defense mechanisms. For instance, the schizoid and manic defenses against anxiety and guilt both involve splitting and projection mechanisms, and, through projection, a link with the outside world. When external objects are shared with others and used in common for purposes of projection, fantasy social relationships may be established through projective identification with the common object. These fantasy relationships are further elaborated by introjection; and the two-way character of social relationships is mediated by virtue of the two-way play of projective and introjective identification.

I shall speak of the "fantasy social form and content of an institution" to refer to the form and content of social relationships at the level of the common individual fantasies which the members of an institution share by projective and introjective identifica-tion. Fantasy is used in the sense of completely unconscious intra-psychic activity, as defined by Susan Isaacs.[13] From this point of view the character of institutions is determined and colored not only by their explicit or consciously agreed and accepted functions but also by their manifold unrecognized functions at the fantasy level.

## Illustrations of Socially Structured Defense Mechanisms

It is not my intention in this article to explore either systematically or comprehensively the manner in which social defense mechanisms operate. I shall first examine certain paranoid anxieties and defenses, and then depressive anxieties and defenses, keeping them to some extent separate for purposes of explication and giving illustrations from everyday experience. Then I shall present case material from a social study in industry, which may make clearer some of the theoretical considerations by showing the interaction of paranoid and depressive phenomena.

### Defenses against Paranoid Anxiety

One example of social mechanisms of defense against paranoid anxieties is that of putting bad internal objects[14]

---

[12] Cf. "Functions of Introjection and Projection" in J. Riviere, ed., *Developments in Psycho-Analysis*, p. 129: "Such taking in and expelling consists of an active interplay between the organism and the outer world; on this primordial pattern rests all intercourse between subject and object, no matter how complex and sophisticated such intercourse appears. (I believe that in the last analysis we may find it at the bottom of all our complicated dealings with one another.) The patterns Nature uses seem to be few, but she is inexhaustible in their variation."

[13] "The Nature and Function of Phantasy," in J. Riviere, ed., *Developments in Psycho-Analysis*.

[14] The nature of the objects projected and introjected (e.g., feces, penis, breast), the medium of introjection and projection (e.g., anal, urethral, oral) and the sensory mechanism of introjection and projection (kinæsthetic, visual, auditory, etc.), are variables of fundamental importance in the analysis of group relationships. I shall not, however, consider these variables to any extent here, but I hope to show in subsequent publications that their introduction makes possible a systematic explanation of differences between many types of institution.

and impulses into particular members of an institution who, whatever their explicit function in a society, are unconsciously selected, or themselves choose to introject these projected objects and impulses and either to *absorb* them or *deflect* them. By absorption is meant the process of introjecting the objects and impulses and containing them, whereas in deflection they are again projected but not into the same members from whom they were introjected.

The fantasy social structuring of the process of absorption may be seen, for example, in the case of a first officer in a ship, who, in addition to his normal duty, is held responsible for many things that go wrong, but for which he was not actually responsible. Everyone's bad objects and impulses may unconsciously be put into the first officer, who is consciously regarded by common consent as the source of the trouble. By this mechanism the members of the crew can unconsciously find relief from their own internal persecutors. And the ship's captain can thereby be more readily idealized and identified with as a good protective figure. The anal content of the fantasy attack on the first officer is indicated in the colloquialism that "the first officer must take all the shit; and he must be prepared to be a shit." Naval officers in the normal course of promotion are expected to accept this masochistic role; and the norm is to accept it without demurring.

The process of deflection may be seen in certain aspects of the complex situation of nations at war. The manifest social structure is that of two opposing armies, each backed and supported by its community. At the fantasy level, however, we may consider the following possibility. The members of each community put their bad objects and sadistic impulses into the commonly shared and accepted external enemy. They rid themselves of their hostile, destructive impulses by projecting them into their armies for deflection against the enemy. Paranoid anxiety in the total community, Army and civilian alike, may be alleviated, or at least transmuted into fear of known and identifiable enemies, since the bad impulses and objects projected into the enemy return, not in the form of introjected fantastic persecutors, but of actual physical attack, which can be experienced in reality. Under appropriate conditions, objective fear may be more readily coped with than fantasy persecution. The bad sadistic enemy is fought against, not in the solitary isolation of the unconscious inner world, but in cooperation with comrades-in-arms in real life. Individuals not only rid themselves of fantastic persecution in this way; but further, the members of the Army are temporarily freed from depressive anxiety because their own sadistic impulses can be denied by attributing their aggressiveness to doing their duty, that is, expressing the aggressive impulses collected and introjected from all the community. And members of the community may also avoid guilt by introjecting the socially sanctioned hatred of the enemy. Such introjected sanction reinforces the denial of unconscious hatred and destructive impulses against good objects by allowing for conscious expression of these impulses against a commonly shared and publicly hated real external enemy.

Social cooperation at the reality level may thus allow for a redistribution of the bad objects and impulses in the fantasy relations obtaining among the members of a society.[15] In conjunction with such a redistribution, introjective identification makes it possible for individuals to take in social sanction and

---

[15] Cf. Freud's description of the redistribution of libido in the group, *Group Psychology*, p. 43.

support. The primitive aim of the absorption and deflection mechanisms is to achieve a non-return at the fantasy level of the projected fantasy bad objects and impulses.

But even where absorption and deflection are not entirely successful (and mechanisms at the fantasy level can never be completely controlled), the social defense mechanisms provide some gain. Paula Heimann[16] has described the introjection of projected bad objects, and their related impulses, into the ego, where they are maintained in a split-off state, subjected to intrapsychic projection, and kept under attack. In the cases described above, the ego receives support from the social sanctions which are introjected, and which legitimize the intra-psychic projection and aggression. The first officer, for example, may be introjected, and the impulses projected into him introjected as well. But in the fantasy social situation other members of the crew who also attack the first officer are identified with by introjection, partly into the ego, and partly into the super-ego. Hence the ego is reinforced by possession of the internalized members of the crew, all of whom take part in the attack on the segregated bad objects within the ego. And there is an alleviation of the harshness of the super-ego by adding to it objects that socially sanction and legitimize the attack.

These illustrations are obviously not completely elaborated; nor are they intended to be so. They are abstractions from real life situations in which a fuller analysis would show defenses against persecutory and depressive anxiety interacting with each other and with other more explicit functions of the group. But perhaps they suffice to indicate how the use of the concepts of introjective and projective identifications, regarded as interacting mechanisms, may serve to add further dimensions to Freud's analysis of the army and the church. We may also note that the social mechanisms described contain in their most primitive aspects features which may be related to the earliest attempts of the infant, described by Melanie Klein,[17] to deal with persecutory anxiety in relation to part objects by means of splitting and projection and introjection of both the good and bad objects and impulses. If we now turn to the question of social defenses against depressive anxieties, we shall be able to illustrate further some of the general points.

### Defenses against Depressive Anxiety

Let us consider first certain aspects of the problems of the scapegoating of a minority group. As seen from the viewpoint of the community at large, the community is split into a good majority and a bad minority—a split consistent with the splitting of internal objects into good and bad, and the creation of a good and bad internal world. The persecuting group's belief in its own good is preserved by heaping contempt upon and attacking the scapegoated group. The internal splitting mechanisms and preservation of the internal good objects of individuals, and the attack upon, and contempt for, internal, bad persecutory objects, are reinforced by introjective identification of individuals with other members taking part in the group-sanctioned attack upon the scapegoat.[18]

[16] "Preliminary Notes on Some Defence Mechanisms in Paranoid States, *International Journal of Psycho-Analysis*, XXXIII (1952), 208-13.

[17] Cf. "The Œdipus Complex in the Light of Early Anxieties," *Contributions to Psycho-Analysis*, pp. 339-90 and "Notes on Some Schizoid Mechanisms," in J. Riviere, ed., *Developments in Psycho-Analysis*.

[18] Cf. Melanie Klein's description of the operation of splitting mechanisms in the depressive position, "A Contribution to the

If we now turn to the minority groups, we may ask why only some minorities are selected for persecution while others are not. Here a feature often overlooked in consideration of minority problems may be of help. The members of the persecuted minority commonly entertain a precise and defined hatred and contempt for their persecutors matching in intensity the contempt and aggression to which they are themselves subjected. That this should be so is perhaps not surprising. But in view of the selective factor in choice of persecuted minorities, we must consider the possibility that one of the operative factors in this selection is the consensus in the minority group, at the fantasy level, to seek contempt and suffering in order to alleviate unconscious guilt. That is to say, there is an unconscious cooperation (or collusion) at the fantasy level between persecutor and persecuted. For the members of the minority group, such a collusion reinforces their own defenses against depressive anxiety—by such mechanisms as social justification for feelings of contempt and hatred for an external persecutor, with consequent alleviation of guilt and reinforcement of denial in the protection of internal good objects.

Another way in which depressive anxiety may be alleviated by social mechanisms is through manic denial of destructive impulses, and destroyed good objects, and the reinforcement of good impulses and good objects, by participation in group idealization. These social mechanisms are the reflection in the group of mechanisms of denial and idealization shown by Melanie Klein to be important mechanisms of defense against depressive anxiety.[19]

The operation of these social mechanisms may be seen in mourning ceremonies. The bereaved are joined by others in common display of grief and public reiteration of the good qualities of the deceased. There is a common sharing of guilt, through comparison of the shortcomings of the survivors with the good qualities of the deceased. Bad objects and impulses are gotten rid of by unconscious projection into the corpse, disguised by the decoration of the corpse, and safely put out of the way through projective identification with the dead during the burial ceremony, such mechanisms are unconsciously aimed at the avoidance of persecution by demonic figures. At the same time good objects and impulses are also projected into the dead person. Public and socially sanctioned idealization of the deceased then reinforces the sense that the good object has after all not been destroyed, for "his good works" are held to live on in the memory of the community as well as the surviving family, a memory which is reified in the tombstone. These mechanisms are unconsciously aimed at the avoidance of haunting by guilt-provoking ghosts. Hence, through mourning ceremonies, the community and the bereaved are provided with the opportunity of unconsciously cooperating in splitting the destroyed bad part of the loved object from the loved part, of burying the destroyed bad objects and impulses, and of protecting the good loved part as an eternal memory.

One general feature of each of the instances cited is that the fantasy social systems established have survival value for the group as well as affording protection against anxiety in the individual. Thus, for example, in the case of the mourning ceremony the social idealizing and manic denial make it possible for a bereaved person to reduce the internal chaos, to weather the immediate and intense impact of

Psychogenesis of Manic-Depressive States." *Contributions to Psycho-Analysis*, pp. 282-310.
  [19] "Mourning and Its Relation to Manic-Depressive States," *ibid.*, pp. 311-38.

death, and to undertake the process of mature internal mourning at his own time and his own pace.[20] But there is a general social gain as well, in that all those associated in the mourning ceremony can further their internal mourning and continue the lifelong process of working through the unresolved conflicts of the infantile depressive position. As Melanie Klein has described the process, "It seems that every advance in the process of mourning results in a deepening in the individual's relation to his inner objects, in the happiness of regaining them after they were felt to be lost ('Paradise Lost and Regained'), in an increased trust in them and love for them because they proved to be good and helpful after all."[21] Hence, through the mourning ceremony, the toleration of ambivalence is increased and friendship in the community can be strengthened. Or again, in the case of the first officer, the ship's crew, in a situation made difficult by close confinement and isolation from other groups, is enabled to cooperate with the captain in carrying out the required and consciously planned tasks by isolating and concentrating their bad objects and impulses within an available human receptacle.

## Case Study

I shall now turn to a more detailed and precise examination of fantasy social systems as defense mechanisms for the individual and as mechanisms allowing the group to proceed with its sophisticated or survival tasks, by examining a case study from industry. It may be noted that the conception of sophisticated tasks derives from Bion's conception of the sophisticated task of the work or W group.[22] I am refraining from using Bion's more elaborate conceptual scheme defining what he terms the "basic assumptions" of groups, since the relationship between the operation of basic assumptions and of depressive and persecutory phenomena remains to be worked out.

The case to be presented is one part of a larger study carried out in a light engineering factory, the Glacier Metal Company, between June, 1948, and the present time. The relationship with the firm is a therapeutic one; work is done only on request, from groups or individuals within the firm, for assistance in working through intra-group stresses or in dealing with organizational problems. The relationship between the social consultant (or therapist) and the people with whom he works is a confidential one; and the only reports published are those which have been worked through with the people concerned and agreed by them for publication. Within these terms of reference, I have published a detailed report on the first three years of the project.[23]

The illustration I shall use is taken from work done with one department in the factory.[24] The department employs roughly sixty people. It was organized with a departmental manager as head. Under him was a supcrinten-

[20] Cf. Melanie Klein, "Many Mourners Can Only Make Slow Steps in Reestablishing the Bonds with the External World Because They Are Struggling Against the Chaos Inside," *ibid.*, p. 329.
[21] *Ibid.*, p. 328.

[22] "Group Dynamics: A Re-View."
[23] *The Changing Culture of a Factory.*
[24] This case material is a condensation of material which is given in much greater detail in two published articles: E. Jaques, "Collaborative Group Methods in a Wage Negotiation Situation," *Human Relations*, III (1950), 223-49; and E. Jaques, A. K. Rice, and J. M. M. Hill, "The Social and Psychological Impact of a Change in Method of Wage Payment," *Human Relations*, IV (1951), 315-40.

dent, who was in turn responsible for four foremen, each of whom had a working group of ten to sixteen operatives. The operatives had elected five representatives, two of whom were shop stewards, to negotiate with the departmental manager on matters affecting the department. One such matter had to do with a change in methods of wages payment. The shop had been on piece rates (i.e., the operatives were paid a basic wage, plus a bonus dependent on their output). This method of payment had, for a number of years, been felt to be unsatisfactory. From the workers' point of view it meant uncertainty about the amount of their weekly wage, and for the management it meant complicated rate-fixing, and administrative arrangements. For all concerned, the not infrequent wrangling about rates that took place was felt to be unnecessarily disturbing. The possibility of changing over to a flat rate method of payment had been discussed for over a year before the project began. In spite of the fact that the change was commonly desired they had not been able to come to a decision.

A *Period of Negotiation*

Work with the department began in January, 1949, by attendance at discussions of a sub-committee composed of the departmental manager, the superintendent, and three workers' representatives. The general tone of the discussions was friendly. The committee members laid stress upon the fact that good relationships existed in the department and that they all wanted to strive for further improvement. From time to time, however, there was sharp disagreement over specific points, and these disagreements led the workers' representatives to state that there were many matters on which they felt they could not trust the management. This statement of suspicion was answered by the management members, who emphasized that they for their part had great trust in the workers' sense of responsibility.

The workers' suspicion of management also revealed itself in discussions held at shop floor level between the elected representatives and their worker constituents. The purpose of these discussions was to elicit in a detailed and concrete manner the views of the workers about the proposed change-over. The workers were on the whole in favor of the change-over, but they had some doubt as to whether they could trust the management to implement and to administer the change-over in a fair manner. What guarantees did they have, they asked, that management had nothing up its sleeve? At the same time, the workers showed an ambivalent attitude toward their own representatives. They urged and trusted them to carry on negotiations with management, but at the same time suspected that the representatives were management "stooges" and did not take the workers' views sufficiently into account. This negative attitude toward their representatives came out more clearly in interviews with the workers alone, in which opinions were expressed that although the elected representatives were known as militant trade unionists, nevertheless they were seen as liable to be outwitted by the management and as not carrying their representative role as effectively as they might.

The day-to-day working relationships between supervisors and workers were quite different from what would be expected as the consequence of these views. Work in the shop was carried out with good morale, and the supervisors were felt to do their best for the workers. A high proportion of the shop had been employed in the company for five years or more, and genuinely good personal relationships had been established.

The discussions in the committee composed of the managers and elected representatives went on for seven months, between January and July, 1949. They had a great deal of difficulty in working toward a decision, becoming embroiled in arguments that were sometimes quite heated and had no obvious cause—other than the workers' suspicion of the management, counterbalanced by the management's idealization of the workers. Much of the suspicion and idealization, however, was autistic, in the sense that although consciously experienced, it was not expressed openly as between managers and workers. These attitudes came out much more sharply when the elected representatives and the managers were meeting separately. The workers expressed deep suspicion and mistrust, while the managers expressed some of their anxieties about how responsible the workers could be—anxieties which existed alongside their strong sense of the workers' responsibility and of their faith in them.

## Analysis of the Negotiation Phase

I now wish to apply certain of our theoretical formulations to the above data. This is in no sense intended to be a complete analysis of the material. Many important factors, such as changes in the executive organization of the shop, personal attitudes, changes in personnel, and variations in the economic and production situation all played a part in determining the changes which occurred. I do wish, however, to demonstrate how, if we assume the operation of defenses against paranoid and depressive anxiety at the fantasy social level, we may be able to explain some of the very great difficulties encountered by the members of the department. And I would

emphasize here that these difficulties were encountered in spite of the high morale implied in the willingness of those concerned to face, and to work through in a serious manner, the group stresses they experienced in trying to arrive at a commonly desired goal.

The degree of inhibition of the autistic suspicion and idealization becomes understandable, I think, if we make the following assumptions about unconscious attitudes at the fantasy level. The workers in the shop had split the managers into good and bad —the good managers being the ones with whom they worked and the bad being the same managers but in the negotiation situation. They had unconsciously projected their hostile destructive impulses into their elected representatives so that the representatives could deflect, or redirect, these impulses against the bad "management" with whom negotiations were carried on, while the good objects and impulses could be put into individual real managers in the day-to-day work situation. This splitting of the management into good and bad and the projective identification with the elected representatives against the bad management served two purposes. At the reality level it allowed the good relations necessary to the work task of the department to be maintained; at the fantasy level it provided a system of social relationships reinforcing individual defenses against paranoid and depressive anxiety.

Putting their good impulses into managers in the work situation allowed the workers to reintroject the good relations with management, and hence to preserve an undamaged good object and alleviate depressive anxiety. This depressive anxiety was further avoided by reversion to the paranoid position in the negotiating situation.[25] During

---

[25] Melanie Klein has described how paranoid fears and suspicions are often used as a

the negotiations paranoid anxiety was partially avoided by the workers by putting their bad impulses into their elected representatives. The representatives, while consciously the negotiating representatives of the workers, became unconsciously the representatives of their bad impulses. These split-off bad impulses were partially dealt with and avoided because they were directed against the bad objects put into management in the negotiation situation by the workers and their representatives.

Another mechanism for dealing with the workers' own projected bad objects and impulses was to attack their representatives, with an accompanying despair that not much good would come of the negotiations. These feelings tended to be expressed privately by individuals. The workers who felt like this had introjected their representatives as bad objects and maintained them as a segregated part of the ego. Intra-psychic projection and aggression against these internal bad objects were supported by introjective identification with other workers, who held that the representatives were not doing their job properly. That is to say, other members of the department were introjected to reinforce the intra-psychic projection and as protection against the internal bad representatives attacking back. In addition to defense against internal persecution, the introjection of the other workers provided social sanction for considering the internalized representatives as bad, offsetting the harshness of super-ego recrimination for attacking objects containing a good as well as a persecuting component.

From the point of view of the elected representatives, anxiety about bad impulses was diminished by unconsciously accepting the bad impulses and objects of all the workers they represented. They could feel that their own hostile and aggressive impulses did not belong to them but belonged to the people on whose behalf they were acting. They were thus able to derive external social sanction for their aggression and hostile suspicion. But the mechanism did not operate with complete success, for there still remained their own unconscious suspicion and hostility to be dealt with, and the reality of what they considered to be the good external management. Hence, there was some anxiety and guilt about damaging the good managers. The primary defense mechanism against the onset of depressive anxiety was that of retreat to the paranoid position. This came out as a rigid clinging to attitudes of suspicion and hostility even in circumstances where they consciously felt that some of this suspicion was not justified by the situation they were actually experiencing.

From the management side, the paranoid attitude of the elected representatives was countered by the reiteration of the view that the workers could be trusted to do their part. This positive attitude unconsciously contained both idealization of the workers and placation of the hostile representatives. The idealization can be understood as an unconscious mechanism for diminishing guilt, stimulated by fears of injuring or destroying workers in the day-to-day work situation through the exercise of managerial authority—an authority which there is good reason to believe is, at least to some extent, felt unconsciously to be uncontrolled and omnipotent. To the extent that managers unconsciously felt their authority to be bad, they feared retaliation by the operatives. This in turn led to a reinforcement of the idealization

---

defense against the depressive position. Cf., for instance "The Psychogenesis of Manic-Depressive States," *Contributions to Psycho-Analysis*, p. 293.

of the elected representatives as a defense against paranoid anxiety, that is to say, as a means of placating the hostility of the workers and hence of placating internal persecutors. These idealizing and placatory mechanisms were employed in the meetings with the elected representatives, so that reality mechanisms could operate in the relationships with workers in the work situation, less encumbered with the content of uncontrolled fantasy.

It can thus be seen that the unconscious use of paranoid attitudes by the workers and idealizing and placatory attitudes by the management were complementary and reinforced each other. A circular process was set in motion. The more the workers' representatives attacked the managers, the more the managers idealized them in order to placate them. The greater the concessions given by management to the workers, the greater was the guilt and fear of depressive anxiety in the workers and hence the greater the retreat to paranoid attitudes as a means of avoiding depressive anxiety.

### Description and Analysis of the Post-Negotiation Phase

In June, six months after the discussions began, these attitudes, rather than the wages problem, were for a time taken as the main focus of consideration. A partial resolution occurred,[26] and the workers decided, after a ballot in the whole department, to try out a flat-rate method of payment. The condition for the change-over, however, was the setting up of a council, composed of managers and elected representatives, which would have the authority to determine departmental policy—a procedure for which the principles had already been established in the company. The prime principle was that of unanimous agreement on all decisions, and the agreement to work through all obstacles to unanimous decision by discovering sources of disagreement so that they could be resolved.

It appeared as though the open discussion of autistic attitudes facilitated a restructuring of the fantasy social relations in the department—a restructuring which brought with it a greater degree of conscious or ego control over their relationships. The fact, however, that there was only a partial restructuring of social relations at the fantasy level showed itself in the subsequent history of the shop council. For, following the change-over to a flat-rate method of payment, the council came up against the major question of reassessing the times in which given jobs ought to be done.

Under piece rates such assessment of times was necessary, both for calculation of the bonus to operatives and for giving estimated prices to customers. On the flat rates, it was required only for estimating to customers, but the times thus set inevitably constituted targets for the workers. Under piece rates, if a worker did not achieve the target, it meant that he lost his bonus; in other words, he himself paid for any drop in effort. Under flat rates, however, a drop below the target meant that the worker was getting paid for work that he was not doing. A detailed exploration of workers' attitudes[27] showed that the change-over from piece rates to flat rates had in no way

---

[26] The work-through process is in part described in the articles referred to above, and includes an account of the manner in which transference phenomena were handled in the face-to-face group situation. An analysis of the work-through process is outside the scope of the present paper, and hence there is only passing reference to it in the text.

[27] Cf. "The Social and Psychological Impact of a Change in Method of Wage Payment."

altered their personal targets and personal rate of work. They felt guilty whenever they fell below their estimated targets, because they were no longer paying for the difference. In order to avoid this guilt, the workers applied strong pressure to keep the estimated times on jobs as high as possible, as well as pressure to get the so-called tight times (times on jobs that were difficult to achieve), re-assessed. There were strong resistances to any changes in job assessment methods which the workers suspected might set difficult targets for them.

On the management side, the change-over to flat rates inevitably stirred whatever unconscious anxieties they might have about authority. For under piece rates, the bonus payment itself acted as an impersonal and independent disciplinarian, ensuring that workers put in the necessary effort. Under flat rates it was up to managers to see that a reasonable rate of work was carried on. This forced upon them more direct responsibility for the supervision of their subordinates and brought them more directly into contact with the authority that they held.

The newly constituted council, with its managers and elected representatives, had great difficulty in coping with the more manifest depressive anxiety both in the managers and in the workers. This showed in managers' views that the council might possibly turn out to be a bad thing because it slowed down administrative developments in the department. Similar opinions that the council would not work and might not prove worthwhile played some part in the decision of five out of six of the elected representatives not to stand for re-election in the shop elections which occurred sixteen months after the setting up of the council. These five were replaced by five newly elected representatives, who in turn brought with them a considerable amount of suspi-

cion. That is, there was again a retreat to the paranoid position while the managers' depressive anxiety continued to show to some extent in the form of depressive feelings that the council would not work. It has only been slowly, over a period of two years, that the council has been able to operate in the new situation as a constitutional mechanism for getting agreement on policy and at the same time intuitively to be used for the containment of fantasy social relationships. An exploration of the re-rating problem has been agreed and is being carried on with the assistance of an outside industrial consultant.

This case study, then, illustrates the development of an explicit social institution, that of meetings between management and elected representatives, which allowed for the establishment of unconscious mechanisms at the fantasy level for dealing with paranoid and depressive anxieties. The main mechanisms were those of management idealizing the hostile workers and the workers maintaining an attitude of suspicion toward the idealizing management. To the extent that splitting and projective identification operated successfully, these unconscious mechanisms helped individuals to deal with anxiety, by getting their anxieties into the fantasy social relations structured in the management elected-representative group. In this way the anxieties were eliminated from the day-to-day work situation and allowed for the efficient operation of the sophisticated work task and the achievement of good working relationships.

However, it will be noted that the elected representative-management group was also charged with a sophisticated work task—that of negotiating new methods of wages payment. They found it difficult to get on with the sophisticated task itself. In terms of the theory here propounded, these difficulties have been explained as arising from the manner in which the predominant unconscious fantasy relations in the negotiating group ran counter to the requirements of the sophisticated task. In other words, an essentially constitutional procedure, that of elected representatives meeting with an executive body, was difficult to operate because it was being used in an unrecognized fashion at the fantasy level to help deal with the depressive and paranoid anxieties of the members of the department as a whole.

## Some Observations on Social Change

In the above case study, it might be said that social change was sought when the structure and culture no longer met the requirements of the individual members of the department and in particular of the managers and the elected representatives. Manifest changes were brought about and in turn appeared to lead to a considerable restructuring of the fantasy social form and content of the institution. Change having taken place, however, the individual members found themselves in the grip of new relationships, to which they had to conform because they were self made. But they had brought about more than they had bargained for, in the sense that the new relationships under flat rates and the policy-making council had to be experienced before their implications could be fully appreciated.

The effects of the change on individuals were different according to the roles they occupied. The elected representatives were able to change roles by the simple expedient of not standing for re-election. And this expedient, it will be noted, was resorted to by five of the six representatives. The managers, however, were in a very different position. They could not relinquish or

change their roles without in a major sense changing their positions, and possibly status, in the organization as a whole. They had, therefore, individually to bear considerable personal stress in adjusting themselves to the new situation.

It is unlikely that members of an institution can ever bring about social changes that suit perfectly the needs of each individual. Once change is undertaken, it is more than likely that individuals will have to adjust and change personally in order to catch up with the changes they have produced. And until some readjustment is made at the fantasy level, the individual's social defenses against psychotic anxiety are likely to be weakened. It may well be because of the effects on the unconscious defense systems of individuals against psychotic anxiety that social change is resisted—and in particular, imposed social change. For it is one thing to readjust to changes that the individual has himself helped to bring about. It is quite another to be required to adjust one's internal defense systems in order to conform to changes brought about by some outside agency.

## Summary and Conclusions

Freud has argued that two main processes operate in the formation of what he calls artificial groups, like the army and the church; one is identification by introjection, and the other is replacement of the ego-ideal by an object. I have suggested that this latter process implicitly contains the concept, formulated by Melanie Klein, of identification by projection. Further, Melanie Klein states explicitly that in the interaction between introjective and projective identification lies the basis of the infant's earliest relations with its objects. The character of these early relations is determined by the way in which the infant attempts to deal with its paranoid and depressive anxieties and by the intensity of these anxieties.

Taking these conceptions of Freud and Melanie Klein, the view has here been advanced that one of the primary dynamic forces pulling individuals into institutionalized human association is that of defense against paranoid and depressive anxiety, and, conversely, that all institutions are unconsciously used by their members as mechanisms of defense against these psychotic anxieties. Individuals may put their internal conflicts into persons in the external world, unconsciously follow the course of the conflict by means of projective identification, and re-internalize the course and outcome of the externally perceived conflict by means of introjective identification. Societies provide institutionalized roles whose occupants are sanctioned, or required, to take into themselves the projected objects or impulses of other members. The occupants of such roles may absorb the objects and impulses—take them into themselves and become either the good or bad object with corresponding impulses; or, they may deflect the objects and impulses—put them into an externally perceived ally, or enemy, who is then loved, or attacked. The gain for the individual in projecting objects and impulses and introjecting their careers in the external world lies in the unconscious cooperation with other members of the institution or group who are using similar projection mechanisms. Introjective identification then allows more than the return of the projected objects and impulses. The other members are also taken inside and legitimize and reinforce attacks upon internal persecutors or support manic idealization of loved objects, thereby reinforcing the denial of destructive impulses against them.

The unconscious cooperation at the fantasy level among members of an institution is structured in terms of what is here called the fantasy social form and content of institutions. The form and content of institutions may thus be considered from two distinct levels: that of the manifest and consciously agreed form and content (including structure and function, which, although possibly unrecognized, are nevertheless in the preconscious of members of the institution, and hence are relatively accessible to identification by means of conscious study); and that of the fantasy form and content, which are unconsciously avoided and denied, and, because they are totally unconscious, remain unidentified by members of the institution.

A case study is presented to illustrate how within one department in a factory a sub-institution, a committee of managers and elected workers' representatives, was used at the fantasy level for segregating hostile relations from good relations, which were maintained in the day-to-day production work of the department. When, however, the committee was charged with a serious and conscious negotiating task, its members encountered great difficulties because of the socially sanctioned fantasy content of their relationships with each other.

Some observations are made on the dynamics of social change. Change occurs where the fantasy social relations within an institution no longer serve to reinforce individual defenses against psychotic anxiety. The institution may be restructured at the manifest and fantasy level; or the manifest structure may be maintained, but the fantasy structure modified. Individuals may change roles or leave the institution altogether. Or, apparent change at the manifest level may often conceal the fact that no real change has taken place, the fantasy social form and content of the institution being left untouched. Imposed social change which does not take account of the use of institutions by individuals, to cope with unconscious psychotic anxieties, is likely to be resisted.

Finally, if the mechanisms herein described have any validity, then at least two consequences may follow. First, observation of social processes may provide one means of studying, as through a magnifying glass, the operation of paranoid and depressive anxieties and the defenses built up against them. Unlike the psycho-analytical situation, such observations can be made by more than one person at the same time. And second, it may become more clear why social change is so difficult to achieve, and why many social problems are so intractable. For from the point of view here elaborated, changes in social relationships and procedures call for a restructuring of relationships at the fantasy level, with a consequent demand upon individuals to accept and tolerate changes in their existing pattern of defenses against psychotic anxiety. Effective social change is likely to require analysis of the common anxieties and unconscious collusions underlying the social defenses determining fantasy social relationships.

# Part 5
## change and
## growth in
## groups

The final selections analyze major trends in human-relations training groups from their inception to their dissolution. The goal in such groups is to develop a "mature group"—a group that "knows very well what it is doing." Both selections describe the fundamental and often traumatic changes that occur as the group struggles toward that goal, and the reader will see that many issues treated more or less separately in previous sections are considered in their dynamic relation to each other.

In no sense do we choose the training group, or the learning group, to portray these relations because it is typical of most groups. Quite the contrary. In its goal and in the freedom it enjoys from outside pressures, the training (learning) group is more exceptional than typical. Yet the members' goal of creating a group that is capable of becoming aware of its own processes casts their experience into a special perspective that can be instructive both to group members and to students of groups. For one thing, members quickly realize that their traditional orientation to the group situation is inadequate: their dependence upon the person in charge, their competition with their peers, their tendency to dispose of problems intellectually, and so on. These habitual ways must be given up and new ones adopted. The old authority as well as peer and work relations are gradually broken down, and the group approaches an anomic or null state, during which all ways become uncertain and from which an entirely new social system and culture must be created. Now, it is precisely this transformation from old, to null, to a new system that makes the training-group experience of general importance. Because nothing can be taken for granted and any new attempt is immediately put to the test, one learns which issues are the critical ones to address and which means actually advance the group toward its goal.

In the description of the dynamics of the training (learning) groups, the reader will find the interplay among personality, system, and culture (outlined by Parsons et al.), the sequential orientation to system problems (suggested by Bales), the primordial issues of authority and intimacy (referred to by Freud and by Brown), the differentiation into instrumental and emotional orientations (seen by Bales and Leik), the creation of myths in response to interpersonal stress (Slater), the collective mechanisms for relieving anxiety (Jaques), and the mechanisms for discovering group potentials and boundaries (Dentler and Erikson). All are aspects of the overall effort to achieve group self-awareness—a goal corresponding to a remarkable degree with the concept of system-consciousness in Deutsch's cybernetic model.

# chapter seventeen

## A Theory of Group Development

WARREN G. BENNIS                    HERBERT A. SHEPARD

If attention is focused on the organic properties of groups, criteria can be established by which phenomena of development, learning, or movement toward maturity can be identified. From this point of view, maturity for the group means something analogous to maturity for the person: a mature group knows very well what it is doing. The group can resolve its internal conflicts, mobilize its resources, and take intelligent action only if it has means for consensually validating its experience. The person can resolve his internal conflicts, mobilize his resources, and take intelligent action only if anxiety does not interfere with his ability to profit from his experience, to analyse, discriminate, and foresee. Anxiety pre-

Reprinted from Warren G. Bennis and Herbert A. Shepard, "A Theory of Group Development," *Human Relations,* IX, No. 4 (1956), 415-57, as abridged in Warren G. Bennis, Kenneth D. Benne, and Robert Chin, eds., *The Planning of Change: Readings in the Applied Behavioral Sciences* (New York: Holt, Rinehart & Winston, Inc., 1961), pp. 321-40, by permission of The Research Center for Group Dynamics, Ann Arbor, Michigan, and Holt, Rinehart & Winston, Inc. Copyright © 1961 by Holt, Rinehart & Winston, Inc. This theory is based for the most part on observations made over a 5-year period of teaching graduate students "group dynamics." The main function of the seminar as it was set forth by the instructors was to improve the internal communication system of the group, hence, a self-study group.

vents the person's internal communication system from functioning appropriately, and improvements in his ability to profit from experience hinge upon overcoming anxiety as a source of distortion. Similarly, group development involves the overcoming of obstacles to valid communication among the members, or the development of methods for achieving and testing consensus. Extrapolating from Sullivan's definition of personal maturity we can say a group has reached a state of valid communication when its members are armed with

. . . referential tools for analyzing interpersonal experience, so that its significant differences from, as well as its resemblances to, past experience, are discriminable, and the foresight of relatively near future events will be adequate and appropriate to maintaining one's security and securing one's satisfactions without useless or ultimately troublesome disturbance of self-esteem [13, p. 111].

Relatively few investigations of the phenomena of group development have been undertaken. This paper outlines a theory of development in groups that have as their explicit goal improvement of their internal communication systems.

A group of strangers, meeting for the first time, has within it many obstacles to valid communication. The more heterogeneous the membership, the more accurately does the group become, for each member, a microcosm of the rest of his interpersonal experience. The problems of understanding, the relationships, that develop in any given group are from one aspect a unique product of the particular constellation of personalities assembled. But to construct a broadly useful theory of group development, it is necessary to identify major areas of internal uncertainty, or obstacles to valid communication, which are common to and important in all groups meeting under a given set of environmental conditions. These areas must be strategic in the sense that until the group has developed methods for reducing uncertainty in them, it cannot reduce uncertainty in other areas, and in its external relations.

### The Two Major Areas of Internal Uncertainty: Dependence (Authority Relations) and Interdependence (Personal Relations)

Two major areas of uncertainty can be identified by induction from common experience, at least within our own culture. The first of these is the area of group members' orientations toward authority, or more generally toward the handling and distribution of power in the group. The second is the area of members' orientations toward one another. These areas are not independent of each other: a particular set of inter-member orientations will be associated with a particular authority structure. But the two sets of orientations are as distinct from each other as are the concepts of power and love. A number of authorities have used them as a starting-point for the analysis of group behavior.

In his *Group Psychology and the Analysis of the Ego*, Freud noted that "each member is bound by libidinal ties on the one hand to the leader . . . and on the other hand to the other members of the group" (3, p. 45). Although he described both ties as libidinal, he was uncertain "how these two ties are related to each other, whether they are of the same kind and the same value, and how they are to be described psychologically." Without resolving this question, he noted that (for the Church and the Army) "one of these, the tie with the leader, seems . . . to be more of a ruling factor than the other, which holds between members of the group" (3, p. 52).

More recently, Schutz (11) has made these two dimensions central to his theory of group compatibility. For him, the strategic determinant of compatibility is the particular blend of orientations toward authority and orientations toward personal intimacy. Bion (1, 2) conceptualizes the major dimensions of the group somewhat differently. His "dependency" and "pairing" modalities correspond to our "dependence" and "interdependence" areas; to them he adds a "fight-flight" modality. For him these modalities are simply alternative modes of behavior; for us, the fight-flight categorization has been useful for characterizing the means used by the group for maintaining a stereotyped orientation during a given subphase.

The core of the theory of group development is that the principal obstacles to the development of valid communication are to be found in the orientations toward authority and intimacy that members bring to the group. Rebelliousness, submissiveness, or withdrawal as the characteristic response to authority figures; destructive competitiveness, emotional exploitiveness, or withdrawal as the characteristic response to peers prevent consensual validation of experience. The behaviors determined by these orientations are directed toward enslavement of the other in the service of the self, enslavement of the self in the service of the other, or disintegration of the situation. Hence, they prevent the setting, clarification of, and movement toward group-shared goals.

In accord with Freud's observation, the orientations toward authority are regarded as being prior to, or partially determining of, orientations toward other members. In its development, the group moves from preoccupation with authority relations to preoccupation with personal relations. This movement defines the two major phases of group development. Within each phase are three subphases, determined by the ambivalence of orientations in each area. That is, during the authority ("dependence") phase, the group moves from preoccupation with submission to preoccupation with rebellion, to resolution of the dependence problem. Within the personal (or "interdependence") phase the group moves from a preoccupation with intermember identification to a preoccupation with individual identity to a resolution of the interdependence problem.

### The Relevant Aspects of Personality in Group Development

The aspects of member personality most heavily involved in group development are called, following Schutz, the dependence and personal aspects.

The dependence aspect is comprised by the member's characteristic patterns related to a leader or to a structure of rules. Members who find comfort in rules of procedure, an agenda, an expert, etc. are called "dependent." Members who are discomfited by authoritative structures are called "counterdependent."

The personal aspect is comprised by the member's characteristic patterns with respect to interpersonal intimacy. Members who cannot rest until they have stabilized a relatively high degree of intimacy with all the others are called "overpersonal." Members who tend to avoid intimacy with any of the others are called "counterpersonal."

Psychodynamically, members who evidence some compulsiveness in the adoption of highly dependent, highly counterdependent, highly personal, or highly counterpersonal roles are regarded as "conflicted." Thus, the person who persists in being dependent upon any and all authorities thereby provides himself with ample evidence that authorities should not be so trustingly relied upon; yet he cannot profit from this experience in governing his future action. Hence, a deep, but unrecognized, distrust is likely to accompany the manifestly submissive behavior, and the highly dependent or highly counterdependent person is thus a person in conflict. The existence of the conflict accounts for the sometimes dramatic movement from extreme dependence to extreme rebelliousness. In this way counterdependence and dependence, while logically the extremes of a scale, are psychologically very close together.

The "unconflicted" person or "independent," who is better able to profit from his experience and assess the present situation more adequately, may of course act at times in rebellious or submissive ways. Psychodynamically, the difference between him and the conflicted is easy to understand. In terms of observable behavior, he lacks the compulsiveness and, significantly, does not create the communicative confusion so characteristic of, say, the conflicted dependent, who manifests submission in that part of his communication of which he is aware, and distrust or rebellion in that part of his communication of which he is unaware.[1]

---

[1] Schutz has developed a test, Fundamental Interpersonal Relations Orientations

Persons who are unconflicted with respect to the dependence or personal aspect are considered to be responsible for the major movements of the group toward valid communication. That is, the actions of members unconflicted with respect to the problems of a given phase of group development move the group to the next phase. Such actions are called barometric events, and the initiators are called catalysts. This part of the theory of group development is based on Redl's thesis concerning the "infectiousness of the unconflicted on the conflicted personality constellation" (see 9). The catalysts (Redl calls them "central persons") are the persons capable of reducing the uncertainty characterizing a given phase. "Leadership" from the standpoint of group development can be defined in terms of catalysts responsible for group movement from one phase to the next. This consideration provides a basis for determining what membership roles are needed for group development. For example, it is expected that a group will have great difficulty in resolving problems of power and authority if it lacks members who are unconflicted with respect to dependence.

**Phase Movements**

The foregoing summary has introduced the major propositions in the theory of group development. While it is not possible to reproduce the concrete group experience from which the theory is drawn, we can take a step in this direction by discussing in more detail what seem to us to be the domi-

(FIRO), which is capable of measuring "conflictedness" and "independence" with respect to each of the dimensions, dependency and intimacy, as well as a third, "assertiveness" or the degree to which an individual will make his views felt in expressing himself in a group. See (10).

nant features of each phase. The description given below is highly interpretive, and we emphasize what seem to us to be the major themes of each phase, even though many minor themes are present. In the process of abstracting, stereotyping, and interpreting, certain obvious facts about group process are lost. For example, each group meeting is to some extent a recapitulation of its past and a forecast of its future. This means that behavior that is "regressive" or "advanced" often appears.

*Phase I: Dependence*

*Subphase 1: Dependence-Flight.* The first days of group life are filled with behavior whose remote, as well as immediate, aim is to ward off anxiety. Much of the discussion content consists of fruitless searching for a common goal. Some of the security-seeking behavior is group-shared—for example, members may reassure one another by providing interesting and harmless facts about themselves. Some is idiosyncratic—for example, doodling, yawning, intellectualizing.

The search for a common goal is aimed at reducing the cause of anxiety, thus going beyond the satisfaction of immediate security needs. But just as evidencing boredom in this situation is a method of warding off anxiety by denying its proximity, so group goal-seeking is not quite what it is claimed to be. It can best be understood as a dependence plea. The trainer, not the lack of a goal, is the cause of insecurity. This interpretation is likely to be vigorously contested by the group, but it is probably valid. The characteristic expectations of group members are that the trainer will establish rules of the game and distribute rewards. He is presumed to know what the goals are or ought to be. Hence his behavior is regarded as a "technique"; he is merely playing hard to get. The pretense of a fruitless search for goals is a plea for him to tell the group what to do, by simultaneously demonstrating its helplessness without him, and its willingness to work under his direction for his approval and protection.

We are here talking about the dominant theme in group life. Many minor themes are present, and even in connection with the major theme there are differences among members. For some, testing the power of the trainer to affect their futures is the major concern. In others, anxiety may be aroused through a sense of helplessness in a situation made threatening by the protector's desertion. These alternatives can be seen as the beginnings of the counterdependent and dependent adaptations. Those with a dependent orientation look vainly for cues from the trainer for procedure and direction, sometimes paradoxically they infer that the leader must want it that way. Those with a counterdependent orientation strive to detect in the trainer's action elements that would offer ground for rebellion, and may even paradoxically demand rules and leadership from him because he is failing to provide them.

The ambiguity of the situation at this stage quickly becomes intolerable for some, and a variety of ultimately unserviceable resolutions may be invented, many of them idiosyncratic. Alarm at the prospect of future meetings is likely to be group-shared, and at least a gesture may be made in the direction of formulating an agenda for subsequent meetings.

This phase is characterized by behavior that has gained approval from authorities in the past. Since the meetings are to be concerned with groups or with human relations, members offer information on these topics, to satisfy the presumed expectations of the trainer and to indicate expertise, interest, or achievement in these topics (ex-officers from the armed services, from fraternities, etc. have the floor). Topics such as business or political leadership, discrimination and desegregation, are likely to be discussed. During this phase the contributions made by members are designed to gain approval from the trainer, whose reaction to each comment is surreptitiously watched. If the trainer comments that this seems to be the case, or if he notes that the subject under discussion (say, discrimination) may be related to some concerns about membership in this group, he fails again to satisfy the needs of members. Not that the validity of this interpretation is held in much doubt. No one is misled by the "flight" behavior involved in discussing problems external to the group, least of all the group members. Discussion of these matters is filled with perilous uncertainties, however, and so the trainer's observation is politely ignored, as one would ignore a *faux-pas* at a tea-party. The attempts to gain approval based on implicit hypotheses about the potential power of the trainer for good and evil are continued until the active members have run through the repertoire of behaviors that have gained them favor in the past.

*Subphase 2: Counterdependence-Flight.* As the trainer continues to fail miserably in satisfying the needs of the group, discussion takes on a different tone, and counterdependent expressions begin to replace overt dependency. In many ways this subphase is the most stressful and unpleasant in the life of the group. It is marked by a paradoxical development of the trainer's role into one of omnipotence and powerlessness, and by division of the group into two warring subgroups. In subphase 1, feelings of hostility were strongly defended; if a slip were made that suggested hostility, particularly toward the trainer, the group members were embarrassed. Now expressions of hostility are more frequent, and are more likely to be supported by other members, or to be met with equally hostile responses. Power is much more overtly the concern of group members in this subphase. A topic such as leadership may again be discussed, but the undertones of the discussion are no longer dependence pleas. Discussion of leadership in subphase 2 is in part a vehicle for making explicit the trainer's failure as a leader. In part it is perceived by other members as a bid for leadership on the part of any member who participates in it.

The major themes of this subphase are as follows:

1. Two opposed subgroups emerge, together incorporating most of the group members. Characteristically, the subgroups are in disagreement about the group's need for leadership or "structure." One subgroup attempts to elect a chairman, nominate working committees, establish agenda, or otherwise "structure" the meetings; the other subgroup opposes all such efforts. At first this appears to be merely an intellectual disagreement concerning the future organization of group activity. But soon it becomes the basis for destroying any semblance of group unity. Fragmentation is expressed and brought about in many ways: voting is a favorite way of dramatizing the schism; suggestions that the group is too large and should be divided into subgroups for the meetings are frequent; a chairman may be elected and then ignored as a demonstration of the group's ineffectualness. Although control mechanisms are sorely needed and desired, no one is willing to relinquish the rights of leadership and control to anyone else. The trainer's abdication has created a power gap, but no one is allowed to fill it.

2. Disenthrallment with the trainer proceeds rapidly. Group members see him as at best ineffectual, at worst damaging, to group progress. He is ignored and bullied almost simultaneously. His interventions are perceived by the counterdependents as an attempt to interrupt group progress; by the dependents, as weak and incorrect statements. His silences are regarded by the dependents as desertion; by the counterdependents as manipulation. Much of the group activity is to be understood as punishment of the trainer, for his failure to meet needs and expectations, for getting the group into an unpleasant situation, for being the worst kind of authority figure—a weak and incompetent one, or a manipulative, insincere one. Misunderstanding or ignoring his comments, implying that his observations are paranoid fantasies, demonstrations that the group is cracking up, references to him in the past tense as though he were no longer present—these are the punishments for his failure.

As, in the first subphase, the trainer's wisdom, power, and competence were overtly unquestioned, but secretly suspected; so, in the second subphase, the conviction that he is incompetent and helpless is clearly dramatized, but secretly doubted. Out of this secret doubt arises the belief in the trainer's omnipotence. None of the punishments meted out to the trainer are recognized as such by the group members; in fact, if the trainer suggests that the members feel a need to punish him, they are most likely to respond in injured tones or in tones of contempt that what is going on has nothing to do with him and that he had best stay out of it. The trainer is still too imposing and threatening to challenge directly. There is a secret hope that the chaos in the group is in fact part of the master plan, that he is really leading them in the direction they should be going. That he may really be helpless as they imply, or that the failure may be theirs rather than his, are frightening possibilities. For this reason subphase 2 differs very little in its fundamental dynamics from subphase 1. There is still the secret wish that the trainer will stop all the bedlam which has replaced polite uncertainty, by taking his proper role (so that dependent members can cooperate with him and counterdependent can rebel in the usual ways).

Subphase 2 thus brings the group to the brink of catastrophe. The trainer has consistently failed to meet the group's needs. Not daring to turn directly on him, the group members engage in mutually destructive behavior: in fact, the group threatens suicide as the most extreme expression of dependence. The need to punish the trainer is so strong, however, that his act of salvation would have to be magical indeed.

*Subphase 3: Resolution-Catharsis.* No such magic is available to the trainer. Resolution of the group's difficulties at this point depends upon the presence in the group of other forces, which have until this time been inoperative, or ineffective. Only the degenerative aspects of the chain of events in subphases 1 and 2 have been presented up to this point and they are in fact the salient ones. But there has been a simultaneous, though less obvious, mobilization of constructive forces. First, within each of the warring subgroups bonds of mutual support have grown. The group member no longer feels helpless and isolated. Second, the trainer's role, seen as weak or manipulative in the dependence orientation, can also be perceived as permissive. Third, his interpretations, though openly ignored, have been secretly attended to. And, as the second and third points imply, some members of the group are less the prisoners of the dependence-counterdependence dilemma than others. These members, called the independents, have been relatively ineffective in the group for two reasons. First, they have not developed firm bonds with other members in either of the warring subgroups, because they have not identified with either cause. Typically, they have devoted their energies to an unsuccessful search for a compromise settlement of the disagreements in the group. Since their attitudes toward authority are less ambivalent than those of other members, they have accepted the alleged reason for disagreement in the group—for example, whether a chairman should be elected—at face value, and tried to mediate. Similarly, they have tended to accept the trainer's role and interpretations more nearly at face value. However, his interpretations have seemed inaccurate to them, since in fact the interpretations have applied much less to them than to the rest of the group.

Subphase 3 is the most crucial and fragile in group life up to this point. What occurs is a sudden shift in the whole basis of group action. It is truly a bridging phase; if it occurs at all, it is so rapid and mercurial that the end of subphase 2 appears to give way directly to the first subphase of Phase II. If it does not occur thus rapidly and dramatically, a halting and arduous process of vacillation between Phases I and II is likely to persist for a long period, the total group movement being very gradual.

To summarize the state of affairs at the beginning of subphase 3: 1. The group is polarized into two competing groups, each unable to gain or relinquish power. 2. Those group members who are uncommitted to either subgroup are ineffective in their attempts to resolve the conflict. 3. The trainer's contributions only serve to deepen the cleavage in the group.

As the group enters subphase 3, it is

moving rapidly toward extinction: that is, splintering into two or three subgroups. The independents, who have until now been passive or ineffectual, become the only hope for survival, since they have thus far avoided polarization and stereotypic behavior. The imminence of dissolution forces them to recognize the fruitlessness of their attempts at mediation. For this reason, the trainer's hypothesis that fighting one another is off-target behavior is likely to be acted upon at this point. A group member may openly express the opinion that the trainer's presence and comments are holding the group back, suggest that "as an experiment" the trainer leaves the group "to see how things go without him." When the trainer is thus directly challenged, the whole atmosphere of the meeting changes. There is a sudden increase in alertness and tension. Previously, there had been much acting out of the wish that the trainer were absent, but at the same time a conviction that he was the *raison d'être* of the group's existence —that it would fall apart without him. Previously, absence of the trainer would have constituted desertion, or defeat, fulfilment of the members' worst fears as to their own inadequacy or the trainer's. But now leaving the group can have a different meaning. General agreement that the trainer should leave is rarely achieved. However, after a little further discussion it becomes clear that he is at liberty to leave, with the understanding that he wishes to be a member of the group, and will return if and when the group is willing to accept him.

The principal function of the symbolic removal of the trainer is in its effect of freeing the group to bring into awareness the hitherto carefully ignored feelings toward him as an authority figure, and toward the group activity as an off-target dramatization of the ambivalence toward authority.

The leadership provided by the independents (whom the group sees as having no vested interest in power) leads to a new orientation toward membership in the group. In the discussion that follows the exit of the trainer, the dependents' assertion that the trainer deserted and the counterdependents' assertion that he was kicked out are soon replaced by consideration of whether his behavior was "responsible" or "irresponsible." The power problem is resolved by being defined in terms of member responsibilities, and the terms of the trainer's return to the group are settled by the requirement that he behave as "just another member of the group." This phrase is then explained as meaning that he should take neither more nor less responsibility for what happens in the group than any other member.

The above description of the process does not do justice to the excitement and involvement characteristic of this period. How much transferable insight ambivalent members acquire from it is difficult to assess. At least within the life of the group, later activity is rarely perceived in terms of submission and rebellion.

An interesting parallel, which throws light on the order of events in group development, is given in Freud's discussion of the myth of the primal horde. In his version:

These many individuals eventually banded themselves together, killed [the father], and cut him in pieces. . . . They then formed the totemistic community of brothers all with equal rights and united by the totem prohibitions which were to preserve and to expiate the memory of the murder [3, p. 112].

The horde's act, according to Freud, was soon distorted into an heroic myth: instead of murder by the group, the myth held that the father had been overthrown single-handed by one person, usually the youngest son. In this attribution of the group act to one individual (the hero) Freud saw the "emergence of the individual from group psychology." His definition of a hero is ". . . a man who stands up manfully against his father and in the end victoriously overthrows him" (4, p. 9). (The heroic myth of Freud thus shares much in common with Sullivan's "delusion of unique individuality.")

In the training group, the member who initiates the events leading to the trainer's exit is sometimes referred to as a "hero" by the other members. Responsibility for the act is felt to be shared by the group, however, and out of their experience comes the first strong sense of group solidarity and involvement—a reversal of the original version, where the individual emerges from the group. This turn of events clarifies Freud's remark concerning the libidinal ties to the leader and to the other group members. Libidinal ties toward the other group members cannot be adequately developed until there is a resolution of the ties with the leader. In our terms, those components of group life having to do with intimacy and interdependence cannot be dealt with until those components having to do with authority and dependence have been resolved.

Other aspects of subphase 3 may be understood by investigating the dramatic significance of the revolt. The event is always marked in group history as "a turning-point," "the time we became a group," "when I first got involved," etc. The mounting tension, followed by sometimes uproarious euphoria, cannot be entirely explained by the surface events. It may be that the revolt represents a realization of important fantasies individuals hold in all organizations, that the emotions involved are undercurrents wherever rebellious and submissive tendencies toward existing authorities must be con-

trolled. These are the themes of some of our great dramas—*Antigone, Billy Budd, Hamlet,* and our most recent folk-tale, *The Caine Mutiny.* But the event is more than the presentation of a drama, or an acting-out of fantasies. For it can be argued that the moments of stress and catharsis, when emotions are labile and intense, are the times in the group life when there is readiness for change. Leighton's analysis of a minor revolution at a Japanese relocation camp is worth quoting in full on this point:

While this [cathartic] situation is fraught with danger because of trends which may make the stress become worse before it gets better, there is also an opportunity for administrative action that is not likely to be found in more secure times. It is fairly well recognized in psychology that at periods of great emotional stir the individual human being can undergo far-reaching and permanent changes in his personality. It is as if the bone structure of his systems of belief and of his habitual patterns of behavior becomes soft, is fused into new shapes and hardens there when the period of tension is over. . . . Possibly the same can be true of whole groups of people, and there are historical examples of social changes and movements occurring when there was widespread emotional tension, usually some form of anxiety. The Crusades, parts of the Reformation, the French Revolution, the change in Zulu life in the reign of Chaca, the Meiji Restoration, the Mormon movement, the Russian Revolution, the rise of Fascism, and alterations in the social sentiments of the United States going on at present are all to some extent examples [7, p. 360].

Observers of industrial relations have made similar observations. When strikes result from hostile labor-management relations (as contrasted to straight wage demands), there is a fluidity of relationships and a wide repertoire of structural changes during this period not available before the strike act.[2]

So it is, we believe, with the training group. But what are the new values and behavior patterns that emerge out of the emotional experience of Phase I? Principally, they are acceptance by each member of his full share of responsibility for what happens in the group. The outcome is autonomy for the group. After the events of subphase 3, there is no more attribution of magical powers to the trainer—either the dependent fantasy that he sees farther, knows better, is mysteriously guiding the group and protecting it from evil, or the very similar counterdependent fantasy that he is manipulating the group, exploiting it in his own interests, that the experience is one of "brain-washing." The criterion for evaluating a contribution is no longer who said it, but what is said. Thereafter, such power fantasies as the trainer himself may have present no different problem from the power fantasies of any other group member. At the same time, the illusion that there is a struggle for power in the group is suddenly dissipated, and the contributions of other members are evaluated in terms of their relevance to shared group goals.

*Summary of Phase I*

The very word development implies not only movement through time, but also a definite order of progression. The group must traverse subphase 1 to reach subphase 2, and subphase 3 before it can move into Phase II. At the same time, lower levels of development coexist with more advanced levels. Blocking and regression occur fre-

quently, and the group may be "stuck" at a certain phase of development. It would, of course, be difficult to imagine a group remaining long in subphase 3—the situation is too tense to be permanent. But the group may founder for some time in subphase 2 with little movement. In short, groups do not inevitably develop through the resolution of the dependence phase to Phase II. This movement may be retarded indefinitely. Obviously much depends upon the trainer's role. In fact, the whole dependence modality may be submerged by certain styles of trainer behavior. The trainer has a certain range of choice as to whether dependency as a source of communication distortion is to be highlighted and made the subject of special experiential and conceptual consideration. The personality and training philosophy of the trainer determine his interest in introducing or avoiding explicit consideration of dependency.

There are other important forces in the group besides the trainer, and these may serve to facilitate or block the development that has been described as typical of Phase I. Occasionally there may be no strong independents capable of bringing about the barometric events that precipitate movement. Or the leaders of opposing subgroups may be the most assertive members of the group. In such cases the group may founder permanently in subphase 2. If a group has the misfortune to experience a "traumatic" event early in its existence—exceedingly schizoid behavior by some member during the first few meetings, for example—anxieties of other members may be aroused to such an extent that all culturally suspect behavior, particularly open expression of feelings, is strongly inhibited in subsequent meetings.

Table 1 summarizes the major events of Phase I, as it typically proceeds. This phase has dealt primarily with the

---

[2] See A. Gouldner (6), W. F. Whyte, Jr. (14). Robert E. Park, writing in 1928, had considerable insight on some functions of revolution and change. See (8).

TABLE 1   Phase I: Dependence-Power Relations[a]

| | Subphase 1 dependence-submission | Subphase 2 counterdependence | Subphase 3 resolution |
|---|---|---|---|
| 1. Emotional Modality | Dependence—Flight. | Counterdependence—Fight. Off-target fighting among members. Distrust of staff member. Ambivalence. | Pairing. Intense involvement in group task. |
| 2. Content Themes | Discussion of interpersonal problems external to training groups. | Discussion of group organization; i.e., what degree of structuring devices is needed for "effective" group behavior? | Discussion and definition of trainer role. |
| 3. Dominant Roles (Central Persons) | Assertive, aggressive members with rich previous organizational or social science experience. | Most assertive counterdependent and dependent members. Withdrawal of less assertive independents and dependents. | Assertive independents. |
| 4. Group Structure | Organized mainly into multi-subgroups based on members' past experiences. | Two tight subcliques consisting of leaders and members, of counterdependents and dependents. | Group unifies in pursuit of goal and develops internal authority system. |
| 5. Group Activity | Self-oriented behavior reminiscent of most new social gatherings. | Search for consensus mechanism: Voting, setting up chairmen, search for "valid" content subjects. | Group members take over leadership roles formerly perceived as held by trainer. |
| 6. Group movement facilitated by: | Staff member abnegation of traditional role of structuring situation, setting up rules of fair play, regulation of participation. | Disenthrallment with staff member coupled with absorption of uncertainty by most assertive counterdependent and dependent individuals. Subgroups form to ward off anxiety. | Revolt by assertive independents (catalysts) who fuse subgroups into unity by initiating and engineering trainer exit (barometric event). Group moves into Phase II. |
| 7. Main Defenses | Projection. Denigration of authority. | | |

[a] Course terminates at the end of 17 weeks. It is not uncommon for groups to remain throughout the course in this phase.

resolution of dependence needs. It ends with acceptance of mutual responsibility for the fate of the group and a sense of solidarity, but the implications of shared responsibility have yet to be explored. This exploration is reserved for Phase II, which we have chosen to call the Interdependence Phase.

## Phase II: Interdependence

The resolution of dependence problems marks the transfer of group attention (and inattention) to the problems of shared responsibility.

Sullivan's description of the change from childhood to the juvenile era seems pertinent here:

The juvenile era is marked off from childhood by the appearance of an urgent need for compeers with whom to have one's existence. By "compeers" I mean people who are on our level, and have generically similar attitudes toward authoritative figures, activities and the like. This marks the beginning of the juvenile era, the great developments in which are the talents for cooperation, competition and compromise [12, pp. 17-18. Emphasis ours].

The remaining barriers to valid communication are those associated with orientations toward interdependence: i.e. intimacy, friendship, identification. While the distribution of power was the cardinal issue during Phase I, the distribution of affection occupies the group during Phase II.

*Subphase 4: Enchantment-Flight.* At the outset of subphase 4, the group is happy, cohesive, relaxed. The atmosphere is one of "sweetness and light." Any slight increase in tension is instantly dissipated by joking and laughter. The fighting of Phase I is still fresh in the memory of the group, and the group's efforts are devoted to patching up differences, healing wounds, and maintaining a harmonious atmosphere.

Typically, this is a time of merrymaking and group minstrelsy. Coffee and cake may be served at the meetings. Hours may be passed in organizing a group party. Poetry or songs commemorating the important events and persons in the group's history may be composed by individuals or, more commonly, as a group project. All decisions must be unanimous during this period, since everyone must be happy, but the issues on which decisions are made are mostly ones about which group members have no strong feelings. At first the cathartic, healing function of these activities is clear; there is much spontaneity, playfulness, and pleasure. Soon the pleasures begin to wear thin.

The myth of mutual acceptance and universal harmony must eventually be recognized for what it is. From the beginning of this phase there are frequent evidences of underlying hostilities, unresolved issues in the group. But they are quickly, nervously smoothed over by laughter or misinterpretation. Subphase 4 begins with catharsis, but that is followed by the development of a rigid norm to which all members are forced to conform: "Nothing must be allowed to disturb our harmony in the future; we must avoid the mistakes of the painful past." Not that members have forgotten that the painful past was a necessary preliminary to the autonomous and (it is said) delightful present, though that fact is carefully overlooked. Rather, there is a dim realization that all members must have an experience somewhat analogous to the trainer's in subphase 3, before a mutually understood, accepted, and realistic definition of their own roles in the group can be arrived at.

Resistance of members to the requirement that harmony be maintained at all costs appears in subtle ways. In open group discussion the requirement is imperative: either the member does not dare to endanger harmony with the group or to disturb the *status quo* by denying that all problems have been solved. Much as members may dislike the tedious work of maintaining the appearance of harmony, the alternative is worse. The house of cards would come tumbling down, and the painful and exacting work of building something more substantial would have to begin. The flight from these problems takes a number of forms. Group members may say, "We've had our fighting and are now a group. Thus, further self-study is unnecessary." Very commonly, the possibility of any change may be prevented by not coming together as a total group at all. Thus the members may subgroup through an entire meeting. Those who would disturb the friendly subgroups are accused of "rocking the boat."

The solidarity and harmony become more and more illusory, but the group still clings to the illusion. This perseveration is in a way a consequence of the deprivation that members have experienced in maintaining the atmosphere of harmony. Maintaining it forces members to behave in ways alien to their own feelings; to go still further in group involvement would mean a complete loss of self. The group is therefore torn by a new ambivalence, which might be verbalized as follows: 1. "We all love one another and therefore we must maintain the solidarity of the group and give up whatever is necessary of our selfish desires." 2. "The group demands that I sacrifice my identity as a person; but the group is an evil mechanism which satisfies no dominant needs." As this subphase comes to a close, the happiness that marked its beginning is maintained only as a mask. The "innocent" splitting of the group into subgroups has gone so far that members will even walk around the meeting table to join in the conversation of a subgroup rather than speak across the table at the risk of bringing the whole group together. There is a certain uneasiness about the group; there is a feeling that "we should work together but cannot." There may be a tendency to regress to the orientation of subphase 1: group members would like the trainer to take over.

To recapitulate: subphase 4 begins with a happy sense of group belongingness. Individual identity is eclipsed by a "the group is bigger than all of us" sentiment. But this integration is short lived: it soon becomes perceived as a fake attempt to resolve interpersonal problems by denying their reality. In the later stages of this subphase, enchantment with the total group is replaced by enchantment with one's subgroup, and out of this breakdown of the group emerges a new organization based on the anxieties aroused out of this first, suffocating, involvement.

*Subphase 5: Disenchantment-Fight.* This subphase is marked by a division into two subgroups—paralleling the experience of subphase 2—but this time based upon orientations toward the degree of intimacy required by group membership. Membership in the two subgroups is not necessarily the same as in subphase 2: for now the fragmentation occurs as a result of opposite and extreme attitudes toward the degree of intimacy desired in interpersonal relations. The counterpersonal members band together to resist further involvement. The overpersonal members band together in a demand for unconditional love. While these subgroups appear as divergent as possible, a common theme underlies them. For the one group, the only means seen for maintaining self-esteem is to avoid any real commitment to others; for the other group, the only way to maintain self-esteem is to obtain a commitment from others to forgive everything. The subgroups share in common the fear that intimacy breeds contempt.

This anxiety is reflected in many ways during subphase 5. For the first time openly disparaging remarks are made about the group. Invidious comparisons are made between it and other groups. Similarly, psychology and social science may be attacked. The inadequacy of the group as a basis for self-esteem is dramatized in many ways —from stating "I don't care what you think," to boredom, to absenteeism. The overpersonals insist that they are happy and comfortable, while the counterpersonals complain about the lack of group morale. Intellectualization by the overpersonals frequently takes on religious overtones concerning Christian love, consideration for others, etc. In explanations of member behavior, the counterpersonal members account for all in terms of motives having nothing to do with the present group; the overpersonals explain all in terms of acceptance and rejection in the present group.

Subphase 5 belongs to the counterpersonals as subphase 4 belonged to the overpersonals. Subphase 4 might be caricatured as hiding in the womb of the group; subphase 5 as hiding out of sight of the group. It seems probable that both of these modalities serve to ward off anxieties associated with intimate interpersonal relations. A theme that links them together can be verbalized as follows: "If others really knew me, they would reject me." The overpersonal's formula for avoiding this rejection seems to be accepting all others so as to be protected by the others' guilt; the counterpersonal's way is by rejecting all others before they have a chance to reject him. Another way of characterizing the counterpersonal orientation is in the phrase, "I would lose my identity as a member of the group."

The corresponding overpersonal orientation reads, "I have nothing to lose by identifying with the group." We can now look back on the past two subphases as countermeasures against loss of self-esteem; what Sullivan once referred to as the greatest inhibition to the understanding of what is distinctly human, "the overwhelming conviction of self-hood—this amounts to a delusion of unique individuality." The sharp swings and fluctuations that occurred between the enchantment and euphoria of subphase 4 and the disenchantment of subphase 5 can be seen as a struggle between the "institutionalization of complacency" on the one hand and anxiety associated with fantasy speculations about intimacy and involvement on the other. This dissociative behavior serves a purpose of its own: a generalized denial of the group and its meaning for individuals. For if the group is important and valid then it has to be taken seriously. If it can wallow in the enchantment of subphase 4, it is safe; if it can continually vilify the goals and objectives of the group, it is also safe. The disenchantment theme in subphase 5 is perhaps a less skilful and more desperate security provision with its elaborate wall of defenses than the "group mind" theme of subphase 4. What should be stressed is that both subphase defenses were created almost entirely on fantastic expectations about the consequences of group involvement. These defenses are homologous to anxiety as it is experienced by the individual; i.e. the state of "anxiety arises as a response to a situation of danger and which will be reproduced thenceforward whenever such a situation recurs" (5, p. 72). In sum, the past two subphases were marked by a conviction that further group involvement would be injurious to members' self-esteem.

*Subphase 6: Consensual Validation.*

In the groups of which we write, two forces combine to press the group toward a resolution of the interdependency problem. These are the approaching end of the training course, and the need to establish a method of evaluation (including course grades).

There are, of course, ways of denying or avoiding these realities. The group can agree to continue to meet after the course ends. It can extricate itself from evaluation activities by asking the trainer to perform the task, or by awarding a blanket grade. But turning this job over to the trainer is a regression to dependence; and refusal to discriminate and reward is a failure to resolve the problems of interdependence. If the group has developed in general as we have described, the reality of termination and evaluation cannot be denied, and these regressive modes of adaptation cannot be tolerated.

The characteristic defenses of the two subgroups at first fuse to prevent any movement toward the accomplishment of the evaluation and grading task. The counterpersonals resist evaluation as an invasion of privacy: they foresee catastrophe if members begin to say what they think of one another. The overpersonals resist grading since it involves discriminating among the group members. At the same time, all members have a stake in the outcome of evaluation and grading. In avoiding the task, members of each subgroup are perceived by members of the other as "rationalizing," and the group becomes involved in a vicious circle of mutual disparagement. In this process, the fear of loss of self-esteem through group involvement is near to being realized. As in subphase 3, it is the independents —in this case those whose self-esteem is not threatened by the prospect of intimacy—who restore members' confidence in the group. Sometimes all that is required to reverse the vicious circle quite dramatically is a request by an independent for assessment of his own role. Or it may be an expression of confidence in the group's ability to accomplish the task.

The activity that follows group commitment to the evaluation task does not conform to the expectations of the overpersonal or counterpersonal members. Its chief characteristic is the willingness and ability of group members to validate their self-concepts with other members. The fear of rejection fades when tested against reality. The tensions that developed as a result of these fears diminish in the light of actual discussion of member roles. At the same time, there is revulsion against "capsule evaluations" and "curbstone psychoanalysis." Instead, what ensues is a serious attempt by each group member to verbalize his private conceptual scheme for understanding human behavior—his own and that of others. Bringing these assumptions into explicit communication is the main work of subphase 6. This activity demands a high level of work and of communicative skill. Some of the values that appear to underlie the group's work during this subphase are as follows:

1. Members can accept one another's differences without associating "good" and "bad" with the differences.
2. Conflict exists but is over substantive issues rather than emotional issues.
3. Consensus is reached as a result of rational discussion rather than through a compulsive attempt at unanimity.
4. Members are aware of their own involvement, and of other aspects of group process, without being overwhelmed or alarmed.
5. Through the evaluation process, members take on greater personal meaning to each other. This facilitates communication and creates a deeper understanding of how the other person thinks, feels, behaves; it creates a series of personal expectations, as distin-

guished from the previous, more stereotyped, role expectations.

The above values, and some concomitant values, are of course very close to the authors' conception of a "good group." In actuality they are not always achieved by the end of the group life. The prospect of the death of the group, after much procrastination in the secret hope that it will be over before anything can be done, is likely to force the group into strenuous last-minute efforts to overcome the obstacles that have blocked its progress. As a result, the sixth subphase is too often hurried and incomplete. If the hurdles are not overcome in time, grading is likely to be an exercise that confirms members' worst suspicions about the group. And if role evaluation is attempted, either the initial evaluations contain so much hostile material as to block further efforts, or evaluations are so flowery and vacuous that no one, least of all the recipient, believes them.

In the resolution of interdependence problems, member-personalities count for even more than they do in the resolution of dependence problems. The trainer's behavior is crucial in determining the group's ability to resolve the dependence issue, but in the interdependence issue the group is, so to speak, only as strong as its weakest link. The exceedingly dependent group member can ride through Phase I with a fixed belief in the existence of a private relationship between himself and the trainer; but the person whose anxieties are intense under the threats associated with intimacy can immobilize the group. (Table 2 summarizes the major events of Phase II.)

## Conclusions

Dependence and interdependence—power and love, authority and intimacy

—are regarded as the central problems of group life. In most organizations and societies, the rules governing the distribution of authority and the degree of intimacy among members are prescribed. In the human relations training group, they are major areas of uncertainty. While the choice of these matters as the focus of group attention and experience rests to some extent with the trainer, his choice is predicated on the belief that they are the core of interpersonal experience. As such, the principal obstacles to valid interpersonal communication lie in rigidities of interpretation and response carried over from the anxious experiences with particular love or power figures into new situations in which they are inappropriate. The existence of such autisms complicates all discussion unduly and in some instances makes an exchange of meanings impossible.

Stating the training goal as the establishment of valid communication means that the relevance of the autistic response to authority and intimacy on the part of any member can be explicitly examined, and at least a provisional alternative formulated by him. Whether this makes a lasting change in the member's flexibility, or whether he will return to his more restricted formula when confronted with a new situation, we do not know, but we expect that it varies with the success of his group experience—particularly his success in understanding it.

We have attempted to portray what we believe to be the typical pattern of group development, and to show the relationship of member orientations and changes in member orientations to the major movements of the group. In this connection, we have emphasized the catalytic role of persons unconflicted with respect to one or the other of the dependence and interdependence areas. This power to move the group

TABLE 2   Phase II: Interdependence-Personal Relations

| | Subphase 4: enchantment | Subphase 5: disenchantment | Subphase 6: consensual validation |
|---|---|---|---|
| 1. Emotional Modality | Pairing-Flight. Group becomes a respected icon beyond further analysis. | Fight-Flight. Anxiety reactions. Distrust and suspicion of various group members. | Pairing, understanding, acceptance. |
| 2. Content Themes | Discussion of "group history," and generally salutary aspects of course, group, and membership. | Revival of content themes used in Subphase 1: What is a group? What are we doing here? What are the goals of the group? What do I have to give up—personally—to belong to this group? (How much intimacy and affection is required?) Invasion of privacy vs. "group giving." Setting up proper codes of social behavior. | Course grading system. Discussion and assessment of member roles. |
| 3. Dominant Roles (Central Persons) | General distribution of participation for first time. Overpersonals have salience. | Most assertive counterpersonal and overpersonal individuals, with counterpersonals especially salient. | Assertive independents. |
| 4. Group Structure | Solidarity, fusion. High degree of camaraderie and suggestibility. Le Bon's description of "group mind" would apply here. | Restructuring of membership into two competing predominant subgroups made up of individuals who share similar attitudes concerning degree of intimacy required in social interaction, i.e., the counterpersonal and overpersonal groups. The personal individuals remain uncommitted but act according to needs of situation. | Diminishing of ties based on personal orientation. Group structure now presumably appropriate to needs of situation based on predominantly substantive rather than emotional orientations. Consensus significantly easier on important issues. |
| 5. Group Activity | Laughter, joking, humor. Planning out-of-class activities such as parties. The institutionalization of happiness to be accomplished by "fun" activities. High rate of interaction and participation. | Disparagement of group in a variety of ways: high rate of absenteeism, tardiness, balkiness in initiating total group interaction, frequent statements concerning worthlessness of group, denial of importance of group. Occasional member asking for individual help finally rejected by the group. | Communication to others of self-system of interpersonal relations; i.e., making conscious to self, and others aware of, conceptual system one uses to predict consequences of personal behavior. Acceptance of group on reality terms. |
| 6. Group movement facilitated by: | Independence and achievement attained by trainer-rejection and its concomitant, deriving consensually some effective means for authority and control. (Subphase 3 rebellion bridges gap between Subphases 2 and 4.) | Disenchantment of group as a result of **fantasied expectations of group life.** The perceived threat to self-esteem that further group involvement signifies creates schism of group according to amount of affection and intimacy desired. The counterpersonal and overpersonal assertive individuals alleviate source of anxiety by disparaging or abnegating further group involvement. Subgroups form to ward off anxiety. | The external realities, group termination and the prescribed need for a course grading system, comprise the barometric event. Led by the personal individuals, the group tests reality and reduces autistic convictions concerning group involvement. |
| 7. Main Defenses | Denial, isolation, intellectualization, and alienation. | | |

lies mainly in his freedom from anxiety-based reactions to problems of authority (or intimacy): he has the freedom to be creative in searching for a way to reduce tension.

We have also emphasized the "barometric event" or event capable of moving the group from one phase to the next. The major events of this kind are the removal of the trainer as part of the resolution of the dependence problem; and the evaluation-grading requirements at the termination of the course. Both these barometric events require a catalytic agent in the group to bring them about. That is to say, the trainer-exit can take place only at the moment when it is capable of symbolizing the attainment of group autonomy, and it requires a catalytic agent in the group to give it this meaning. And the grading assignment can move the group forward only if the catalytic agent can reverse the vicious circle of disparagement that precedes it.

Whether the incorporation of these barometric events into the training design merely makes our picture of group development a self-fulfilling prophecy, or whether, as we wish to believe, these elements make dramatically clear the major forward movements of the group, and open the gate for a flood of new understanding and communication, can only be decided on the basis of more, and more varied, experience.

The evolution from Phase I to Phase II represents not only a change in emphasis from power to affection, but also from role to personality. Phase I activity generally centers on broad role distinctions such as class, ethnic background, professional interests, etc.; Phase II activity involves a deeper concern with personality modalities, such as reaction to failure, warmth, retaliation, anxiety, etc. This development presents an interesting paradox. For the group in Phase I emerged out of a heterogeneous collectivity of individuals; the individual in Phase II emerged out of the group. This suggests that group therapy, where attention is focused on individual movement, begins at the least enabling time. It is possible that, before group members are able to help each other, the barriers to communication must be partially understood.

## Bibliography

1. BION, W. R., "Experiences in Groups: I," *Human Relations*, I, No. 3 (1948), 314-20.
2. ———, "Experience in Groups: II," *Human Relations*, I, No. 4 (1948), 487-96.
3. FREUD, SIGMUND, *Group Psychology and the Analysis of the Ego*, trans. J. Strachey. London: International Psycho-Analytical Press, 1922; New York: Liveright, 1949.
4. ———, *Moses and Monotheism*. London: Hogarth Press, 1939; New York: Vintage Books, 1955.
5. ———, *The Problem of Anxiety*, trans. H. A. Bunker. New York: Psychoanalytic Quarterly Press and W. W. Norton, 1936.
6. GOULDNER, ALVIN, *Wildcat Strike*. Yellow Springs, Ohio: Antioch Press, 1954; London: Routledge, 1955.
7. LEIGHTON, A. H., *The Governing of Men*. Princeton, N.J.: Princeton Univ. Press, 1946.
8. PARK, ROBERT E., "The Strike," in *Society*. New York: The Free Press, 1955.
9. REDL, F., "Group Emotion and Leadership," *Psychiatry*, V (1942), 573-96.
10. SCHUTZ, W. C., *FIRO: A Three-Dimensional Theory of Interpersonal Behavior*. New York: Holt, Rinehart & Winston, 1958.
11. ———, "What Makes Groups Productive?" *Human Relations*, VIII, No. 4 (1955), 429.
12. SULLIVAN, H. S., *Conceptions of Modern Psychiatry*. Washington,

D.C.: William Alanson White Psychiatric Foundation, 1940, 1945; London: Tavistock Publications, 1955.

13. ———, "Tensions, Interpersonal and International," in Hadley Cantril, ed., *Tensions That Cause Wars*. Urbana, Ill.: Univ. of Illinois Press, 1950.

14. WHYTE, W. F., JR., *Patterns for Industrial Peace*. New York: Harper & Row, Publishers, 1951.

# chapter eighteen

## Toward a Conception of the Life Cycle of Groups

THEODORE M. MILLS

One of the more deeply perplexing and taxing experiences for the person entering a learning group . . . is the speed at which events, in kaleidoscopic confusion, appear. Often it is expressed in images of "jungle noises," "being at sea," "horses off in all directions," "being shot at from all quarters," "a mess, a mess, a mess," and so on. "We have never, don't now, and will never know what is going on, and if someone says he can untangle it, that just makes it worse." One might imagine similar images going through the mind of a totally naïve person at his first baseball game. Events appear strangely confused, disordered, and unpredictable. Only after one conceives *the game* do these events take their meaningful and enjoyable place in an ordered pattern. Only then do certain events become significant, central, and exciting—though perhaps still unpredictable.

Reprinted from Theodore M. Mills, *Group Transformation: An Analysis of a Learning Group* (Englewood Cliffs, N.J.: Prentice-Hall, Inc., 1964), pp. 65-80, by permission of Prentice-Hall, Inc. Copyright © 1964 by Prentice-Hall, Inc.

The experienced group leader, or the well-trained observer, has at least an implicit conception of what goes on in men's minds and something of what transpires in groups. By deciphering the multifaceted meaning of comments, he discerns more order and patterns than can the initiate. In fact, a number of teachers, therapists, observers, and social scientists have sensed the existence of certain structures and of ordered change in these structures. Currently, there is a variety of formulations which attempt to make clear the phases, developmental sequences, cycles, or the like through which groups tend to go. The authors of these schemes perhaps share the assumption that a "game"—albeit ingenious and complicated—is being played and that random-like events will become more ordered, more meaningful, more significant once the "game" is conceived, formulated, and understood.

Quite appropriately, these preliminary conceptions of systems in change vary according to the type of group and its goal and according to the professional role or theoretical interest of their authors. For example, for short-term, intellectual, problem-solving groups, Bales conceives of phases in terms of

the intellectual processes of orientation, evaluation, and decision, these being paralleled by an increase in socio-
emotional issues.[1] For groups training
normal adults in human relations,
Thelen and Dickerman formulate four
phases: (1) members' attempt to establish their customary place in the
power hierarchy; (2) leader's rejection
of this hierarchy and of authoritarian
goals, resulting in frustration and conflict; (3) cohesion and complacency;
harmony at all costs; (4) combination
of group-centeredness and serious efforts at "work."[2] Phases in his therapy
groups are formulated by Mann as (1)
hostility serving to bind members
through mutuality of feelings, (2) anxiety about closeness, (3) personal mutual analysis, and (4) personal mutual
synthesis.[3] . . . Aiming at a more abstract level, Parsons, Bales, and Shils
suggest an ever-ascending spiral created
by four-stage cycles, the stages being
addressed to the problems of (1) adaptation, (2) goal reduction, (3) integration, and (4) emotional expression and
maintenance of patterns[4]; more recently
Parsons has presented a more refined
conception of the cycle.[5]

Perhaps these examples are enough
to suggest the enormous utility of a
clearly conceived, comprehensive model
of the major sequences in group structure and process. Enough is known
from observation and experience to say
that groups are inherently complex systems with a vast number of variables
changing simultaneously. Valuable as
knowledge of the correlation between
two or three of them might be, there
remains the question of the place of
one correlation within a set of many;
and insightful though the comprehensive clinical analysis of the motivation
of one event, or of the motivational
system of one member, might be, there
remains the question of its ramifications in an interdependent system.
Though current models may be open
to justifiable criticism because of bias
and gaps, as they are improved they
can help the practitioner place a single
event or variable within a multivariate
context and relate the here and now
both to the past and to the future,
much as the fan does with his fairly
complex model of the game of baseball.

The discussion of the life cycle of
learning groups presented [below] was
prompted, first, by the desire to understand more clearly how readings in
content analysis are associated with
major changes in the group and, second, by the need, in my opinion, to
emphasize certain processes which
have been observed in learning groups
but which have not found their way
into current conceptions of phases,
cycles, and developmental sequences.
The first of these is the process of forming indigenous norms, that is, of giving
up preconceived normative notions, of

---

[1] Robert F. Bales and F. L. Strodtbeck,
"Phases in Group Problem Solving," *Journal
of Abnormal and Social Psychology*, XLVI
(1951), 485-95.

[2] H. Thelen and W. Dickerman, "The
Growth of a Group," *Educational Leadership*, VI (1949), 300-316. In these references
on group development, I am indebted to the
work of Warren G. Bennis in working papers
on group development and some problems
and research gaps in group development,
Group Research Project, Massachusetts Mental Health Center.

[3] James Mann, "Group Therapy with
Adults," *American Journal of Orthopsychiatry*,
XXIII (1953), 332-37.

[4] Talcott Parsons, Robert F. Bales, and
Edward A. Shils, *Working Papers in the
Theory of Action* (New York: The Free
Press, 1953), pp. 163-269.

[5] Talcott Parsons, "Pattern Variables Re-
visited," *American Sociological Review*, XXV

(August, 1960), 467-83. See also Talcott
Parsons, "The Point of View of the Author,"
in Max Black, ed., *The Social Theories of
Talcott Parsons* (Englewood Cliffs, N.J.:
Prentice-Hall, 1961), pp. 311-63.

creating normlessness, of experimenting with and selecting new ones, and of refashioning them through experience. One part of this process of course is the creation and modification of the full set of role relations within the group. In most current formulations, these processes, which are difficult to tie down empirically, are excluded. Problem-solving sequences, such as those of Bales, for example, deal with frequencies of types of behavior in an extranormative sense. Unincorporated within the hypothesis are questions of what members believe the behavior should be and whether or not it coincides with contractual relations within the group. Moreover, although sequences in therapy groups may trace the rise and fall of anxiety, rarely is there consideration of the anxiety-reducing function of entering into a contract with one's "rival" or with one's "master." Changes in norms and changes in motivational states are intimately related. For these reasons, the discussion of the life cycle emphasizes normative processes.

The second emphasis is upon *partial* consummation. Until much more is understood about human behavior, and insofar as members of learning groups realize what is *not* known by them or by anyone else, there is an incompleteness to their experience. They may have started on an enterprise, but by no means do many groups feel that they have gained total wisdom. In terms of initial and even subsequent expectations, members ordinarily feel that they have fallen short of the group goal. Consummation in learning groups is partial and fragmentary, as it may be in therapy groups. In spite of this limitation, however, current formulations, without an important exception, portray in the way persons and the group change an eventual climb to an ideal peak. The picture is of members who express themselves freely and discern accurately while they listen, comprehend, and achieve consensual validation—this while the group becomes integrated. Some characteristic final phases illustrate the point: *The Working Group* (Bach),[6] *Combination of Group-Centeredness* and *Serious Efforts at "Work"* (Thelen and Dickerman),[7] *Focus of Responsibility Becomes Fixed in Group* (Gordon)[8] *Personal Mutual Synthesis* (Mann),[9] *Productive Collaboration* (Semrad and Arsenian),[10] *Integrative* (Coffey and Leary).[11]

Whether the formulations refer to groups far more successful than those observed by the author, or whether the formulation expresses what should happen rather than what in fact does happen, remains to be learned from further rigorous empirical examination. Until such time, the discussion of the life cycle notes some of the effects partial consummation has had upon the learning groups observed by the author.

The third emphasis is upon the fact that most learning groups terminate. Anticipating this death and handling its reality is an important issue to those who commit themselves to the group. Though separation anxiety and the process of termination are familiar to many therapists and trainers, they have not gained an important place in the

6 George R. Bach, *Intensive Group Psychotherapy* (New York: Ronald, 1954), pp. 268-93.

7 Thelen and Dickerman, *op. cit.*

8 Thomas Gordon, *Group-Centered Leadership* (Boston: Houghton Mifflin, 1955), Chap. 10.

9 Mann, *op. cit.*

10 Elvin V. Semrad and John Arsenian, "The Use of Group Processes in Teaching Group Dynamics," in Warren G. Bennis, Kenneth D. Benne, and Robert Chin, eds., *The Planning of Change* (New York: Holt, Rinehart & Winston, 1961), pp. 737-43.

11 H. S. Coffey *et al.*, "Community Service and Social Research," *Journal of Social Issues*, VI (1950), 25-37.

formulations of group development, phase sequences, and so forth. Why this is so is probably not a simple matter. It may be associated with the desire to think only about positive aspects at the end of the group's life; it may result from the pervasive and culturally patterned denial of death in our society; or it may be rooted in an underlying sociological assumption that while persons die, institutions and societies live on. In any case, no formulation, to my knowledge, adequately accommodates group mortality. Some, in fact, would seem to require fundamental modification to make room for processes of dissolution, liquidation, and separation.

Emphasis upon norms, imperfect consummation, and dissolution should not be interpreted as an exclusion of other issues and processes which have already been summarized in developmental sequences. The following discussion, in fact, assumes, is indebted to, and builds upon the perceptive and stimulating conceptions of Bennis and Shepard, Semrad and Arsenian, Parsons, Bales, and Shils, and seeks by its special emphasis to add its contribution to a comprehensive formulation. At the same time, the emphases are based upon the belief that the realities of group process are such that a comprehensive model must be in terms of a life cycle—group formation and group dissolution—rather than simply a progressive development toward some implicitly desired state.

## Issues and Activities in the Life Cycle of Learning Groups

There are five principal periods: (1) the encounter, (2) testing boundaries and modeling roles, (3) negotiating an indigenous normative system, (4) production, and (5) separation. For each period, the central issues, the predominant activity, and the group properties which emerge as a consequence are briefly suggested. The discussion does not attempt to include all areas, issues, or mechanisms—for example, certain sources of personal anxiety and their defenses, the progress of role differentiation and the probable structures, the more complex patterns of symbolic manipulation, and the process of member and group clarification. Instead, it presents a likely course in terms of selected variables. Moreover, it does not attempt to follow through the fate of groups which vary from this particular course or to specify the fate of those which become arrested at particular points along the way.

### The Encounter

*Issues.* The first issue is whether or not a group will actually materialize. Will a sufficient number of persons return and continue to attend? Second, and if they do, to what degree will the arrangements and procedures that are worked out be conducive to accomplishing the announced aim.

For a prospective member, the first issue is: Do I want to belong to the group in view of what the experience might demand and what it might give? Second, am I capable of being a member? Am I, for example, able to see what I don't want to see, to do what I prefer not to do, to be appraised by those I don't want to judge me? Looking far ahead, will what I can give be valued by others?

*Activities.* Among characteristic responses to these issues are the following:

NAÏVE ACTIVISM. Based upon preconceptions of group discussion, of human behavior, of one's role in similar contexts, and supported by the hope that these conceptions handle most contingencies, members rush into the task.

DISILLUSIONMENT. Due to the almost universal inadequacy of the pre-conceptions, to a growing awareness that embracing a task is not the same as performing it, and to an uncertainty arising from the value differences among members, disillusionment occurs.

RETRENCHMENT. As a consequence of disillusionment, members withdraw from the more complicated areas of the task and suppress their more personal thoughts.

*Emergent Properties.* If the enterprise continues, the following new components or states are likely to exist.

Within the group, there is a state of anomie. Preconceived notions about what should be felt, said, and done and about the roles of member and instructor are found inadequate and inappropriate and hence must be given up. Since there is no indication from any authoritative source concerning what notions might or should take their place, anomie exists.

Persons arrange a new contract with themselves, as it were. They enter an arrangement whereby they agree to give more to the group than they receive immediately, and they leave themselves more than usually vulnerable, intellectually and emotionally.

In short, the group emerges from the encounter with certain members making long-term investments and committing themselves to a state of anomie.

## Testing Boundaries and Modeling Roles

*Issues.* A central issue of a group in such a state is to determine the scope of anomie. Of the previous ideas about what the group should be and about what should be done, how many are to be given up, how many modified, how many retained? How extensive is the uncertainty? how deep the involvement? how threatening the process? A second issue is the character of the arrangement that might replace anomie.

What constitutes a learning group? What is involved in creating a productive and satisfying arrangement?

For a group member, the central issue is: Can I try new stances, new roles, when chance of success is low and risk of failure is high? Can I go ahead without authoritative approval and disapproval as a guide? To what extent dare I risk being called a fool?

*Activities.* With a distant goal, but with no normative guides from any source, one likely set of responses is (1) to retest pragmatically the limits of preconceived ideas, and (2) to model new behavioral roles so that their scope, their effectiveness, and their appropriateness may be experienced and judged by members. Boundary testing and role modeling are likely to be oriented to the following issues:

COMMITMENT. The importance of the group to oneself may be tested by being absent; the importance of one's own performance, by giving one's very best ideas or by remaining silent; the worth of the performance of others, by overt challenge or by silent critique. The strength of others' commitment is tested and gauged.

AUTHORITY. The apparent discrepancy between the expected and the announced role of the instructor is tested by attempts to manipulate him into the more conventional active, directive, appraising, and nurturant role, or by taking his role, or by organizing a substitute authority structure. Tests are made of the members' fantasy of him as omnipotent and omniscient and of them, in relationship to him, as ignorant and impotent. Unbelieving, they test, above all, the instructor's assertion that he will not legislate for them and give to them a new system. In the course of these attempts, the roles modeled include the rebellious, the recalcitrant, the doctor's helper, the usurper, the silent supporter, and the independent student.

INTIMACY. Tests are made for an

equitable, comfortable distance between members, often by approaching too close and pulling too far away. Similar tests are made of (1) the limits of self-revelation and of what one can tolerate seeing in others, (2) the range of tolerance of similarities and of differences among members, (3) the lasting power of one's initial likes and dislikes and of one's admiration and devaluation of others, and (4) the solidarity of subgroups which might offer security. Modeled roles may include the cold and the detached, the intimate and the anaclitic, the open and the personal, the fellow student and the colleague. Testing and modeling are oriented to the definition of acceptable boundaries of particularistic, diffuse, and affective interpersonal relations.

WORK. What more exactly is involved in "understanding human behavior"? The process of seeking knowledge is tested by trying to let the facts speak for themselves, by simply accepting or rejecting a case instead of understanding it, by trying to explain a case from the application of a single theory or set of concepts, and by attempting to exhaust the material from an analysis of only the conscious level. Testing all the way, the group members move facing backward into work. Tests seek those circumstances which give absolute certainty to one's interpretation. Tests explore how infinite the regression is when one attempts to understand another's attempt to understand someone's attempt to report events. Modeled roles are those of jurist, academician, romanticist, scientist, poet, philosopher, and artist. Since the issue of exploring what the group might or wants to become is critical, discussion of external matters, such as cases or events of community and nation, become screen discussions within which the exploration of the group's future continues. Issues of commitment and authority are explored and tested in this substitute context. For this reason, there is ambiguity concerning what a speaker is referring to, and there is no distinction between the feelings about external objects and about internal ones.

In summary, processes during this second phase are devoted to testing boundaries and modeling possibilities in respect to *personal commitment, authority, intimacy,* and *work.* Exploration permeates the boundary between the group and the external situation so that these distinctions are not clear.

*Emergent Properties.* The following new components, or states, are likely to exist as residues of experimentation.

Since testing boundaries, modeling roles, and formulating conclusions from these activities *are* part of the process of learning about human behavior, there exists—though perhaps still unformulated—a notion of what it takes to be productive and a feeling of satisfaction in having begun to learn. Therefore, there vaguely exists a sense of goal direction, a sense that is based pragmatically upon the group's experience.

Consequently, there also exist grounds not only for selecting those issues which are relevant to the goal but for evaluating the possible alternative ways of handling issues. There exist, in other words, both motivation and a rudimentary set of values to guide the formation of a new normative system.

### Negotiating an Indigenous Normative System

*Issues.* Having dropped certain preconceptions, displayed a range of possibilities, experienced progress in learning, intellectually and emotionally, and gained a sense of goal direction, the group's central issue is to legislate an enabling set of norms. How are values and preferences to be formulated into ideas concerning what should and should not be done, and concerning what sorts of interpersonal relations should prevail?

For a group member, the central issues are: Can I perform the student role in this group and still be the kind of person I am and want to be? Is the role which is preferred both creative and compatible with my needs and capacities?

*Activities.* With a rudimentary but pragmatically based sense of the legitimate and the preferred, the group is likely to negotiate a new set of norms and to select agents who sanction and control on behalf of these norms. Whereas earlier roles of experimenter and explorer were modeled, now roles of sanctioner and controller are modeled. Negotiations focus upon the following familiar issues:

COMMITMENT. Attempts are made to establish the criteria for group membership. The right of members to consume time to make a personal point, the right of silent members to receive without giving, the right of absent members to return without paying a price, these rights are all challenged. The uncommitted portions of the group and of persons are sought out, and loyalty tests are administered. Members testify to their own loyalty.

AUTHORITY. The group revolts overtly against the instructor, thereby transforming the fantasy of instructor-omnipotence and member-impotence into a new set of ideas concerning what members can and should do independently of the instructor. Membership entails guilt over revolt and responsibility for making decisions. Both students and instructor now have a right and an obligation to make decisions instrumental to the group goal, and the instructor is obligated to protect those who seek to engineer such decisions. The taboo against expressing negative reactions against the instructor is attenuated.

INTIMACY. The experience of learning something by collaborating results in the inhibition of intimacy is its aim; that is, being close for its own sake is differentiated from being close enough to produce something of value. The latter becomes the basis of the new normative relationship. Differences among members, as persons and in their roles, tend to become tolerable and admitted (providing there is some indication that each contributes toward effective goal reduction). Persons who remain alien in this respect become crucial issues; they either come around or are ostracized. These negotiations eventuate, first, in roles which approximate collaborating ones and, second, in an attenuation of the taboo against expressing positive feelings.

WORK. Having discovered that some behavior of some members is insightful, instructive, and productive, the group attempts to follow their lead. It practices creating fantasy material and interpreting it as a means of discovering more about what is going on in the group. In another direction, it examines carefully the basic facts in cases and expresses a desire to hear tape recordings of its own procedures. On the one hand, all data (ideally) become relevant; on the other, the canons of observation, interpretation, and formulation are (ideally) retained.

*Emergent Properties.* From the viewpoint of the group as a whole, the following new components are important.

A nucleus of persons is committed to a rudimentary normative system. These norms are based both upon pragmatic tests of what the group can do and what it needs to do to accomplish its goal.

A set of conditions are formulated which members must fulfill before they take group time and before their roles are allowed to become differentiated.

A new role relationship arises between member and instructor which replaces the previous image of impotence confronting omnipotence. Members are obligated to inquire and to decide; the instructor is obliged both to protect the innovator and to back up those who exercise control in behalf of the new norms.

A new role relationship among members distinguishes the instrumental from the personal. Though obliged to work together, members are not obliged to like one another, nor are they prevented from doing so. Though obliged to reveal those feelings which are essential to an understanding of the cases and the group's processes, members remain free to express or not to express those personal likes and dislikes peripheral to the group's task.

A new conception of the group's task arises. Figure and ground begin to separate. Replacing the image of a formless, boundless mass of data, projections, interpretations, and fantasies is a notion of the relevance of facts, the value of interpretations, and the fruitfulness of formulations. Usefulness replaces certainty as a criterion.

A concept arises of the group as a unique entity distinct from the constituent personalities and from all other groups. It could now be named. The boundary between group and nongroup is confirmed, as evidenced, for example, by the impossibility of admitting a stranger and by the unavoidable pain at the loss of a member.

In short, in this phase the group seeks to define and to legislate what it should be. As it evaluates, selects, and decides, it inadvertently becomes something special—it becomes a unique system with its own values, norms, internal arrangements, and outlook on the external world.

## Production

*Issues.* Having become a group of a special kind, its new issue is what it can produce. Can its observations and interpretations stand up to tests against reality? Can its formulations be communicated, understood, remembered, and transmitted to others? Can it create something of lasting value?

For a member, the issues are: Can I communicate ideas which are both relevant and in such a form that they can be tested against reality? Can I hear, evaluate, and test someone else's ideas?

*Activities.* Though by no means for the first time, but with new determination, members apply what they know about the processes of observation, emotional expression, interpretation, formulation, and testing.

OBSERVATION. To what extent are observations complete and accurate? What cues and signals does one tend to miss?

EMOTIONAL EXPRESSIONS. To what extent are the feelings experienced by members, by authors, or by persons in the cases conveyed for what they are? What is repressed? What is distorted? What is projected?

INTERPRETATION. On how many levels and in terms of what facets might one interpret an event? What is a statement saying about the case? about the speaker? about the group?

FORMULATION. By what gift or skill are ideas which come from the concrete and the particular transformed into ones which are helpful in clarifying or explaining disparate data? How does one translate what is learned into ideas that can be conveyed and tested for both their relevance and their lasting value?

TESTING. By reference to basic data —whether it be tapes of their own sessions, facts as reported in cases, or of some other sort—observations, interpretations, and formulations are impersonally tested for completion, accuracy, and usefulness.

INTERNAL CHECKS. Since tests show the effect of various defenses upon the working processes, the group tends to establish internal checks against denial, distortion, intellectualization, and projection. Statements are screened as they are produced, and members are ranked according to their contact with reality.

DIAGNOSIS. Members attempt to assess what is in the here and now that either disrupts or facilitates the working process and, consequently, they seek to understand more fully how group process affects the learning process.

*Emergent Properties.* Ordinarily, the production test causes a revision of certain components:

The nature of the task is redefined. It is more difficult than it seemed.

The aspiration level of the group is lowered. The revised goal is to understand something about limited aspects of human and group processes.

Norms governing what should or should not be expressed are relaxed. ("Deviant" behavior might be productive after all.)

Central cultural themes are formed around those interpretations and formulations which have been found insightful, helpful, and apparently of lasting value. Since these themes have, in a sense, saved the group, members gather them and husband them. They symbolize what the group wishes itself to be.

The group as a whole becomes an object of negative feelings. Members are disillusioned with its resources and its potential.

At the same time, the intellectual boundaries between fact and fantasy, between group process and content of statements, between the internal group and the external objects, and between a gratifying statement and one based on reality are clearer. The distinctions have been clarified by the testing that has gone on.

In short, during this phase the group puts itself to the test of producing something of general and lasting value. Rallying around a set of central insights, salvaged from the test, it emerges disillusioned and less ambitious, but intellectually keener.

## Separation

Most training and learning groups run by a fixed schedule. The first and last meeting date is known. Consequently, quite irrespective of how the group has done and what it aspires to do, the fact of separation forces a complex set of demands and issues, some of which are briefly noted below.

*Issues.* Two central issues exist for the group as a whole. First, can it create something of value that will not die; and, second, how are the boundaries between the group and other objects to be dissolved in time for the last meeting?

For a member, the first issue is: How can I recollect within the allotted time my attachments to others and to the group? Second, am I able to carry away the group's valuables, as well as its finished and unfinished business?

*Activities.*

WORK. Effort, sometimes compulsive, is spent generating new interpretations and formulations which might hold the key or the secret. The history of the group is reviewed and successful episodes are codified. Paralleling this effort is an attempt to understand what the group is (more than what it can do) by understanding the way it dies.

INTIMACY. Members withdraw first by expressing their deepest feelings, positive or negative, about one another, then by expressing positive feelings. The boundary between group members and others is dissolved by bringing friends in as visitors and by recounting fully to outside friends what is going on in the group.

AUTHORITY. The attempt to dissolve the boundary between the instructor as authority and other authorities takes the form of asking him to state once and for all that his role is artificial, not real, that the course from the beginning has been an experiment, and that if he were truly himself he would not do what he has done.

COMMITMENT.    Members review their roles and what they have given and received from one another. They seek a confirmation that their choice to join the enterprise was a wise one. Positive feelings about the experience are aroused and members thank one another for contributions.

Yearning for a benediction from some source, the group dies.

*Emergent Properties.*    What is left: A group that is dead and cannot be revived. Individual fantasies of a future reunion.

Within persons, a tendency, on occasion, to model their emotional and intellectual processes of experiencing, observing, interpreting, formulating, and so forth after the pattern of processes which occurred in the group. Individual members tend, on occasion, to operate as the group as a system operated.

A tendency in some members to create groups in which they can re-enact the instructor's role.

A tendency in some members to induce their friends to re-enact their own role by joining the course.

Angry feelings toward the instructor for beginning something he should know could not be finished. Anger toward themselves for committing themselves to such an enterprise.

Some sense of accomplishment.

301.18    100327

**DATE DUE** M65

| DEC 8 1971 | | | | |
|---|---|---|---|---|
| | | | | |
| | | | | |
| | | | | |
| | | | | |
| | | | | |
| | | | | |
| | | | | |
| | | | | |
| | | | | |
| | | | | |
| | | | | |
| | | | | |
| | | | | |
| | | | | |